The
NORTH TOWER

Controlled Demolition
and the
Bush, Cheney, Giuliani Cover-up

DAVID ALDEN

LIBERTY BELL BOOKS

Published in 2018 by
Liberty Bell Books, LLC
P.O. Box 3846
Chandler, AZ 85244
E-mail: libertybellbooks@outlook.com
Copyright © David Alden 2018

ISBN 978-0-578-15554-8

Permission to use photographs and illustrations that appear in this publication has been sought in all cases where they are not in the public domain. None has been included against the express wish of the owner. The following owners have granted rights: AP Wide World Photos, Corbis/Sygma, Reuters, Jeff Mock and Jean-Philipe Boulet.

Cover photographic sequence by Ray Stubblebine/Reuters.

Book Formatting by Jera Publishing

Manufactured in the United States of America.

To order directly from Liberty Bell Books, please add $4.50 shipping and handling to the price of the first copy, and $1.00 for each additional copy.

Contents

Acknowledgments.. i

Introduction.. 1

1   The Cover-up 17

2   The Explosions on B4 .... .80

3   The Secret Plans.. 106

4   More Explosions 128

5   More Witnesses... 164

6   Further Evidence of Controlled Demolition........................ 183

Epilogue.. 324

Appendix A: The Force Needed to Displace a Perimeter Panel 331

Appendix B: The Force Needed to Shear NIST Samples C-46 and C-24 .. 339

Appendix C: The 50-, 6- and 7-Shafts 341

Appendix D: The Factor of Safety 359

Appendix E: The Strange Case of Building 7 362

Appendix F: 9/11 Contradictions 372

Notes 443

Select Bibliography 483

Index 485

About the Author 490

Acknowledgments

FIRST AND FOREMOST, I must thank two people in particular who granted me interviews that helped me to gain a fuller understanding of what happened inside the North Tower at the World Trade Center during the terrorist attacks of September 11, 2001. One is former maintenance man Hursley Lever, whose description of a massive explosion he witnessed in the B4 subbasement level convinced me that the official explanation for it could not possibly be the truth. The other is Jules Naudet, codirector of the award-winning film *9/11*, who arrived in the main lobby minutes after the plane crash, with his camera in hand, and filmed there for about an hour, until the collapse of the South Tower forced his evacuation.

My deep appreciation is also due to former WKPHX radio talk show host Jeff Farias. The first pages of this book were written with his encouragement.

A very special note of thanks is due to Dr. Thomas Skeen, PhD, who teaches English composition at Grand Canyon University. Due to the subject matter, a significant portion of the information contained in this book tends to be of a very technical nature and is, perhaps, not exactly the right cup of tea for the average person. Dr. Skeen was very helpful as far as offering useful ideas for structuring the presentation of that material, which helped make the final product more readable.

Last, but certainly not least, I am particularly indebted to my alma mater, Worcester Polytechnic Institute (WPI). That exceptional New England college made it possible for me to gain an education and real-life work experience in several different aspects of the civil engineering field that, as it turned out all these many years later, proved invaluable in the daunting task of writing this book.

Introduction

THREE SKYSCRAPERS COLLAPSED at the World Trade Center (WTC) in New York City after the terrorist attacks of September 11, 2001—the colossal North and South Towers, each 110 stories tall, and the 47-storied Building 7.

Three Buildings Fell at the WTC on 9/11
Copyright: Jeff Mock

They were the most bizarre structural failures that have ever occurred in the history of modern engineering. Each of the towers was supported by a 180-million-pound structural steel framework that was three times

1

stronger than necessary.[1] And, due to their height—a quarter of a mile— and their proximity to major airports in the area, they were specifically designed to withstand the damage caused by the hijacked commercial airliners that slammed into them.[2] So, it is not surprising that they both remained standing for a very long time after being hit. Yet, when they finally did collapse, they fell like a house of cards. They were gone in about ten seconds. That is about the same time it would have taken a brick to hit the ground if dropped off their roofs. Building 7, which was similarly steel-framed, was completely down in about seven seconds. And it was not even hit by a plane.

Two billion pounds of material made up the combined 220 floors of the towers.[3] But it was all reduced to a debris pile less than three stories high.[4] To comprehend the scale of that, compare the following photograph, which was taken soon after those two buildings collapsed, to the previous one of them standing.

After the Collapses
Photo by Michael Rieger/FEMA

In the words of cleanup crew member Danny Doyle, "Where the hell did everything go?"[5]

"We Have Some Planes"

The official story is that the collapses were the result of a series of events that began at about 8:13 that morning. That was when American Airlines Flight 11, a Boeing 767-200ER commercial airliner, which had taken off from Boston's Logan Airport fourteen minutes earlier carrying eighty-one passengers and a crew of eleven, did not acknowledge a flight controller's order to climb to a higher altitude.[6] At 8:24 a.m., a hijack was confirmed when a man's voice, speaking with a distinctive Middle Eastern accent, was heard over an open mic in the cockpit, saying, "We have some planes. Just stay quiet, and you'll be okay. We are returning to the airport." And then, moments later: "Nobody move. Everything will be okay. If you try to make any moves, you'll endanger yourself and the airplane. Just stay quiet."[7]

Five young Islamic terrorists had taken control of the aircraft. During the course of those early morning hours, fourteen others of their group would hijack three more planes. Allegedly, they were America-hating members of al Qaeda, a militant group essentially operating out of a cave in Afghanistan, whose inspirational leader and financier was a multimillionaire sheik from Saudi Arabia named Osama bin Laden.

Osama bin Laden
Source: US Government

Bin Laden was a leading figure in the Islamic community who was notorious in the West for his extremist views. He had made it no secret in the past that he was angered by the US's refusal to remove its troops from his homeland after the 1990 Gulf War, particularly the Islamic holy sites of Mecca and Medina. For him, the continued stationing of "Infidel" troops in the heart of Islam was the ultimate insult, and he had taken part in issuing two fatwas calling for all Muslims in the Middle East to increase terrorist activities and drive western interests out of the region.

It is also alleged that he financed and directed the bombing of two US Embassies in East Africa in the summer of 1998 as well as the assault on an American navy ship, the USS *Cole*, in the Gulf of Aden in October of 2000. Those attacks killed hundreds of people, including seventeen US sailors.

The 9/11 attacks, it is said, were an extension of bin Laden's "Holy War." Flight 11 was the first to hit. At just before 8:47 a.m., it flew into the 96th floor of the North Tower, killing everyone onboard as well as many who were at work in the building. Sixteen minutes after that, at 9:03, the second hijacked plane, United Airlines Flight 175, another Boeing 767, with fifty-six passengers and nine crew, hit the South Tower at about the 81st floor with similarly tragic results.[8]

The crash of Flight 175 was followed about thirty-four minutes later by the impact of American Airlines Flight 77, a Boeing 757, onto the south face of the Pentagon, located just outside the nation's capital. That crash killed sixty-four people on the plane and 125 in the building.[9]

Finally, it all came to an abrupt end when, at about 10:03, the fourth plane, United Airlines Flight 93, another Boeing 757, carrying thirty-seven people and a crew of seven, crashed into a Pennsylvania field while some of the passengers put up a heroic struggle to retake control of the aircraft.[10]

Fifty-six minutes after being hit, the South Tower was the first to go. It collapsed at 9:59 a.m. The North Tower survived for 102 minutes and fell at 10:29. Building 7 suddenly collapsed seven hours later, at 5:20 p.m. No deaths were recorded as a result of that last collapse, but an estimated 2,100 people were lost when the towers fell.[11]

A Stark Reality

The official explanation for the tower collapses says that their steel support columns in the plane impact zones failed from being overheated by intensely burning fires fed by jet fuel.[12] Allegedly, this allowed the top block of floors above to fall with such force that it crushed the undamaged floors below it to the ground. It is said that Building 7 also collapsed in a somewhat similar manner due to fires that were ignited when it was hit by flaming debris from the collapsing North Tower.

But this was unprecedented. Never before had such steel-framed structures ever been collapsed by fire, let alone be so devastatingly disintegrated.[13] And here, there were three in the same day. Previously, this kind of freefall collapse of a steel-framed building had only been seen in controlled demolitions in which the lower part of the structure is eliminated by very powerful explosives so that it offers no resistance to the upper part falling on it. And whether that was the case at the WTC has been a controversial issue ever since. In fact, there is a group consisting of 2,900 professional architects and engineers, many of whom have PhDs in structural engineering, who are convinced that all three buildings had to have been brought down by explosives. That committed group of technical experts feel so strongly about the science supporting their finding that they have banded together and, since the year 2010, have been continually putting their careers on the line by doggedly petitioning Congress for a complete reinvestigation.[14]

Obviously, as of this writing, they have not been successful. But that is not because their argument is a complicated one. Actually, once boiled down, it is deceptively simple. It is as easy as understanding the difference between having *zero* evidence or having a *ton* of evidence. Incredible as it may seem to the uninitiated, there has been exactly zero hard evidence ever presented that has definitively proven that the jet fuel-fed fires caused the collapses. In actual fact, a close reading of the nearly 10,000 pages of the official reports reveals that that conclusion is based entirely on hypothetical computer simulations of the plane crashes, which is a method that past practice has shown to be highly unreliable.[15]

What is doubly troubling, and more than a little ironic, is that the reports themselves actually acknowledge that deficiency. For instance, the first report on the tower collapses done by the Federal Emergency Management Agency (FEMA)—released in May 2002—says that there

5

was *"uncertainty"* in its simulations due to a "limited amount of physical evidence" and a "scarcity of data."[16] Three years later, another report done by the National Institute of Standards and Technology (NIST) was even more to the point, admitting that "another important source of *uncertainty* in this analysis is the inaccuracy associated with mathematical and numerical models."[17]

FEMA was also ambiguous on the mystery of Building 7. At first, it said that that collapse "appears" to have been "due to fire."[18] Then, in a later section, it admits that that conclusion is only "a hypothesis based on potential rather than on demonstrated fact" and that "the specifics of the fires in WTC7 and how they caused the building to collapse remain unknown at this time."[19] And it called for further investigation. But, after having six years with which to study it, NIST would be likewise frustratingly vague. In a 2008 public presentation, a spokesman for the institute would report that its collapse was "primarily due to fire," but then in the next breath he would admit that that finding was also based completely on a computer simulation, not hard evidence.[20]

So, if the only evidence on which the official findings were based came from analyses that were admittedly flawed, how could the writers of those reports *honestly* make the assertion that their conclusions were reliable? The answer, of course, is that they could not.

On the other hand, as you will see from the pages of this book, the claim that explosives caused the collapses has a *ton* of hard evidence to back it up. Not the least of which are the observations of more than a hundred witnesses who said they saw the explosions. For just one example take the Fire Department of New York (FDNY). It completed its own investigation within three months of the attacks. That so-called World Trade Center Task Force (WTCTF) collected recorded statements from 118 of its members who said that they saw, heard and felt explosions going off at the WTC both before and during the collapses.[21] Many of them were high officers in the department with many years of experience who know an explosion when they see one. Typical of them was FDNY *Deputy Commissioner* Thomas

Fitzpatrick who said this about the collapse of the South Tower: "My initial reaction was that this was exactly the way it looks when they show you those implosions on TV."[22]

Then there was FDNY *Battalion Chief* Dominick DeRubbio, who described the fall of one of the towers this way: "It looked like a timed explosion."[23]

Assistant Fire Commissioner Stephen Gregory also saw the explosions. This is what he said about the collapse of one of the towers: "I saw a flash, flash, flash at the lower level of the building. You know, like when they demolish a building."[24]

Other first responders had the same impression. This is what *paramedic* Daniel Rivera said about the collapse of one of the towers: "Do you ever see a professional demolition where they set the charges on certain floors and then you hear, "Pop, pop, pop, pop, pop?" I thought it was that."[25]

Firefighter Richard Banaciski described the collapse of one of the towers this way: "It seemed like on television [when] they blow up these buildings. It seemed like it was going all the way around like a belt—all these explosions."[26]

Another *firefighter*, Kenneth Rogers, who saw the South Tower come down, said this: "I kept watching. Floor after floor, after floor...One floor under another—after another. And when it hit about the fifth floor, I figured it was a bomb because it looked like a synchronized deliberate kind of thing."[27]

Karin Deshore, a *commander* of the FDNY's Emergency Medical Services was outside the North Tower just as it began to come down. This is how she described it:

Somewhere around the middle of the North Tower, there was this orange and red flash coming out. Initially, it was just one flash. Then this flash just kept popping all the way around the building and that building had started to explode. The popping sound...And with each popping sound, it was initially an orange and then a red flash came out of the building and then it would just go all around the building on both sides as far as I could see. These popping sounds and the explosions were getting bigger—going both up and down and then all around the building.[28]

All of this presents a stark reality; if those 2,100 people who died in the collapses were killed by explosives planted in the buildings, it means that what we are faced with here is an unsolved case of premeditated mass murder.

A Voice from the Towers

Consider, if you will, for one unflinching moment, the enormity of that; if the WTC collapses were indeed due to controlled demolitions, imagine the heartless indifference to human suffering that it must have taken for those who planted and detonated the explosives. The horror of that is reflected in the desperate calls for help heard on the 9-1-1 tapes. To get just a glimpse of what it must have been like, consider the voice of Kevin Cosgrove, one of the over 600 people who were above the plane impact zone of the South Tower when Flight 175 hit.

Kevin Cosgrove
Source: Wikipedia

At about 9:53 a.m., having concluded that he was trapped on the 105th floor, Cosgrove made the last of several calls for help. By then, it had been about fifty minutes since the plane crash. What follows is the final minutes of his conversation with a sympathetic female police dispatcher, who has just assured him that the first responders from the fire department have everything they need to know to rescue him. Choking on thick, black smoke and fearing for his life, he answers, hoarsely:

I know [they] do, but it doesn't feel like it, man. We got... You got lots of people up here. I know you got a lot in the building, but we're on the top. Smoke rises, too. We're on the floor. We're in the window. I can barely breathe, now. Can't see... (Told to hang in there.) You can say that. You're in an air-conditioned building. What the hell happened?! (Again, told help is on the way.) Doesn't feel like it...Tell God to blow the wind from the west. It's really bad. It's black. It's arid. (To others, nearby.) Does anyone else wanna chime in, here? (No answer.) We're young men. We're not ready to die. 105! Two Tower! (Long pause.) How the hell are you gonna get my ass down? I need oxygen. (Told again help is on the way.) It doesn't feel like it, lady. You get'em in from all over. You get'em in from Jersey! I DON'T GIVE A SHIT! OHIO! (Asked his last name.) Mine's Cosgrove. I must have called about a dozen times, (Spelling it out.) C.O.S.G.R.O.V.E. My wife thinks I'm alright. I called and told her I was leaving the building and that I was fine, and then BANG! (Long pause.) Cherry. Doug Cherry. Doug Cherry is next to me. 105! Whose office? John Ostaru's office. We're in John Ostaru's office, O.S.T.A.R.U. (Dispatcher also spells it out.) Right! That's the office we're in. There's three of us here. We're looking at the Financial Center. Three of us. Two broken windows.[29]

Just then, at 9:59, there are the rumbling sounds in the background. He lets out a blood-curdling scream, "OH, GOD! OH...," that is abruptly cut off. The line goes dead. What appears to be explosions have just gone off in the plane impact zone, and the top block of floors above is tipping to the south.

The South Tower Collapse Begins
Source: Unknown

The building begins collapsing from the plane impact zone down, floor by floor in succession, killing everyone inside. Cosgrove's body would be found in the debris pile.

Why the North Tower?

For the normal, average, everyday person, it is difficult, if not impossible, to comprehend how the final blow that killed Kevin Cosgrove and the over 600 other people in the South Tower could have been caused by explosives that were planted in the building by other human beings. But, tragically, the evidence for it is overwhelming.

In the first place, to appreciate how unlikely it would have been for fire to cause that building to collapse, it is important to know how it was specifically designed to resist such conditions. Its construction consisted of an exoskeleton of 240 steel columns about 2 feet apart around its entire perimeter (including one each for the four chamfered corners), together with a central core of 47 other columns that were massive in size.

Note the following illustration.

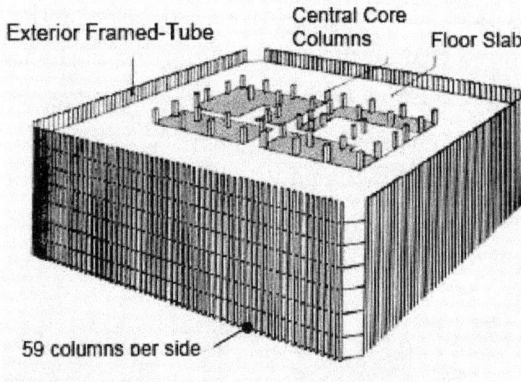

Twin Tower Design
Source: FEMA

All of those columns were overdesigned beyond normal engineering practice, with the perimeter columns having a factor of safety of 5.40 and the core columns 1.80, which means that they could handle 540% and 180% of their predicted load, respectively.[30] This gave the tower an average factor of safety of about 3, which means that on the day of the attacks, where there was no wind, it was utilizing only one third of its overall load bearing capacity.

Under ideal conditions with adequate ventilation, ordinary hydrocarbon-based fires, such as those at the WTC, which were fed by jet fuel and furnishings, can burn at about 900°C.[31] At that temperature, steel loses 90% of its strength, and structural failure can occur. But realistically, such fires usually only *average* about 500°C, due to their inefficient, oxygen-starved, diffuse-flame nature.[32] According to Massachusetts Institute of Technology (MIT) professor Dr. Thomas Eagar, PhD, such fires, which are commonly accompanied by the kind of thick, black, heat-smothering smoke seen in the WTC towers, will likely burn at a *maximum* temperature of no more than 650°C.[33] But at that temperature, steel only loses about *half* its strength.

With the tower utilizing only a third of its load bearing capacity before the plane hit, that means that, even if the steel temperatures in the plane impact zone reached that uppermost 650° level, the support columns would still have been able to handle the load, because the government's own analysis shows that an insignificant portion of the total number of columns in the plane impact zone were taken out by the plane crash.[34] Thus, fire could not have caused the collapse.[35]

Secondly, note the following photos. They show that Flight 175 hit the southeast corner of the of the building, causing fire damage to only the east half of the floors 78 to 84 (arrows).

SE Corner - Impact
Source: NIST

NE Corner - Exit
Source: NIST

The west side of those floors remained free of fire and structural damage for the full fifty-three minutes that the tower stood after plane impact. This indicates that only those columns on the east side could have been weakened by fire and that the building should have, therefore, tipped to the east, if those columns had buckled. But, as the photo of collapse initiation above shows, the building tipped to the south. This also indicates that fire was *not* the cause.

Thirdly, actual eyewitness testimony from the plane impact zone, together with other visual evidence, disproves the official account. By about 9:53 a.m., some six minutes before collapse, one heroic firefighter, Battalion Chief Orio J Palmer, had made his way to the lowest level of the plane impact zone at the 78th floor and did not encounter a significant fire condition.[36] After checking out the situation, Palmer, a decorated fire department employee with many years' experience, radioed back that there were only "two to three isolated pockets of fire," and "we should be able to knock it down with two lines."

At that same time, color photos and videos show that the fires in the center of the impact zone on the 81st floor, where the nose of the plane hit, were dying down to a similar condition. Note the following photo. It was taken by the New York Police Department (NYPD) at 9:58:02, fifty-eight seconds before collapse.

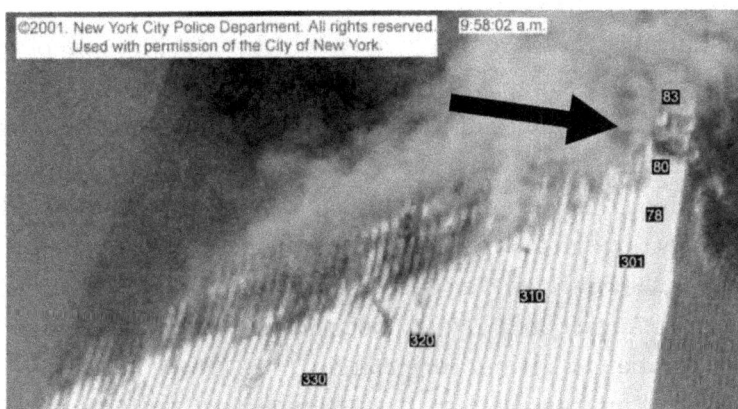

9:58:02 a.m.

**East Side of South Tower
58 seconds before collapse**
Source: NYPD

This shows that the whole range of perimeter columns on the east side of the building, columns that had been fully engulfed by jet fuel fireballs upon plane impact, had now cooled to where there was only one significant pocket of fire. That was at the northeast corner at the 82nd floor (arrow). But, if so, then how could the official explanation for collapse be correct? Clearly, this photo does not support it. It shows that the fires here had *decreased* to the paltriness that Palmer had observed at the 78th floor. Thus, the east-side perimeter columns had to have been *cooling* down, not heating up, and, therefore, could not have buckled due to the fire.

All of this circumstantial evidence indicates that it is highly unlikely that fire caused the South Tower to collapse. But, as convincing as this abbreviated look is, as you are about to see, there is exponentially more evidence surrounding the collapse of the North Tower that disproves the official account, much of it hard evidence. Indeed, the amount and clarity of that evidence literally demands that there be a compete reinvestigation of whether explosives were involved in the collapses. And that is why I chose to concentrate mainly on the North Tower for the subject of this book.

Stranger than Fiction

Understandably, there are those who are highly sensitive to reopening this wound. They say that having a new investigation would be irresponsible: that it would be disrespectful to the families of the victims to make them relive that day; that it would be a waste of time and resources; that rehashing the 9/11 attacks this many years after the fact would put the country through an unnecessary emotional turmoil; and so on. But polling has shown that that anxiety is *not* shared by most Americans. For example, an August 2013 YouGov poll showed that the public supports a reinvestigation by a two-to-one margin.[37]

In fact, a significant block of the public goes even further, saying that the whole 9/11 event very well could have been entirely an inside job of *domestic* terror.[38] For example, a 2006 Scripps/Howard poll performed by Ohio State University found that that belief was held in some regard by thirty-three percent of adult Americans. If conservatively based on the 2000 Census, that figures to about 70 million people.[39,40]

And that number has only grown since due to a virtual flood of additional circumstantial evidence that has surfaced over the years.[41] In fact, that additional evidence is so extensive that to do it justice would take a volume of its own. But, as intriguing as that alternative scenario is, it runs far afield of the intended premise of this book. The singular approach of this work is to stick to only those things that can be proven. However, that provocative evidence pointing to a wider conspiracy cries out for consideration, and it is at the peril of the truth that it be overlooked. In consideration of that, some of its major aspects have been added herein as Appendix F, entitled "9/11 Contradictions." It is highly recommended that anyone seriously interested in studying the events of 9/11 take a close look at it.

Having said that, hopefully, anyone reading this book will recognize that one of the distinguishing characteristics of its actual chapters is that they studiously avoid discussing unsubstantiated theories. Their mission is specific. Using the North Tower as a prime example, they walk the reader step by step through the body of hard evidence that proves that the WTC collapses were the direct result of explosives, and that it was covered up at the highest levels of government, both local and federal.

Granted, this story is so full of intrigue that it seems stranger than fiction; that certain powerful people, for whatever reason, could be so corrupt as to have an agenda that required covering up the cold-blooded murder of thousands of their fellow citizens is a hard thing to grasp. The natural tendency is to close one's eyes to it. But it is a testament to the volume of evidence proving it to be so that a clear majority of Americans have overcome that reticence and, as the YouGov poll showed, favor a complete reinvestigation. So, at this point in time, although you will not see much about it in the mainstream media, most of the public is way ahead of the powers that be on this issue. What has now become the most critical question for most Americans is not whether the buildings were brought down by explosives, but who did it?

No doubt, this is an unnerving business to try to wrap one's head around. But the saving grace for anyone intent on exposing it is the universal truth that there is no such thing as a "perfect" crime; in even the wiliest of criminal enterprises, there will always be clues found that point to the guilty. In this case, the most important clue is knowing how key evidence pointing to the use of explosives was destroyed. Normal police practice dictates that who had the motive and opportunity to do that becomes a prime area of investigation. This is so because a search for who was involved in the cover-up often leads to the perpetrator, or, at least, to someone who was trying to protect the culprit.

With respect to that, the first chapter of this book, "The Cover-up," presents evidence showing that officials at the highest levels of New York's City Hall, mainly in the person of Mayor Rudolph Giuliani, and the White House, represented by Vice President Richard "Dick" Cheney, working under the authority granted to him by President George W. Bush, conspired to see that the most direct evidence pointing to the use of explosives—the *structural steel* from the buildings—did not see the light of day.

1

The Cover-up

THIS IS HOW NIST described the initiation of the North Tower collapse in its 2005 report:

> In WTC 1 [North Tower], the *fires* [in the plane impact zone] weakened the [steel] core columns and caused the floors on the south side of the building to sag. The floors pulled the heated south perimeter columns inward, reducing their capacity to support the building above. Their neighboring columns quickly became overloaded as columns on the south wall buckled. The top section [about 20 floors] of the building tilted to the south and began its descent [crushing the lower, undamaged ninety-six floors below to the ground]. The time from aircraft impact to collapse initiation was largely determined by how long it took for the fires to weaken the building core and to reach the south side of the building and weaken the perimeter columns and floors.[42]

The Steel Smoking Gun

In a circumstance such as this—where fire is said to have initiated the collapse of a steel-framed building—it is essential to have its *structural steel* available for an in-depth metallurgical analysis. This is so because steel undergoes specific internal changes when subjected to high temperatures. It starts to lose strength once it is heated to about 300°C. And it progressively weakens as its temperature rises. When it reaches about 1200°C, it essentially has no strength left. But the temperature that steel ultimately reaches in any fire condition becomes accurately recorded in explicit changes that occur to its granular structure as different precipitates appear, internally. And those compounds can be observed using a

17

special technique of electron microscopy called electron-backscattered diffraction (EBSD).[43]

So, if you have the steel from the fire-damaged area of a building to physically examine, there is nothing at all hypothetical about determining the actual degree of temperature that it reached and thus be able to determine how much its strength may have been degraded. Therefore, in an investigation of a collapse like that of the North Tower, the first thing the investigating engineers would do would be to physically gather the structural steel from the area of the plane impact zone and have a metallurgist examine it. The results of that, together with the construction drawings for the building—which would have revealed the factor of safety built into its design—would have allowed them to determine whether the support columns in the impact zone could have buckled due to the fires and allowed the top block of floors to fall as a unit.

With respect to that, it is not unreasonable to ask why the structural steel from the North Tower debris pile would ever be intentionally destroyed by government officials. On the face of it, that would seem paradoxical because, without that steel being available for metallurgical analysis, it would be impossible to verify the official explanation for the collapse; i.e., that steel had been sufficiently weakened by the fires.

But on the other hand, having the structural steel available for analysis could have proven the contrary—that it did *not* get hot enough to initiate collapse, and, therefore, the building should have remained standing, indefinitely. If that was found, then the next thing called for would be something that investigators all over the country routinely do, even in the case of a suspicious house fire—test for residues of explosives. But, if that were done and such residues were discovered, it would have turned the official explanation for the collapse on its head. It would have been the proverbial "smoking gun."

And that is precisely why the steel had to be destroyed.

The Cheney Cabal

Vice President Cheney's involvement in the WTC investigations had a peculiar dynamic behind it, a study of which strongly suggests how the cover-up was initiated.

Vice President Cheney
Source: The White House

His authority to get involved in the aftermath of the collapses was made possible by a special directive issued by President Bush four months *prior* to the 9/11 attacks.[44]

President George W. Bush
Source: The White House

That presidential edict specifically ordered the head of FEMA, Joseph Allbaugh, to create a new, so-called Office of National Preparedness (ONP) inside the agency. The role of the ONP was to deal with the "consequences" of any future terrorist attack upon the United States in a manner to be determined by Cheney.

In part, that directive reads:

Protecting the American homeland and citizens from the threat of weapons of mass destruction is one of our Nation's important national security challenges...Today, *numerous Federal departments and agencies* have programs to deal with the *consequences* of a potential use of a chemical, biological, radiological, or nuclear weapon in the United States...But to maximize their effectiveness, these efforts need to be *seamlessly integrated*, harmonious and comprehensive.

Therefore, I have asked Vice President Cheney to oversee the development of a coordinated national effort...I have also asked Joe Allbaugh, the Director of the Federal Emergency Management Agency, to create an *Office of National Preparedness*. This Office will be responsible for *implementing* the results of those parts of the national effort overseen by Vice President Cheney that deal with *crisis management*...[45] (Italics added.)

This set the stage for the WTC cover-up by making Cheney superior to Allbaugh in overseeing the allocation of FEMA resources when dealing with the aftermath (i.e., the "consequences") of any future terrorist attack.

An indication that the cover-up was seriously underway on 9/11 was when, within only hours of the attacks, Bush further overrode Allbaugh's authority and personally hand-selected a man named Ted Monette to head up FEMA/ONP's activities at the WTC.

As reported by FEMA:

Monette was appointed by President Bush, September 11, 2001, to serve as the FCO [Federal Control Officer] for the attack on the World Trade Center in New York City. He was the senior federal official responsible for establishing the immediate federal presence on the scene, establishing command and control of federal resources, and coordinating all federal assets supporting the City of New York.[46]

This took Allbaugh completely out of the picture. After this, he would have virtually no input into the operation. From then on, all of FEMA's activities at the WTC—including overseeing any investigation of the collapses that might occur—would be set by Cheney and implemented by the ONP through Monette. In other words, the effort would be run out of the White House by what will be referred to here as the "Cheney cabal."

Indeed, on the evening of the attacks, a White House press release confirmed that "FEMA support is working closely with the White House" to "assist local...governments" to "insure [sic] coordination and management of the consequences of the events." [47] No doubt, that meant that Cheney (the *White House*) was assisting the City of New York (the *local governments*) in dealing with the collapses at the WTC (the *consequences of the events*).

Bush's directive also said that *all* the federal agencies which would traditionally be responsible for dealing with the aftermath of a terrorist attack were to be "seamlessly integrated" into the ONP. This suggests that Cheney would have supervisory control over the Federal Bureau of Investigation (FBI).[48] This is likewise troubling, because, as it was, only two months previous to the attacks, in July 2001, Bush had also handpicked a new director for that bureau. The evidence shows that, in the immediate aftermath of the attack on the WTC, under this new director, Robert Mueller, the FBI, which past precedent dictated would have normally taken charge of the investigation by first freezing the scene of the crime and then beginning a search for evidence, completely relinquished its authority to the Cheney cabal.

Considering that nearly 2,100 people were murdered in cold blood by the collapses, that lack of effort shown by the FBI under Mueller is astonishing. Its laboratory in Quantico, Virginia, which is universally accepted as one of the most comprehensive crime labs in the world, no doubt has experts who understand the importance of preserving the steel from such a crime scene. Yet, although over 1,000 of its agents would be, at one time or another, in close proximity to the WTC steel in the weeks and months after the attacks, not one would ever step forward to take control of it as evidence.[49]

Nor would the bureau ever conduct any of the basic forensic examinations that were normal for such a crime scene, including that thing that local investigators all over the country routinely do—test for residues of explosives.

The Destruction of Evidence

In the wake of the WTC collapses, there was naturally a great deal of public concern for the safety of other high-rise buildings. Subsequently, the Bush administration was pressured to sponsor a study that could precisely explain the structural failures that occurred and offer recommendations on how to improve building safety in the future. In a pretentious effort to make it appear that they were concerned about that, the Cheney cabal, under cover of FEMA, called on the foremost authority available—the American Society of Civil Engineers (ASCE).[50]

To its credit, the ASCE made a good-faith effort and organized a contingent of twenty-six of some of the top civil engineering experts available.[51] Called the Building Performance Study (BPS) team, most of them arrived in New York from their places of employment all over the country within two weeks of the attacks, ready to go to work.[52]

Giuliani's Speedy Steel Recycling Program

But once at the WTC, the BPS engineers were alarmed to discover that the structural steel from the debris pile—the most important evidence that could aid in their investigation—was already in the process of being hauled out of the site and sold off for scrap. This, they soon discovered, was being done at the direction of Mayor Giuliani, who, strangely enough, had also ordered the NYPD to lock them out of the site.[53]

Mayor Rudolph Giuliani
Source: The City of New York

There can be no doubt that Giuliani was responsible for this tampering with evidence from the crime scene. In the first place, as mayor, he controlled the police and, thus, access to the trade center. Secondly, he was also the only one who could approve the high-price contracts to have the debris cleaned up. In addition, his culpability would be indisputably carved out in no uncertain terms by a House Select Committee on Science (HSCS) in Washington. Having received complaints about the destruction of the steel, the HSCS finally held a hearing on March 6, 2002, in which they called on the leader of the BPS team, Dr. W. Gene Corley, PhD. Corley testified that when he arrived at the site three weeks after the attack, the steel was already being recycled. When asked who was responsible, he stated frankly, "That was determined, I understand, by the City of New York."[54] There can be no doubt that he was referring to Mayor Giuliani, who had a well-known reputation for running the city like an autocracy.

Also notable is the uncanny speed of that removal. According to at least one FBI report: "The City of New York started moving the debris to a closed landfill on Staten Island, *right away*." [55] Indeed, as early as late in the afternoon on the very day of the attacks—even before the collapse of Building 7—local contractors familiar to the city were seen jamming up the streets around the trade center with their trucks and heavy equipment.[56] Then, beginning that night—working under hastily issued, multi-million-dollar verbal contracts, done with just a handshake with Giuliani's deputies—they began trucking the debris from the collapsed buildings twenty-nine miles away to Staten Island and dumping it there, at the Fresh Kills landfill.[57]

Giuliani himself would boast about the swiftness of that at a news conference the very next day, saying, "*We* were able to move 120 dump trucks of debris out of the city last night. Which will give you a sense of the work that was done overnight."[58]

But the swiftness of that begs a few questions. One might think that, as a former federal prosecutor, the mayor would be more sensitive with respect to meddling with a crime scene, especially one in which thousands of people had been murdered in cold blood. But one would be wrong.

There was virtually no pause by Giuliani to seek meaningful scientific advice. Some may argue that he was justified in acting with such haste because this was also a search and rescue operation and the lives of some who could be still trapped under the debris were at stake. But what the mayor failed to reveal in his news conference was that, as soon as the debris arrived at Fresh Kills, the structural steel—vital evidence in a crime of mass murder—was being straightaway separated out and sold off by his deputies to four New Jersey scrap yards.[59]

WTC Steel at Fresh Kills
Photo by Andrea Booher/FEMA

In turn, the scrap dealers were quickly cutting the steel into three-foot sections for easy storage on freighting ships and selling it off to various Asian countries for recycling.[60, 61]Most of it was going to China—and at a twenty percent discount from the prevailing market rate, which guaranteed a quick sale.[62]

This brazen tampering with evidence was itself a serious crime, and it threw up a huge red flag that something peculiar was going on behind the scenes that did not quite meet the eye. For anyone else, it no doubt would have meant risking serious consequences, and the fact that Giuliani could get away with it is telling. For one thing, even as scrap, the steel was valuable. At the going market rate at the time of $150.60 a ton, the twenty percent discount on the 300,000 tons from the WTC meant this hasty recycling effort would be giving away close to a whopping $9 million.[63] And the steel did not even belong to the city. It belonged to a state agency, the Port Authority of New York and New Jersey (PANYNJ), which had developed the WTC and only leased out the buildings.[64]

But, without any argument whatsoever from Governor George Pataki, Giuliani was allowed complete freedom to quickly dispose of that valuable steel—and, apparently, at any cost.[65,66]But, you might ask, why the rush?

One might excuse Pataki's negligence for not asserting his authority and taking charge of the situation by saying he was as thunderstruck by the collapses as everyone else and froze up. Then again, perhaps, it was just a matter of convenience to have locals take care of the mess. But either way, Giuliani's act of locking the ASCE's BPS team of investigating engineers out of the site was pretty audacious; it took things to a whole new level.

But where did he get the nerve? Presumably, Bush's handpicked FCO on the scene, Ted Monette, could have asserted his authority and intervened to get the BPS investigators onto the site and save the steel, but the fact that he did not is a strong indication that the mayor must have been given tacit approval by the Cheney cabal to get rid of it.

The DDC Coup d'état

The strategy that Giuliani employed to accomplish that destruction is also telling. Normal protocol for dealing with the aftermath of a terrorist attack is for local authorities stand aside and let federal agencies take the lead. A prime example of that is the 1995 bombing of the Alfred E. Murrah Building in Oklahoma City.[67]In that case, almost before the smoke cleared, the FBI took control of the site and headed up the criminal investigation, FEMA deployed search and rescue teams, and the Army Corps of Engineers provided engineering expertise to help clear the debris and perform any needed engineering analysis.[68]However, at the WTC, Giuliani wielded his power as mayor to short-circuit that process.

This little-known fact was born out in a sworn court deposition obtained in 2007 by *New York Times* reporter Anthony DePalma, who wrote:

> Officials from the Federal Emergency Management Agency, the Army Corps of Engineers and the Occupational Safety and Health

25

Administration, all with extensive disaster response experience, arrived almost immediately, only to be placed on the sideline. One Army Corps official said Mr. Giuliani acted like a "benevolent dictator."

Despite the presence of those federal experts, Mr. Giuliani assigned the ground zero cleanup to a largely unknown city agency, the *Department of Design and Construction*. Kenneth Holden, the department's commissioner until January 2004, said in a deposition in the federal lawsuit against the city that he initially expected FEMA or the Army Corps to try to take over the cleanup operation. Mr. Giuliani never let them.[69] (Italics added.)

But handing off the WTC site to the Department of Design and Construction (DDC) not only undermined federal policy for dealing with a terrorist attack, it literally represented a coup d'état of long-established city planning for dealing with emergencies—planning in which Giuliani himself had expended a lot of his own political capital, as well as tens of millions of dollars of hard-earned taxpayers' money. In February 1993, there had been a previous terrorist attack on the WTC in which a truck bomb had been detonated in a B2 subbasement parking area. It killed six people and injured over a thousand. As a candidate for mayor at the time, Giuliani was critical of the city's response to it, which he saw as slow and uncoordinated. After he won election the following November, he began talking about how the city could have responded more efficiently by having a strong central command center that could have taken *control* of the site of the tragedy and better managed first responders.

In light of the newly-emerged threat of a terrorist attack, the need for a strong central command had become an imperative, the mayor stressed, because disasters like the one in '93 required a "hybrid response" from a variety of both city and federal agencies, all of which, out of necessity, operated on different radio frequencies.[70]Subsequently, in 1995, he called for the city to create a so-called Mayor's Office of Emergency Management (OEM). This new office would be precisely designed, he said, to be an "overarching organizational structure equipped to take control of the scene of any disaster and coordinate the many different responding departments."[71] And a year later, with a lot of fanfare, he announced that its design had been completed and that the state legislature had funded it to the tune of $200,000.[72]

Then, two years later, on December 28, 1998, at a staggering total cost to the city, including rent and renovations, of close to $61 million, he moved the OEM into a hi-tech command center he had constructed in the 23rd floor of the ill-fated Building 7, at the WTC.[73, 74]

In his 2002 book, *Leadership*, Giuliani would tout that "state-of-the-art" command center as "one of the most important decisions I made [as mayor]."[75] It was, he said,

> packed with computers and television screens to monitor conditions all over the city and beyond. It had generators in case the power failed, sleeping accommodations in case we had to stay overnight, storage tanks with water and fuel, and stockpiles of various antidotes.[76]

In addition, it had a bomb shelter-like design that could resist hurricane force winds. The following photograph shows the extensive technical scope of that operation.

The OEM in Building 7
Source: City of New York

In contrast, the DDC had none of that. It was an obscure city department that operated out of a rehabbed former Chiclets factory across the East River in a rundown industrial area of Queens.[77] And it was not even hands-on. Its function was merely administrative, being concerned with making contracts for the construction of municipal infrastructure, such as streets, sidewalks, jails and daycare centers, etc. Moreover, it had no assigned responsibilities whatsoever in the city's emergency response plans.

And Building 7 was still standing when the switch was done. So it would come as a shock to those who followed New York City politics to learn how Giuliani had canceled out his vaunted OEM command center and turned the WTC disaster over to the DDC, charging those glorified paper-pushers with the awesome task of rescuing survivors, recovering the remains of victims, and cleaning up the site.

Adding to this intrigue is the secretive manner with which the mayor accomplished his coup. Journalist William Langewiesche offered some insight into that. Being the only reporter who was allowed access to the WTC after the collapses, he had exclusive contact with both city officials and those working at the site, the details of which he recounted in a series of articles for the *Atlantic Monthly* magazine; articles which later became basis for his book, *American Ground; Unbuilding the World Trade Center.*[78] In the course of his reporting, Langewiesche would learn how Giuliani had made a "backroom" decision to "finesse" the OEM to ensure that a "shift in power in the direction of the DDC" took place.[79]

Also suspicious was the speed of it. That Giuliani executed this take-over quickly is evidenced by the fact that, by 9:30 a.m.—just twenty-seven minutes after the second plane crash—the DDC's deputy director, Mike Burton, was already on the phone, making his first expenditure of city funds.

As Burton himself would later explain it:

On the morning of September the 11th, shortly after I got to city hall, let's say at about 9:30, I called Regional Scaffold. At that point in time, I thought that all I needed was some scaffolding and netting and some sidewalk bridging because all I saw was that a plane had hit the building and there was going to be some hazardous structural elements hanging off the building. And I knew I would need to protect the public from walking in and around the trade center complex. Never realizing that the towers would actually collapse.[80]

But the second plane crash at 9:03 had already signaled that the city was under a terrorist attack. That should have automatically thrown the situation firmly into the realm of the OEM command center in Building 7 and its affiliated federal experts, not an untried city department, like the DDC.

Having been privileged with insider details of how stealthily the mayor had managed to wrangle this takeover, at one point, Langewiesche was inspired to ask DDC Director Holden how the federal people felt about being cut out of the action. Holden acted as if this strange arrangement was standard procedure, saying, "We had the equipment. We had the connections. We could handle it. We just went and did what we had to do. And no one said no."[81]

No doubt suspecting that as less than credible, Langewiesche probed further, asking if any of any of the federal people agreed with that decision and said yes. In response, Holden let the cat out of the bag, saying, "No. But then again, *we weren't asking*."[82]

The "Skeleton in the Closet"

Adding further to the mystery surrounding these shenanigans is the fact that, if normal OEM protocol had been followed after the first plane crash, Giuliani's handoff of the scene of the crime to the DDC should not even have been possible. The mayor admitted as much in his book, saying that, in the past, the OEM "had conducted tabletop exercises designed to rehearse our response to a wide variety of contingencies." Referring to Flight 11 hitting the North Tower, he added, "As shocking as this crash was, we had actually planned for just such a catastrophe."[83]

Accordingly, one would expect that the mayor's hi-tech command center in Building 7 would have been manned immediately after the first plane crash and its procedures activated. Part of that would have included alerting its contacts in the several federal agencies with which it had drilled. If the protocol that was developed during those practice exercises had been followed on 9/11, once the second plane hit, and it became clear that a terrorist attack was underway, there would not have been any vacancy at the WTC for the DDC to fill; the scene of the crime would have been physically taken over by the OEM's federal experts, just like at Oklahoma City.

However, the evidence shows that none of the OEM's standard procedures were ever activated on 9/11. This was mainly because, although minor staff members did show up at the command center after the first plane crash, none of the top brass ever went there.[84] Both Mayor Giuliani, who should have been acting as the commander-in-chief of the operation, and his OEM director, Richard Sheirer, along with practically all his top deputies, who should have been coordinating the city's response to the tragedy, literally avoided Building 7 like the plague.

This is not conjecture. It is known by their own admissions. In *Leadership*, Giuliani frankly admitted that he failed to do his duty. He wrote that instead of going to the OEM command center in Building 7 immediately after the plane crashes, he went to a makeshift, replacement command post that had been hastily thrown together for him by his police commissioner, Bernard Kerik.[85] It was located at 75 Barclay Street, which, oddly enough, was, for all practical purposes, just across the street from Building 7, at the northeast corner of Barclay and West Broadway.[86]

As for Sheirer, in an appearance before the 9/11 Commission—an investigation into the attacks later conducted by Congress—he would admit that instead of going to his command center after the first plane crash, he, along with most of his top deputies in tow, broke with protocol and went directly to the lobby of the North Tower, where the fire department had set up its own temporary command post.[87] And they stayed there for almost a solid hour, all the while never attempting to coordinate with any of the OEM's other members, or the mayor, or any of the federal disaster experts with which they had trained for, as the mayor has acknowledged, "just such a catastrophe."[88]

This is no small matter. It had dire consequences. Post-9/11, Giuliani was praised left and right in TV news reports for the "courage" he had apparently shown, trudging through the dust clouds of the collapsed buildings, allegedly with the safety of the people of New York utmost in his mind. That image won him nationwide admiration as "America's Mayor." Likewise, Sheirer would be featured in *New York* magazine as the "unsung hero of the hot zone" for the supposed fearless, quick response OEM had to the attack under his direction.[89] But nothing could be further from the truth. The skeleton in the closet of their official stories is that their negligence of not showing up at their command center in Building 7 directly contributed to the unnecessary deaths of hundreds of people.

When the 9/11 Commission opened its public hearings into the attacks in November of 2002, one expert witness who testified, Edward Plaugher, was profoundly disturbed by that. As chief of the Arlington County Fire Department in Virginia, he was praised for the way his organization handled the emergency response to the Pentagon attack. But, when asked by Commissioner Jamie Gorelick what he thought of New York's response at the WTC, Plaugher was unapologetically harsh, declaring that "the lack of a unified command" due to the OEM command center in Building 7 not being properly activated "dramatically impacted the loss of first responder lives on 9/11."[90]

And the commission's senior counsel, John Farmer, agreed with that damning assessment. In one internal staff report, he pointed out how a properly functioning OEM could have "kept a record of which floors were searched in the towers" and eliminated "the redundancy" of police and fire units "checking same floors, over and over again."[91] This, in turn, would have reduced the number of first responders in those two buildings, which, at one point, was estimated to have been 600 firefighters and scores of police officers.[92] And thus, fewer would have died in the collapses.

Another commission report would second that emotion, saying, "If anybody kept record of which floors were searched, they wouldn't have needed half those firefighters."[93] In other words, having a properly functioning command center very likely could have spared the lives of at least

43 of the 343 firefighters who perished in the collapses, as well as all 60 police officers who were killed.[94]

Yet another report from the 9/11 Commission tells how the fire department ordered the immediate evacuation of the North Tower after it was hit, but due to a lack of coordination by the OEM, 9-1-1 police dispatchers were telling people in the building to stay put until firefighters got to them.[95] A later study done by the *New York Times* found that, of 130 callers to 9-1-1 that were reviewed, only two were told to leave their workstations and exit the building.[96] All who stayed died in the collapse.

In addition, another commission staff report would note how that lack of OEM coordination very likely resulted in the deaths of many office workers in the South Tower. It tells how the fire department had discovered that the A stairwell, one of three in the building, was clear all the way past the plane impact zone. But, because the police were operating on a different radio frequency and the OEM was not coordinating rescue efforts, 9-1-1 police dispatchers did not get that information and could not relay it to people calling in who thought they were hopelessly trapped in the upper floors.[97] An estimated 619 people who were above the plane impact zone died when that building collapsed.[98] Most likely, some of them would have survived if the command center had been operating properly.

Typical of those victims is Kevin Cosgrove, whose last desperate call for help from the South Tower was presented in the Introduction. He and the others on the 105th floor very well might have escaped death during the 56 minutes the building stood after the plane crash had they known that they were less than 100 feet away from that open A stairwell.[99]

The Hidden Agenda

The OEM command center in Building 7 was designed especially for the emergency that Giuliani and Sheirer found themselves in after the plane crashes, and, under the circumstances, it was the most logical place to be to save lives. That they knowingly put so many lives at risk by avoiding it is a strong indication that they had to have been acting according to some kind of secret, overriding agenda.

For instance, consider the circumstances surrounding Sheirer's move to the North Tower lobby. What is inexplicable about it is that that location was not more secure than the command center. Well before his arrival, it had become a scene of complete disaster. Within seconds of Flight 11 impacting the building, that lobby was hit by an enormously powerful fireball/explosion.[100] The detonation blew out several elevators, dislodged massive marble panels from a wall, and blasted huge safety glass windows two to three inches thick out of the west side of the building. In addition, at least five people were basically incinerated, on the spot.[101] As firefighter Joe Casaliggi put it, "It looked like the plane hit the lobby."[102]

But in contrast, at that same time, the OEM command center in Building 7 was, by all accounts, very secure. It had a bomb shelter-like design, and, being that it was on the north end of the WTC and a breeze was blowing smoke from the towers' fires in a southerly direction, it afforded a perfect view of the situation. In fact, a staff report from the 9/11 Commission would consequently find Sheirer's decision to avoid going there, not just inexplicable, but inexcusable, saying, "Everybody from OEM was with him [at the North Tower], virtually the whole chain of command. Some of them *should* have been at the command center."[103]

And the FDNY's Captain Kevin Culley agreed. As an OEM field responder, he went directly to the North Tower lobby after the first plane crash. But when he arrived, he was surprised to see that Sheirer and his deputies were also there. Asked by the commission what they were doing, he was at a loss, saying,

That's a good question. I don't know what they were doing. The command center would normally be the focus of a major event. And that would be where I would expect the director to be.[104]

Another commission staff report seems just as mystified, saying, "We tried to get sense of what Sheirer was really doing. We tried to figure it out from the videos. We couldn't tell."[105]

Even more bizarre is how the only direct action Sheirer took while in the North Tower lobby virtually ensured that his OEM command center would be rendered completely useless for dealing with the tragedy that was unfolding. According to the commission, within about twenty minutes of the second plane crash, he created out of thin air the ruse of a third attacking plane, and, using that as an excuse, phoned in an order to evacuate.[106] Under that so-called "threat," those minor staffers who had gone to the command center were forced to make a hasty, panic-driven exit.[107,108]

Another commission staff report would be highly critical of that development, saying,

> Any attempt to establish a unified command on 9/11 would have been frustrated by the lack of communication and coordination among responding agencies. The Office of Emergency Management headquarters, which *could* have served as a focal point for information-sharing, was evacuated. [109] (Italics added.)

The obvious implication here is that something very dark was going on behind the scenes with Sheirer. For some reason, yet to be explained, he really did think the command center was a dangerous place to be; he did not want to go there, himself, and he wanted everybody else out, too.

But what was the threat? He had no credible report of a third attacking plane. While air traffic controllers at nearby La Guardia Airport did detect a low, fast-moving Navy interceptor jet approaching in that general timeframe to provide air support, Sheirer did not get that report. He got his information from one of his deputies, Richard Rotanz, who called from the lobby of Building 7 to relay second-hand information he got from an unidentified "Secret Service agent" who had offhandedly told him that up to seven other hijacks might still be out there, somewhere.[110] But it was a big stretch for Sheirer to say that that was confirmation that another plane was heading to attack the WTC. He could have easily disproven that false threat by contacting any one of his FBI OEM members, but he did not. Instead, he used that weak information to cause the immediate evacuation of the most important office critical to the lives of the thousands still trapped in the towers.

A similar cloud hangs over Giuliani's move to 75 Barclay because it was also not a more secure location from which to operate. It was merely a standard office setting at street level with ordinary glass windows. In addition, a critical amount of time had to be spent in trying to organize a working phone bank. Moreover, Giuliani wrote in his book that, by the time he started setting up there, he had already observed victims jumping from the North Tower to escape fires in its upper floors.[111] Under the circumstances, there can be no question that the OEM command center in Building 7, with its bullet-proof, bomb shelter-like design and hi-tech communication equipment, was the more logical place for the commander-in-chief of the operation to be in order to save lives. But he did not want to go there. Again, what was the threat?

Like Sheirer's move to the North Tower lobby, Giuliani's move to 75 Barclay demands some serious justification. But his attempts at that fail miserably. For instance, in his book, he initially says this:

> Now that the *second* plane had hit, the command center was being evacuated—it was too *near* the attacked buildings and could itself be a *target*. I immediately devised two priorities. *We had to set up a new command center.* And we had to find a way to communicate with people in the city.[112] (Italics added.)

In the first place, this can only be seen as a transparent attempt to provide cover for Sheirer's fake, third-plane "threat" that caused the OEM evacuation, because neither Giuliani nor Sheirer had received any specific, verified threat of an incoming third plane that necessitated it. Secondly, with 75 Barclay being right across the street from Building 7, for all practical purposes, it was just as close to the towers.

But more significant in this statement is Giuliani's assertion that his decision to avoid going to the OEM command center was made *after* it was ordered evacuated. And indeed, *if* the decision to go to 75 Barclay was made after the command center was determined to be a dangerous location, that would provide some justification for avoiding it, regardless of whether the reason for the evacuation made sense. However, two pages later, the mayor contradicts himself by saying this:

Within minutes of the *first* plane hitting the towers, the decision was made to establish two command posts—one for the fire department and one for the police department. The fire department…set up their command post [on West Street] so they had the buildings in their line of sight. *The police department had already begun setting up at 75 Barclay...*[113] (Italics added.)

Here, he says that the "police" (Kerik) had "already" begun setting up at 75 Barclay near the time of the "first" plane crash. But the OEM evacuation took place after the *second* crash. This seems to indicate that Giuliani actually made his decision to go to 75 Barclay *before* the command center was evacuated. The difference here is huge. If he made his decision to avoid going to the OEM command center before it was judged unsafe, what could have been his reason?

This raises suspicion that, like Sheirer, Giuliani and Kerik had to have been highly motivated to avoid Building 7 by something other than concern for the safety of the thousands of lives at risk. With respect to that, there is testimony by a minor OEM staff member—Emergency Medical Technician (EMT) Richard Zarillo—that is particularly devastating to them.

In the later inquiry conducted by the fire department's WTCTF, Zarillo would describe how he and FDNY Captain Abdo Nahmod immediately began driving to Building 7 from their office in Brooklyn, after the first plane crash.[114] He said that he saw the second plane crash as they were crossing the Brooklyn Bridge.[115] After parking near the intersection of Broadway and Vesey Street, they sprinted the two blocks down Vesey and entered the front entrance of Building 7. Anticipating that Giuliani and Sheirer would show up, once upstairs in the command center, they started activation procedures.

And they would have continued doing that if not for Sheirer's false report of third plane, which, Zarillo said, occurred between "five and ten minutes" after they arrived.[116]

So, if Zarillo saw the second plane crash as he was driving across the Brooklyn Bridge, judging by the distance from the bridge to Building 7, which was in the vicinity, he could not have made it to Building 7 sooner than about ten minutes after that 9:03 a.m. crash. This would put his arrival there at about 9:13, at the earliest. And if Sheirer's order to evacuate came as little as five minutes after Zarillo entered the command center, that would put the evacuation at no sooner than 9:18.

But, in *Leadership*, Giuliani wrote that he met Police Commissioner Kerik on Barclay Street near the WTC "one minute" after the *second* tower was hit, which would have put him there at about 9:04.[117] And per Kerik's account, the exact location where they met was near the rear of Building 7, at the intersection of Barclay Street and West Broadway.[118] But at 9:04, Zarillo must have just crossed the Brooklyn Bridge and was still rushing to get there. So, he could not have arrived at the front entrance to Building 7 before Giuliani arrived to meet Kerik. This means that, if Kerik had "already" been setting up at 75 Barclay by the time of Giuliani's arrival, the decision to avoid going to the OEM command center had to have been made *before* it was evacuated; very likely, as much as fourteen minutes before (9:18 - 9:04).

Again, as with the case of Sheirer, what could have been the reason for Kerik and Giuliani to avoid entering Building 7?

The Explosion

The peculiar determination that Giuliani, Sheirer, and Kerik individually showed in not following their long-established OEM protocol after the first plane crash can only lead to the strong suspicion that they shared some level of foreknowledge that something even more sinister than a terrorist attack was going on that morning. And whatever that "something" was, it made it an absolute imperative that they avoid entering Building 7, even if it cost hundreds of other people their lives.

Some may argue that the evidence for this is merely circumstantial. But as it turned out, if they were not tipped-off to avoid the OEM command center, they each had to have been lucky to a degree beyond any normal human expectation, because, only minutes after Sheirer phoned in his fake third-plane threat and the command center was evacuated, Building 7 was hammered by a massive internal explosion.

The magnitude of that blast was to such an extent that it knocked out all the building's elevators and collapsed the stairwells, rendering the command center inaccessible. There can be no doubt that, if Giuliani,

Sheirer, and Kerik had followed protocol and went there after the first plane crash, they would have ended up being trapped in the building by that explosion, if not killed by it.

The fact of this explosion was never revealed by any of the Bush investigations, but it was verified by two very credible, high-level city officials. One was a man named Barry Jennings.

Barry Jennings
Source: Wikispooks

By the time of the attacks, he had been a thirty-three-year veteran employee of the New York Housing Authority, and, as the deputy director of its Emergency Service Department, was an OEM member.

The other was Michael Hess. He was New York's corporation counsel, a job where he supervised the city's legal team of 600 lawyers.[119]

Michael Hess
Source: New York Law Journal

In 2007, Jennings consented to a video-recorded interview with independent investigators Dylan Avery and Jason Bermas in which he recounted testimony he had previously given in secret three years previously, behind closed doors, to the 9/11 Commission.[120] In that video, he describes how he told the commission that he was on his way to work that morning when he received a call that a small Cessna aircraft had hit the WTC, and he was directed to go help man the OEM.

He went on to describe how everything seemed normal at Building 7 when he arrived, except that there were a lot of police in the lobby. He subsequently met Hess there. He did not know Hess at the time, but Hess told him that he was expecting to meet Giuliani at the command center, so they ended up taking an elevator to the 23rd floor, together. But, when they got up there, the door to the command center was locked. They subsequently went back down to the lobby and enlisted the help of a security guard and a police officer, who got them in via a freight elevator.

Once inside, they realized that the command center had just been evacuated. This was evidenced, Jennings said, by "half-eaten sandwiches" and cups of hot coffee still "smoking" on the desks.

Since the command center was manned twenty-four hours a day, it is most likely that those food items had been left there by the night watch crew, who, along with Zarillo and Nahmod, had just made their hasty exit.[121] But, being unaware of Sheirer's fake third-plane threat, Jennings and Hess could see no obvious reason for that; the only thing happening were fires burning in the North and South Towers, which were about 400 and 800 feet away, respectively, and the command center had a hurricane-resistant design. In addition, neither the security guard nor the officer who let them in had warned them of any other danger.

But this is what Jennings said happened next:

> After I called several individuals, one individual told me that we *need to leave right away*. Mr. Hess came running back in and said we were the only ones in there and he found a stairwell. So we subsequently went to the stairwell, and we were going [down] the stairs. When we reached the sixth floor, the landing that we were

39

standing on gave way. There was an *explosion*, and the landing gave way. And I was left there, hanging. I had to climb back up and now had to walk back up to the eighth floor.[122] (Italics added.)

Jennings did not say who warned him to get out of the building or what the danger was, but he confirmed that the explosion happened before the 9:59 a.m. collapse of the South Tower, saying, "When I made it back to the eighth floor, both buildings [the towers] were still standing." He added that, as a result of the explosion, he and Hess remained "trapped" on the eighth floor for several hours before they were rescued by firefighters.

During that time, it got very hot and smoky, so Jennings used a fire extinguisher to break out a window. The following photograph was actually found in the NIST report. It shows Hess, calling for help through that broken window.

Michael Hess, 8th Floor, WTC 7
Source: NIST

Also according to Jennings, during the time they were trapped, they heard "other explosions." And eventually, both towers collapsed. When their rescuers finally got them down to the lobby, it was unrecognizable. It was, he said, in "total ruins," and they had to step over "[dead] people" on their way out of the building. (For more on this, see Appendix E, "The Strange Case of Building 7.")

Hess also confirmed the explosion. After being rescued, he started walking north on Broadway, making his way to City Hall, which was about five or six blocks away.[123] At one point, he was stopped and interviewed by a TV news crew from New York's Channel 9. Obviously still shaken by the experience, this is what he said in a breathless voice:

> I was up in the Emergency Management Center on the 23rd floor. And when all the power went out in the building, another gentleman and I walked down to the eighth floor where there was an *explosion*. And we were trapped on the eighth floor with smoke...thick smoke, all around us for about an hour and a half.[124] (Italics added.)

Mysteriously, in August 2008, a year after giving the Avery/Bermas interview, Barry Jennings, at the relatively young age of 53 and, by all outward appearances, an otherwise healthy, vibrant individual, suddenly died.[125] It was two days before the release of NIST's report on the collapse of Building 7, a report that would make no mention of him or Hess, or the explosion they witnessed.

The cause of Jennings death has never been made public. Suspiciously enough, about the same time he died, his entire family—a wife and four children—dropped out of sight and became untraceable.[126]

As for Hess, he was a longtime friend of Giuliani's and after 9/11 was given the highly-paid position of managing partner in Giuliani Partners, a security consultant firm that the mayor started after his term ran out in 2002.[127] As far as is known, he has never again spoken publicly about the explosion.

The Mystery of 75 Barclay Street

The question of who chose the 75 Barclay Street location for an alternate OEM command center to the one on the 23rd floor of Building 7 is also full of intrigue. It remains one of the deepest mysteries of this whole saga. No one seems to want to own up to it. Giuliani laid it off on Kerik. And

Kerik passed it off on his bodyguard, Detective Hector Santiago. Problem is, in Santiago's only known interview that he gave about his movements that day, he did not recall having anything to do with it.

Note the following illustration for 75 Barclay's location at the WTC.

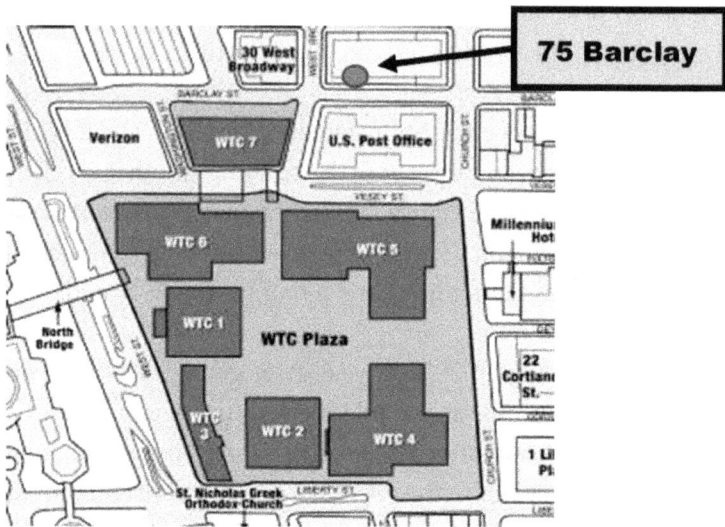

75 Barclay at the WTC
Source: FEMA

Giuliani's official explanation for 75 Barclay began about 8:00 a.m. In *Leadership*, he wrote that his normal habit was to hold morning staff meetings at City Hall, but, on the morning of attacks, he had instead arranged to have breakfast at a restaurant a couple of miles north of the WTC with his lawyer, Dennison Young, and others. That gettogether was cut short just before 9:00 when his first deputy, Joe Lhota, called to say that a plane had hit the WTC.[128] Immediately, he and Young, who would be with the mayor every step of the way that morning, piled into his van and, being driven by one of his assistants, Richard Godfrey, headed to the scene at top speed. Also with them was NYPD Detective Patty Varrone, part of Giuliani's security detail. Varrone got Kerik on the phone he and Giuliani arranged to meet in front of Building 7, on Vesey Street, just north of the North Tower.[129] Along the way, at 9:03, the second plane hit the South Tower, making it clear that the first crash was no accident; the city was under attack.

According to Giuliani, "one minute" after that second crash, his van sped to a stop near 75 Barclay, at the intersection of Barclay Street and West Broadway. This was one block north of Vesey, right across from the rear, northeast corner of Building 7.[130] Kerik was there. Giuliani got out and they had a conversation in which Kerik informed the mayor that he did not think the Building 7 OEM command center was safe because it was too close to the burning towers.

Giuliani wrote in his book that that conversation also included the following:

Bernie and his staff had already identified a building at 75 Barclay Street, just northeast of 7 World Trade Center, as a possible site [for a new command post]. 'The security guard here is on the job,' said Bernie, meaning he was a former cop. He's got phones, we commandeered the place.'[131]

But Kerik's version of this conversation was significantly different. In his 2001 book, *The Lost Son*, he said that, after the first plane crash, he was waiting for Giuliani in front of Building 7 as planned, with Lhota and Santiago, when Flight 175 hit the other side of the South Tower.[132] To avoid debris flying in their direction, they all ran the one block up West Broadway to Barclay street. But contrary to what the mayor said, Kerik claimed that he did not have anything to do with discovering the 75 Barclay location. He passed that off on Santiago, writing,

A man ran out of the main floor of 75 Barclay Street and told Hector that he was a retired cop and that we could use his office [for a command post]. Hector ran in to make sure the phones were set up.[133]

At that point, it was about 9:04, and the mayor was arriving.[134] Kerik set the scene, saying this:

The mayor's car was racing down Broadway. I flagged him down...The mayor and I talked about setting up a command post and someone again suggested that we go to the bunker at the office of Emergency Management Center at 7 World Trade Center. The mayor and I agreed that it wasn't safe, so we walked [west] toward the West Side Highway where the firefighters and cops had set up a deployment area [at the corner of West Street and Vesey].[135]

Notice that, in the version Kerik gives here of his actual conversation with the mayor, there is no discussion about 75 Barclay or a "retired cop." Nor was there anything said about Santiago checking for phones, or that that location had already been commandeered.

The suspicious nature of Giuliani's explanation for the Barclay location is further fueled by Santiago's recollection. In an interview for a 2002 book, *Never Forget*, he said that, after the second plane hit, he and Kerik did indeed run together up to the intersection of Barclay and West Broadway. And, at a certain point, they became separated when, to escape the debris, Santiago ducked into a garage. It took only seconds for the air to clear, and by then Giuliani's van was speeding up to the intersection. This is what Santiago said happened next:

I run back out and I see the commissioner. At this point, he meets up with the mayor. We go from Vesey onto the West Side Highway and we go over to where the fire department had their temporary headquarters.[136]

Here, Santiago's story conflicts with Kerik's in that he says nothing about a retired cop coming out of 75 Barclay, or that he went in to check on the phone situation. But he does agree with Kerik in that, at this point, nothing was said to Giuliani about 75 Barclay Street, or that it had been commandeered. They all just simply left the area and started walking towards West Street, where the fire department had set up its temporary command post.

All accounts agree that, once they were at the fire department post at West and Vesey, Giuliani met with head of operations, FDNY Chief Peter Ganci, and others, and they discussed tactics of how to handle the fires in the towers. In Santiago and Kerik's recollections of events, they next discussed whether to have their command center at City Hall. But it was decided that that could be another target. Then, without any explanation of why or who made the decision, Santiago says simply, "We decide to go over to 75 Barclay Street."[137] Per his and Kerik's accounts, this is the first mention of that location, by anyone, at any time, to Giuliani. But still, nothing is said about it having phones, or that it had been commandeered.

By the time Giuliani left West and Vesey, it was, according to his book, 9:44, and he had been at the scene for forty minutes.[138] For all that time, he and his entourage had watched in horror as scores of people jumped from the upper floors of the North Tower to escape the fires. And also for all that time, as has been discussed previously, the hi-tech command center in Building 7, with its bomb shelter-like design and clear view of the trade center, was the superior location from which to operate. That that was exactly the case is confirmed by the many OEM staffers who did go there. Those previously mentioned—Zarillo, Nahmod, Jennings and Hess—certainly thought so. As did John Peruggia, chief of the EMTs.[139] Also arriving was Mike Maggio, a FDNY battalion chief.[140] OEM Deputy Director Richard Rotanz also showed up.[141] As did FDNY Captain James Yakimovich.[142] And activation procedures were initiated with the expectation that Giuliani, Sheirer and all his other OEM deputies would show up. But, however suitable that Building 7 location was, instead of following their protocol for emergencies and going there, Giuliani's entourage, which by now included virtually every high-ranking police official, started walking back to the Barclay location.

Significantly, though, *no* fire department officials or OEM leaders were a part the mayor's group. This, of course, defied Giuliani's logic for creating the OEM in the first place. Having the police commanders separate from those of the fire department, and with no OEM personnel present to coordinate them, would make it logistically impossible to organize an effective response from the 75 Barclay Street location, because the fire and police departments, whose members were by now swarming to the trade center, were operating on different radio frequencies. As has also been discussed previously, that lack of coordination would contribute in a major way to the unnecessary deaths of over a hundred of them.

At one point in his book, Giuliani tried to counter criticism about going to the Barclay location with only police officials by claiming that OEM Director Sheirer was with his entourage when they left West and Vesey, and that he (Giuliani) had instructed Ganci to tell Fire Commissioner Tom Von Essen to join him at 75 Barclay when he arrived on the scene.[143] But both of those things are blatantly false. As described previously, Sheirer admitted to the 9/11 Commission that he went directly to the North Tower lobby after the first plane crash, and that he stayed there for almost a solid hour. He only left when Giuliani finally got a message to him to come over to 75 Barclay, minutes before the collapse of the South Tower.

As for Von Essen, in 2002, he wrote an autobiography entitled *Strong of Heart*. In it, he describes how he did arrive later at Ganci's post, but he could not even locate Giuliani because the mayor, in fact, did *not* tell Ganci, or anyone else for that matter, where he was going.[144] It was not until after the 9:59 fall of the South Tower that Von Essen happened to run into Giuliani's group as they were trudging north on Broadway, trying to escape the dust cloud after a narrow escape from 75 Barclay Street, where the windows had been blown in by the force of the collapse.

The fact that Giuliani did not make an effort to see that these two vital members of the OEM team joined his entourage, and then that he later lied about it in an attempt to justify going to 75 Barclay, suggests that he never really intended for that location to become an effective command post. This fits with the notion that it was chosen merely as an excuse to avoid entering Building 7.

As to the question of who chose 75 Barclay Street: Kerik's story picks up after Giuliani's entourage left Chief Ganci at the fire department post. In his book, he says,

We walked north on West Street. Our immediate problem was set-ting up a command post...We moved back toward the building on

Barclay Street, and I sent Hector and Pitch [Detective John Picciano] inside to get it ready.[145]

But Giuliani's conflicted version says that it was Kerik's decision alone, and that he (Kerik) had already commandeered that location some forty minutes earlier. Even years after the fact, Giuliani would still be sticking to that claim; and with a vengeance. In his May 19, 2004 testimony before the 9/11 Commission, he would emphatically insist, to the point of committing perjury, that it was Kerik who nailed down that location. In actual fact, the bizarre story he gave about that, with all of its extravagant enhancements, was wholly made up. In describing for the commission the conversation he had with Kerik upon his 9:04 arrival at the WTC on the morning of the attacks, he said this:

[The] commissioner pointed to an emergency truck that was pulling up to in front of 70 Barclay Street, and he said, "That will be our command post. We're attaching hard lines into this building, and we're taking over this building." And they were literally taking people out of 75 Barclay Street and setting up a command post. And I said, "Is this going to be our main command post?" And he said, "Yes, that'll be our command post. We'll operate out of there. We've evacuated 7 World Trade Center." I said, "OK." I said, "Where is the, where is the fire department set up? Where are they fighting the fire?" He said, "Over on West Street." So, we began to walk and talk going toward West Street, which was a block and half to two blocks away.[146]

Here, the mayor again wipes his hands of the decision-making process and lays it all at the feet of Kerik. But where did the rest of this scenario come from? Kerik, in his book, and Santiago, in his *Never Forget* interview, did not mention anything about an emergency truck or attaching hard phone lines into any building. Nor did they say anything about taking people out of 75 Barclay. Kerik did write that he was trying to set up a police command post at that time, but he said that was being done by officers Sean Crowley and Eddie Aswad all the way over on the other side of the trade center at the intersection of Liberty and West Streets.[147]

Moreover, it would have been physically impossible to be setting up at 75 Barclay by the time Giuliani arrived, because the alleged "retired cop" of Kerik's version did not come out of 75 Barkley to offer his office until after the 9:03 second plane crash, and Giuliani said he arrived at about the same time. So, unless *Star Trek's* Captain Kirk had magically beamed down the "emergency truck" from his Enterprise spaceship, as well as the police crew and the "people" they were allegedly moving out of the building, it could not have happened.

Neither could the OEM command center in Building 7 have been evacuated at that point in time. According to Richard Zarillo's testimony, that did not occur until 9:18, at the very earliest, which would have been fourteen minutes after Giuliani's van sped up to the scene.

This stark disconnect between Giuliani's so-called "recollection" of what happened and reality—under oath, no less—brings into deep relief his desperate need to absolve himself of any suspicion that he was the one who chose the Barclay location. However, that it was Kerik's choice does not fly. In his book, Kerik admits that, if he had his druthers, he never would have gone there. He actually lamented the fact that it was a totally inadequate location for a command center. About that tucked away, first-floor office two blocks from the heart of the trade center, he would write:

> But while we had a number of top officials, we didn't have any federal numbers and we weren't sure we had any phones that would work... Unfortunately, at that point, there was absolutely nothing we could do to get a complete picture of what was really happening. [Meaning that there was no line of sight to the burning towers.] We couldn't even find a television to turn on the news to see what the media was reporting. Finally, someone found a radio.[148]

Adding to this intrigue is the fact that Giuliani and Kerik could not get their stories straight about the basic fact of *when* 75 Barclay was chosen. As pointed out previously, Giuliani wrote that "Within minutes of the *first* plane hitting the towers...the Police department had *already* begun setting up at 75 Barclay."[149] But Kerik wrote that that location had not been discovered until after the *second* plane crash; when the retired cop came out to offer it. In fact, as mentioned above, the only police command center he was setting up after the first plane crash was located at Liberty and West streets, on the other side of the trade center.

Then Santiago put the lie to them both. In his accounting, he did not recall anything being said about the Barclay location until after they left Chief Ganci at West and Vesey, some forty minutes after Giuliani arrived.

Above and beyond the questions of who chose the Barclay location and when, there remains the burning key question of *why* it was even needed. The Building 7 command center was the logical place to go. But Giuliani's masterminding of the DDC coup d'état and the destruction of the steel makes is clear that he had no intention of letting the OEM take over the WTC after the collapses. So, it would not be surprising if it turned out that he preplanned the 75 Barclay location to further that goal.

It is hard to understand how someone like Kerik could also be capable of such treachery. By all accounts, he was a person so dedicated to personal integrity that, through hard work and determination, he had pulled himself up by his bootstraps and overcame a severely disadvantaged childhood to achieve an otherwise sterling career in law enforcement; rising from patrolman to detective, and then to police commissioner. But, sadly, that he could have fallen to such a disturbing low level in this instance is substantially confirmed by an article that he wrote years later for the Online news magazine, *Newsmax*. In that September 9, 2011 piece entitled "Bernard Kerik: 'I Was Looking Into the Gates of Hell,'" he said this about the time he was waiting for Giuliani in front of Building 7, after the first plane crash:

Within minutes, I was there, standing right next to 7 World Trade Center that housed Mayor Rudy Giuliani's Office of Emergency

Management. *The front had been damaged by the explosion and there was no way for me to get in.*[150] (Italics added)

Here, he implies that he would have followed protocol and would have gone to the OEM command center, if it had only been possible. However, the main entrance to the building, he claimed, had been extensively damaged. But by what explosion? While it is true that Jennings and Hess witnessed an explosion in Building 7, that one could not have occurred until after 9:18—the earliest time that Richard Zarillo could have evacuated. And, as has been noted, plenty of people got into the building before that. Not the least of whom was also Tony Carbonetti, Giuliani's chief of staff. Before the second crash, he was actually up in the command center on the 23rd floor, talking on the phone to President Bush's chief of staff, Andy Card, in Florida.[151] Later, he would come out and join Giuliani's entourage in their walk to West Street.[152]

Even more troubling with respect to Kerik is something that Lhota said passed between them while they were waiting for Giuliani in front of Building 7, after the first plane crash. He said that, at one point, Kerik said to him, "This has got to be *al Qaeda*."[153] Moments later, Flight 175 plowed into the South Tower, signaling that it was a terrorist attack, and "the building explodes right over us," Lhota recalled.[154] But how could Kerik have known after the first crash something that the rest of the world only deduced after the second crash—that al Qaeda was involved—unless he had some secret insider information about what was really going on?

Compounding that suspicion is that, when Kerik came to write about this event in his book—which was literally only a couple months after the fact, in the late fall of 2001—he falsely claimed that he thought the first plane crash was an accident, stating,

First, I had believed that a small plane hit the first tower, and then I thought a passenger jet *accidently* hit the first tower, but now, with both towers engulfed in flames, I could see that this was something else entirely. Terrorism.[155] (Italics added)

Tragically, like his patron, the mayor, it appears that Kerik had also become entangled in a web of lies.

So, *who* chose 75 Barclay Street? *When* was it chosen? And, most importantly, *why*? Could it be that the likely answers to these questions are tied to the same hidden agenda that allowed for Giuliani and Kerik to escape possibly being killed by the explosion that Barry Jennings and Michael Hess said disabled the OEM command center in Building 7? If so, that would certainly offer some explanation for why the mayor felt the need to have his lawyer at his side every step of the way that morning.

The Tri-POD II "Shell Game"

Also mysterious is that, even *before* Building 7 collapsed, a replacement command center for Giuliani's 23rd floor OEM was already being organized far from the scene of the disaster. This represents one more piece of the puzzle that further leads to the suspicion that Vice President Cheney had intimate foreknowledge of, not only the collapses, but the plane crashes, as well.

Specifically, several months before 9/11, Cheney/ONP had teamed up with Giuliani to create a so-called "war game" exercise, allegedly to test the city's emergency response to an act of biological terrorism. Called Tri-POD II (Trial Point of Dispensing II), one stage of it was to take place on September 12.[156, 157] While the WTC was being attacked on the 11th, the command center for TriPOD II was in the process of being created two miles away in a warehouse at Pier 92, on the Hudson River.

Meanwhile, the collapse of the South Tower would force Giuliani and his police entourage out of their 75 Barclay Street "command post." Then, after the North Tower collapsed, they would set up temporarily at the Police Academy building on 20th Street for the purpose of having news conferences. Later that day, there was the complete collapse of Building 7. After that, Tri-POD II was suspended, and all the federal agencies involved with it, together with what was left of Giuliani's OEM personnel, were regrouped at the Pier 92 location, supposedly to deal with the cleanup/recovery operation at the WTC. But this last development seems all too convenient and brings up the possibility that it was part of a plan. This is how Giuliani explained it to the 9/11 Commission:

The reason Pier 92 was selected as a command center was because on the next day, on September 12, Pier 92 was going to have a drill, it had hundreds of people here, from FEMA, from the Federal Government, from the State, from the State Emergency Management Office, and they [FEMA]were getting ready for a drill for biochemical attack. So that was gonna be the place they were going to have the drill. The equipment was already there, so we were able to establish a command center there, within three days, that was two and a half to three times bigger than the command center that we had lost at 7 World Trade Center. And it was from there that the rest of the search and rescue effort was completed.[158]

This, of course, was not the whole truth. What the mayor failed to mention was that, by at least 9:30 a.m.—the time of Mike Burton's call to Regional Scaffold, before any building collapse and well *before* Pier 92 was reassigned to allegedly deal with the disaster—he had already, as reporter Langewiesche put it, unjustifiably made a "backroom" decision to "finesse" the OEM and allow the DDC to control the WTC site and proceed with the cleanup/recovery operation, on its own. In fact, immediately after the towers collapsed, the DDC would establish its own independent command post a few blocks north of the trade center, at Public School 89, and, with the NYPD standing guard at the WTC, would never relinquish control of the crime scene to anyone.

Another troubling aspect of Giuliani's statement to the commission is the omission that he had also placed Tri-POD II's federal disaster experts—as *Times* reporter Anthony DePalma put it—on the "sideline" almost "immediately" after the second plane crash. As a result, those federal experts from Tri-POD II, being the same ones that were connected to the mayor's OEM, would subsequently have no input into the disaster, not ever.

These two strategic moves—the DDC coup d'état and the banning of Tri-POD II's federal experts to the remote Pier 92 location—cemented Giuliani's unfettered control of the steel evidence. So essentially, Cheney's Pier 92 "OEM" location was reduced to being no more than just a prop in a thinly disguised shell game. It was, in effect, acting as a slight-of-hand diversion while the real action was taking place at the WTC, with the DDC destroying the evidence of controlled demolition. This, of course, was a direct result of Bush creating the ONP and putting Cheney in charge; all this four months *prior* to the 9/11 attacks.

A Battleground of Resentment

And so it was that, by nightfall on the day of the attacks, with the city's OEM members and its federal experts exiled to Cheney's Pier 92, Giuliani had the DDC positioned to begin something for which it had absolutely no qualifications or experience—dealing with a crime scene of mass murder, allegedly perpetrated by international terrorism.

The claim that this was part of a hidden agenda to cover up controlled demolitions by destroying the steel is also given credibility by the abysmal state of affairs that developed at the WTC because of that takeover. From the very beginning, DDC incompetence and its desperate rush to destroy the steel would lead to chaos and confrontation at the site. In effect, the WTC would progressively become a battleground of resentment between two warring factions, with the construction workers and firefighter-recovery crew on one side and DDC bosses on the other.

One early witness to that dysfunction was Marty Corcoran. He was a construction manager for Weeks Marine, the company whose barges would later be used to ship some of the debris to Fresh Kills.[159] On the day after the attacks, with Building 7 down, he made his way to what he thought was the OEM's new command post at the Public School 89 location. But this is what he found:

It was unbelievable. There are ten thousand meetings going on. The OEM had lost everything. It's like their preparations were thrown out the window. It was insane.[160]

He was also more than a little surprised to learn that the DDC, a city department he had never heard of, was in charge. He was told to see Mike

Burton, who was heading up day-to-day operations. Upon meeting him, it was obvious to Corcoran that Burton was in over his head:

> I tried to explain to him what we do and don't do. I can remember the look on his face. It was like he was a deer caught in the headlights. Like, where's the next shot coming from? And I felt embarrassed, because it was like I was speaking another language to him.[161]

Charlie Vitchers was one of the construction supervisors for the cleanup. In the 2006 book, *Nine Months at Ground Zero* (which he co-wrote), he offered this insight into the situation:

> Basically, what the DDC normally does is observe and report. On a normal project, they walk the site with the contractor to make sure equipment that they are paying for is on-site and that the man counts are correct...But in the real world the DDC doesn't really have a role in logistics or scheduling activities on the job.[162]

And that led to a cleanup/recovery process that was annoying, at best. "People," he said, "were frustrated because they didn't have any authority to dictate to somebody what should be done."[163]

Crane operator Bobby Gray agreed, saying,

> Public servants [the DDC] were acting like construction experts. [But] they had no field experience, no practical experience in doing what they were trying to do.[164]

Due to that, Vitchers ended up taking charge, holding morning work-scheduling sessions with key people in his trailer. According to firefighter recovery team member, Sam Melisi, operations then became smoother:

> When they started getting the construction crews into that trailer that established some type of order, some idea of what's going to

happen. Those meetings were totally different than the meetings with DDC and the fire department, or the police. It started to get so much more coordinated.[165]

Burton, however, turned out to be no wallflower. He began pushing for a quick cleanup with such extraordinary zeal that it was obvious to all that his orders were coming from City Hall; meaning Giuliani (the "benevolent dictator"). It was not long before he was being referred to as "Czar."[166] Crews were forced to work around the clock, in twelve-hour shifts.[167] Daily goals were set for debris removal, measured in tons, and anybody who missed the mark had hell to pay.[168] Reportedly, on more than one occasion, Burton's relations with the workers and firefighters were so sour that it was awkward for him to even show his face at the site.[169]

This is how Gray described it:

At points, it looked to me like the DDC was only concerned with trying to get this thing done—get the pile down to street level— before Giuliani left office at the end of the year...It started to smell like politics and business...The DDC was just sitting down and just screaming at the contractors.[170]

What is not well-known among the public is the degree to which this contentious infighting characterized the DDC cleanup/recovery operation. The general feeling in the country was that those working the site were a harmonious group; united in sympathy for the victims and selflessly devoted to the work they were doing—rescuing survivors, searching for the remains of victims, and clearing the site. But under the surface, the real state of affairs was far from that. While a noble spirit certainly was the driving force for the firefighters and construction workers to be there, and they remained devoted to that, as time went on, all too many of them found that working on a day-to-day basis under Giuliani's DDC became a progressively miserable situation.

The main bone of contention was over the DDC's overriding need for a speedy cleanup which, all too often, was without any regard whatsoever to the recovery of the remains of the victims.[171] Those working the site found that disrespectful, and it often led to heated confrontations. Vitchers, a potent individual in his own right, was not shy about voicing in painfully vivid detail some of the several clashes he had with DDC officials. One example he wrote about in his book was how Burton's deputy, Lou Mendes, a bulldog of a man, would frequently appear at their morning meetings and berate them:

He would come in and start screaming at everybody, call everybody an idiot: "You guys don't know what the fuck you're doing! Why is it taking so long to do this? Why is it taking so long to do that? What the fuck is wrong with you?"[172]

But Vitchers also understood that, ultimately, Giuliani was the instigator. As he also wrote, "I knew that he [Mendes] had to answer to the higher authorities, Mike Burton of the DDC and the mayor's office."[173]

As for the steel, Burton had an education and background in engineering and must have known how vital it was as evidence, but he displayed little concern for its preservation.[174] His indifferent attitude toward that was noted by New York Times reporters James Glanz and Eric Lipton in their 2003 book, City in the Sky. In it, they wrote:

Burton, who had become the effective czar for the cleanup job, had made it clear that he cared very little about engineering subtleties like the question of why the towers first stood, then collapsed on September 11. But he was deeply immersed in the details of hauling steel out of the debris pile.[175]

Years later, both Burton and his boss, Ken Holden, would confirm that they were acting on orders from Giuliani, whose overriding concern, above all else, was a quick cleanup. With respect to Holden, that subject came up in his response to questions he was asked about a health and safety issue at the site. By September 13, two days after the attack, the US Department of Labor's Occupational Safety and Health Administration

(OSHA) had declared that the air around the WTC was hazardous to breathe due to the amount of cancer-causing asbestos fibers and chemical fumes that were floating around. And they recommended that all workers wear dual-cartridge, air-purifying masks.[176]

But in those early days, only about thirty percent of them were doing so.[177] In a 2006 interview, Holden was asked why he did not force the people under him to wear protective gear when he became aware of that OSHA report. He responded that he would have "loved to have the authority to throw out people who would not wear protective equipment."[178] But, he indicated, the mayor was that final authority. And Giuliani, he said,

was mostly interested in reports on the tons of debris and steel that was shipped out and the bodies that were found. [He wanted] numbers and results, not what type of work problems and risks were behind those numbers. [He wanted] us to clean it up quickly. The sooner the better.[179]

Actually, there were several reasons why most of those working the site stopped using the masks. In the first place, they were not adequately informed of the OSHA report and were unaware of the seriousness of the situation.[180] In addition, the masks they were given were defective and when using them for any length of time, they found it difficult to breathe and had to take frequent breaks, which was annoying.[181]

But taking breaks slowed things down. So, when most of the firefighters and construction workers stopped wearing the masks, entirely, Holden, knowing the mayor's desire for a speedy clean-up, did not enforce the OSHA rule. And the mayor, knowing full-well the danger involved, also let it slide.

In fact, at one point, Giuliani went the extra mile and actively encouraged that unsafe behavior by falsely insinuating at a news conference that the masks were not necessary, saying,

The health department has run tests and, at this point, are not concerned. So far, all the tests that we have done do not show an undue amount of asbestos, doesn't show any particular chemical agent that we have to be concerned about. The accumulation of it for people who are down there can become very, very irritating. There are a lot of people whose eyes have been burned. But I don't think there's any chemical agent that we have to worry about.[182]

And whenever he made a short visit to the site, the mayor made a big display of his own lack of concern by not wearing a mask, himself, which reinforced the feeling among those working there that the masks were not necessary.[183]

Burton's confirmation that Giuliani was ultimately responsible for the destruction of the steel came years later at a hearing concerning a health issue that arose as a direct result of that. Tragically, nearly 35,000 people who worked the site, or nearby to it, ended up suffering from debilitating upper respiratory ailments and/or had developed cancers.[184] Those injured said that they were not adequately advised about the OSHA report, nor were they given proper masks, and they said the city should be held liable. But the city, by then under the administration of new mayor Michael Bloomberg, was balking on funding their healthcare. Burton's testimony at a hearing concerning that included this damning statement:

> Ultimately, the mayor [meaning Giuliani] gets the responsibility for what happened down there [at the WTC]. *Everything* was coordinated through the mayor's deputies and the mayor.[185] (Italics added.)

The BPS Team "Iced"

By September 25, two weeks after the attacks, with the DDC now firmly in control of the WTC, most of the BPS engineers had arrived to begin their investigation only to find to their utter astonishment that, not only were they barred from entering the site and the steel was being destroyed, but their investigation was going to be put on hold, indefinitely. They were informed by the Cheney cabal (aka, FEMA/ONP) that, although they were to officially remain as the chief investigators of the collapses, they were not going to be allowed to collect steel samples for their study. That job, they were told, had already been arranged to be done on their behalf by a separate group of local engineers associated with the Structural Engineers Association of New York (SEAoNY).[186]

FEMA's final report would later confirm this curious bit of obstructionism, saying, "Collection and storage of steel members from the WTC site was *not* part of the BPS Team efforts sponsored by FEMA and the American Society of Civil Engineers (ASCE)."[187] While the BPS team was being organized and traveling to New York, the report explained, "Engineers from SEAoNY had *offered* to collect certain WTC steel pieces for future building performance studies."[188] The powers that be had apparently accepted that "offer" and had further decided that that procedure would continue for the duration of the investigation.

The essential effect of this bizarre arrangement was that none of the BPS team of technical experts would be able to view the steel from the collapsed buildings before beginning their investigation. But that simply defied logic. To conduct a proper study, it was vital that they have up-close and personal access to that evidence. That meant deciding on and picking out from the debris pile and the scrap yards those steel samples that *they* thought were unusual and that might inform *them* of how the buildings came down.

However, that was not on the agenda. Immediately after their arrival, that BPS team—top experts in their field who had left their places of employment all over the country to travel to New York specifically to discover what caused the deaths of close to 2,100 of their fellow citizens—were forced to sign *nondisclosure* agreements and told to stand down, until further notice.

Understandably, frustration set in. As one dismayed team member would anonymously complain to the *New York Times*, "This is almost the Dream Team of engineers in the country working on this, and our hands are tied. FEMA is controlling everything."[189]

All Attempts to Save the Steel Failed

Meanwhile, all the BPS team members could do was stand by and watch as the WTC steel continued to be shipped out of the country at an alarming rate. And let there be no mistake that this blatant tampering with evidence was being done out of ignorance. Several experts made attempts to apprise Giuliani of the seriousness of retaining that key evidence, but they all ran into a stone wall; inexplicably, time after time, their complaints were met with silence from officials at City Hall.

One expert who was especially disturbed by that was Glenn Corbett. As an associate professor of fire science at New York's John Jay College of Criminal Justice, he had volunteered to assist the BPS team and, due to that, had a front-row seat into what was going on. This is how he later described it:

> We pressed early on for full-scale investigation. And, of course, one of the issues was—while we were doing that—the evidence from the buildings was being destroyed as we were talking about it. And we were advocating early on back then that the process of removing the steel, certainly, that was not an issue; that wasn't an issue, because this was a rescue and recovery operation. But once it was off the site, there was no real need for speed, basically, to get the steel cut up into small pieces and shipped overseas for scrap. We were concerned about that. And again, we understood early on that those [pieces of steel] were going to hold the keys to knowing exactly how the buildings came down. And, unfortunately, we were not successful in getting the *elected officials*—the powers that be—to do that [save the steel].[190] (Italics added.)

Another unsuccessful attempt was made by Dr. Abolhassan-Asl Astaneh, PhD, a professor of civil and environmental engineering at the University of California, Berkeley. He was sent to the WTC under auspices of the National Science Foundation (NSF) specifically to study the collapses. But he was also barred from the site by the NYPD. As a result, during his first few weeks in New York, the only chance he had to get a look at the steel was when trucks hauling it to Fresh Kills happened to be briefly stopped in traffic in front of his hotel.

The HSCS hearing in Washington would take special note of Professor Astaneh's failed efforts, saying,

An NSF-funded independent researcher [Astaneh], recognizing that valuable evidence [the steel] was being destroyed, attempted to intervene with the City of New York to save the valuable artifacts, but the city was *unwilling* to suspend the recycling contract.[191] (Italics added.)

About that, Professor Astaneh would later explain:

When there is a car accident and two people are killed, you keep the car until the trial is over. If a plane crashes, not only do you keep the plane, but you assemble all the pieces, take it to a hangar, and put it together. That's only for 200, 300 people, when they die. In this case, you had 3,000 people dead. You had a major machine, a major manmade structure. My wish was that we had spent whatever it takes, maybe $50 million, $100 million, and maybe two years, get all this steel, carry it to a lot. Instead of recycling it, put it horizontally, and assemble it. You have maybe 200 engineers, not just myself running around, trying to figure out what's going on. After all, this is a crime scene and you have to figure out exactly what happened for this crime, and learn from it. But that was my wish. My wish is not what happens.[192]

Unquestionably, the most valiant attempt to stop the destruction of the steel was made by James A Rossberg, the director of the ASCE's Structural Engineering Institute. The BPS team did not have subpoena power and could not force Giuliani to stop destroying evidence, but during the week of September 24, Rossberg took matters into his own hands and tried contacting the mayor by phone to lodge a complaint.[193,194] After repeated tries and getting no response, on Friday, September 28, he sent a request in writing, via fax.[195] Still, there was no answer.

No doubt exasperated by this stonewalling and realizing that literally tons of vital evidence was being destroyed by the minute, Rossberg decided to take desperate measures. A few hours after sending the unanswered fax, he took his complaint to the *New York Times*.[196]

The next day, after first confirming Rossberg's complaints with lower-level city officials, reporters James Glanz and Kenneth Chang, who were also alarmed by the situation, broke the story in no uncertain terms, saying this:

> The huge steel in columns and beams of the World Trade Center are being hauled off to be melted and recycled *before* engineers can inspect the twisted metal, which they say could hold important clues on how to build safer skyscrapers in the future.

> The city has signed a contract that allows two New Jersey firms to recycle the estimated 310,000 tons of steel from the trade center site, including some 90,000 tons from each tower...But some engineers, including a team assembled by the American Society of Civil Engineers, say that examination of the steel could allow them to piece together the *precise* chain of events that led to the collapse of the buildings...How the girders bent could tell the engineers which part of the buildings failed first. Microscopic analysis of the steel could tell them how hot the fires burned.[197] (Italics added.)

But the steel continued to be shipped out of the country as fast as humanly possible. Even if the mayor had deaf ears on this issue, one might think that this negative publicity shined on the situation for the whole world to see might inspire some reaction on the part of local and state law enforcement agencies, or certainly the FBI. But it did not.

The "Scoop and Dump"

However, it is apparent that the *Times* investigation did have an effect on Giuliani. Only, it was not the kind that the BPS team would have preferred; instead of inspiring caution, the mayor became even more determined to destroy the steel quickly and took desperate measures to see to that. The object of his wrath was the firefighter recovery crew.

From the very beginning of the cleanup operation, it had become apparent to everyone working the site that the single most troubling aspect of it for the mayor was the work stoppage that was often caused by the special care the firefighter recovery crew took in searching for remains. But exercising such diligence was no small matter to those who cared. Of the close to 2,100 people killed in the tower collapses, only 293 bodies would ever be found intact.[198] Many of the victims had been horribly torn apart and their body parts buried beneath tons of debris. As the cranes dug through the pile, arms and legs or pieces of bones and flesh, some as small as a fraction of an inch, would be uncovered. Out of respect, firefighters could often be seen down on their hands and knees with garden tools, meticulously combing through the debris, bagging up small pieces as they went along. For first responder recoveries, they were especially reverential. All work at the site would stop, and the firefighters would line up at attention and salute as the remains were carried out on a flag-draped stretcher.

This meticulous process required a lot of time and personnel. But, on September 28, the same day Rossberg went to the *New York Times*, Giuliani—in order, he said, to "speed" the cleanup—suddenly fired off an order drastically reducing the firefighter recovery crew from sixty-four members to twenty-five.[199] This was, of course, especially disturbing to the firefighters. Working with such a small crew, they argued, would reduce their recovery effort to a mere "scoop and dump" operation in which body parts would not be discovered until they ended up at Fresh Kills with the rest of the debris.[200] If carried out, they argued, that would be disrespectful to the over 1,000 victims not yet found, which no doubt included most of their 343 brother firefighters who had perished in the collapses.[201]

Suspiciously, at that same exact time, the DDC bosses, citing undefined so-called "safety" concerns, suddenly began ordering recovery crew members to stay fifty feet away from the grappling cranes that were digging out debris. Again, the firefighters protested, arguing that that was too far away to spot body parts before they were ripped through by the cranes' massive-toothed buckets.

Now, the fight was on in earnest. Disgusted by what they saw as an unconscionable emphasis on speed coming from City Hall, the now undermanned firefighter crew rebelled and refused to obey the fifty-foot rule; whenever they spotted something that looked suspicious, they would step in front of the cranes, forcing them to pause—which, being in complete sympathy, their operators were more than willing to do—then, other firefighters would climb onto the pile and take their time, patiently picking through the debris.

Invariably, frustrated DDC officials would step forward and complain about the continued slow-down of work. But when they did, they were bitterly told, in no uncertain terms, to—as firefighter Sam Melisi more politely put it—"Buzz off."[202]

"Rudy Must Go!"

Naturally, this inbred hostility could not help but feed on itself, and throughout October the atmosphere at the site thickened with tension. Finally, it reached a breaking point and the inevitable happened. On November 2, an angry group of 1,000 off-duty firefighters staged a loud protest at the site.[203] Predictably, tempers erupted, and eleven were arrested when some tried to force entry and a cop got punched in the face during a scuffle that broke out with the NYPD.[204]

The firefighters called for the release of those arrested. When that did not happen, they marched the five blocks up Broadway to City Hall, chanting, "Rudy must go!"[205]

Giuliani was furious.[206] The next day, in what the firefighters called a "Stalinist tactic," he had the president of the Uniformed Firefighters Association, Kevin Gallagher, arrested on a charge of criminal trespass.[207] That prompted an angry response from one union official, who said,

> The mayor fails to realize that New York City is not a dictatorship, where if you don't like what a union is doing you can just go and lock up a union's president. The message being sent from City Hall is that if you don't agree with this administration, we will get you.[208]

In the end, the mayor had charges dropped against all but one of those arrested and agreed to the firefighters' demand not to reduce the size of their recovery crew.[209] But he generally won that round; the search for remains would continue, only on a less ambitious scale than before. And, if push came to shove, the firefighters would have little say about whether some body parts might end up at Fresh Kills.[210]

This uneasy compromise did little to resolve the edgy atmosphere at the site, and, according to Langewiesche's first-person account, that bad feeling never went away. Indeed, as he reported, it "escalated toward the very end."[211]

The Bogus "Bovis Road"

That increase in pent-up pressure near the end of the cleanup operation was due in no small part to another of Giuliani's heartless decisions. Over a thousand victims of the collapses had not yet been found, but, in a last-ditch effort to speed up the debris removal even more, his DDC bosses ordered the workers to build a dirt-ramped roadway into the center of the pile so trucks could more easily be loaded. Derisively referred to by those working the site as the "Bovis Road" after its main contractor, Bovis Lend Lease, this road, due to the geography of the site, needed to go over a certain area that had been previously red-flagged by the firefighters to very likely contain a great number of the buried bodies of their fellow firefighters and civilians who they had tried to rescue.[212]

Langewiesche recounted an incident which was typical of the level of anguish this caused. He described how one older, grizzled firefighter verbally attacked Holden, one day. Approaching in wild-eyed desperation, the man got right in his face, shouting, "You stop these guys from pushing dirt in here! I've got two friends out there. And I've got my son buried right here."[213]

But the road was built, regardless. The site ended up resembling an open-pit mining operation, with it reaching down deep into the heart of the trade center. And from then on, until the end of the cleanup operation, the removal of remains buried beneath that road had to be delayed, and all those working the site were forced to watch daily as heavy trucks rolled across those victims' graves.[214]

But, as for the debris removal—and thus the recycling of the steel—it did, indeed, proceed at a noticeably more rapid pace.[215]

BPS Team "Iced," Again

By the time of the firefighters' demonstration, certain family members of the victims of the collapses had become just as restless. By now, having been made aware of the destruction of the steel by several negative articles in the *New York Times,* many of them had come to the sneaking suspicion that the deaths of their loved ones were not being properly investigated. And they started pressuring Giuliani; with some even carrying signs and demonstrating in front of City Hall.

No doubt aware of the sinking politics of the situation, on October 7, Giuliani finally agreed to allow the BPS engineers onto the WTC site for the first time.[216] But the team's so-called "access" was apparently just for show; by then, almost a month after the attacks, eighty percent of the steel had already been shipped out of the country, and the team was only allowed a three-day walkthrough of the WTC site and the four New Jersey salvage yards.[217]

In those short and sweet trips, the BPS engineers were only able to locate ten columns that they found significant as potential evidence for their investigation, and they set them aside for future examination, marking them in red paint with the word "SAVE." But to add insult to injury, just three days later, on October 10, the SEAoNY engineers would note in their log that all ten of them had been "accidentally" processed in salvage yard operations.[218] In other words, they were destroyed.

Immediately after that, the BPS team was, once again, put on ice by the Cheney cabal. This time, it would be for *three months.*[219]

During that whole period of inactivity, those engineering experts were denied access to basic information they needed to begin a proper investigation. They were not allowed to inspect the steel that the SEAoNY engineers were ostensibly selecting on their behalf.[220] They were also denied access to the vitally important architectural drawings of the buildings.[221] They were prohibited from talking to witnesses.[222] Even looking at the hundreds of photographs and videos that had been taken of the buildings before, during, and after the collapses was prohibited.[223]

In addition, being reminded of the nondisclosure agreements hanging over their heads, they were threatened with dismissal, or worse, if they ever contacted the press again.[224]

"No Holidays!"

Another incident that illustrates just how attached Giuliani must have been to seeing that the steel was totally destroyed—and quickly—occurred in mid-November. It started when Holden decided to give those working the site the day off for Veterans Day. When the mayor got wind of it, he sent his deputies down to make it clear in no uncertain terms that work stoppage for holidays was never to happen again.[225]

This led to his getting into a heated argument during his radio show later that month.[226] Having worked on Thanksgiving, one worker called in and pressed him about why they were not going to have Christmas off to spend with their families. It seemed a reasonable request, but Giuliani refused, saying that it was more important for the families who lost loved ones that the recovery of victims continue "around the clock."

Of course, the mayor was being disingenuous. According to the later statements by Holden and Burton, he did not even care about the health risks to which he was subjecting those working the site. If so, then how could the feelings of the families possibly be of any concern to him?

"A Half-baked Farce"

By the end of January, Bill Manning, a reporter for *Fire Engineering* magazine, a 125-year-old firefighter trade publication, had become so incensed by the whole affair that he wrote these scathing words:

> *Fire Engineering* has good reason to believe that the "official investigation" blessed by FEMA...is a half-baked farce that may already have been commandeered by political forces whose primary interests, to put it mildly, lie far afield of full disclosure. Except for the

marginal benefit obtained from a three-day, visual walk-through of evidence sites conducted by ASCE (American Society of Civil Engineers) investigation committee members—described by one close source as a "tourist trip"—no one's checking the evidence for anything.[227]

"This Was a Crime Scene"

Giuliani's push to get the steel shipped out quickly would be successful. His take-charge attitude resulted in the WTC site being completely cleared in less than nine months, instead of the thirty months predicted. It would officially end on May 28, 2002, when a ceremony attended by the mayor marked the moment when the last piece of debris—a column—was hauled out of the site to be, as usual, sold off for scrap.[228]

But such destruction of evidence is a serious crime. And it can have serious consequences. In a case like the 9/11 attacks, it was a federal offense that can result in heavy prison time. That is spelled out in Title 18, Section 1519 of the US Code, which says:

Whoever knowingly alters, destroys, mutilates, conceals, covers up, falsifies, or makes a false entry in any record, document, or tangible object with the intent to impede, obstruct, or influence the investigation or proper administration of any matter within the jurisdiction of any department or agency of the United States or any case filed under title 11, or in relation to or contemplation of any such matter or case, shall be fined under this title, imprisoned not more than 20 years, or both.[229]

An example of that is what happened later during the Bush administration to a man who was accused of taking home small pieces of the space shuttle Columbia that disintegrated upon reentry. He was arrested and indicted. And in that case, prosecutors were asking for a prison sentence of fifteen years and a fine of $500,000.[230]

And there can be little doubt that Giuliani was fully aware that his meddling with the steel was illegal. For instance, on September 27, 2001, the *Associated Press* and the *Washington Post* teamed up for an article on the WTC disaster. In that piece, they reported that Giuliani, during an interview, had personally referred to the WTC site as a "crime scene."[231] Also, about the site of the disaster in *Leadership*, the mayor would pointedly write, "This was a crime scene."[232] Being a former federal prosecutor, one can safely assume, then, that he must have been keenly aware that his destruction of the steel could expose him to severe penalties.

But somehow, he must have also known that, regarding the WTC, the normal rules did not apply—at least not to him.

White House Deception

Despite being publicized in every possible way—from the *New York Times* to the HSCS hearing in Washington—the criminal act of destroying the steel that was set in motion by Giuliani was allowed to continue under the Cheney cabal's watch and in plain view of the FBI. This suggests that a high-level cover-up was well underway that had its origins in the White House. In turn, that puts a dark cloud of suspicion over the subsequent official investigations. So, is there any evidence that those investigations were, in fact, not honest searches for the truth?

The quick answer to that question is yes. Take the FEMA investigation, for one. Right off the bat, President Bush showed a singular lack of commitment by allotting it a pitiful, shoe-string budget. Typically, investigations of this scope have cost tens of millions of dollars. For example, earlier, in 1996, the Clinton administration had authorized $50 million for the investigation of TWA Flight 800, which crashed off the coast of Long Island, killing 230 people.[233] And after the 9/11 attacks, in 2003, Bush himself would support a similar budget for NASA's investigation after the space shuttle Columbia would burn up on re-entry to the earth's atmosphere, killing seven astronauts.[234] But incredibly, in the case of the WTC—where 2,100 innocent people had been mercilessly slaughtered in the collapses—Bush only gave FEMA's BPS team a paltry $600,000.[235]

Even worse, when that meager allowance was quickly eaten up, the White House refused to refund it. Due to that, the ASCE itself had to chip in with a $500,000 donation to finish the investigation and complete the writing of the report.[236]

In addition, not only did the White House restrain the BPS investigators by limiting their funding, but it set a time limit to finish the work. As a result, the team's report had to be delivered in lightning speed for such investigations—just seven months.[237]

Together, these two restrictions crippled the investigation.[238] At one point, this fact was testified to by BPS lead investigator Gene Corley. At the March 2002 HSCS hearing in Washington, Corley, who held a PhD in structural engineering, was asked about his report's conclusions that were going to be released within a couple of months. In response, he did not mince words. He confessed that "the scope of the investigation was not to come to final conclusions." His team, he said, "simply did not have the resources or the time to do that."[239]

NIST; the $22 Million Scam

Not surprisingly, FEMA's May 2002 final report was not well-received among those who thought that the deaths of the over 2,000 innocent victims of the collapses deserved a more concentrated effort. At only a couple hundred pages, the sketchy, preliminary nature of it caused a firestorm of criticism. And the plot thickened considerably when Gene Corley's own credibility came into question.

As it turned out, although he was being honest about the lack of time and money in his HSCS testimony, contrary to what he told the committee about those obvious limitations, even a cursory look at FEMA's later report revealed that the agency did, in fact, come to "final conclusions." For example, that report's opening Executive Summary, which Corley himself wrote, states categorically that "the structural damage sustained by each tower from the [plane] impact, combined with the ensuing fires, *resulted* in the total collapse of each building."[240] No matter how you look at it, this is a pretty definitive statement. But it seems odd coming from a guy whose so-called "investigation" was, as he had testified, fatally stunted by restrictions of time and money.

Also unsettling was the discovery that Corley had a special relationship with the White House. It was learned that he had not been selected by the ASCE to head the BPS team. Instead, he had been secretly chosen for that position by the Bush administration. This was after he had also been previously hand-picked to head up the engineering assessment of the Oklahoma City bombing case.[241] For many, this ongoing, cozy relationship with the administration explains why he never attempted to intervene on behalf of his BPS team to attempt to stop Giuliani's destruction of the steel.[242]

Later incidents would confirm that suspicion. For one thing, despite his critical assessment of the value of the FEMA investigation in his HSCS testimony, Corley would make a complete reversal and become an avid spokesperson for its so-called "final conclusions" in a documentary produced by the Public Broadcasting Service (PBS). In that film, called *How the Towers Fell*, he would unequivocally state that "it was the combination of the [plane] impact load doing great damage to the building, followed by the fire, that caused collapse," cynically adding that he hoped FEMA's so-called "findings" would have lasting significance in the future "to develop buildings that will provide more safety for those who are in those buildings."[243]

But the real nail in the coffin of Corley's poor credibility would come during the NIST investigation. At one point during its proceedings, he was recorded on video posing as a "reporter" at a news conference held by the institute and suspiciously asking softball questions that were obviously meant to rally public support for the official theory for the collapses.[244]

That kind of transparent duplicity is also revealed in FEMA's final report. A close reading of it shows that Corley's personal "finding" that the plane crashes caused the collapses is wholly inconsistent with the conclusions of other investigators working under his supervision. For example, Chapter 2, which was written by a team headed by Ronald Hamburger, contradicts him, saying, "the specific chain of events that led to the eventual collapse [of the North Tower] will probably *never* be identified."[245] And later, that chapter says that those same conditions were "likely" to have occurred in the South Tower.[246] And still later, its

"Recommendations" section admitted that "additional studies" should be conducted in order to determine the actual mechanism for the collapses.[247] Having learned of those discrepancies in the FEMA report, family members of the victims kept up the pressure for a new investigation.[248] After several months of pretentious hand-wringing in the media—led primarily by Cheney—over how another investigation might detract resources from the administration's newly-minted "War on Terror," the White House finally agreed to one.[249] But once again, the administration neglected to adequately fund it. When questioned under oath about the cost of a second, more complete scientific investigation during his HSCS testimony, Corley had frankly stated that it would take about $40 million.[250] And by historical standards, that seems about right. But in August 2002, when the White House first publicly announced that the second investigation would be done, only $16 million was authorized for it.[251] Later, that would be increased to $20 million. In the end, it would end up costing about $22 million. But still, that was wholly inadequate.

According to that August 2002 White House announcement, this second underfunded investigation was officially to begin in October 2002 by NIST and was going to be headed by Dr. Sivarage Shyam-Sunder, a decade-long employee of the institute, who, like Corley, also held a PhD in structural engineering. Not surprisingly for many of the administration's critics, Sunder's report, which appeared three years later, unequivocally affirmed Corley's finding that the tower collapses were caused by the jet fuel-fed fires from the plane crashes.[252, 253] As for Building 7, Sunder took six years before releasing a separate report on that collapse, which essentially said the same thing.[254, 255]

But, as was highlighted in the Introduction, the most troubling aspect of both the FEMA and NIST reports is that their conclusions were based solely on *hypothetical* computer simulations of the plane crashes, not hard evidence; which, of course, was necessitated by the destruction of the steel.

How FEMA developed its models was not revealed in its report, which had the effect of blocking any critical analysis of its methods. On the other hand, NIST did reveal its methods. But a close reading of its section on the North Tower reveals that the final simulation it used to illustrate that collapse was artificially manipulated to give a predetermined result.[256]

For instance, the institute started by determining its most "reasonable" parameters for its computer simulation of the crash of Flight 11 into the North Tower and variously called that the "Base Case," or "Case A." But, when it ran that simulation, the tower did *not* collapse.[257] So what did Dr. Sunder do? Did he act like a neutral, unbiased investigator and reassess his original assumptions about the collapse and maybe look elsewhere for the cause than the plane crash? No, he simply adjusted the parameters of the model, creating out of thin air a new, more severe "Case B" simulation that did make the tower collapse.[258]

This was accomplished, his report admits, by "making the tower structure weaker and the aircraft structure stronger."[259] And then, he had the unconscionable audacity to reverse his original finding and say that that corrupted Case B simulation is now the one that "reasonably" matches the evidence.[260] The only proof of its accuracy being that the computer made the tower collapse due to an unrealistic plane crash.

This process cannot, in any way, be called a true scientific study. It is more properly called a fraud—a $22 million scam cooked-up by Sunder et al to hide the true cause of the cold-blooded murder of 2,100 innocent people.

The Simultaneous Investigations

That the White House was behind that hypocrisy is nailed down considerably by the discovery that that second so-called "investigation" done by NIST was, actually, *not* born independently from that of FEMA, as the country was cynically led to believe. A close examination of the facts reveals that a scheme had been hammered out in the very beginning of the process, at the highest levels of the White House, to use simultaneous investigations by FEMA and NIST to hide the use of explosives.

In other words, the administration created the ruse that the second investigation done by NIST was a reaction to public pressure, when it was actually planned all along as an elaborate emergency-backstop should FEMA's superficial, preliminary report stir up a public backlash (which it did).

FEMA gave a clue to this scheme in its May 2002 final report when it said this regarding the fires in the North Tower:

Using the Computational Fluid Dynamics (CFD) fire model, *Fire Dynamics Simulator* Ver. 1 (FDS1), fire scientists at the *National Institute of Standards and Technology* (*NIST*) (Rehm, et al. 2002) were able to mathematically approximate the size of fires...[261] (Italics added.)

By revealing here that NIST had already done its Fire Dynamics Simulator (FDS) computer modeling of the fire temperatures in the North Tower, FEMA inadvertently admitted that NIST had already concluded the major part of its investigation—the trumped-up "Case B" simulation of the crash of Flight 11— prior to May 2002. This is so because a major principle of fire engineering dictates that the temperature of a fire in a building is directly proportional to the free flow of air/oxygen throughout the structure. Thus, an important parameter needed for input into the FDS would have been a figure for the amount of air flow throughout the North Tower that was due to the destruction allegedly done to the building's internal floors and walls by the plane crash. That number could only have been determined by running a separate simulation for the bogus Case B plane impact damage. Therefore, this statement by FEMA is direct confirmation that NIST's Case B simulation must have already been cooked-up at some point in time before the release of FEMA's report.

This proves that NIST's investigation was geared up long *before* the release of the FEMA report, not five months after it in reaction to public pressure, as the White House pretended.

NIST's Engineering Laboratory released a later document in 2011 that sheds some light on when the NIST investigation actually began. That paper, entitled, "Questions and answers about the NIST WTC Towers Investigation," says this:

The Federal Emergency Management Agency (FEMA), which had launched its Building Performance Assessment Team (BPAT) [*sic*]

Study in early *October 2001*, sent a team of experts to review the steel at the WTC site and the salvage yards. These experts, *including one from NIST*, identified pieces of steel of potential interest to a follow-on investigation. Beginning in February 2002, NIST, on its own initiative, began identifying additional steel pieces of potential interest at the salvage yards and transporting them to NIST to preserve and secure the evidence in *anticipation* of launching its own investigation, which it announced in *August 2002*.[262] (Italics added.)

The key to understanding the importance of this passage is knowing that NIST is not, as its title might suggest, an independent investigative agency. It is, in fact, a division of a White House Cabinet member—the US Department of Commerce. As such, Dr. Sunder would not begin his own investigation into such a politically charged matter as the WTC collapses by sending one of his "experts" to study the "steel" unless he was directed to do so by the president.

This confirms that the NIST investigation was launched by the Bush White House *simultaneously* with that of FEMA, in October 2001, about one month after the attacks, not a year later in August 2002, as a reaction to public pressure.

Conclusion
Regrettably, one can only conclude from the existence of that elaborate, tandem FEMA/NIST cover-up scheme that it was known at the highest levels of the Bush White House that the deaths of those 2,100 people who died in the collapses were due to explosives, not the al Qaeda plane crashes. In turn, that suggests that, for whatever reason, the endgame of this ruse of having simultaneous "investigations" was to hang blame for the collapses on Osama bin Laden.

Among the many other startling revelations in this chapter, the most prominent is the OEM-disabling blast in Building 7, as witnessed by Barry Jennings and Michael Hess. It provides undeniable proof that explosives were, without any doubt, planted at the WTC. Obviously, the device that caused that explosion did not plant itself. It had to have been planted by a human being. And that person had to have had a purpose. So what could that have been? To find an answer to that, following normal police procedure is, again, helpful. That dictates that we look for who *benefited* from the crime.

Obviously, that explosion was a seminal event. With their command center put out of action, OEM personnel and their associated federal disaster experts were spun off in disarray. This prevented an Oklahoma City bombing situation from occurring, where federal agencies could get control of the crime scene. Clearly, that benefited the cover-up by making it possible for Giuliani to affect the DDC coup d'état and get rid of the steel. The later demolition of Building 7 would put a neat little bow on that betrayal; with the steel from that building hauled off and recycled with that of the towers, a critical amount of the most direct physical evidence of mass murder using explosives would disappear.

The fact of that OEM explosion also links up with the suspicion that Sheirer was, at least to some degree, involved with Giuliani in the cover-up. For instance, in his 9/11 Commission testimony, he said that he did not communicate for the *first* time with the mayor that morning until about an hour after the first plane crash. That was when Giuliani got a message to him in the North Tower lobby, asking that he join him at the 75 Barclay Street police "command" post.[263] Yet, immediately after that *first* plane crash, he and Giuliani—the two top leaders of the OEM—had, in chorus, made the disastrous decision to shirk their duties and avoid entering Building 7, thus avoiding being possibly killed by the explosion. This indicates that they likely had a previous conversation *before* the attacks in which they discussed the danger of entering Building 7. That, in turn, suggests foreknowledge.

It is not known how deep their level of foreknowledge went; just because they both avoided Building 7 does not mean that they had to have known the full extent of what was going to happen—i.e., the collapses—but only what they needed to know to stay safe and available to assist in the later cover-up. In fact, it is unlikely that either of them did know the full extent of what was about to happen that morning, because, clearly, if Sheirer knew that all three buildings were going to collapse, he would not have gone to the North Tower lobby. Certainly, he would not have stayed there for an hour, waiting for the building to come down.

Likewise, if Giuliani knew Building 7 was going to completely collapse, he would not have chosen 75 Barclay, which was basically right across the street, for an alternate command post. But the fact that they both shirked their duties in harmony suggests that at least one of them—most likely Giuliani—had been forewarned about entering Building 7, and that he had subsequently passed that along to Sheirer, at some point in time, *before* the attacks.

Police Commissioner Kerik's actions after the first plane crash strongly suggests that he also had some involvement in the cover-up. His statement to Joe Lhota about the first crash being the work of "al Qaeda" is telling. As was his claim in *Newsmax* that the front entrance to Building 7 was impassable, and that is why he could not go the command center. In that same vein: Was there really a "retired cop" who "offered" the totally inadequate 75 Barclay location? Santiago, for one, did not confirm it. And, in his book, Kerik actually complained about the inadequacy of that location.

That there was also some level of collusion between Giuliani and people high up in the Bush administration involves an early phone call that the mayor made to the White House that morning. In *Leadership*, he says that, while driving to the WTC after the *first* plane crash, he had asked Detective Vallone to put in that call.[264] But he also said that he thought the first plane crash was because "some nut had crashed a small plane" into the North Tower *accidentally*, which hardly would have constituted a national emergency.[265] He did not say whether Vallone got the call through to the White House, who she talked to, or what was said, but why call the White House at all, unless he knew that the first plane crash was more than just an accident?

A second call Mayor Giuliani made to the White House's main number later that morning adds to the suspicion of collusion. In *Leadership*, he wrote that he made it from 75 Barclay Street at about 9:50 a.m. He said his purpose was to ask about air support for the city.[266] But the facts belie that. In the first place, only the president can order up Air Force jets, and Bush was in Florida, at the time. Giuliani claimed in his book that when he made this call he was unaware that Bush was not at the White House. But that does not ring true because—as was previously noted in this chapter—his chief of staff, Tony Carbonetti, had already called the White House from the OEM command center in Building 7 some forty-seven minutes earlier. At that time, Carbonetti had been told by the president's chief of staff, Andy Card, that, if Giuliani wanted to talk to the president, he had to call the Situation Room conference center in the White House and be "patched" through to him; the inference being that Bush was not at the White House where he could normally be reached through the main switchboard. And Card gave Carbonetti the number to call. Giuliani also wrote that Carbonetti was with his entourage at Chief Ganci's post on West Street at 9:44 and had joined them in their walk back to 75 Barclay. The need for air support being such a vital question, it is inconceivable that Carbonetti did not tell Giuliani then about his conversation with Card. But, when Giuliani got to 75 Barclay, instead of immediately calling the Situation Room to contact Bush as Card directed, he called the main White House number.

Cheney was holding down the fort there that morning in Bush's absence. But the vice-president does not have any standing in the military chain of command. Thus, it is more likely that Giuliani's real reason for contacting the White House—including the call he had previously ordered Detective Vallone to make—was to touch base with his co-conspirator, Cheney, not to get air support.

As for Cheney, his overall foreknowledge of the entire WTC attack scenario is strongly indicated by the existence of the Tri-POD II war game. Obviously, that exercise had to have been scheduled cooperatively with Giuliani months before the attacks. But, if he (Cheney) was unaware of the attacks, why was its command center planned to be headquartered two miles away from the WTC when the hi-tech command center in Building 7 was specifically designed precisely for that purpose? Creating that Building 7 location was, as Giuliani admitted in his book, "the most important decision" he had made as mayor. Tens of millions of dollars of taxpayer money was tied up in it. In fact, several times in the past, he had presided over the same kind of drills that were headquartered at that command center. So why not run Tri-POD II out of there as well, unless he had been influenced by Cheney to locate it elsewhere? This does not mean that Cheney had to have told Giuliani the full extent about the attack on the WTC, or even about the collapses, but only what he needed to know to be available later for the cover-up.

This would, of course, make Cheney a major player. The circumstances surrounding Tri-POD II forces the question: Was it merely coincidental that it was Bush's May 2001 directive to Allbaugh that put Cheney in a position to conspire with Giuliani to destroy the steel? If so, that would have had to have been one monumental happenstance. On the other hand, if not a coincidence, that presidential edict would be prima facia evidence that Bush, as well as Cheney, had foreknowledge of the plane attacks, knew the WTC buildings were rigged for demolitions, knew that thousands of people were going to die, and that they let it happen.

In summary, having now proven that at least one explosive device was planted at the WTC—*the OEM-disabling blast in Building 7*—and having also outlined the activities of three of the major suspects involved in covering that up—*Bush, Cheney, and Giuliani*—the rest of this book now lays out the hard evidence that proves explosives were also planted in the North Tower.

2

The Explosions on B4

AS DISCUSSED IN CHAPTER 1, the *only* evidence that could have been used to prove the Bush administration's claim that the WTC collapses were due to the plane crashes and the fires that subsequently developed was a metallurgical examination of the steel from the twin towers. But the alternative proposition that says explosives were involved does not suffer from that limitation. Whereas the official explanation requires a microscopic investigation of the granular structure of the steel from the plane impact zones to determine how much it was weakened by the fires, the manifestations of explosions are obvious to the human senses—they can be seen, heard, and felt. And that can be embedded in the memories of witnesses.

The most significant examples of that are the statements of five maintenance workers who experienced explosions in the North Tower's B4 subbasement level—four stories below ground—when Flight 11 hit the 96th floor, a quarter of a mile above them. The confluence of their observations provide indisputable proof that explosives were planted in the building.

The Explosions
The WTC had its own law enforcement agency, the Port Authority Police Department (PAPD). Its main desk was in a nine-story building adjacent to the North Tower, called WTC 5. Flight 11 crashed into the tower at about 8:47 a.m. Three minutes later, at 8:50, the PAPD main desk received this urgent call:

PAPD:	Port Authority Police, Officer Brady.
Male Caller:	Officer, help. We're down on the B4 level. This

	is Turner's field office. There's been a big explosion. We've got water lines open. There seems to be steam and smoke in the area.
PAPD:	OK. Where? Where exactly on B4?
Male Caller:	Turner Construction, right outside the 50-Car. We're across the hall from the 50-Car.
PAPD:	Is there any smoke condition in the area?
Male Caller:	It's...yeah, we got smoke. I don't know how, whether it's from fire or just dust.[266]

The Official Explanations

The first official version of what caused all of the explosions in the lower levels of the North Tower—including the one the PAPD caller was referring to—was given by FEMA. This is what that agency said in its final report of May 2002:

As the aircraft crashed into and plowed across the buildings, they distributed jet fuel throughout the impact area to form a *flammable "cloud."* Ignition of this cloud resulted in a rapid pressure rise, expelling a fuel rich material from the impact area into shafts and through other openings caused by the crashes, resulting in dramatic fireballs.[267] (Italics added)

By July 2004, the 9/11 Commission had come out with this more detailed version:

A jet fuel *fireball* erupted upon impact and shot down at least one bank of elevators. The fireball exploded onto numerous lower floors, including the 77th and 22nd; the West Street lobby level; and the B4 level, four stories below ground.[268] (Italics added)

This became the standard for discussion in the mainstream media. The following graphic depicts its incredible sequence of events.

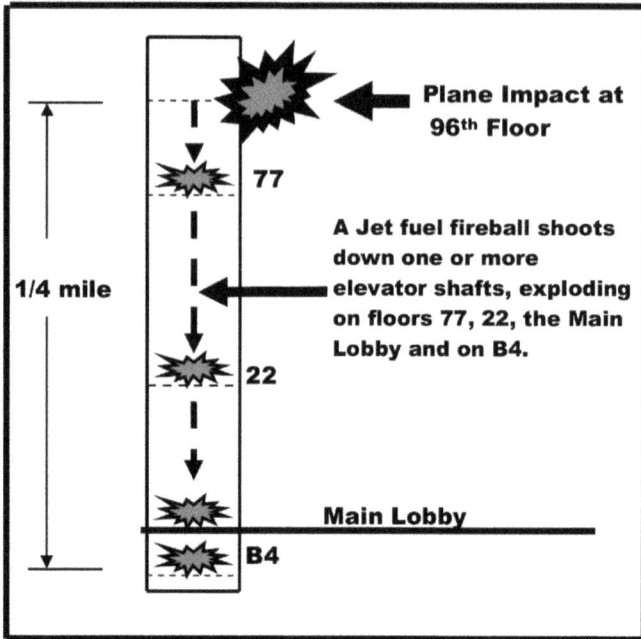

The Fireball-Down-A-Shaft Theory

Finally, in December 2005, NIST's final report said this (please note that WTC 1 refers to the North Tower):

> In addition, the jet fuel distribution through the buildings and down the elevator shafts generated large fires. The elevator shafts inside WTC 1 contained a fast moving jet fuel *droplet cloud fire* which damaged the shaft walls, elevator doors, and floors near the elevator shafts due to the overpressures that were generated.[269] (Italics added)

But it stands to reason that these official reports could only have been speculating about what caused the lower level damage. There can be no evidence that supports their conclusion that a "flammable cloud," a "fireball," or a "droplet cloud fire" went down one or more elevator shafts. Although several witnesses did see a fireball explode out of at least one bank of elevators in the main lobby at the time of plane impact, none has ever come forward to testify to actually seeing a fireball coming down a shaft. Indeed, it is quite certain that even if someone was actually inside a shaft and in a position to observe such a thing, that person would not have lived to tell about it.

Moreover, those official explanations are weakened considerably by the very nature of jet fuel, itself.

The Question of Jet Fuel

To begin with, although the term may sound exotic, jet fuel is essentially just plain old, ordinary kerosene, a nonexplosive, low volatility fuel. It is considered low volatility because it has a very high flash point. The flash point of a liquid fuel refers to the temperature at which vapors will form on its surface that are capable of being ignited; not that it will explode, just that it can be made to sustain burning on its own. The flash point of kerosene jet fuel ranges from 100 to 160°F, depending on factors such as barometric pressure, humidity, etc.[270] That means that unless a pool of it is raised to at least 100°, if you throw a match into it, the flame will quickly burn out with the match. By contrast, gasoline is a highly volatile fuel with a flash point of minus 45°F, which means that even on a freezing cold winter day, if it is lit, it will continue to burn. That is why kerosene is used as jet fuel and gasoline is not. It is a lot safer.

In addition, kerosene jet fuel, under moderate temperature conditions, can only be made to "explode" if it is dispersed in the form of a vapor cloud. The official story relies on that for its fireball-down-a-shaft theory. But even then, the conditions have to be almost perfect. A kerosene cloud is only explosive within a narrow range of densities. If the density of the vapor is below 0.7 percent by volume, it will be too lean (not having enough fuel) to explode, and if it is above 5 percent by volume it will be too rich (having too much fuel). And even within that range, there must be an ignition source—a spark or a flame. The only way the cloud could spontaneously ignite itself is if its temperature reaches what is called its auto ignition temperature. For kerosene, that is 428°F.[271]

Some supporters of the official story like to excuse the fireball-down-a-shaft theory by saying that it was actually liquid jet fuel that fell down a bank of elevator shafts and later formed a cloud of fumes, which was somehow ignited and caused all of the explosions in the lower levels of the tower, at the time of plane impact. However, under this theory it would have taken some period of time for a flammable cloud to form at the lowest level to which the liquid fuel had settled. And that does not fit the rapidity with which the explosions occurred after plane impact. In addition, no source is ever given for the ignition of that imagined vapor cloud.

In addition, the ambient air temperature outside the tower on the day of the 9/11 attacks was about 71°F. Given that fact, it is impossible to think that the air temperature in any of the North Tower elevator shafts could be above the 100°F minimum needed for jet fuel to even sustain burning, let alone the 428°F needed for it to self-ignite. So, the notion that liquid jet fuel fell down a shaft to the lower floors and the basement levels and then formed a vapor cloud that subsequently exploded on all those different levels so quickly after plane impact is not a likely possibility and can be discounted.

Moreover, when a kerosene vapor cloud does "explode," the fireball formed is more in line with a low energy deflagration—an intensely burning fire—than with a true explosive event. FEMA made this point crystal clear when it said this about the initial fireballs created by the impact of Flight 11 on the North Tower:

> Although dramatic, these fireballs (in the impact zone) did not explode or generate a shock wave. If an explosion or detonation had occurred, the expansion of the burning gases would have taken place in microseconds, not the two seconds observed.[272]

In other words, strictly speaking, a jet fuel-fed fireball is not considered a true explosive event, because it is not accompanied by a shock wave. So right off the bat, this brings into question the official theory, which says that a jet fuel-fed fireball could shoot a quarter of a mile down an elevator shaft, blowing up on three levels on the way down, and would still have enough energy left to explode with incredible fury on B4.

No Trace of Jet Fuel on B4

The PAPD caller reported that an "explosion" had occurred on B4, but there is no evidence that jet fuel was present.

The office that the caller was referring to belonged to Turner Construction, a company that was doing work on the tower. According to the architectural drawings, Turner's office had to be located in a "Support Services" area across from the 50-car's elevator shaft, in the southeastern part of B4; as a 1984 site plan drawing shows, all other areas were either designated for "Port Authority (PA) Maintenance," "National Engineering" or for "Broadway Electrical."[273]

The 50-car was the main freight elevator for the building and the only elevator that serviced B4 and had door openings there. Refer to the following B4 detail drawing done in 1968.

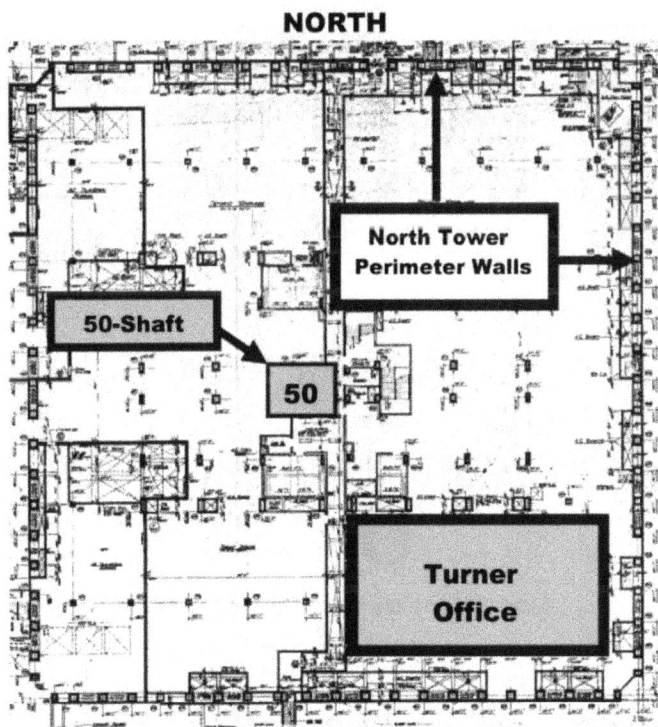

North Tower B4 Level
(1968 Drawing)

85

The following view of the previous plan indicates the location of the PAPD caller in relation to the elevator shafts.[274] Note how close his location was to the elevators and to Turner's office.

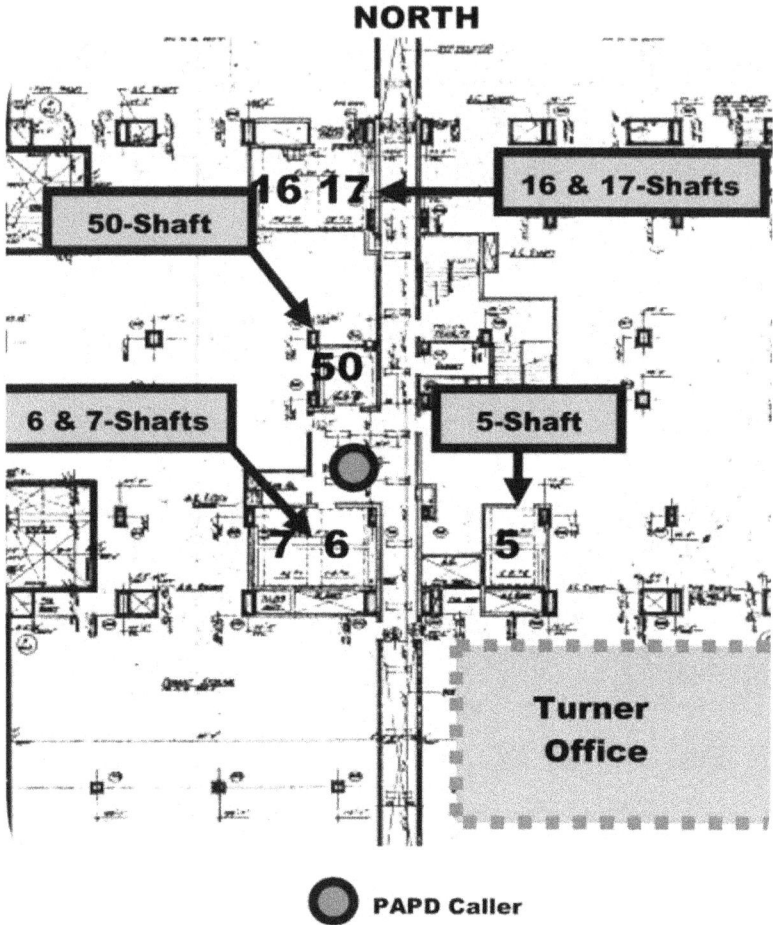

Location of the PAPD Caller
(1968 B4 Detail)

The PAPD caller was located pretty close to all of the elevator shafts. If the explosion he was calling about was caused by a jet fuel fireball exploding out from one of them, as the official accounts claim, there should have been obvious signs near him that a fireball had hit the area, because his call came only three minutes after the plane crash and thus had to have been made very shortly after the alleged fireball supposedly swept through this level of the tower. But, by questioning whether the smoke was from "fire or just dust," the caller was indicating that he did not see any sign of fire in the area, or the aftereffects of a fire. In other words, if the "smoke" was caused by a fireball that had shot out of an elevator shaft, he would not have questioned the source of the smoke. It would have been obvious to him.

Secondly, he does not mention a *kerosene* smell, which would also have been obvious to him if jet fuel had been involved. The whole B4 area would have been filled with its unmistakable, pungent odor.

And thirdly, the caller talks of a "big" explosion, which indicates a lot of physical destruction and, thus, the presence of a *shock wave*. As has been explained, that is not characteristic of a jet fuel fireball, which creates more on the order of a mere deflagration than a true explosive event.

No fire, no kerosene odor and the presence of a shock wave all add up to one thing: Jet fuel was not involved in the "big explosion."

The following statements of the five North Tower workers who were on B4 also bear that out.

The Witnesses

Building engineer **Edward McCabe** was one who personally observed the enormous power of the explosion the PAPD caller was talking about. He was in the B4 operating level of the refrigeration room when the explosion occurred. That was located just beyond the North Tower's south perimeter wall. To better understand his location, note the following drawing, showing the layout of the subbasement levels of the WTC.

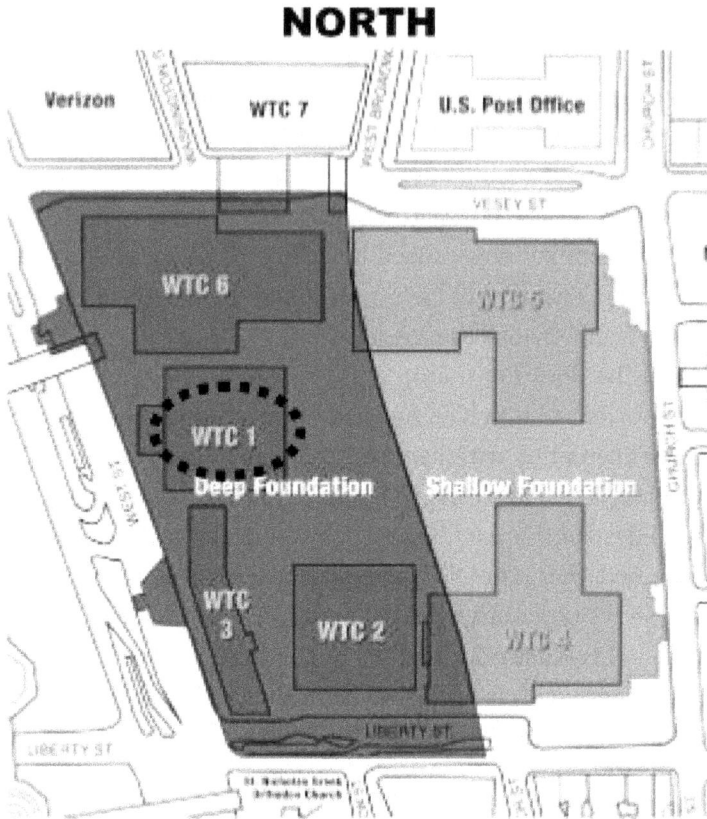

NORTH

WTC Subbasement
Source: FEMA

The area marked "Deep Foundation" had six basement levels, from B1 down to B6. The area marked "Shallow Foundation" only had two basement levels, B1 and B2. So the B4 level of the WTC extended beyond the footprint of the North Tower (WTC 1), itself. On B4, it was possible to walk from the North Tower to the South Tower (WTC 2), to the Marriot Hotel (WTC 3), and to the Customs House (WTC 6).

Also on B4, just outside the actual perimeter walls of the North Tower, there were parking areas, access to the PATH subway system that ran under the complex, and the refrigeration room where McCabe was located. His position is shown in the following drawing.

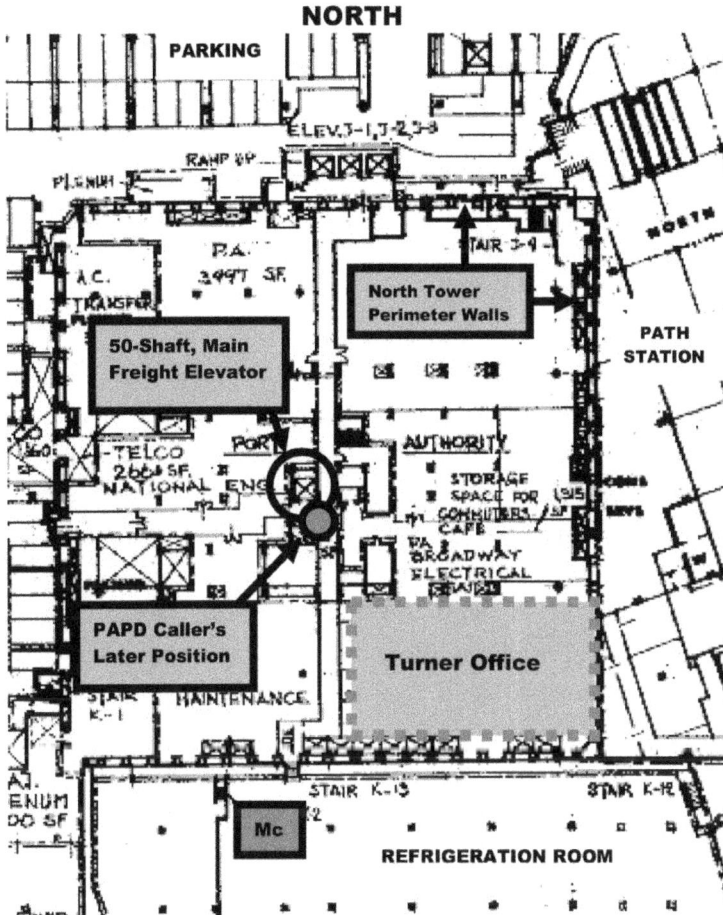

McCabe's Location
(1984 Site Plan)

This is what McCabe said:

I was in the refrigeration plant in Tower One, Subbasement 4. I was passing through when I felt a slight shifting of the building. I froze right where I stood and listened...nothing. About 30 seconds pass and to my left about 30 feet from me was a stairway leading up to a door. This door explodes off its hinges and white smoke came into the plant.

I later on found out the reason there was an explosion was the jet fuel filled the elevator shaft and seconds later a spark triggered an explosion.

I stood at the bottom of this staircase wondering what happened. Seconds later, through the smoke came people who worked beyond that door for the construction company. They were all secretaries. They walked like zombies, not speaking. I can smell their burnt flesh. One was bleeding pretty bad, and I started to walk her to path train station across the plant. One woman seemed unharmed, and I asked her what happened. She told me a bomb blew up their offices. When we got to the PATH platform, I laid the woman down, she thanked me, and I returned to the blown door to see if I could find anyone else.[275]

(In a subsequent interview, McCabe added that when he entered the office, he could see that all of the walls within fifty feet of the door had been blown down.[276])

Sure enough, there were more. The smoke was being sucked up the shaft now, and I can see there were no longer any walls just rubble. One woman was under her desk, refusing to come out. After a little coaxing, she came, and, at this point, a few of my colleagues were sifting through the rubble, trying to find anybody. We did about 3 trips. Everyone was out.[277]

Note that the part of his statement where he says the cause of the explosion was jet fuel that had come down an elevator shaft is not something that he personally observed. That was something he learned later from news reports. This is a common misperception expressed by many 9/11 witnesses who were influenced by the official story and later wove that thread into their recollection of events.

Above and beyond that, his statement exhibits the same notable contradictions from the official account that were made by the PAPD caller. First, he did not report seeing a fire. One would think that if a jet fuel fireball had hit the Turner office, there would be a fire raging there due to all the combustibles that are normally in an office setting. He would have seen it, and people would be making a mad scramble to escape it. But what McCabe described was something completely different; nothing was burning, and people were moving slowly, like "zombies."

Secondly, he did not mention smelling kerosene, which would have been obvious to him if jet fuel had been involved.

Thirdly, he described the second blast as being accompanied by a tremendously powerful shock wave; Turner's office was completely leveled, and all the walls within fifty feet of the door that had gotten "blown off its hinges" were down.

McCabe also makes a fourth point here. He indicates that there were *two* explosive events, not one. The first explosion caused a "slight shifting of the building." And the second was a powerful blast happening about "thirty seconds" after that.

In addition, McCabe made an astute observation when he returned to the office. He said he could see "smoke being sucked up the shaft." It is most likely that he was referring to the 50-shaft, which the plans indicate was the only elevator that serviced B4 and had door openings there. This indicates that there was more destruction done by the second blast than just to Turner's office. Because for him to actually see the 50-shaft from inside the office, a lot of additional walls that had been between the office and that shaft also had to be down.

On that point, note the following drawing, which shows what must have been his minimum line of sight to the 50-shaft from inside the office.

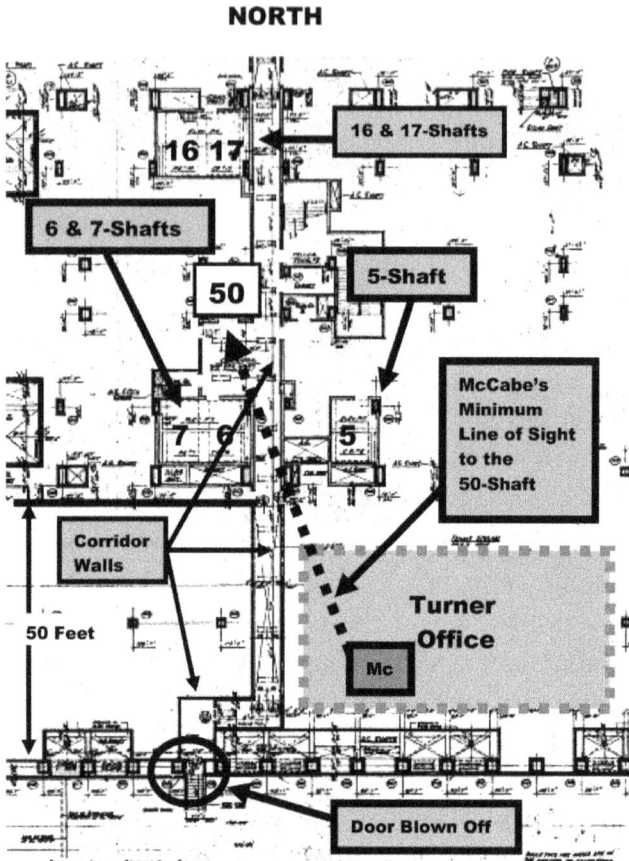

McCabe's Line of Sight to the 50-Shaft
(1968 B4 Detail)

At a minimum, in order for McCabe to see smoke getting sucked up the 50-shaft from inside the Turner office and also to account for all the walls being down within fifty feet of the door that got "blown off its hinges," all of the corridor walls would have to be down from the door to the 50-shaft (and possibly also parts of the 6-shaft). At the extreme, if his point of view was from the east side of the office, the walls of the 5-shaft would also have had to be down.

And even if McCabe was referring to either the 5-, 6-, or 7-shaft as the one that smoke was being sucked up, that would mean that the walls of that particular shaft would have to have been blown down. In fact, if any of these cases were true, that would have been a lot of destruction. And it is impossible to think that it could have been caused by a jet fuel fireball, which does not produce a shock wave.

McCabe's observations coincide with the statements of two maintenance men, **Hursley "Chino" Lever** and **Jose Sanchez.** They worked for American Building Maintenance (ABM), the company that held the service contract on the WTC. According to my interview with Lever, they were in a metal shop just on the west side of the 50-shaft, in an area occupied by National Engineering.[278] The following portion of the previous drawing shows their location and their eventual escape route.

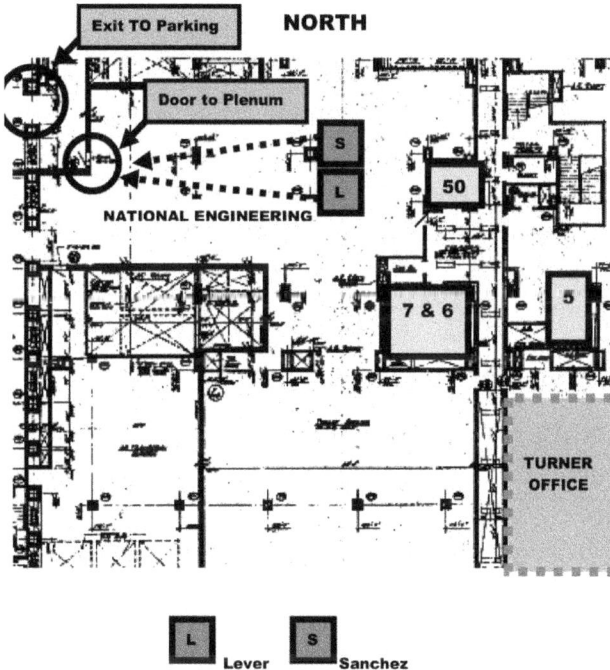

Lever and Sanchez's Location
(1968 B4 Detail)

Lever was working on a piece of metal at a grinding machine when he said this happened:

I heard a bomb. So, I says, "Probably a transformer again blew up." So I step back, finish what I had to finish, and I started towards the door again. And there came a big blast with a big ball of fire. And that's when I got hit. It hit me right back down on the ground and I realized my ankle was shattered.

(Also in my interview with him, Lever said that he had actually stepped out into the hallway and was standing just outside the shop door and in front of the 50-shaft, when the blast hit him.[279])

I can't walk. I'm shot. So, I crawl on my left side up to a door and into a plenum [a room that serves as the return for the building's air conditioning system]. And there was a door over there. So, I hold onto the door and I stand up. I limp to the door, hoping it would open. Well luckily the doors open.[280]

Lever and Sanchez made it to a parking area on the west side of the building, where Lever was rescued and driven up to the street level and put into an ambulance.

This account by Sanchez coincides with Lever's:

It sounded like a bomb and the lights went on and off. We started to walk to the exit, and a huge ball of fire went through the freight elevator. The hot air from the ball of fire dropped Chino to the floor and my hair got burned. The room then got full of smoke. And I remember saying out loud I believe it was a bomb that blew up inside the building.[281]

First, note here that there is a repeat of that same mantra that gets repeated over and over again by witnesses who were convinced by the mainstream media that a fireball came down an elevator shaft. However, from his position inside the shop Sanchez could not have actually seen that.

Furthermore, in my interview with Lever, he also said that a fire did not erupt in their shop.[282] So whatever it was that hit him and Sanchez, it could not have been a jet fuel-fed fireball. Otherwise, their shop would have been turned into a howling inferno, and they likely would have been horribly burned by it.

As for the "ball of fire" they saw, that is something that is commonly seen in true explosive events. It is caused by rapidly expanding hot gases that shoot out in all directions from the center of the blast. And that must have been what they saw.

That is further backed up by the fact that, like McCabe and the PAPD caller, neither Lever nor Sanchez reported a kerosene odor in the area. They did, however, report that there was a significant shock wave associated with the "ball of fire."

Also, note that they both confirmed McCabe's claim that there were two explosive events, the second one being much more powerful than the first.

Another witness was their fellow maintenance worker, **Philip Morelli**. This is what he said in an interview with New York television station TV1, shortly after the attack:

I go downstairs. The foreman tells me to remove some containers. As I'm walking by the main freight car of the building in the corridor that's when I got blown. I mean the impact of the explosion, or whatever happened, it threw me to the floor. And that's when everything started happening. It knocked me right to the floor. You didn't know what it was. You're assuming something just fell over in the loading dock. Something very heavy. Something very big. You don't know what happened. And all of a sudden you just felt the floor moving. And you get…And the walls…Then…I mean you heard that coming towards you.

I was racing. I was going toward the bathroom. All of a sudden…I opened the door. I didn't know it was the bathroom. And all of a sudden, the big impact happened again. And all the ceiling tiles were falling, swinging out of the ceiling. And (when) I come running out the door, the walls were down.[283]

In a second video interview with an independent researcher, Morelli would add that he then ran directly out the east exit of the tower.[284]

Also in that second interview, Morelli said that he was ten feet away from the 50-shaft when he was knocked down by the first blast.[285] This makes it possible to fix his location. As mentioned, the plans for the North Tower show that the 50-car was the only elevator that serviced B4. And other evidence, which will be presented shortly, will show that it was in use at the time of plane impact.[286] That means Morelli must have come down the B Stairway (which the plans also show was the only stairway that went to B4) to remove the containers. He must have then walked south in the main north-south corridor past the 50-shaft, which would have been to his right. And if he was ten feet from the 50-shaft when the first explosion knocked him down, that would put him in the hallway directly across from it. (This is also where the PAPD caller would be, later.)

Note the following drawing, showing Morelli's position at the time of the first explosion.

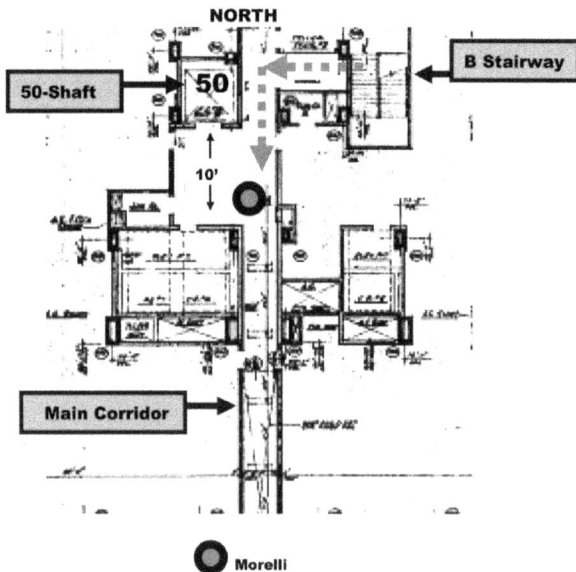

Morelli at the First Explosion
(1968 B4 Detail)

Lever also told me that when he went out into the hallway to investigate the first explosion, he did not see Morelli.[287] So Morelli must have disappeared into a nearby room quite quickly after he was knocked down by the first explosion.

However, I was unable to locate Morelli and interview him to find out exactly where he went. So at this point, I have made what I think is a reasonable assumption as to where he went after he was knocked down. After that first explosion, Morelli said he ran to a "bathroom," which he didn't know was a bathroom. And that was where he was when the second more powerful blast hit. The plans for B4, however, do not show an actual bathroom on that level. But they do show a "Janitor's Closet" only a few feet from where he fell from the first explosion. Note the following drawing:

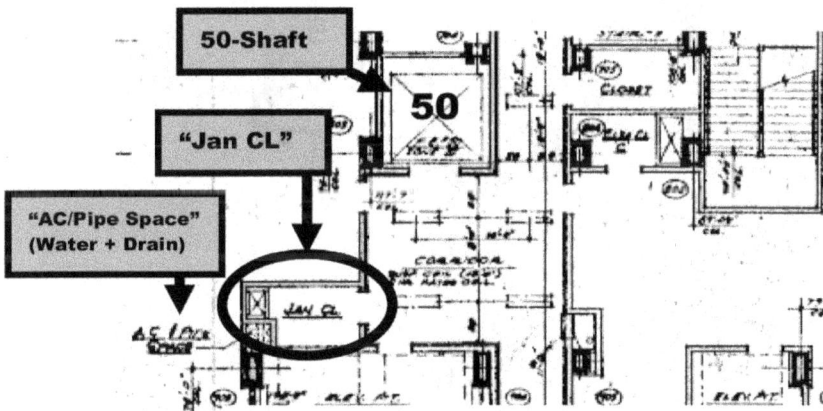

Janitor Closet on B4
(1968 B4 Detail)

It is likely that this was where he took shelter. This room probably had at least a sink for washing up, and that is why he mistook it for an actual bathroom. In any case, there was no other room where Morelli could have taken shelter in the short time that Lever said he took to step out into the hallway to investigate the first blast. So assuming that was where Morelli went, this next drawing shows his location, together with that of Lever and Sanchez, when the second blast hit.

NORTH

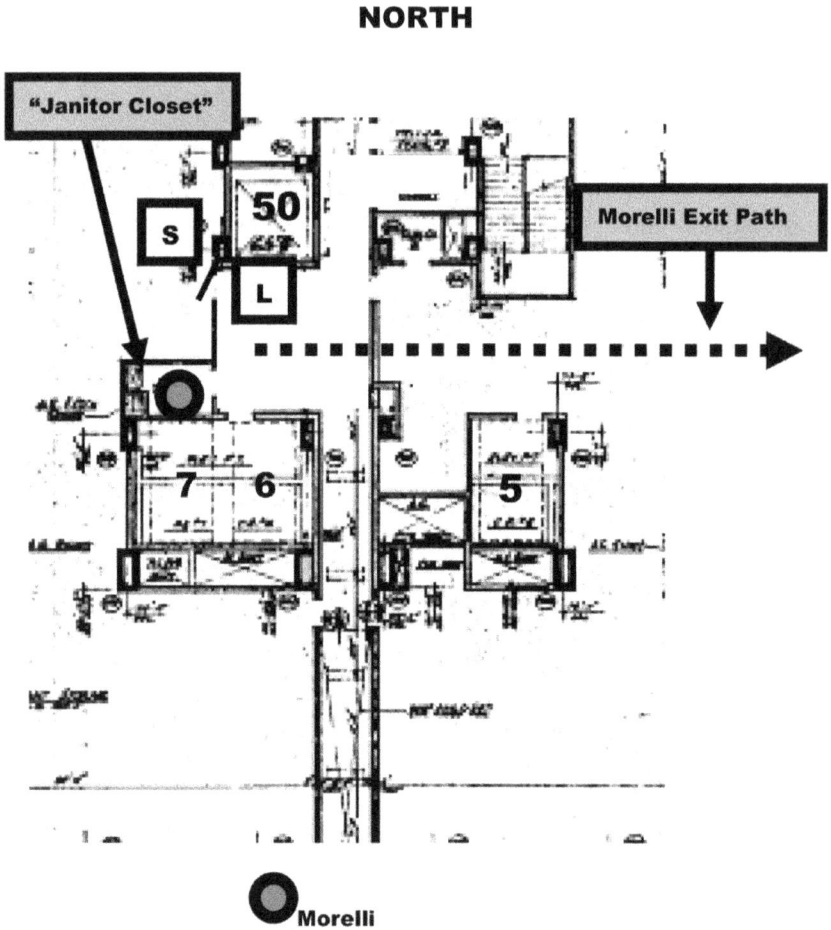

Morelli at the Second Blast
(1968 B4 Detail)

While Morelli was taking shelter in the closet, Lever must have come out into the hallway to investigate the first blast. And that was when all hell broke loose. Lever was blown back into the metal shop.

Seconds later, Morelli came running out of the closet to find a lot of walls down.[288] He then ran toward the east exit.

As to the substance of Morelli's reporting, notice how his account also conforms to the points made by McCabe, Lever, and Sanchez. There was no fire and no kerosene smell associated with this second explosion. But he indicated that there was a pretty significant shock wave when he said "the walls were down."

The fifth witness was **Bobby Hall**, another trade center employee. He was in the north side parking lot, near an entrance to the North Tower. His approximate location is marked in the 1984 site plan.

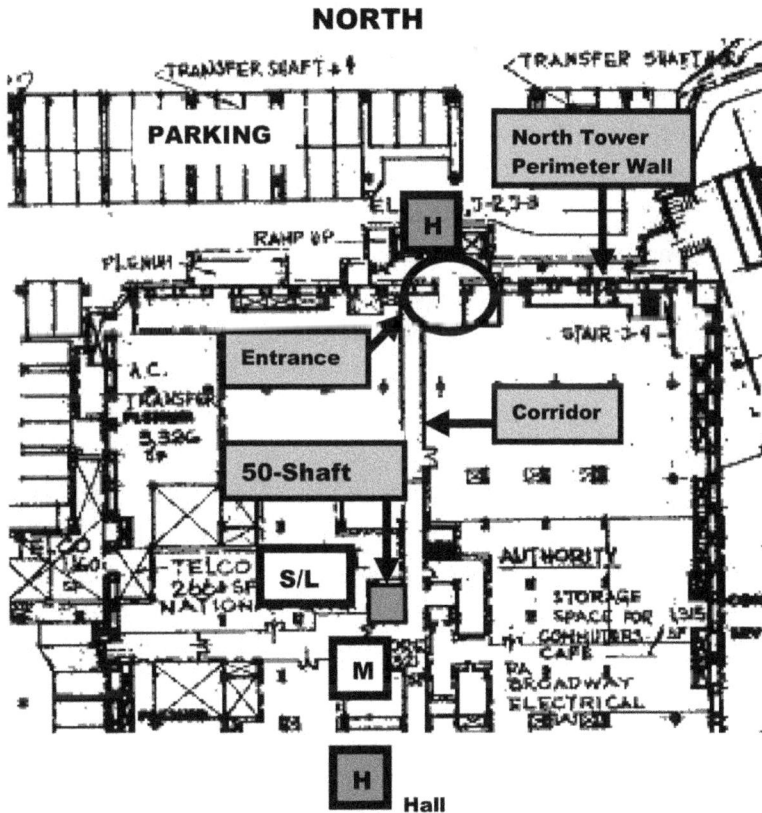

Hall at the Second Explosion
(1984 Site Plan)

While in the parking area, he and a coworker heard an explosion. This is what he said happened next:

> We were going to our shop to make a call and find out what the first explosion was, and the place just came apart on us (and) blew us back into the parking lot. What we found out later was the hot wind was the number 50 freight car falling from the 88th floor and it just came into the parking area where we were and just blew us back out into the parking lot.[289]

Here, Hall admits that he was told later that the "hot wind" that hit him was caused by the 50-car falling down its shaft. But like McCabe and Sanchez, he did not see that happen. However, his actual observations agree with those of the other witnesses: he did not see fire, he did not smell kerosene, there were two explosions, and the second blast had a shock wave.

Taken as a whole, the statements of McCabe, Sanchez, Lever, Morelli, and Hall clearly indicate that whatever blew up on B4 was not a jet fuel-fed fireball, as the official account claims. None of them saw a fire situation erupt, which surely would have occurred if a jet fuel fireball had swept through B4. None of them mentioned smelling kerosene, which would have filled the air if, indeed, jet fuel had been involved. And they all described the tremendous shock wave that was created by the second blast, which is something that is not associated with jet fuel-fed fireballs.

The testimony of these five witnesses (six, if you include the PAPD caller) clearly indicate that what caused the damage on B4 at the time of plane impact could only have been caused by at least two explosive devices, with the second, more powerful one going off about thirty seconds after the first.

It is hard to tell where the first explosion came from. Of the five witnesses, it appears that only Morelli was directly affected by it. He was knocked to the floor. The others—McCabe, Lever, Sanchez, and Hall—only slightly heard or felt it. And what effect the first blast had on Turner's office is not known, because McCabe did not see any damage at that point.

But the second blast was something else, altogether. It hit with enormous power. According to these witnesses, to varying degrees, its heat and shock wave filled the whole B4 area. And their statements make it possible to locate the likely origin of that blast. In the first place, the fact that Lever was thrown in a westerly direction back into the shop indicates that the force of the blast must have come from the east side of B4. Note the following detail drawing which shows Lever's position (L) and that of Sanchez (S), who stayed behind the shop's half-opened door. Also, at this point in time, presumably, Morelli (M) was sheltered in the janitor's closet.

NORTH

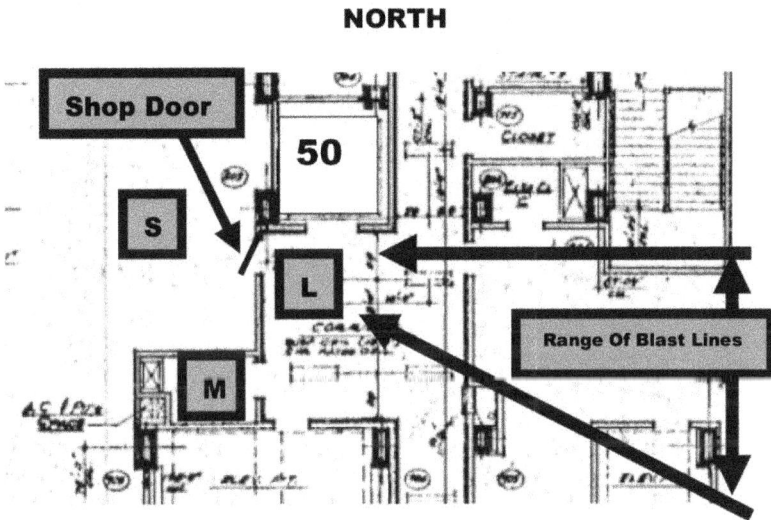

The Second B4 Explosion
(1968 B4 Detail)

The range between the large arrows in this drawing is the only possible direction that the blast would have to come from in order to blow Lever in a westerly direction, back into the shop. Obviously, a blast coming from the 50-shaft would not do the trick. It would have blown him in a southerly direction. Also, if the blast had come from the 50-shaft, it likely would have killed him, because that explosion packed a big punch. It hit hard enough on the other side of B4 to knock down a lot of walls and destroy the Turner office before blowing McCabe's door off its hinges about 100 feet away.

Now, note the following "B4 Damage Assessment Plan." It shows the relative heat experienced by each of the five B4 witnesses and the comparative amount of destruction they observed.

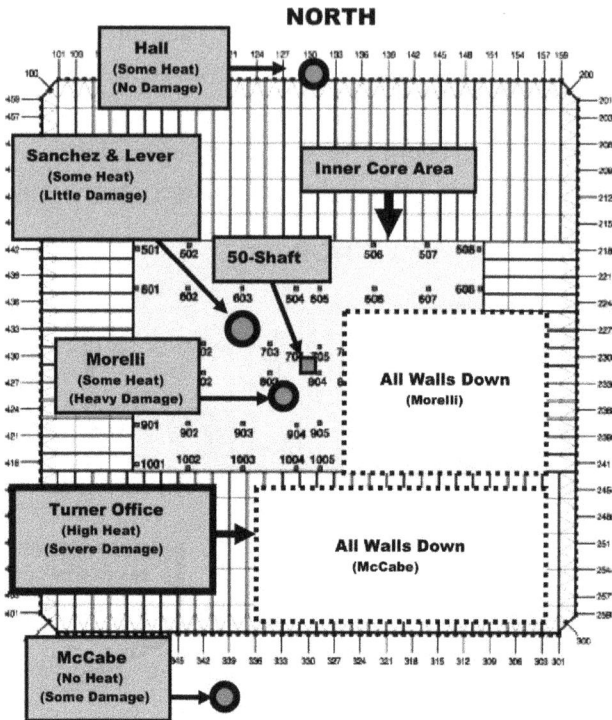

NORTH

Hall
(Some Heat)
(No Damage)

Sanchez & Lever
(Some Heat)
(Little Damage)

Inner Core Area

50-Shaft

Morelli
(Some Heat)
(Heavy Damage)

All Walls Down
(Morelli)

Turner Office
(High Heat)
(Severe Damage)

All Walls Down
(McCabe)

McCabe
(No Heat)
(Some Damage)

B4 Damage Assessment Plan
Original Drawing Source: NIST

This clearly shows that the second explosion did its damage on the east side of B4, with the most severe damage done in the southeast area at Turner's office. This seems to also preclude its originating from inside any of the elevator shafts, including the 50-shaft, which were all basically in the middle of the floor.

The second-most severe degree of damage was done in Morelli's area. He said that when he came running out of the janitor's closet, "the walls were down." This indicates that the walls of the actual room where he took shelter remained intact, and the walls that were down were the ones that he could see in front of him as he was running in an easterly direction toward the exit. So the area of his closet shelter must have been shielded from the major part of the second blast, just like Lever and Sanchez's metal shop.

The third most serious amount of damage occurred at Lever and Sanchez's shop. They saw what appeared to be a "ball of fire" and felt "hot air" that "burned" Sanchez's hair, and Lever was knocked off his feet. But like Morelli's closet, which was near to it, the walls of their shop also stayed intact.[290] So their area was also sheltered from the main force of the second explosion.

As for Hall, he experienced the least of the shock wave. He was thrown backward, but no walls were blown down. He also felt the "hot wind," but he was not burned by it.

Accordingly, the detonation point of the second blast must have been behind a significant barrier of some kind, so that the more northern part of B4—where Lever, Sanchez, Morelli, and Hall were—was partially shielded from the shock wave. But the construction of the tower's interior walls was not substantial enough to resist that kind of force. According to the building's plans, all of the interior partition walls, including the elevator shaft walls, were made out of ordinary sheetrock (drywall), which one would think a powerful blast like what occurred on B4 would have blown through quite easily.[291] So the second explosion must have been shielded by something more substantial than that. The only things in the area that are shown in the drawings that could have served as that kind of a barrier were the steel columns of the inner core area, which at that level of the tower were massive.

The following illustration shows their size.

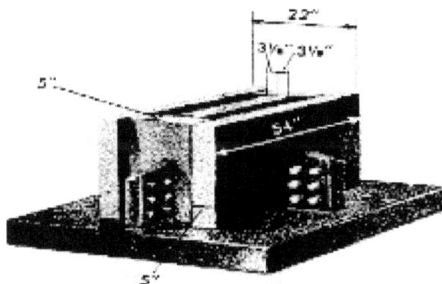

Core Columns at B4
Source: Port Authority of New York and New Jersey

They measured 22 by 54 inches and were almost solid steel.[292]

Note that the Damage Assessment Plan also shows the number designations for the support columns in the core area. An examination of the 1968 detailed drawing in conjunction with that plan indicates that the most likely location of this second explosive device would have been behind either column 907 or 908, which was near the edge of the core, or behind either column 1007 or 1008, just to the south of them.

Please note the following detail.

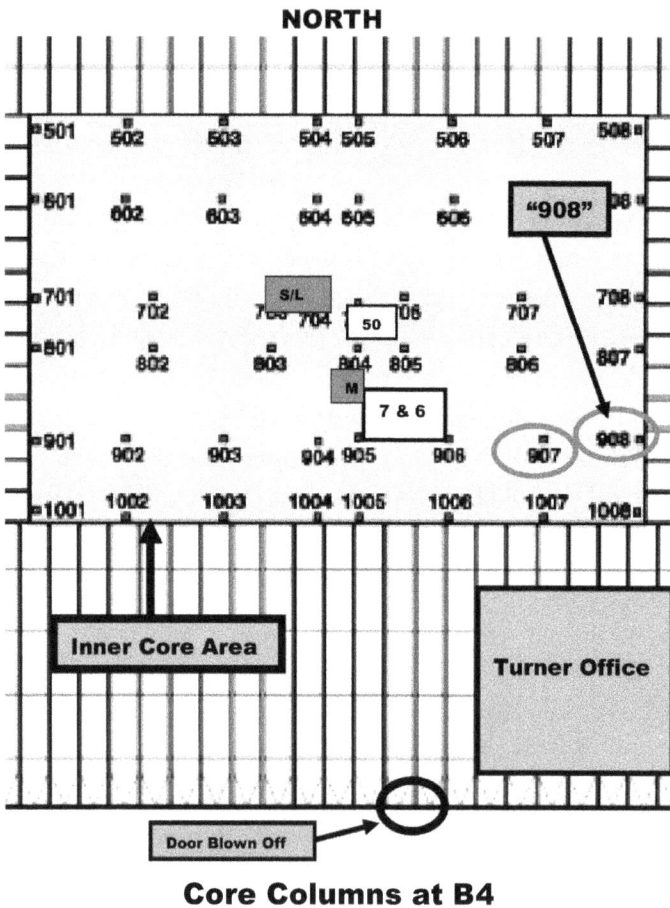

NORTH

Core Columns at B4

It is not likely that the second explosion occurred any further to the west of columns 907 and 1007, because that would have put it too close to Lever, Sanchez, and Morelli, and it probably would have then blown the walls down around them, like it did to the Turner office.

But, if the device that caused that was attached to the south face of either columns 907, 908, 1007 or 1008, it likely would have caused the major destruction done to the Turner office, which would account for McCabe's observations. It also could have then flattened the corridor walls all the way up to the 50-shaft and knocked down the walls around the 5-shaft and possibly part of the 6-shaft. That would account for Morelli's observation that the walls to the east of him were down when he came running out of his closet shelter. Also, it would account for McCabe's observation that smoke was being sucked up one of those shafts. In addition, this would also account for Lever and Sanchez's statements, which indicated that they were only hit with a fraction of the force that the Turner office got. These locations for that explosive device would also account for Hall's statement that said he was hit with a small portion of the shock wave.

Conclusion

The information in this chapter clearly shows that the two explosions observed on the North Tower's B4 basement level were not caused by jet fuel, as the Bush administration's investigations claim. According to the witnesses, those two blasts could only have been caused by explosive devices that were planted there prior to the attacks.

The next chapter nails that down.

3

The Secret Plans

THE PREVIOUS CHAPTER demonstrated through the statements of witnesses that the extensive damage done to the B4 level had to have been caused by two explosive devices that were planted there. This chapter will show that there was no elevator shaft available for a jet fuel fireball to travel down to get that level, leaving explosives as the only alternative. The key to that discovery lies hidden in the blueprints for the building. Perhaps that explains why those plans were kept so secret and made so unavailable to independent researchers for so many years.

WTC Plans Withheld

Normally, without much trouble, any citizen should be able to access any blueprint for any building in his or her area from the local building department. After all, such plans are public information and are not covered by any secrecy laws. But that was not the case with the WTC. As shown, even FEMA's own BPS team of expert engineers from the ASCE could not secure a set of plans for its investigation until almost four months after the attacks.[293]

And other, equally qualified independent investigators were also shut out. The previously mentioned University of California, Berkeley professor, Abolhassan-Asl Astaneh, was one of those. This is how he described FEMA's continued stonewalling in his March 6, 2002, House Select Committee on Science testimony:

> I have not been provided with the information made available to the FEMA Building Performance Assessment Team [sic]. This includes videotapes and photographs taken on 9/11 and the following days and copies of the *engineering drawings*. At this time, having the

videotapes, photographs and copies of the drawings not only is useful, but also is *essential* in enabling us to conduct any analysis of the collapse and to formulate conclusions from our effort.[294] (Italics added)

Naturally, the stubbornness with which the plans were being withheld increased the suspicion among some independent researchers that they likely contained information of an evidentiary nature that might be detrimental to the official explanation for what caused the collapses. One notable interested party was architect Richard Gage, a professional with over twenty years of experience and a member of the American Institute of Architects (AIA). This is how he once described his frustration at being denied those plans:

We cannot truly understand what happened in these historical structural failure events when we are not allowed access to the construction documents. First, they come up with the "pancake theory," then they changed it to the "column failure theory." We don't believe that either of those theories is supported by the available evidence.[295]

Victoria Ashley, the head of a group of three hundred independent investigators affiliated with universities, also protested this mysterious and unprecedented inability to locate and access the plans. This is how she described the stifling effect it had:

Public access to blueprints of the three destroyed skyscrapers—the Twin Towers and WTC Building 7—has been a long-standing goal of the 9/11 research community. The inability to access data on the structural design of the buildings has been an impediment to further investigation.[296]

As it turned out, the problem was complicated by the fact that that the WTC project was built by the Port Authority of New York and New

Jersey (PANYNJ), and, as such, plans did not need to be filed with the city. So, the normal rules did not apply. And, strangely enough, the PANYNJ denied all requests for them under the dubious assertion of "§87(2)(t) of the Public Officer's Law," which prevented disclosure if, "the documents requested *would endanger the life or safety of any person.*"[297] Due to this odd bit of obstructionism, year after year, pleas for the plans fell on deaf ears.

The Holy Grail of Evidences

Then, suddenly, on March 27, 2007, an event occurred that changed the game completely. It was then that, after five and a half years of being zealously guarded from public view, 261 key pages of the original 1200 architectural drawings for the North Tower suddenly appeared.[298] The plans became available when an insider, who preferred to remain anonymous, sent them to Dr. Steven Jones, PhD, a professor of physics at Brigham Young University (BYU). Dr. Jones, who was a well-known critic of the official explanation for the collapses, immediately published them on the Internet.[299] (The North Tower drawings presented in this book were part of that package.)

It didn't take long for independent researchers who could read plans to recognize why they had been so tightly held. As it turned out, that small fraction of drawings turned out to be the "Holy Grail" of evidences. They provide the single most significant proof that the enormously powerful explosions that were observed in several levels of the North Tower—most notably, on the B4 level—had to be due to explosives that were planted in those areas prior to the attacks.

Specifically, with regard to that powerful explosion that occurred on B4, the plans show that of the ninety-nine elevators above ground in the tower, only three shafts—the 50-, 6-, and 7-shafts—were continuous all the way down to that level from the plane impact zone and could have provided a conduit for a potential fireball to travel in, as the official scenario claims. But, when the logistics of the elevator system, as seen in the plans, is considered together with other factors already known from the official reports, and from interviews with certain witnesses, it becomes clear that a fireball did not come down any of those shafts.

That is because all three of those shafts were blocked by their cars a floor or two above B4. And, even if a potential fireball was traveling down any one of them, it would first have caused a massive deflagration on B2 (in the case of the 50-shaft) or B1 (in the case of the 6- and 7-shafts) when it hit the tops of those cars. But according to the witnesses who were there, that did not happen.

The evidence for this was made possible by the discovery in the North Tower's plans of the unique arrangement it had for its elevators. That particular design was called a "Sky Lobby System."

The Sky Lobby System

Normally, in tall commercial buildings, the elevators take up a lot of floor space, resulting in a significant loss of rental income for the owners. The problem was compounded in the twin towers, where getting thousands of people moved up and down a 110-story building presented a logistical nightmare. The designers solved the problem by dividing the height of the building into three zones by what they called "sky lobbies." In this system, passengers would take express elevators from the main lobby to a sky lobby in their zone. Once there, they would then switch to a local elevator that serviced their floor.

But that, in turn, presented challenging structural requirements for buildings so tall. The supervising architect for the project, Minoru Yamasaki and his design engineers from the firm Worthington, Skilling, Helle, and Jackson solved the problem by employing what is called a "framed-tube, lateral force resisting system" for the overall structure. This design utilized a square outer frame of closely-spaced perimeter columns (the outer tube) together with a massively strong arrangement of central core columns (the inner tube). The concentration of columns in the inner core area allowed for all of the elevator shafts and stairwells to be hung on and supported by that enormously strong structure.

Again, here is that concept:

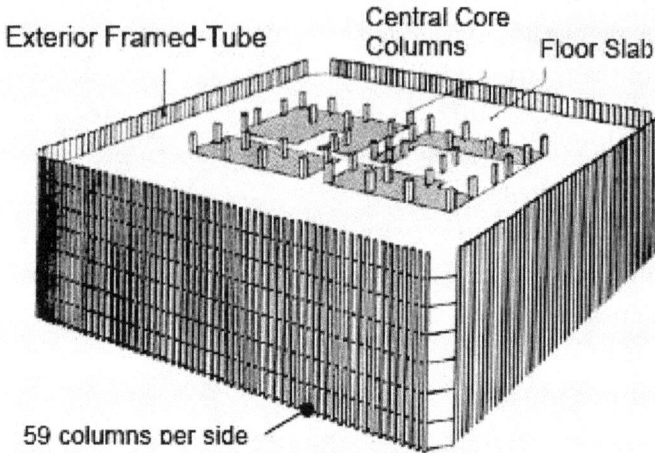

North Tower Design
Source: FEMA

The towers had an outer shell of 240 box-shaped steel perimeter columns and an incredibly strong inner core area made up of 47 huge columns that were 22" by 54" at the foundation and almost solid steel.[300] That core was designed to hold up to 60 percent of the weight of the building and was capable of standing as an independent structure, all by itself. The remaining 40 percent of the gravity load was carried by the perimeter columns, which also took care of 100 percent of the wind resistance.[301]

The following drawing depicts the elevator system in the twin towers from the first floor (plaza/ground level) to the roof. (Please note that this drawing, taken from the NIST report, does not show the six basement levels—B1 to B6—that were below the plaza level. The significance of NIST's negligence in not showing that will be discussed in the next chapter.)

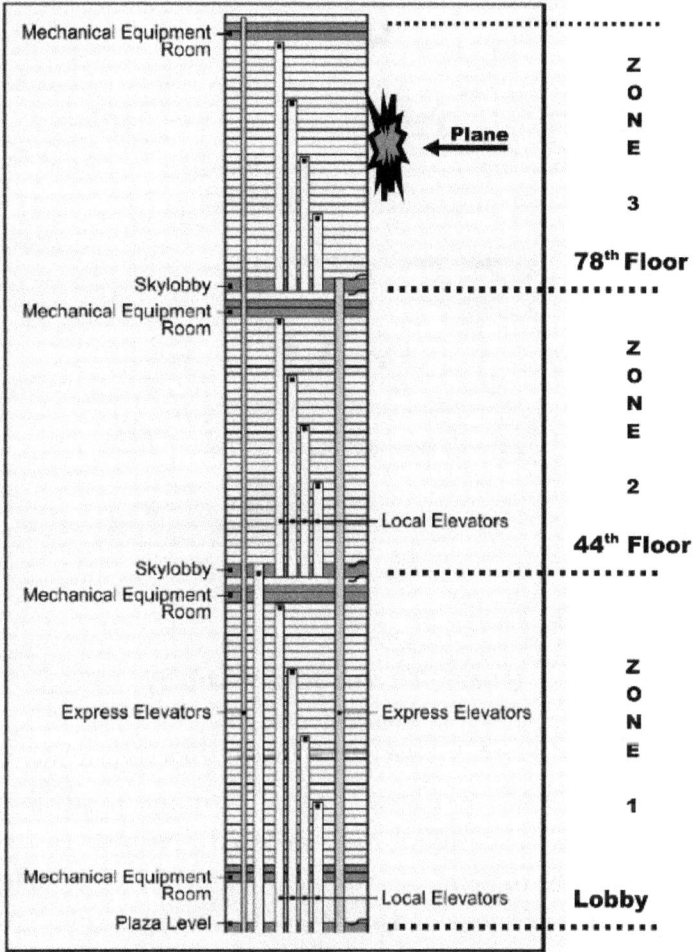

North Tower Elevator System
Source: NIST

The sky lobbies were located at the 44th and 78th floors.[302] The passenger express elevators to the 44th floor sky lobby were accessed via the outer main lobby on the north side of the core. The ones that went to the 78th floor sky lobby were accessed via the outer main lobby on the south side of the core. All of the local elevators for each zone were accessed from inside the core area.

Refer to the following plan.

NORTH

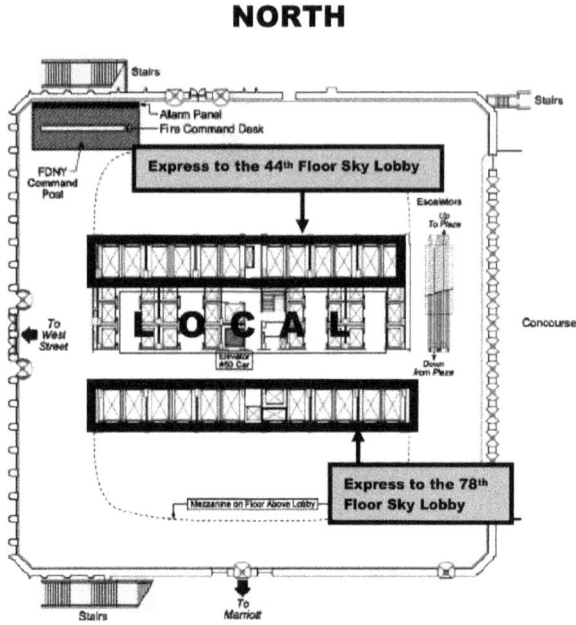

North Tower Main Lobby
Source: NIST

There were 99 elevator cars above ground in the North Tower, but, as this main lobby plan shows, there were only 49 shafts to accommodate them. Due to that, many of the shafts were shared by at least two cars, one in a lower zone and the other in an upper zone. All of the shafts themselves were continuous as far up as needed, but each car that shared any one shaft had to be separated vertically by a floor that accommodated the heavy-duty motor that was required to individually lift it. Those so-called *lift motor room* floors were typically constructed of five inches of steel-reinforced concrete. They were located two floors above the highest floor serviced by any particular elevator car and below the lowest floor that was being used by an upper level car with which it shared a shaft. There would also have to be a so-called "pit" floor of the same construction that housed the return mechanism for each of the cars.

As an example, refer to the following drawing. It depicts the typical arrangement for an elevator that shared a shaft. It is of a lift motor room that was located between the 40th and 42nd floors in the North Tower.

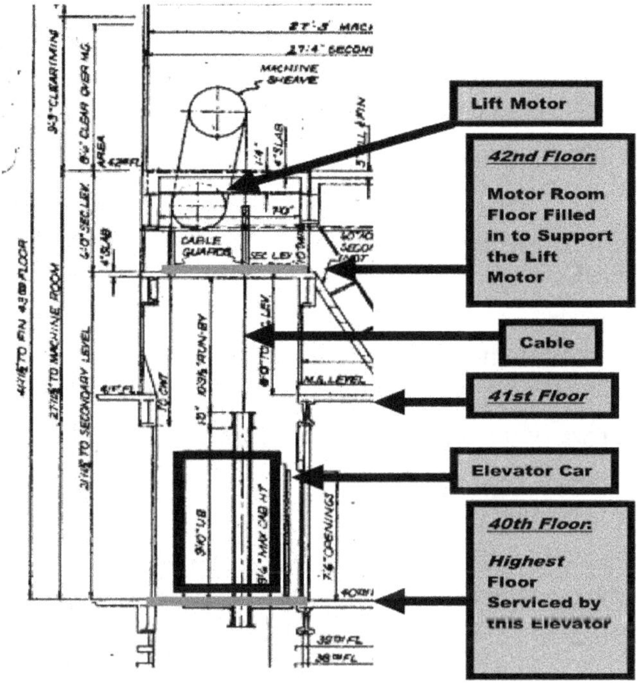

Typical Lift Motor Arrangement
Source: NIST

This indicates that any fireball shooting down this particular shaft would have been blocked by the motor room at the 42nd floor.

Due this arrangement, only the 50-, 6-, or 7-shaft contained just one elevator car with its lift motor room located *above* the plane impact zone and its return pit *below* B4, and could have, therefore, provided an unobstructed path for a fireball to "shoot down" to the B4 level.[303]

The 50-Shaft
As for the 50-shaft, there were two people who were inside its elevator car when the plane hit whose stories confirm that a fireball did not pass on

down to the B4 level in that shaft. One of them was carpenter **Marlene Cruz**. This is what she said:

> I got on the 50-Car, which was the freight elevator. I was going to do a job on the 46th floor. The elevator operator closed the door. It was just him and me in the elevator. I heard that explosion and the doors blew. And the elevator dropped. And there was smoke. Fire. Water all over the place. Debris, Concrete, you name it, fell on top of us. He was out cold for a second. I was caught between the floors. And I was lucky there were some other guys on the B-levels. And they pulled me out.[304]

Note that before she got to her job at the 46th floor, she heard and felt the effects of an "explosion" which occurred above her, and the cable to her elevator was cut and sent the car into freefall. It is possible that the plane crash at the 96th floor caused that, because the motor room for the 50-shaft was located above the plane impact zone. But it is more likely that it was caused by a bomb that was planted in the shaft because she did not mention kerosene jet fuel, which most likely would have fallen down the shaft if it had been breached by remnants of the plane.

All of the elevator cars in the tower were equipped with an automatic braking system. Should a cable be cut, as happened to Cruz's elevator, and it went into free fall, contact points grabbed onto the sides of the shaft after a certain distance and gradually brought the elevator car to a stop via friction. In this way, her 50-car became stuck between the B2 and B3 levels, where it remained.

The fact the 50-car ended up jammed at the B2 level was confirmed by one of Cruz's coworkers, Arthur DelBianco. In an interview with Matt Lauer of NBC-TV News from his hospital bed at Belleview Hospital the next day, DelBianco described how he learned that some of his coworkers were injured in the basement and that he "helped a paramedic to work [his] way down because Marlene [Cruz] was hurt on the second level below ground." Cruz, who was in the bed next to him and holding his hand, interjected, "Right."[305] The second level below ground was the B2 level.

Cruz also said that she laid on the floor on the B2 level for forty minutes before her rescuers wheeled her out of the building on a makeshift dolly.[306] But at no time did she mention that a fireball, or even jet fuel, came down the shaft and hit the top of the elevator car, which was only a few feet away.

The 50-car elevator operator that day, **Arturo Griffith,** offered additional detail:

And as I took off, [it] was a matter of seconds, five, six, seven seconds, I don't know, and there was a loud explosion and the elevator dropped. And when the elevator dropped there was a lot of debris and cables falling on top of the elevator. And I just put my hand over my head and I said, "Oh, God, I'm going to die."

When the elevator finally stopped, they had an explosion that bring the doors inside the elevator. And I think I'm sure that that was what broke my leg. And they had another explosion and the panel that threw me—you know—against the wall. And I guess I was unconscious for a couple of minutes because somebody else was in the elevator with me, and they say that they was trying to get my attention and they didn't get no response from me.[307]

Here, Griffith also confirms that a fireball was not following his elevator car down the shaft after plane impact. If it had, it would have slammed into the top of the car when it stopped, and, most likely, he would have been injured by it, and, no doubt, that would have been the centerpiece of his remarks. But he did not mention a fireball, at that point.

Griffith also said that several seconds *after* the car came to a stop, there were two powerful *explosions*, the first of which caused him to sustain a broken leg. The second one knocked him unconscious. But certain factors indicate that those blasts must have come from below, not from above. Note the following illustration, showing the position of his car after it came to rest.

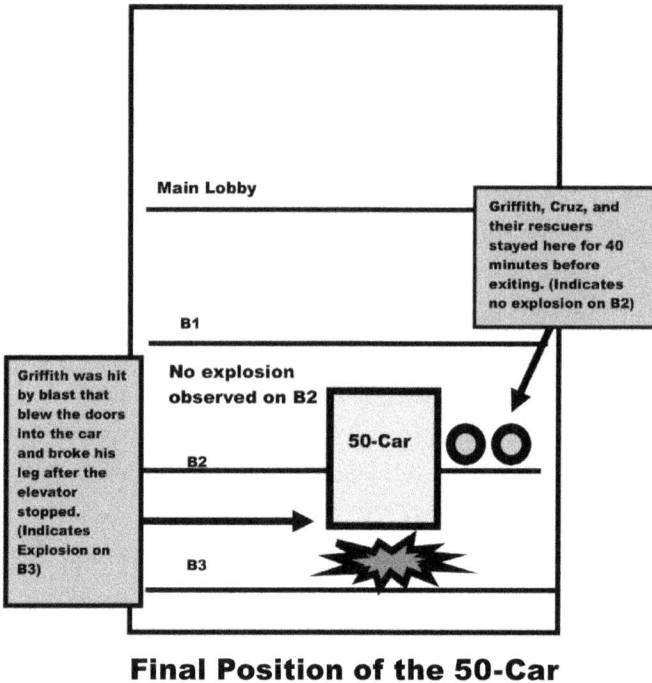

Final Position of the 50-Car

The only possible source for the explosion that caused Griffith to suffer a broken leg would have to be the B3 level, to which the bottom of his elevator car was exposed. If a fireball from the plane impact zone had been chasing the car down the shaft, it would have hit the top of the stopped car and, most likely, both Cruz and Griffith would have been severely burned, or even killed by it. The fireball would also have likely injured their rescuers, who had to be nearby on the B2 level. And then, according to the official story, it would have had to smash through the car and continue down to B4 and cause all of the damage done there.

But that did not happen. Aside from the fact that it would be impossible for a low energy deflagration of a jet fuel fireball to cause that level of destruction, there was no explosion at all seen on B2 by Griffith or Cruz. This proves that the B4 explosions were not caused by a jet fuel-fed fireball coming down the 50-shaft. It also strongly indicates at least three explosive devices were planted in the building: one at some point up the

50-shaft (which cut the cable) and two in the B3 level, near the stopped 50-car (both of which hit Griffith).

The 6- and 7-Shafts

If the fireball did not come down the 50-shaft, the only other possible conduits for it to satisfy the official story and get to B4 from the plane impact zone were the 6- and 7-shafts. But there are several factors that also work against that possibility. In the first place, it is known from the NIST report that on the morning of the 9/11 attacks, *"the 6 and 7-Cars were down for modernization."*[308] This implies extensive remodeling. These two cars were, therefore, expected to be out of service for some time. The blueprints show that, although their shafts went down to B4, the lowest level for which the 6- and 7-shafts had door openings was B1, which was the main service level for doing maintenance work.[309] Therefore, the cars for the 6- and 7-shafts had to be parked there. That was one floor below the main lobby and three floors above B4.

Taking all of the above into account, the following illustration shows what must have been the vertical locations of the 50-, 6-, and 7-cars relative to the main lobby level, B1, B2 and B4, just after plane impact.

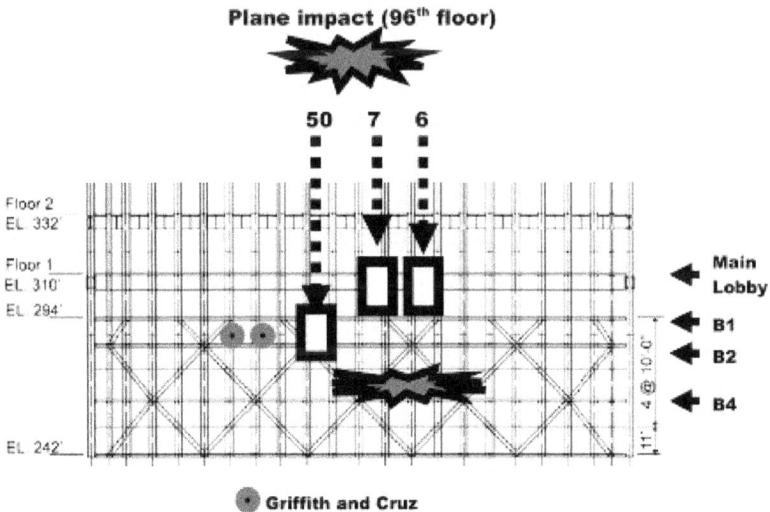

Position of 50-, 6-, and 7-Cars after Plane Impact

This shows that a fireball from the plane impact zone on its way to B4 via the 6- or 7-shafts would have caused a tremendous fireball on B1 as it smashed into the tops of the 6-car and/or the 7- car, since both were parked there. But the witnesses who were on B1 at the time indicated that they did not see that. One of them was **William Rodriquez**.

Note the following illustration.

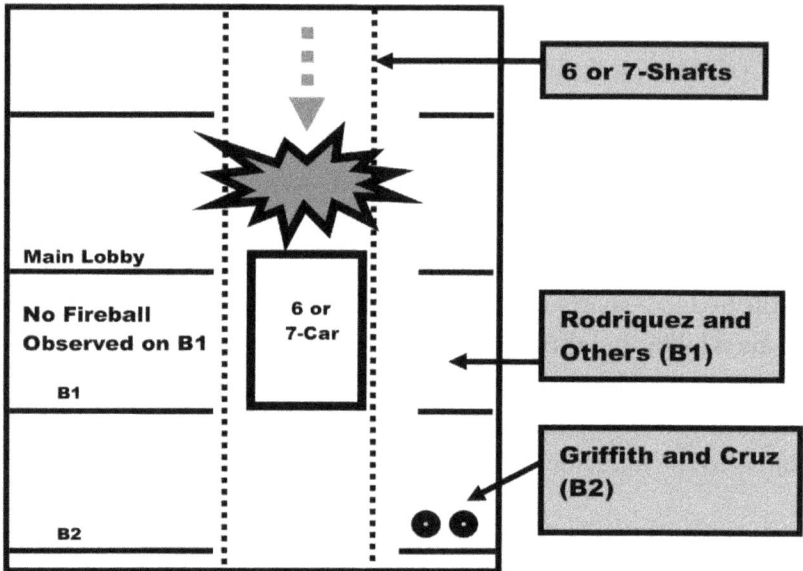

**Possible Fireball
in the 6 or 7-Shafts**

Rodriquez had been an maintenance man in the tower for twenty years. When the plane hit, he was talking to his supervisor outside the ABM main office, which was located in the northeast corner of the B1 level.

Note the following plan for his location with respect to the 50-, 6-, and 7-shafts.

NORTH

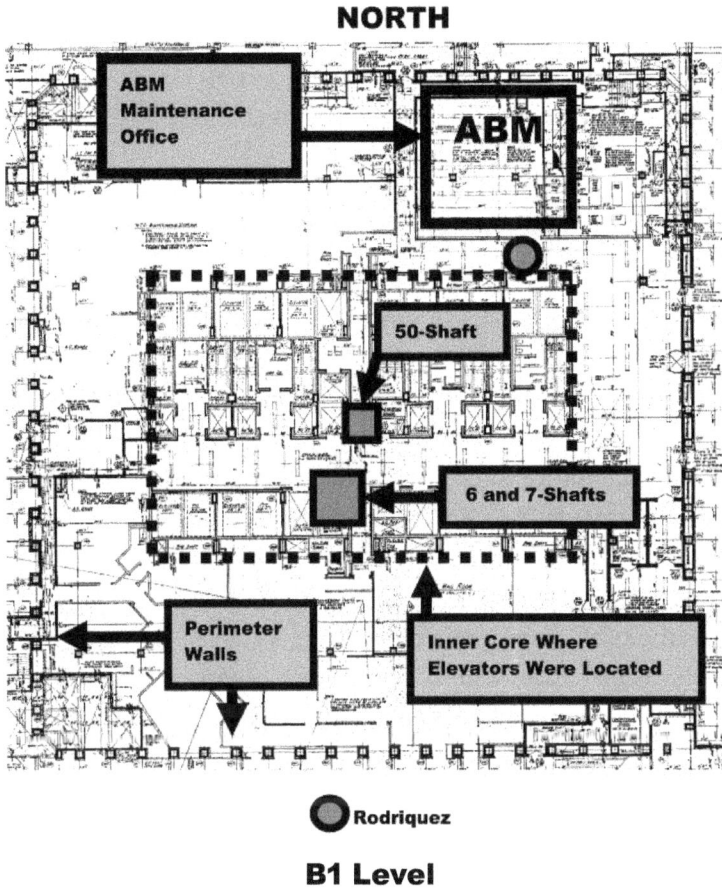

ABM Maintenance Office

ABM

50-Shaft

6 and 7-Shafts

Perimeter Walls

Inner Core Where Elevators Were Located

Rodriquez

B1 Level

This is what Rodriquez said happened:

I was talking to the supervisor in front of the door. There were 14 people there. When all the sudden, at 8:46, we hear BOOOOM! An explosion so powerful and so loud that it pushed us upward in the air, coming from *below*. And it was so powerful that the walls cracked. The false ceiling fell on top of us. The sprinkler system was activated. And everybody started screaming in horror.

The first thing that came to my mind is that a generator blew out in the mechanical room. The mechanical room was located right below us on B2. There were six levels to the basement—B1, B2, and all the way down to B6. When I went to verbalize it, we hear POW! An explosion all the way to the top of the building. And that was the plane hitting the top of the building. Two different events separated by almost 7 seconds.[310] (Italics added)

If Rodriguez's impressions are correct, and there was an explosion below B1 before the plane hit, that would be the strongest evidence possible that explosives were planted in the building. (And in fact, there is convincing seismic evidence that was collected by a laboratory operated by Columbia University that confirms it.[311] That evidence is presented in Chapter 6.)
Rodriguez's statement continued:

At that moment a person comes running into the office yelling, "Explosion! Explosion!" His red shirt was soaked in blood. All his skin was pulled from under his armpits like it was a piece of cloth. And it was hanging off both his hands.

I went to the phone to call the Emergency Medical Unit that was located in the South Tower...When I went to pick up the phone, Pow! Another explosion. The building shaked so much—and the floor started moving below us—that people thought that it was an earthquake. And they started going into the office inside the door frames thinking that it was an earthquake, screaming," Help! Help!" My supervisor, Anthony Saltalamacchia is screaming, "It's a bomb! It's a bomb!"[312]

The injured man was **Felipe David**. He worked for an outside company that supplied the vending machines. At the time of the explosion, he was near an exit door, servicing one of them. This is what he said in a videotaped interview from his hospital bed a few days later:

That day, I was in the basement in sub-level one sometime after 8:30. Everything happened so fast. Everything moved so fast. The building started shaking after I heard the explosion *below*. Dust was flying everywhere. And all of a sudden, it got real hot. We heard something like a bomb. The lights turned out. At the exit door there was this fire that knocked us both down. We were hit by hot air. And the room was full of smoke. At that moment, I believed it was a bomb. (Italics added)

I threw myself onto the floor, covered my face because I felt like I was burned. I sat there for a couple seconds on the floor and felt like I was going to die, saying to myself, "God, please give me the strength."[313]

At that point, he got up and ran to the ABM office. "When I went in, I told them it was an explosion. When people looked at me with my skin hanging, they started crying.[314]

It was David's impression, then, that the fireball came from an "exit door," after he felt an explosion from "below." The only way those two aspects can be reconciled is if he was talking about an exit door leading to a stairwell. The blast could have come up the stairwell and blown the door—which would have typically been a heavy steel fire door—into the B1 area toward where he was standing. But that would have required a tremendous amount of force; in other words, a shock wave.

The following drawings show a typical North Tower stairwell with the doorway detailed.

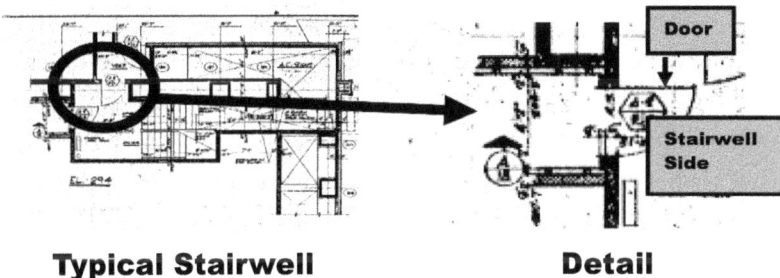

Typical Stairwell   **Detail**
Source: NIST

Notice how the door swings into the stairwell. This is typical. Exit doors to stairwells usually close against a jamb inside the stairwell. An explosion would have to have a very powerful shock wave to get through a heavy-duty steel fire door like this from the stairwell side. As has been explained, that is not a characteristic of jet fuel-fed fireballs.

Furthermore, if the explosion that injured David did come from the plane impact zone via the 6- or 7-shafts, it would have had to perform a seemingly magical task. It would have had to blow past the 6- and/or the 7-car that was parked on B1 and gotten into the B2 level, blown past the fire door on that level, and then it would have had to come back up the stairwell and blow the same type of heavy steel exit door into the B1 level. And, if the official story is to be believed, another fraction of it would have had to continue down to B4 and caused all the damage done there. This is not a likely possibility. Thus, David's impression that the blast that injured him came from below and through an exit door is one more example that indicates that a lower-level explosion occurred that contradicts the official account.

Another witness was **Anthony Saltalamacchia**, Rodriguez's supervisor. He essentially confirmed Rodriguez and David's perception that the explosion came from below B1, not from the plane impact zone. This is what he said:

We heard a massive explosion that was in the WTC about 8:46 am in the morning. The explosion came from...I believe at first...We believed that it came from the mechanical room [one floor down]. And then we heard a series of other explosions that sounded up on the above levels of the building to where I then realized that there was something wrong. And that there was a major problem. And it literally sounded like...people setting off grenades. Picture just multiple grenades just going off. Like BAM, BOUND, BOOM! That's when I thought, "Is there, like, somebody in here, blowing up the place?"[315]

He recalled the pandemonium that ensued as about fifteen coworkers came running to the office, screaming.

As we were doing this, a man who was…I think (his name) was Felipe. He came into our room. And everybody was just like in dead silence. He came in and he was just covered in blood. His skin was like peeling off his arms. His face…I don't know the extent of the burns, but it was just like, wow…So, we're, like, asking him if he's OK. And the man was shaky and in shock. And…we knew we just had to get the man outta here. As much as ourselves.[316]

He further recounted an additional revealing detail that also indicates that there was no fireball near the 6- and 7-shafts on B1 at the time of plane impact. He said that he and the others first attempted to carry David out of the building to safety by going up one floor to the main lobby, as follows:

There's a way out through the lobby and there's way out through the street [loading dock on B1]. We tried going to the lobby first. William and the men tried to go that way. And there was just too much smoke. And there was no way you could go that way.[317]

In order to go out by way of the main lobby, though, they would have had to pass near to the 6- and 7-shafts, because that was where the only stairwell leading up to the main lobby was located. This fact is established by the following two drawings. Note this first one. It is a blowup of the B1 plan.

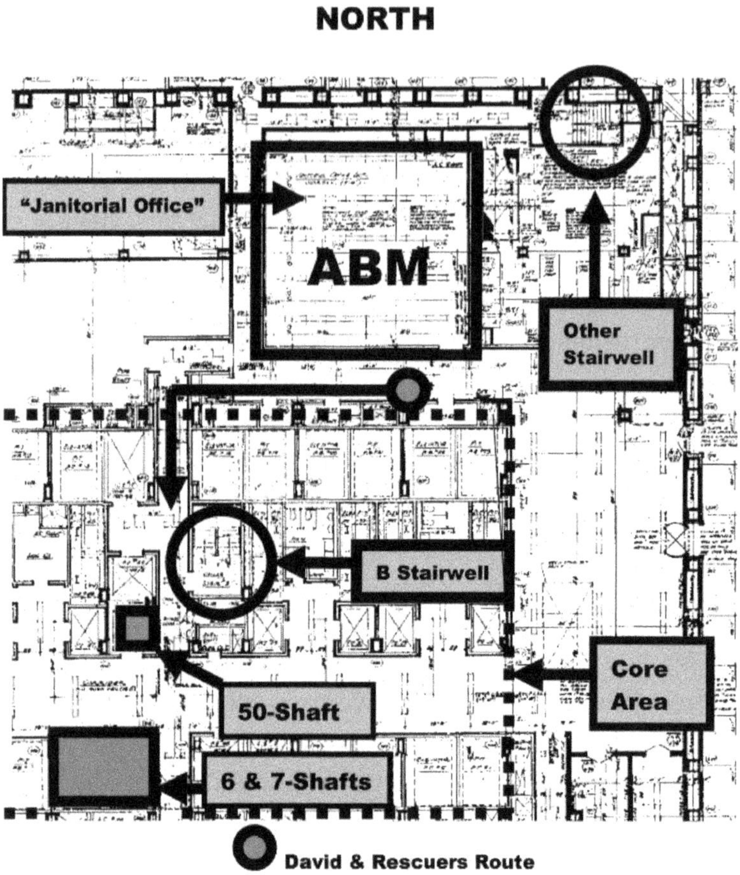

NORTH

"Janitorial Office"

ABM

Other Stairwell

B Stairwell

50-Shaft

6 & 7-Shafts

Core Area

David & Rescuers Route

B1 Level

This plan shows that there were only two possible stairwells on B1. One of them was the main stairwell—the B stairwell—which was located in the middle of the core area, near the 6- and 7-shafts. The other stairwell was the one located in the northeast corner of the outer office area, near the ABM office.

But this next main lobby plan shows that the other stairwell did not go up to the main lobby level.

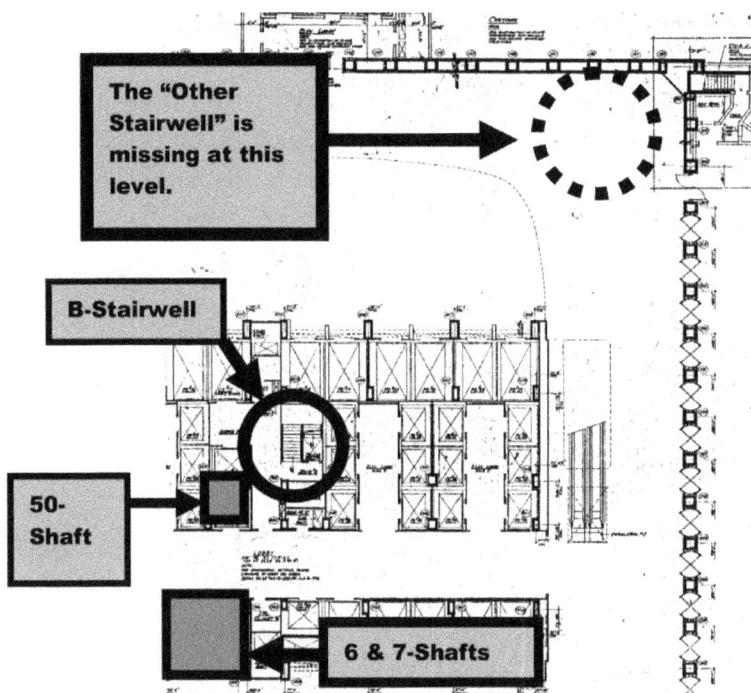

North Tower Main Lobby

Therefore, Rodriguez and the other B1 workers first had to have tried the B stairwell in their attempt to rescue David by way of the main lobby. That would have taken them very near to the 6- and 7-shafts. If a fireball had occurred anywhere near the 6- or 7-shafts, they certainly would have been aware of it. The jet fuel would have caused a tremendous flash fire there and left a strong odor of kerosene hanging in the air. But according to Saltalamacchia, they only encountered smoke. There was no mention of a fire being in the area. Neither was there heat. Nor did he mention seeing damage from a fireball that supposedly had just hit the area. And he did not mention a kerosene smell.

The statement of another maintenance worker, **Salvatore Giambanco,** indicates the same thing. He was just getting off one of the elevators on B1 when he heard an explosion. This is what he said:

We heard the explosion. And the smoke, all of a sudden, came from all over. There was an incredible force of wind that also swept everything away. I remember hearing the scream of a woman, but I couldn't see her. I had just gotten off the elevator and I was standing by it with another man. But I didn't know his name. I remember riding in the ambulance that morning and looking back, thinking it had to be a bomb. If you heard and experienced what I did, it had to be a bomb.[318]

The plans show that if this witness was in an elevator, then he had to be in the inner core area near the 6- and 7-shafts. Note the following plan of the B1 inner core area.

NORTH

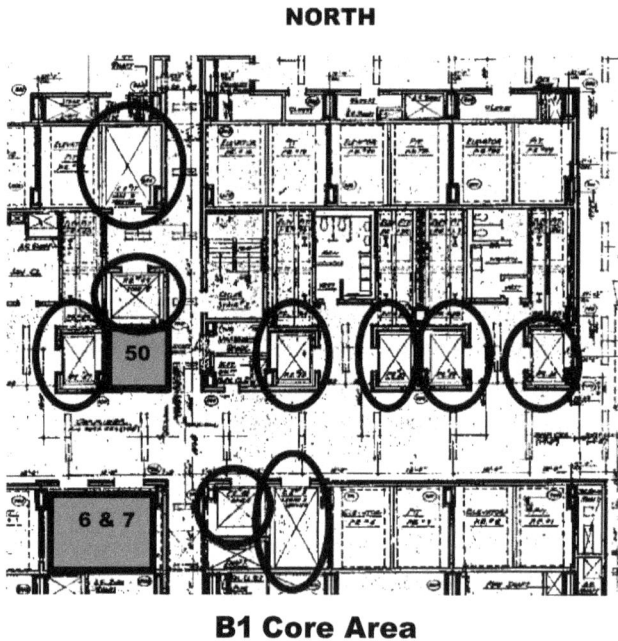

B1 Core Area

Only the nine elevators shown with an "X" and circled in this plan had door openings on B1 and could have been candidates for the one that Giambanco was in. And they were all near the 6- and 7-shafts. If there had been a fireball in either the 6- or 7-shafts, it would have been readily apparent to him. But he confirms Saltalamacchia's observation that there was only a lot of smoke in that area. No evidence of fire or fire damage, no heat, and no kerosene smell means no jet fuel-fed fireball.

Conclusion

This chapter has provided further proof that the Bush investigations' explanation for the two explosions that hit on the B4 level of the North Tower cannot be the truth. All the evidence presented here concurs with the statements of the five workers on B4 and strongly indicates that those two blasts had to have been caused by explosive devices planted there prior to the attack, not jet fuel from the plane.

The next chapter will confirm that explosives were also planted in the upper levels of the tower.

4

More Explosions

IN ADDITION TO THE B4 explosions in the subbasement, there were six other explosions that were observed in upper levels of the North Tower. Those additional explosions occurred:

1. in the main lobby (concourse level) core area;
2. in the 22nd floor core area;
3. in the core area at the 3rd floor;
4. in the core area at some point below the 3rd floor, which caused the collapse of the A Stairwell;
5. at the 44th floor sky lobby, causing floors 65 to 43 in Zone 2 to collapse; and
6. in the 86th floor core area.

While the B4 explosions theoretically could have been due to devices secreted into the basement by people who had access to the parking areas via the outside ramps from the street, these other explosions could only have been accomplished by people who were *allowed* extraordinary access to the upper-levels the building. This presupposes an inside job.

The Explosion in the Main Lobby

Several witnesses came forward to testify to the existence of a powerful detonation that occurred in the main lobby of the North Tower, almost immediately after plane impact. This particular blast had the characteristics of both a jet fuel-fed fireball and an explosive device.

Note the following plan, showing the tower's main lobby. It shows the main entrance from West Street in relation to the 50-, 6-, and 7-shafts and the fire department's Fire Command Center (FCC), a station that was created as a safety precaution after the '93 bombing.

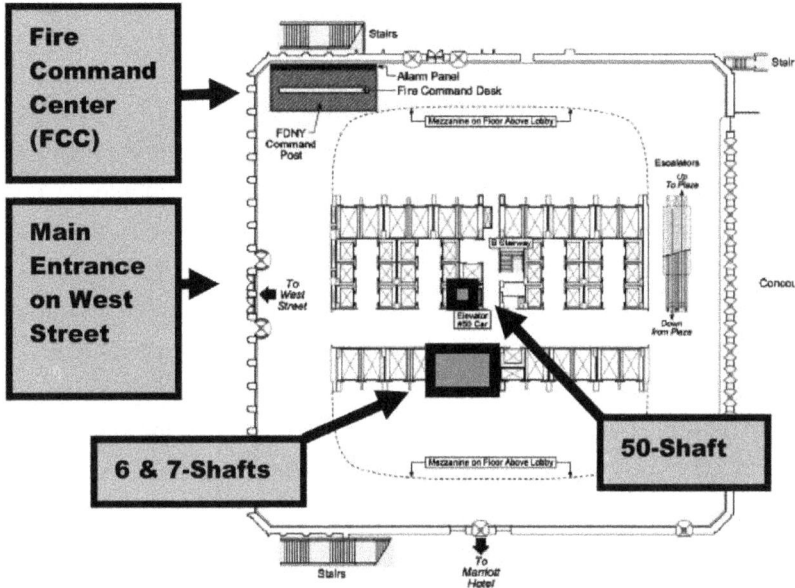

North Tower Main Lobby Plan
Source: NIST

One of the witnesses to this blast was **Lauren Manning**, who suffered severe burns to her face and body. She was interviewed by CNN's Larry King about two weeks after the attack. This is what she said:

LM And as I walked into the building the plane had hit—I imagine—as I was getting out of the cab. And the fuel just poured down.

LK You never got into the building?

LM No, I got into the building. I walked into the lobby. As I was turning toward the elevator banks, the fireball exploded out and caught me from behind and literally pushed me toward the doors as I was running, and...

LK You kept running?

LM   Oh, I kept running through the initial panel of doors, through the revolving doors, outside. And my only desire was to… You know, you think of anything having to do with fire was try to find a way to put it out.[319]

Another witness was **David Kravette.** He was a managing director of Cantor Fitzgerald, a bond trading firm that had offices on floors 101 to 105. This is how he described it: "There was this huge explosion like a fireball exploding out of a bank of elevators. People were engulfed in flames."[320]

Vasana Mutuanot was also inside the main lobby when she heard the explosion. Thinking it was another terrorist attack like the 1993 bombing, she started running. She looked back and saw a fireball coming at her. She described it as "a fireball with sand and heat, like a hurricane of fire" that "swept to my back from my feet up. And then I see fire all over. In my hair, also." "A lot of people," she said, "just blew away, you know, like that."[321]

Another witness, **Ronnie Clifford,** was standing in the lobby of the Marriot Hotel near the glass revolving door that was the south entrance to the North Tower's main lobby.[322] It was about 8:45 a.m., and he was checking his tie in a mirror. Suddenly, he felt a huge explosion. Several seconds later, there was a tremendous shaking of the building. The air on the other side of the glass windows that looked in on the south side of the North Tower lobby was getting hazy. Soon he began to see panicky people, scurrying to escape a "hurricane of flying debris."

The revolving doors to the lobby turned, and there was a hot burst of wind and a suctioning sound. In came a woman who was so badly burned, it was impossible to tell her race. Her clothes had been burnt off except for the zipper of her sweater, which had been melted onto her chest. Her singed hair looked like steel wool. And Ronnie thought he smelled a kerosene-like smell.

He sat the woman down on the marble floor and ran to the bathroom, returning with a black garbage bag filled with water, which he dribbled on her. Incredibly, her mind was clear in spite of her condition. He took out a notepad and got her personal information. Her name, she said, was Jennieanne Maffeo.[323] She was forty, from Brooklyn. She was Italian-American.

Clifford helped firefighters get her to an ambulance, and she was transported to a hospital. She died there on October 12, 2001.

Most of the first responders to the North Tower were firefighters who arrived within minutes of the plane crash. Their descriptions of the damage done to the lobby stands in distinct contradiction to the official story, which says it was caused by a fireball coming down an elevator shaft. To many of them, it seemed more like an explosion had gone off inside the core area where the local elevators were located. One of those was Lieutenant **William Walsh**, from Ladder Company 1. He entered the lobby through the main entrance on West Street. This is what he saw:

> What I observed as I was going through these doors and I got into the lobby of the World Trade Center was that the lobby of the trade center didn't appear that it had any lights. All the glass that abuts West Street was blown out. The glass in the revolving doors was blown out. All the glass in the lobby was blown out...The panels of the walls are made of marble. It's about 2 to 3 inches thick. They're about 10 feet high by 10 feet wide. A lot of those were hanging off the wall.

> Now, the front door is a revolving door. There's a vestibule of about ten feet, let's say. And there's another revolving door. There I noticed two civilians that had more than third degree burns. They were in a pugilistic position. They were black. Burnt. Their skin and their clothes were burnt off. They were smoldering and they were trying to get up. They were just moving around. I estimated that they had less than half a minute in their lives.[324]

On the morning of the attacks, filmmaker **Jules Naudet** happened to be making a documentary about the FDNY with Lt. Walsh and fire department Battalion Chief Joseph Pfeifer. Naudet and Pfeiffer also arrived at the North Tower main lobby within minutes. This is what Naudet said: "A guy from the Port Authority told him [Pfeiffer] the damage was somewhere above the 78th floor. But all you had to do was look around. It was obvious something had happened right there in the lobby."[325]

He also saw the burn victims: "I go in. And I hear screams. And when we go in, right to my right, there was two people on fire, burning. I just didn't want to film them. It was like no one should see this."[326]

William Greene, a firefighter with Engine 6, saw more bodies. This is what he said:

We headed for the B staircase. It was pretty much in the center of the core. We had to go through these turnstiles. I remember there was a lot of rubble on the floor there. There were elevator doors ajar. There were elevator doors missing. I remember I looked up at the ceiling because I thought maybe the ceiling got charred because there was a bunch of rubble on the floor. It was about three feet high in the middle. The ceiling wasn't charred. So I thought the floor blew up. I came to learn later that that was bodies. We had to climb over and around this pile...Right outside the elevators, in the core. We had to climb up and around it. It was like three feet high in the middle.[327]

The following illustration shows Greene's route to the B stairwell.

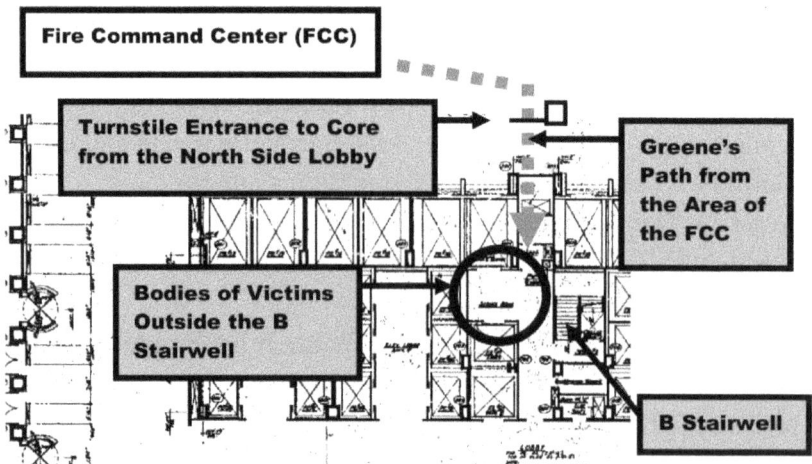

Main Lobby Victims Found by Greene

The following plan shows the location of the burn victims killed by this main lobby blast.

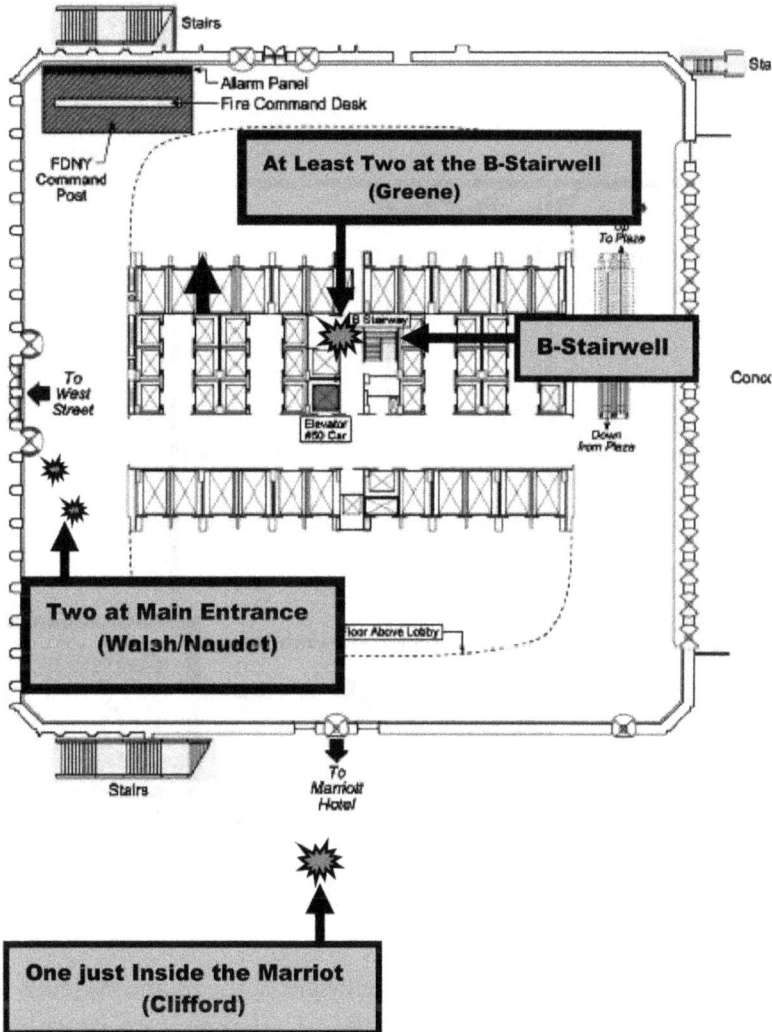

Main Lobby Burn Victims

As the North Tower plans show, the only possible conduit for the official story's alleged fireball from the plane impact zone to reach the main lobby was via the 50-, 6-, or 7-shafts.[328]

What About the 50-Shaft?

Could all this death and destruction have been caused by a fireball coming down the 50-shaft from the plane impact zone, a quarter of a mile up the tower, at breakneck speed, immediately after plane impact?

Recall that the 50-car was stuck between B2 and B3 with Griffith and Cruz inside.

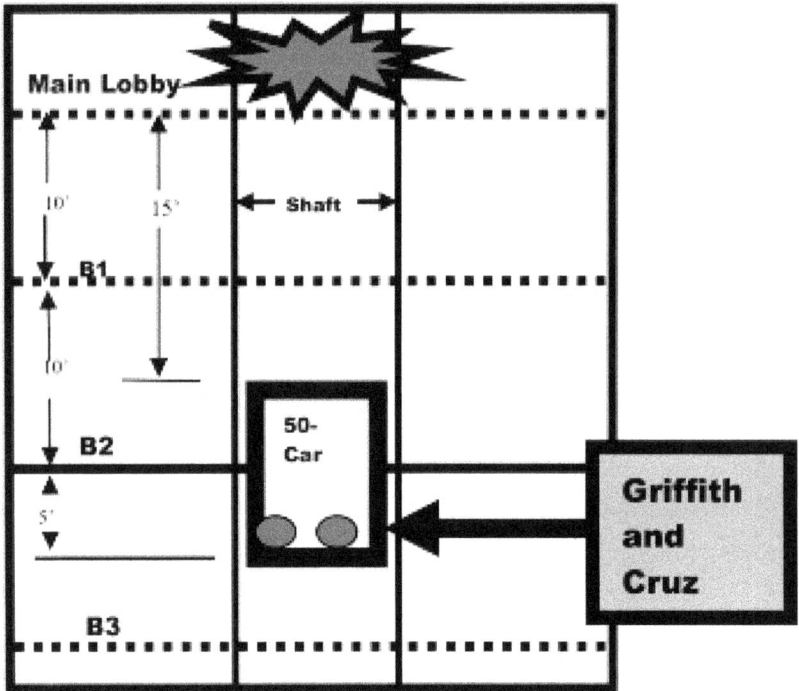

Position of 50-Car After Plane Impact

The blueprints show that the ceiling height of the B1 and B2 levels was ten feet. That would make the top of the 50-car about fifteen feet below the main lobby level, more or less. According to that, the first question that comes up is: Why would a fireball, that was supposedly shooting down the 50-shaft, stop abruptly at the main lobby level and explode out horizontally, rather than take the path of least resistance and continue down to impact the top of the elevator car? The answer is, of course, that it would not.

And we know that such a thing did not happen because Cruz and Griffith both survived the tremendous force of this blast; a force that was strong enough to blow out several elevator cars in the core area, blast heavy marble panels of the west side of the lobby wall, shatter thick exterior glass windows out onto the sidewalk and incinerate several people.

So, the 50-shaft could not have been a source for this main lobby fireball/explosion.

What About the 6- and 7-Shafts?

Other comments made by Lt. Walsh support the conclusion that the 6- and 7-shafts were not the source of this main lobby explosion/fireball, either. He told the fire department's WTCTF investigators that after entering the lobby, he immediately made an inventory of the damage to the elevators, and the 6- and 7-shafts showed no damage. Here is that part of his statement:

What else I observed in the lobby was that...There's basically two areas of elevators. There's elevators off to the left-hand side which are really the express elevators. That would be the elevators that's facing north. Then on the right-hand side there's also elevators that are express elevators, and that would be facing south. In the center of these two elevator shafts would be elevators that go to the lower floors. They were blown off the hinges. That's where the service elevator was also.[329]

At this point, his interviewer took special interest in knowing which elevators he saw "blown off the hinges."

Q.   Were these elevators that went to the upper floors? They weren't side lobby elevators?

W.   No. No, I'd say they went through floors 30 and below.

Q.   And they were blown off?

W.   They were blown off the hinges. And you could see the shafts. The elevators on the extreme north side and the other express elevators on the extreme south side, they looked intact to me from what I could see, the doors anyway.[330]

The interviewer seems surprised that it was the inner core local elevators (see illustration below) that were damaged and not the express elevators that went to the upper sky lobbies, such as the 6- and 7-cars. And well he should have been; those inner core local elevators at the main lobby level did not go any higher than the 44th floor sky lobby. So, none of them could have been a conduit for a fireball to reach the main lobby from the plane impact zone, which was above the 78th floor sky lobby, in zone three.

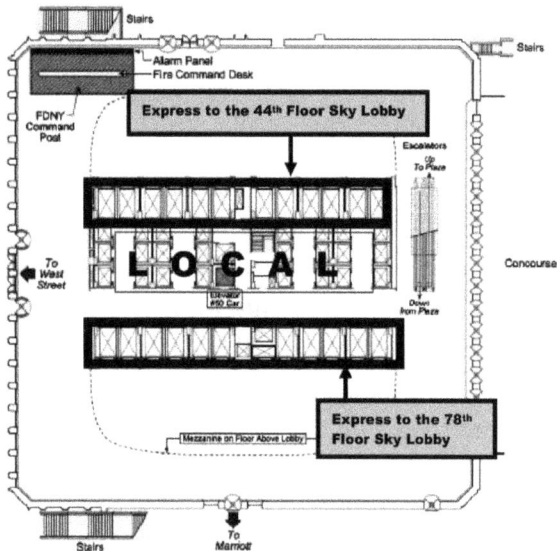

North Tower Main Lobby

Source: NIST

Ronnie Clifford's observations also confirm that this fireball did not originate in the 6- and/or 7-shafts. His vantage point would have put those two elevators in his direct view, through the windows looking into the main lobby from the Marriot. He said that he saw a "hurricane" of debris on the other side of the windows, but he did not mention seeing a fireball. If the 6- and/or the 7-shaft was the source of this first main lobby fireball/explosion, most likely he would have seen it.

Also, that powerful blast would probably have broken the Marriot's window glass in the same way that the windows on the west side of the lobby were blasted outward onto the sidewalk. But the Marriot windows remained intact.

The following plan summarizes the damage done by this main lobby explosion/fireball.

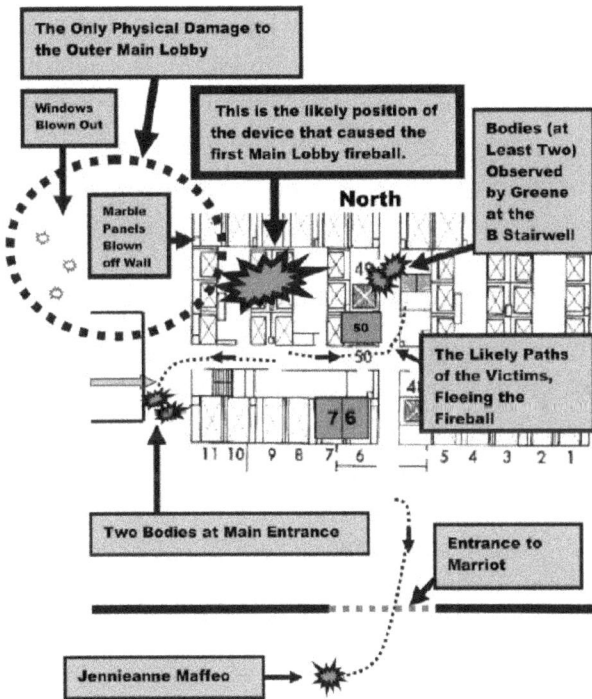

Damage Done by the Main Lobby Blast

In the first place, the facts presented here completely contradict the official account. They indicate that the "fireball" that occurred in the main lobby did not come down from the plane impact zone via the 50-, 6- or 7-shafts. Rather, it had to be due to one or more devices that were planted inside at least one of the passenger local elevator shafts located at the western end of the inner core. From Jules Naudet's video of the damage done to the marble panels in the outer lobby, it appears that the explosives were likely planted near the top of the elevator cars because the vast majority of those panels were blown out about ten feet above the floor, which was the height of the cars.[331]

Secondly, the damage done to the main lobby indicates the presence of a strong *shock wave*. When the detonation occurred, the force of its blast blew out many of the inner core elevators, blasted the heavy marble panels off the west end wall, and shattered the thick safety glass windows out onto the west side sidewalk. That is not something that is associated with jet fuel-fed fireball deflagrations. Only a bomb could have done that.

Thirdly, notice that none of the witnesses mentioned the presence of a *fire* situation being ignited in the lobby. That seems to rule out jet fuel. However, Ronnie Clifford did smell a kerosene-like smell on victim Maffeo, and that cannot be dismissed. Also, some of the witnesses specifically mentioned seeing what they described as a fireball burst out of the core elevators. In addition, at least five people were, for all practical purposes, incinerated on the spot. All of this indicates that a jet fuel/kerosene accelerant may have been present along with some kind of explosive device. It is possible that containers filled with kerosene could have been planted in the core elevator shafts along with an explosive device, and that's what gave the sense that jet fuel was present. This could have been part of the demolition plan meant to give the impression that the lower level fireball/explosions were secondary fireballs caused by jet fuel from the plane crash—a bit of misdirection meant to create a cover story, if you will.

Of course, that is only an educated guess. But in any case, what is very clear is that whatever explosive material it was that blew up in the main lobby, it could not have come from the plane impact zone. That would have been impossible because the elevator shafts that went to the upper floors were not damaged; only the ones to the lower floors were (Walsh). Thus, the explosive power of that detonation had to be due to a very potent device that was planted in the local elevator shafts of the inner core area prior to the plane crash.

And that could only have been done by people who were allowed extraordinary access to the building. Therefore, this is a very strong indication of an inside job.

The Explosion on the 22nd Floor

Damage to the 22nd floor of the North Tower was noted by the 9/11 Commission, but without the detailed comment that it deserved. A huge fire and at least one big explosion occurred there that remains unexplained by the Bush administration's official story.

Moreover, the evidence also shows that the fire had to have been remotely ignited by someone outside the building who was observing Flight 11 as it approached.

In the first place, it is important to know that the 22nd floor housed a hidden office known as the Security Command Center (SCC), from which security personnel managed various vital functions of the twin towers.[332] At the SCC, they controlled such things as the intercom system used to make announcements to workers in case of an emergency; the heating and ventilation system (HVAC); access to the mechanical equipment rooms, which housed various equipment like generators, transformers, and the pumps needed to supply water to the emergency fire suppression system; and access to the roof. Also from the SCC, security personnel monitored the tower's closed circuit TV (CCTV) system, which, after the 1993 bombing, was extensive.[333]

The evidence shows that the SCC office—which was vitally important to the safety of the people in the building, especially in the case of a fire emergency like what happened on 9/11—was intentionally disabled by some kind of incendiary device that started a tremendous fire just outside its door and caused it to be abandoned. At the same time, the highly trained personnel of a backup system at the Operations Control Center (OCC)—located on the B1 level of the South Tower—was, without any justification, ordered by an unknown person to be evacuated. Thus, almost immediately after the first plane hit the North Tower, none of the emergency operating systems that were controlled from the SCC and the OCC could be used to save the lives of people trapped in the building. Due to this, the death toll at the WTC was higher than it would have been had at least one of these two key control centers been able to operate as intended.

The evidence also shows that several of the elevators on the 22nd floor of the North Tower were destroyed by at least one powerful explosion that could not have resulted from jet fuel coming from the plane impact zone at the 96th floor, as the official story says. In addition, the witness statements indicate that the core explosion(s) could not have caused the fire at the SCC. They appear to have been two separate events, caused by two separate and distinct types of devices—one explosive and the other incendiary.

That there was a fire at the SCC is indicated by PAPD recordings of calls that started coming in almost simultaneously with Flight 11 hitting the North Tower. That fire erupted outside the office of the SCC and trapped security staffers inside.

Note the following conversation. According to the time stamp on the recording, it took place at about the same time the plane hit, 8:47 a.m. It was between the PAPD main desk and a woman named **Josie,** who was one of several security staffers inside the SCC. (Please note that "A tower" refers to the North Tower.)

Josie:	There's a fire outside of 22! There's a fire on 22!
PAPD:	Fire on 22? Where? A or B tower?
Josie:	This is the SCC, A tower, the 22nd floor. We see a lot of debris. We are stuck on 22. The door is blocked. There is a fire.
PAPD:	Alright. That's copy.
Male:	This is six-three! We need a (inaudible). We have an injured...He's hurt. Something blew up and (inaudible)
PAPD:	S2 to SCC!
Josie:	Go!
PAPD:	(breaking up) conditions there?
Josie:	Can you repeat that again, please?
PAPD:	Josie, what's the condition on 22?

Josie: 22 is...We cannot leave the area. There is a lot of smoke outside. We are stuck inside...(alarms in background) SCC, S4...S4, this is the SCC, we have (inaudible) running... The air is clearing up just a little bit. But we still can't get out. And we are losing power. We don't have much power.

PAPD: Josie, OK, they are aware that you can't open the door. And they will be up there and get that debris out of the way.

Josie: That's big 10-4, thank you.[334]

Hermina Jones, another SCC worker who survived, also described the fire as intense: "When the fire started, the room was sealed. Flames were shooting off the walls. We started putting wet towels under the door."[335]

The idea that the SCC fire was intentionally set is backed up by the testimonies of firefighters who soon arrived in the area. Although there was fire in the outer office area where the SCC was located, they reported that there was no fire in the core area where the elevators were located, only physical damage. **Michael Yarembinsky** was one of these men. This is how he set the scene: "When we got to 22, we heard there was a Port Authority command post on 22. So we stopped there. My officers wanted to find out some information. My officer, Lieutenant Andy Desperito... he went over to the command post." And he added,

We noticed in the hallway that the elevator shaft had been blown out. There was nothing there. No doors. No framing. Nothing. When you looked down, all you saw was the cables for the elevator and the brick work that was surrounding...*No burning. No smoke* coming out of it.[336] (Italics added)

Kirk Long was another firefighter who was there. This is what he said:

We made it up to the 22nd floor. We stood there for a couple minutes. I believe Andy Desperito talked to the battalion through the fire warden phones. We did locate somebody at the end of the hall. But everything was blown out. The ceiling had fallen. The dropped ceiling had fallen to the floor. Some of the walls were blown out. So, Andy and I had crawled down the hallway to get to the Port Authority command post.[337]

While there was a tremendous fire reported at the SCC, these witnesses described only structural damage from an explosion in the core area, not fire. So obviously, the fire at the SCC could not have been caused by jet fuel from the plane crash, coming down an elevator shaft.

That conclusion is also backed up by the following facts. (1) The SCC was "hidden" in the outer office area, quite some ways from the core elevators. So how could jet fuel get all the way over there without there being a fire at the elevators? (2) The building plans show that none of the local elevators on this floor went past the 44th floor sky lobby. So, they could not even have provided a conduit for jet fuel to get to the 22nd floor. (3) The only elevator shafts that had an unobstructed run up to the plane impact zone from the 22nd floor were the 50-, 6-, and 7-shafts. But it is known that no fireball came down the 50-shaft because Arturo Griffith and Marlene Cruz were in the 50-car, stuck between the B2 and B3 levels, at the time. And they survived. And, from what Yarembinsky said, the 6- and 7-shafts could not be involved either. He said that "everything" was blown out, emphasizing the "doors" and the "framing." But the plans show that the 6- and 7-shafts did not have door openings on the 22nd floor; and thus no doors or framing. So, they could not have been among the ones that he saw blown out.

That it was likely a remotely detonated device that set the fire at the SCC is indicated by the fact that Josie's 8:47 call came in to the PA main desk at almost the exact time of the plane crash, which was pegged by four Air Traffic Control Centers as exactly 8:46:40. The PA transcripts did not show the time to within seconds; however, it can be assumed that Josie's call came no more than one minute and twenty seconds after the plane hit—that is, before the PAPD recording system hit the 8:48 mark. If you figure in a minute or so reaction time for Josie to see the fire erupt, find out that the doors would not open and that the SCC had lost control of their systems, and then make the call to the PAPD, it follows that the fire at the SCC must have erupted very close to the time of plane impact, if not even a little before. This leads to the conclusion that the fire at the SCC was caused by an incendiary device that was ignited remotely by a person who was visually observing the plane coming in.

The question then arises: Why set a fire at the SCC? Many say it was because the fire at the SCC ensured a higher death count, which would make the WTC attack seem as reprehensible as possible for the cabal of conspirators responsible who, presumably, wanted to use it to highlight the involvement of al Qaeda. That, of course, is impossible to prove at this point. But what is undeniably true is that the suspicious circumstances surrounding the fire at the SCC and the equally suspicious evacuation of the backup system at the OCC no doubt had the effect of causing deaths that could otherwise have been prevented.

In support of that charge, note the following facts: Only every fourth door in the North Tower stairwells that accessed the office areas was unlocked, and unless you had a key, the floors in between those could only be unlocked electronically from the SCC. Due to that, many office workers who were unaware of what was going on and did not exit the building or those who were incapacitated and needed assistance were undoubtedly trapped on their floors; The SCC also controlled access to the roof. So, loss of power at the SCC made a rooftop rescue impossible; The SCC controlled the public-address system. With that out of commission, emergency announcements could not be made; The SCC also controlled access to the 75th floor mechanical room, which housed the auxiliary water pumps that were used to fill the building's sprinkler system and emergency firefighting water standpipes and hoses, which were located in the stairwells. Those pumps could only be turned on manually. So, with the SCC out of commission, tower workers on the upper floors could not access that system to fight the fires; The SCC also controlled the smoke purge system of the HVAC heating and air conditioning system which, due to its being inoperable, likely caused many victims to die from smoke inhalation; And the SCC also controlled the manual override of the local elevators, which were designed to return automatically to the sky lobbies at the 78th and 44th floors when the fire alarm was activated. Due to most of the local elevators being unavailable, thousands of victims were forced to file slowly down the building's three narrow stairwells, which many people were still in the process of doing when the building collapsed.

Another disturbing aspect of what happened at the 22nd floor SCC concerns the closed-circuit camera system. Note this snippet of conversation between Josie and the PAPD officer, which took place about 38 minutes after Josie first reported the fire:

Josie: We have, uh, the cameras running on all the perimeter
             outside.

This caused the officer to pause. Then he said:

PAPD: Repeat?
Josie: We have all the cameras up on the outside perimeter.[338]

One would think that the PAPD officer should have been very interested in preserving the recordings from those cameras. They might have contained some interesting information. They might even have shown a close-up of Flight 11 as it flew into the building. They might even have shown who, or what, was flying that plane. Was it really Flight 11 or a drone, as some have suggested? But, inexplicably, the officer ignored what Josie had just said. He merely responded:

OK. We are working our way up to 22.[339]

We will probably never know what was on those recordings, because, apparently, no one in the control room thought to save them. They were the object of some later investigation, but apparently were never found.[340]

It very well could be, however, that one of the purposes of attacking the SCC was to destroy the information from those surveillance cameras.

As mentioned briefly in the beginning of this section, another troubling aspect of the fire on the 22nd floor concerns the SCC's backup system at the OCC. The OCC office was created after the 1993 bombing and was meant to mirror the operations at the SCC, as a safety feature.[341] According to the 9/11 Commission, the "Security Command Center was built on the 22nd floor of 1 WTC, backed up by a new Operations Control Center on the subgrade B1 level at 2 World Trade Center [South Tower]."[342] But the evidence shows that that vitally important office was mysteriously abandoned almost immediately after the North Tower was struck. And due to that, it played no part that day in the emergency response to the attack.[343,344]

One of the PAPD transcripts of emergency calls made that morning indicates that the OCC was manned as per normal operating procedure when the first plane hit the North Tower at 8:47 a.m. As noted in Chapter 2, at 8:50 a.m., three minutes after the crash, a male caller alerted Officer Brady at the PAPD main desk that an explosion had just occurred on the B4 level. Immediately after that, a call came in to another officer at the main desk, named Maggett, from a security officer at the OCC named Edward Calderon, who said, "Maggett, this is Ed at the OCC. I got word that there's an explosion down on B4. We got people hurt down there. B4."[345]

But according to another of the transcripts, the OCC was evacuated about ten minutes later, at just before 9:00 a.m.[346] At that time, a "female" voice coming from the SCC said, "I'm trying to get in contact with the OCC. The phone is just ringing."[347] Presumably, that was Josie, trying to alert the OCC that her office—the SCC—was out of commission.

The fact that the OCC was abandoned very quickly after the first plane crash is also attested to by witness William Rodriguez, who, as mentioned previously, was on the B1 level of the North Tower when Flight 11 hit. Within minutes of that North Tower crash, but before the South Tower was hit sixteen minutes later, he ran to the OCC to alert them to the situation in the North Tower. But when he got there, he saw that the center was empty. This is how he described it:

I run straight to the South Tower where they have the OCC that was created after 1993. They spent $155 million to retrofit the building, and to supposedly straighten it out after the 1993 bombing, and to set up a whole security system, the control center. When I got there and started hitting the window, there was nobody there. There was nobody there—the control center, where they have all the cameras, and the recordings.[348]

The apparent reason why the OCC was empty when Rodriguez got there was explained in a 9:25 call that came in to the PAPD main desk. It was made by an unknown "male" person, who said, "I want to tell you, the OCC is out. They had to evacuate."[349]

There are two disturbing aspects to this last report. First, it insinuates that the evacuation of the OCC was unavoidable. But according to the record of PAPD emergency calls and Rodriguez's statement that is not true. The PAPD transcripts do not mention a fire or an explosion at the OCC at all that morning. And when Rodriquez arrived at the OCC within minutes of the North Tower plane crash, he did not observe any fire or the effects of an explosion there that might have necessitated the evacuation.

Secondly, the OCC, being so critically important to maintaining the safety of the thousands of people in the towers, most certainly was constantly vigilant and was thus expected to be always manned. So, if the North Tower was hit almost simultaneously with Josie's 8:47 call to the PAPD, whoever was manning the OCC (presumably, at least Calderon) at that time had to know that the SCC was out of commission. And they also had to know that their office—the OCC—was, therefore, the only place where vital systems of the North Tower could be controlled to potentially save lives. Yet according to the PAPD transcripts of calls, by ten minutes after the impact of Flight 11 on the North Tower, and before the South Tower was hit, the trained personnel of the OCC had, inexplicably, already evacuated that critically important office.

None of the Bush administration investigations ever attempted to discover who was in the OCC the morning of 9/11. And the only person who is mentioned in the transcripts as being there is Ed Calderon. But, tragically, he was killed by the collapse of the North Tower.[350] So the question remains: Why was the OCC so hastily evacuated?

Again, the likely answer is that it ensured a higher death toll. With the SCC out of commission, the operators at the OCC were the only ones left who had the ability to release all the locked doors in the stairwells and to the roof so firefighters could rescue people from some of the offices, or so they could possibly be rescued by helicopter. They were the only ones who could have unlocked the doors to the mechanical rooms, so any maintenance people up in the tower could turn on the emergency water pumps at the 75th floor mechanical room and begin to attempt to put out the fires. They were the only ones who could have gotten some of the elevators working instead of leaving people trapped on upper floors. They were the only ones who could have attempted to purge the smoke that was suffocating people at the upper levels of the tower. And they were the only ones who could have turned on the PA system right off the bat and tell everybody to get out of the building.

But none of that was done, precisely because almost immediately after the North Tower was hit, somebody ordered the trained personnel at the OCC to evacuate.

Then there remains the question of what happened to the recordings of the surveillance cameras. They were also copied at the OCC and could have been saved from there. Conversely, though, they could have also been destroyed after that control center was evacuated.

Furthermore, as to the possibility that the intentional destruction of the SCC and the ordered evacuation of the OCC may have been done to raise the death toll, it is also important to note that just after the North Tower was hit, people in the South Tower were told by an announcement over the PA system *not* to evacuate the building and to return to their offices. As reported by one TV news reporter:

> In the neighboring South Tower, people were already evacuating, but an announcement over the PA system tells them their building is secure and they can return to their desks; an announcement that will soon have tragic consequences.[351]

According to North Tower, B4-witness Hursley Lever, this PA announcement was heard throughout the whole complex, as well. In my interview with him, he said that he heard it when he was lying in a parking area adjacent to the North Tower while waiting to be evacuated because of the broken ankle he suffered when hit by an explosion upon plane impact. "They were telling people to go back in the building. On the PA system," he said. "I couldn't believe it."[352]

But the PA system for making such announcements was located at only two places—the SCC and the OCC. And if they were both out of commission very early on, who was making that obviously ill-advised announcement, how was it done and why?

This strange PA announcement and the situation surrounding the disabling of the SCC and the premature evacuation of the OCC remain mysteries. But what has been made quite certain here is that the fire that occurred at the SCC, as well as the explosion that occurred upon plane impact in the core elevators on the 22nd floor, could not have been caused by jet fuel coming from the plane impact zone. Those two events could only have been due to two devices that were planted in those two separate and distinct areas prior to plane impact; one incendiary, the other explosive.

So, here we have a second example that points to an inside job of controlled demolition of the North Tower that had to have been perpetrated by people who were allowed extraordinary access to the building.

The Explosion in the 3rd Floor Core Area

There were also badly burned bodies observed in the 3rd floor core area, which the plans show could not have been due to jet fuel from Flight 11. One of the firefighters who discovered the bodies was **Peter Blaich**. This is what he said in his WTCTF interview:

We started going up the B Stairway. As we got to the 3rd floor of the B Stairway, we forced open an elevator door which was burnt on all three sides. The only thing that was remaining was the hoistway door. And inside the elevator were about…I didn't recognize them initially, but a guy from 1 truck said, "Oh, my God, those are people." They were pretty incinerated.[353]

What Blaich is referring to here by "hoistway door" is that a typical office building elevator car has two doors. There is an outer door, which is framed into the hallway wall and, in the case of the North Tower, this one was made of stainless steel buffed to a mirror-like shine. And there is a second, inner door, which is part of the car and moves with it. This so-called hoistway door is only finished on the inside and when seen from the hallway side has more of an industrial look to it. Note the following drawing.

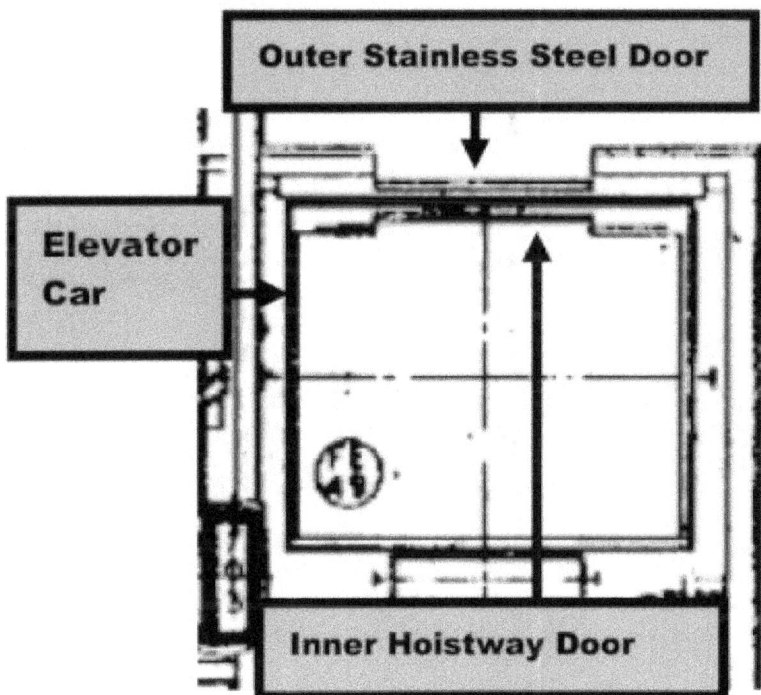

Typical Elevator Doors

Blaich's observation that only the "hoistway door" remained indicates that there was an explosion very near to the elevator car, because the outer stainless steel door had been blown off by the blast. But the logistics of the elevator system on this level indicates that this blast also could not have been caused by jet fuel coming down from the plane impact zone.

Refer to the following plan of the 3rd floor core area.

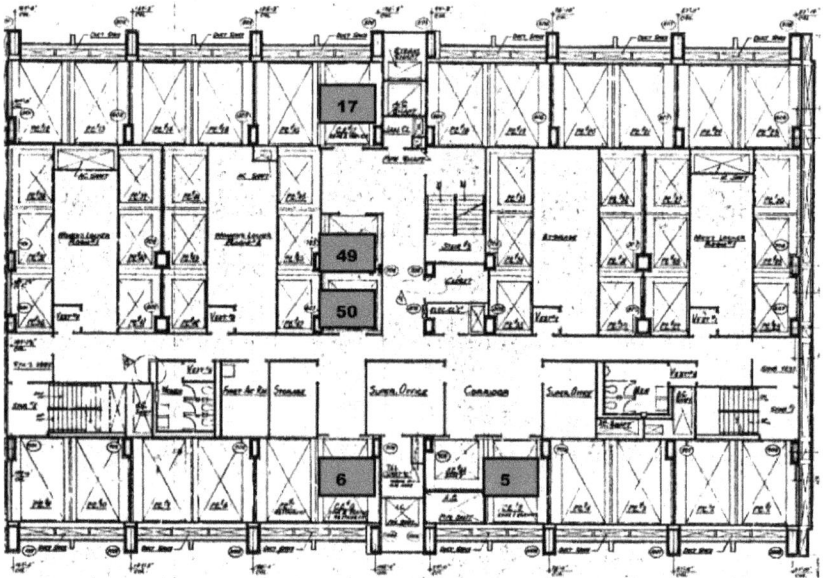

The 3rd Floor Core Area Elevators

This drawing shows that the only elevator cars that could have contained the bodies were the 50-, 49-, 17-, 6-, or 5-cars, because they were the only ones that had doors on this floor that could have been blown out.

The detail below shows how door openings can be determined:

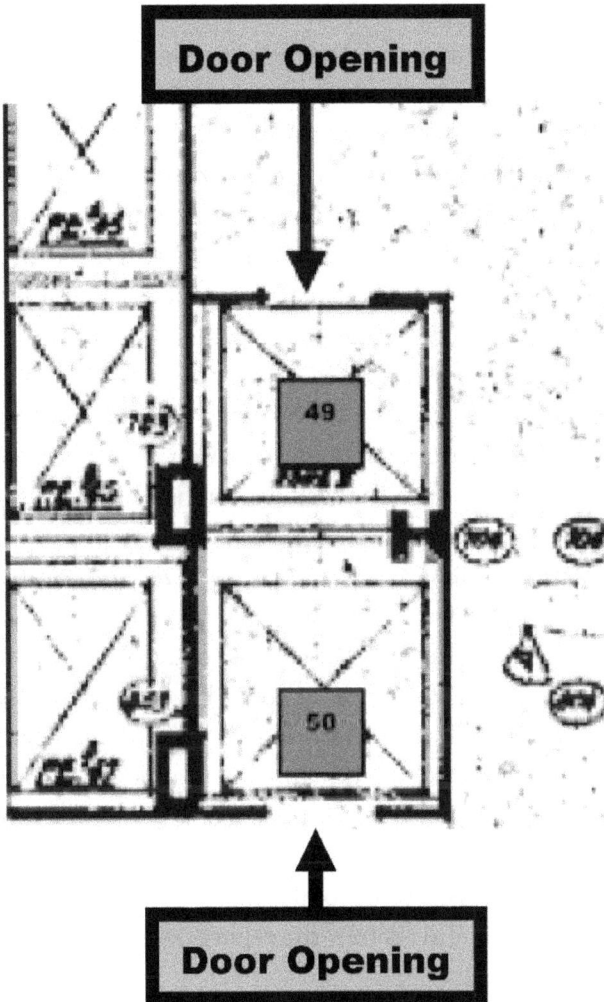

It is known that the 50-car and the 6-car could not have contained the bodies because, as has been previously shown, immediately after plane impact, they were in the basement sublevels. As for the only other cars that were possibilities to have the bodies in them, the plans show that the 49-car did not go any higher than the 74th floor, the 17-car stopped at the 78th floor, and the 5-car only went to the 44th floor.[354] And as has been shown, the lift motor rooms for all the elevators in the tower were located two floors above the highest floor serviced by any car. So, any fireball that might have come down from the plane impact zone in line with the 49-shaft, the 17-shaft or the 5-shaft would have been blocked by motor room floors at the 76th floor, the 80th floor, and the 46th floor, respectively. Therefore, whichever of these cars the bodies were in, it could not have been hit by a jet fuel-fed fireball coming down from the plane impact zone.

So here, once again, we have destruction and deaths that could only have been caused by the detonation of an explosive device that was planted in an elevator shaft below the plane impact zone. This is another example which proves that whoever planted explosives in the North Tower was allowed extraordinary access to the building prior to the attack.

Thus, this is a third example of an explosion occurring in the North Tower that had to have been the result of an inside job.

The Explosion that Collapsed the A Stairwell at the 3rd Floor

Several firefighters who survived the collapse of the North Tower reported that the A Stairwell collapsed at the 3rd floor a long time before the building started to come down. If true, that would be unexplained by the official story, because such a thing could only have happened if core columns below the 3rd floor had been cut and knocked off their bearings by very powerful explosives.

Again, according to NIST, the total collapse of the North Tower began at about the 96th floor. This is how the report described it:

In WTC 1 (North Tower), the fires weakened the core columns and caused the floors on the south side of the building to sag. The floors pulled the heated south perimeter columns inward, reducing their capacity to support the building above. Their neighboring columns quickly became overloaded as columns on the south wall buckled. The *top section* of the building tilted to the south and *began its descent…*[355] (Italics added)

However, this is what firefighter **John Schroeder** said happened to him when he was descending the A Stairwell from the third-floor landing:

> And that's when the stairwell collapsed on us. And we had to dig our way out. Now the building's coming down. We can't see nothing. We start saying our prayers. Tower One was coming down from the interior. Lotta people don't know this. It was coming down from the interior. The inside structure was just disintegrating.[356]

His account of the stairwell collapse was verified by fellow firefighter **Robert Byrne** who was proceeding down behind him.

> Basically, I got as far as the third floor, where I ran into—it looked like there was a collapse down there. It was pretty bad. It was all smoky and dusty. I thought it was smoke, and I got a little nervous. I was at the point where I was going to go up and get another Scott Tank, but I realized it wasn't smoke. That's when I saw it was a collapse. It looked like a collapse. I think it was the second floor, third or second floor, whatever it was. That's where I ran into a Port Authority cop, and he directed me out. It was a good thing I had my flashlight on still, because it was pitch-black.[357]

Greg Hanson, a lieutenant with the FDNY, also saw it. This is what he said:

> We got down to the third floor, and the third floor was partially blocked by some sheetrock. We started to move that when a firefighter from Squad 18—I believe his name is Kelly...He said to me that you can't get down that staircase. There's no exit that way. We made our way to Stairway C, I believe.[358]

Since all three of these men survived to tell their stories, the collapse of that stairwell must have happened a long time before the total collapse of the building. And that contradicts the official account of the collapse in a fundamental way, because it shows that interior support columns were collapsing long before the "top section" of the building "began its descent." This deserves special attention because it appears to follow a technique which is common to many controlled demolitions in central city locations, which is to cut columns close to the foundation to collapse the structure into the basement, thereby minimizing collateral damage to the surrounding area.[359]

According to the North Tower plans, the force needed to accomplish such a thing as Schroeder described had to have been massive, which is a further indication that explosives had to be involved. Note the following drawing. It is a horizontal section through a typical North Tower stairwell, and it gives a good idea of the support system that held throughout the height of the building. The three arrows indicate the vertical support provided by steel columns to which the stairwell was connected.

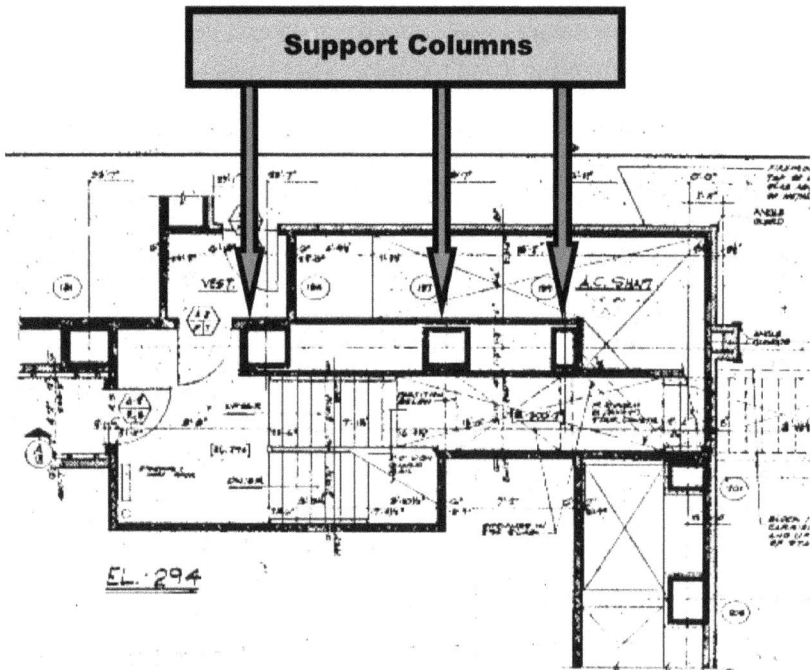

Horizontal Section Through a Typical Stairwell
Source: NIST

The following drawing is a vertical section through a typical stairwell. It shows how the columns that supported the stairwell structure continued down through the building.

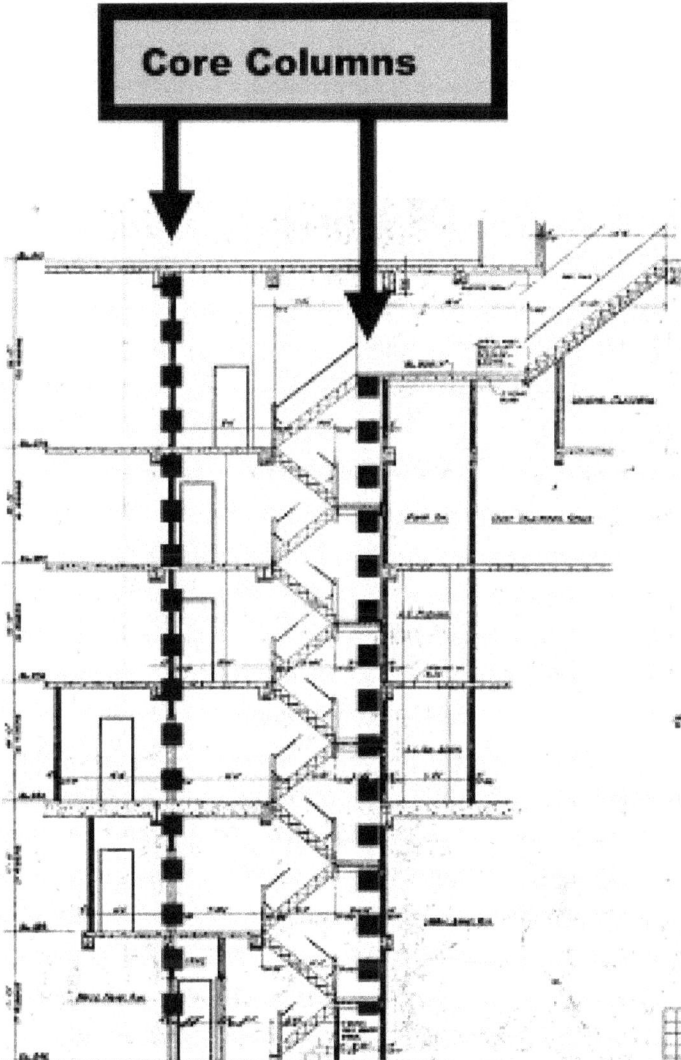

Vertical Section Through a Stairwell
Source: NIST

The next drawing shows how those massive core columns sat on solid bedrock at the foundation of the building.[360]

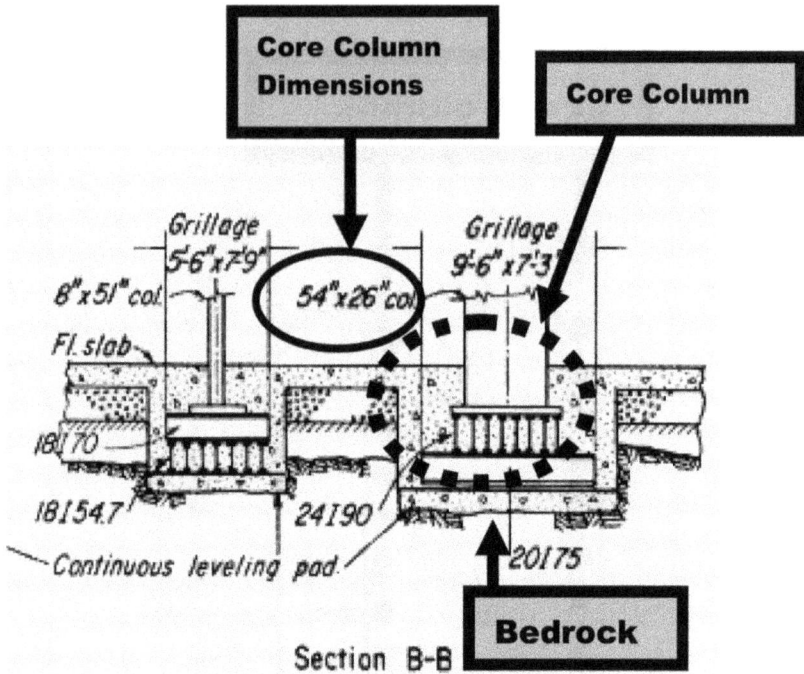

Core Columns at the Foundation

Source: Port Authority of New York and New Jersey

The further they went up the tower, those massive core columns at the foundation transitioned into more common wide-flange shapes of lesser and lesser plate thickness. That is because the upper sections of the columns carried less weight, and thus they could have a smaller profile. The floor level at which the transition took place varied from column to column. Note the following plans. The first one shows the location of the A Stairwell at the 3rd floor. The next floor plan immediately after that shows how the core columns were numbered and at which floor they changed shape. (The numbers below the column numbers in this second drawing indicates the floor level at which the column changes shape.)

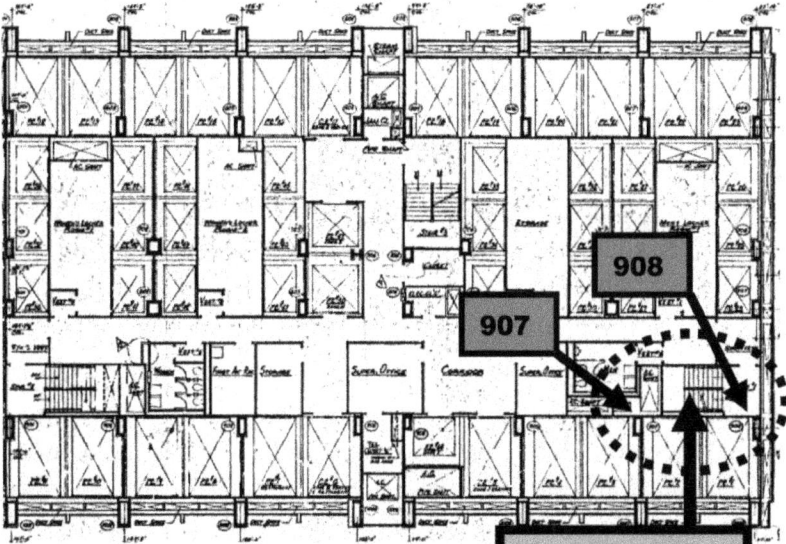

3rd Floor Plan
Source: NIST

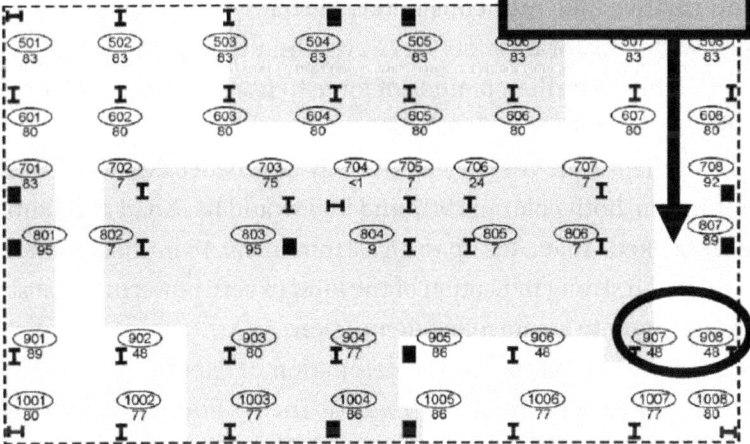

Location of the A Stairwell at the 3rd Floor

502 Column #
83 Floor of Transition from box to Wide Flange columns

Core Area at the 84th Floor
with Column Designations
Source: NIST

The first drawing indicates that the A Stairwell was supported by column lines 907 and 908. The second one shows that those column lines did not transition from their original shape until they reached the 48th floor. Therefore, they would have the same shape at the 3rd floor that they had at the foundation. They measured 22 inches by 54 inches and were almost solid steel.

Then, how much force would it take to fracture them? The total building weight was in the area of 500,000 tons and the columns in the core area held up 60 percent of that, so then, on average, each of the 47 core columns can be calculated to have been holding up 6,383 tons at the foundation [(500,000 x .60)/47], or 12,766,000 pounds each (6,383 x 2000 pounds per ton).[361] That would have been the maximum design gravity load that they were all calculated to withstand at the foundation without experiencing failure, not counting the factor of safety. The columns that supported the A stairwell at the 3rd floor—907 and 908—would have had the same strength since, according to the second plan, their profile did not change until they reached the 48th floor.

If you further take into consideration that the core columns were designed with a factor of safety of 1.8, you find that it would take close to an incredible 23 million pounds of force to fracture either 907 or 908 below the 3rd floor (1.8 x 12,766,000).[362]

And to collapse the A stairwell the way Schroeder described it, at a very minimum, both columns 907 and 908 would have had to be simultaneously blasted. That adds up to an astronomical 46 million pounds of force, which is a strong indication of the kind of very powerful explosives that are common to a controlled demolition.

Also, the notion that it was the detonation of explosive devices that caused the collapse of the A Stairwell at the 3rd floor coincides quite closely with the conclusions of Chapter 2, where it was found that the location of the explosive device that caused the powerful second blast on B4 could have been placed at column either 907 or 908. This suggests the distinct possibility that explosives were also planted on both of those columns at the B4 level.

There are, in fact, two documented witnesses who observed columns in the North Tower's basement after the collapse that appeared to be prime examples of exactly this kind of demolition technique. According to the *New York Times* reporters James Glanz and Eric Lipton, engineers Pablo Lopez and Andrew Pontecorvo observed two massive core columns at the B2 level that had suffered "a compound fracture: the upper sections looked as if they had been kicked, with incalculable fury, about a foot south of the sections they were resting on."[363]

In summary, this collapse of the A stairwell at the third floor is a fourth example which indicates that explosives were planted in the North Tower by people who were allowed extraordinary access to the building. In other words, it had to have been an inside job.

The Explosions that Collapsed Floors 65 Through 43

William Rodriguez also witnessed this phenomenon. This is how he described it:

When I get to the 39th floor, I opened the door. I'm in the corridor. David Lim [a Port Authority Policeman] comes up with 2 firemen and we were talking about what was going to be the next process of rescue when we hear, BOOM! A very strong explosion. Very, very powerful. The building shaked...We lost our footing. And in our building, we hear, BAM! BAM! BAM! BAM! BAM! And a collapse, BOOM! And on the radio we hear, "We lost 65! We lost 65!" Meaning the 65th floor went out floor by floor by floor—down to the 44th floor. Down to the sky lobby, which was on the 44th floor.[364]

As was the case with the collapse of the 3rd floor stairwell, Rodriguez's account given here fundamentally contradicts the official "probable collapse sequence," because he still had enough time to escape the building before it totally collapsed. This means that those upper floors were collapsing inside the building a long time before the "top section" of the building "began its descent."

And it backs up Schroeder's claim that the "inside structure" of the building was "disintegrating." This had to be the case, because the videos taken of the outside of the building at this time show no downward movement or deformation of the perimeter columns. The building continued to stand perfectly still with just black smoke billowing out of the plane impact hole against a blue sky.

This is yet a fifth example indicating an inside job, because those explosives could only have been planted in the tower by people who were allowed extraordinary access.

The Explosion on the 86th floor

North Tower victims **James Gartenburg** and **Patricia Puma** offer dramatic testimony about how they were trapped in their office on the 86th floor by a tremendously powerful explosion that also could not have been caused by a fireball coming down an elevator shaft from the area of the plane crash, as the official story claims.

The following plan of the 86th floor shows their approximate location, which was on the east side of the building, outside the core area.

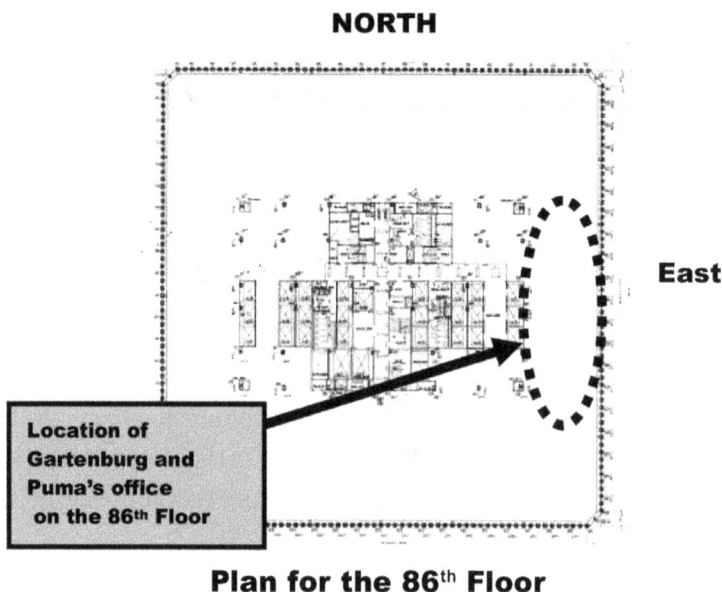

Plan for the 86th Floor

These two people could not get out of the building and were tragically killed when it collapsed. But during the time they were trapped, they had two phone interviews with the media. One took place at about 9:32 a.m., when they were called by ABC-TV News reporter Jim Dwyer. This is how Gartenburg described the situation to him:

I'm stuck on the 86th floor. The fire door has trapped us. Debris has fallen around us. And part of the core of the building is blown out. There is one other person with me. I'm on the east side of the building, on the 86th floor facing east.[365]

I got to work around 8:00 this morning. And I think this happened about 8:45. I felt...I heard a noise, felt the whole building shake and glass blown out. The glass on my floor was blown out from the inside of the building out, rather than the exterior windows of the building blown out. The glass fully shattered. And just the core of the building. The interior core part of the building collapsed. The elevators are blown out. The explosion on the 86th floor seemed to come from the inside out, rather than the outside in. That's why the core of the building is as damaged as it is. The fire door is blocked. It either closed from the force of the explosion or as a fire precaution. The elevators are completely blown out.[366]

Puma then added, "The wall in the ladies' room started to crack. It looked like the explosion came up through the elevator."[367]

Gartenburg indicated that he was in his office when the explosion hit, and Puma indicated that she was in a ladies' room. But notice that neither of them mentioned seeing fire, which is a first indication that the damage to their floor was not caused by jet fuel from the plane. Also, they described a lot of physical damage, indicating that there was a tremendous shock wave associated with the explosion, which is not a characteristic of a jet fuel fireball deflagration. And there was no mention of a kerosene/jet fuel smell.

The following North Tower drawing shows the core area of their floor in more detail:

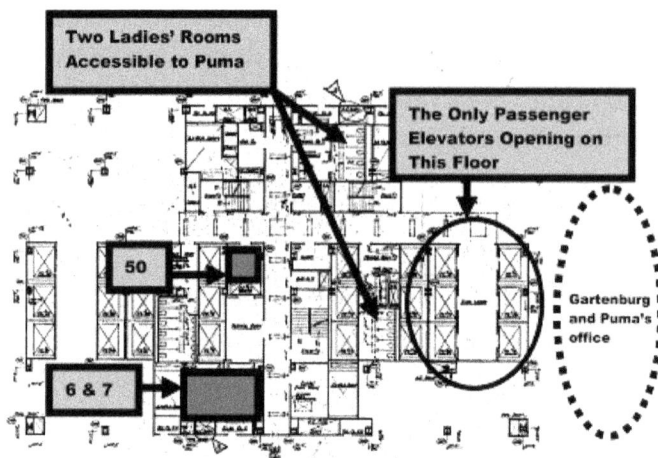

86ᵗʰ Floor Core Area

This plan shows where the only passenger elevators on this floor were located. They must have been the ones that Gartenburg saw blown out. And it is likely that Puma was in the southernmost ladies' room, next to those elevators, when she saw the wall crack.

Now look at this plan of the 94ᵗʰ floor, which was the highest level of the tower where the concrete floor was determined to be undamaged by the plane crash.[368]

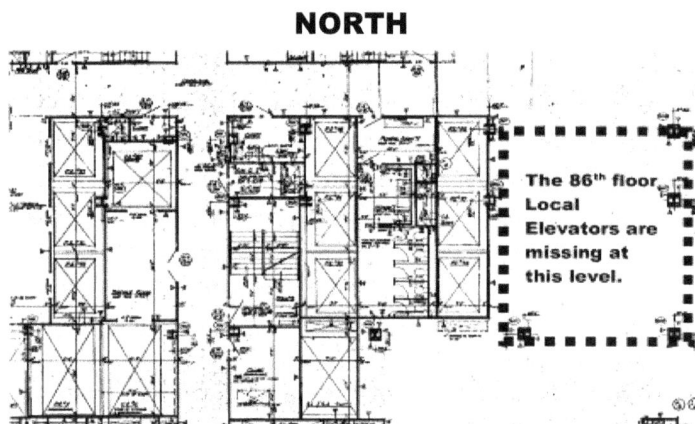

94ᵗʰ Floor Core Area

This shows that those passenger elevators on the 86th floor that were blown out did not extend up to the 94th floor. Therefore, the explosion that destroyed the elevators on the 86th floor could not have been caused by jet fuel-fed fireball coming down from the area of the plane crash, because it would have been blocked by the five-inch thick, steel-reinforced concrete slab at the 94th floor. This indicates that the blast had to have originated below the plane impact zone.

This also conforms to Puma's observation that the explosion came "up" from below the 86th floor.

So, this is yet a sixth example of an explosive event that occurred in the North Tower that had to have been due to an inside job in which a device was planted there prior to the plane crash by people who were allowed extraordinary access to the building.

Conclusion

The widespread nature of the blasts covered in this chapter confirms that explosives were planted, not just in the B4 basement of the North Tower, but throughout the whole building, as well.

This brings up the question of access. After the '93 bombing, the security at the WTC was extremely tight. It had been upgraded to the tune of about $100 million.[369] Under a new protocol, in order to enter the twin towers, either in the main lobbies or in one of the underground parking areas, a visitor first had to be interviewed, photographed, entered into a computer, and given a plastic picture ID card. In addition, video surveillance cameras were installed virtually everywhere, from the outside perimeter of the roofs to the six subbasement levels, and they were constantly being monitored from a security office on the 22nd floor of the North Tower and a second, backup office in the B1 subbasement level of the South Tower. Perhaps most important is that security guards were expected to be always patrolling, often with bomb-sniffing dogs.

Subsequently, planting explosives is something that could only have been perpetrated by people who were *allowed* extraordinary access to the building; i.e., that it was an inside job. The next chapter will detail how the official investigations systematically avoided interviewing anybody who witnessed those upper level explosions.

5

More Witnesses

THE WAY THE FIVE WITNESSES on B4 were handled is a prime example of how the Bush investigations dealt with the charge of controlled
demolition; none of them would be mentioned in either the FEMA or
NIST reports, even though most of them had been interviewed by major
news outlets. The same could be said for virtually anyone who saw the
explosions, including reporters and top officials of the fire department.

B4 Witnesses Ignored

FEMA released its report in May of 2002, but on September 13, 2001, just
two days after the attack, Hursley Lever told his story on national TV
to Matt Lauer on NBC's *Today Show.*[370] He could have led investigators
to Sanchez, who was with him in the metal shop. And shortly after the
attack, Morelli did a video-recorded interview with New York's TV1,
which was broadcast locally.[371] Additionally, on October 1, 2001, about
two weeks after the attack, he was mentioned in an article posted on the
website for McGraw Hill Construction.[372]

As for the 9/11 Commission report, which appeared in 2004, and
NIST's 2005 report, Edward McCabe had contributed a written account
about the B4 explosions to *The September 11 Digital Archive* as early as
July of 2002.[373]

Moreover, before the release of the NIST report, the statements of
McCabe, Lever, Sanchez, Morelli, and Hall, as well as many other witnesses
to the explosions, could be found online. But again, all of that was ignored.

Reporters Ignored

The Bush investigations also refused to consider several contemporaneous
news reports. One who said the North Tower collapse looked just like

a controlled demolition was **John Bussey** from the *Wall Street Journal*. This is what he wrote:

I looked up out of the office window to see what seemed like perfectly synchronized explosions coming from each floor. One after another—from top to bottom—with a fraction of a second between, the floors blew to pieces.[374]

Another who reported the controlled demolition aspect of one of the tower collapses was **Beth Fertig** from New York's WNYC radio. This is what she said:

It just descended like a timed explosion—like when they are deliberately bringing a building down...It was coming down so perfectly that in one part of my brain I was thinking, "They got everybody out, and they're bringing the building down because they have to."[375]

Then there was **Stephen Evans**, a New York-based business correspondent for the British Broadcasting Corporation (BBC). This is how he described the explosive feature of the collapse of the South Tower to his TV audience:

I was at the base of the second tower—the second tower that was hit. There was an explosion. I didn't think it was an explosion, but the building shook. I felt it shake. Then, when we were outside, the second explosion happened. And then there was a series of explosions.[376]

In addition, there was at least one live TV news report from the WTC in which the reporter talked about a high-ranking fire department official who suspected that explosives were planted in one of the towers. That reporter was **Pat Dawson** from NBC News. This is what he said:

Shortly after 9:00, [Chief Turi] received word of the possibility of a secondary device, a bomb, going off. He tried to get his men out as quickly as he could, but he said there was another explosion which took place, and then an hour after the first hit—the first crash that took place—he said there was another explosion that took place in one of the towers here. So, obviously, according to his theory he thinks that there were actually devices that were planted in the building.[377]

Accordingly, it just does not seem possible that the Bush investigations could have innocently missed all this eyewitness testimony. But not a word of it would be mentioned in any of the reports.

FEMA: No Witnesses to Explosions

At only 269 pages, the FEMA report would be the shortest of the Bush investigations and the most egregious as far as describing what occurred. Most significantly, no witnesses to the explosions were mentioned in it. The relevant part of the report merely says,

As the aircraft crashed into and plowed across the buildings, they distributed jet fuel throughout the impact area to form a flammable "cloud." Ignition of this cloud resulted in rapid pressure rise, expelling a fuel rich mixture from the impact area into shafts and through other openings caused by the crashes, resulting in dramatic fireballs.

...The first arriving firefighters observed that the windows of WTC1 [the North Tower] were broken out at the Concourse level. This breakage was most likely caused by overpressure in the elevator shafts. Damage to the walls of the elevator shafts was also observed as low as the 23rd floor, presumably as a result of the overpressures developed by the burning of the vapor cloud on the impact floors.[378]

According to FEMA, the only damage was to the main lobby (the "Concourse level"), where some windows were broken by "fireballs" and to the 23rd floor, where elevator shaft walls were damaged by "overpressures." There is no mention of witnesses to explosions.

The 9/11 Commission: No Witnesses to Explosions

Congress' 9/11 Commission released its report in July of 2004, two years after the FEMA report and almost three years after the attacks. At 571 pages, it was longer than that of FEMA, but as to its coverage of the explosions that occurred, it was also sparse. Again, the commission's extremely truncated account reads, "A jet fuel fireball erupted upon [plane] impact and shot down at least one bank of elevators...The fireball exploded onto numerous floors, the 77th and 22nd; the West Street lobby level; and the B4 level, four stories below ground."[379]

Aside from the passing mention of a fireball that had exploded "on the B4 level," the commission stuck to the pattern established earlier by FEMA—they did not interview the witnesses to it. The lowest level they discussed in any detail was this description of the damage done to the main lobby:

> A battalion chief and two ladder and two engine companies arrived at the North Tower at approximately 8:52. As they entered the lobby, they encountered badly burned civilians who had been caught in the path of the fireball. Floor-to-ceiling windows in the northwest corner of the West Street level of the lobby had been blown out; some large marble tiles had been dislodged from the walls; one entire elevator bank had been destroyed by the fireball.[380]

NIST Protocol was Designed to Avoid Witnesses to Explosions

For all the time that the 9/11 Commission was holding its public hearings and then writing its report in the spring of 2004, NIST was busy with its investigation. So its members no doubt knew before they wrote their report that the commission had expanded somewhat upon FEMA's feeble description of the damage to the North Tower at the time of plane impact. It seems reasonable to expect, therefore, that one of the things that NIST would have done would be to investigate more fully the 9/11 Commission's account of the series of explosions that hit the lower levels of the tower, to verify that it was accurate.

One would think that NIST would especially want to interview the witnesses to the explosion the commission said occurred on B4, since it was the furthest away from where the plane hit and was, therefore, the most suspicious. But NIST did not do that. Instead, its investigators studiously avoided *all* the witnesses to explosions who were in the subbasements. In fact, the evidence shows that there was a self-imposed protocol for interviewing witnesses that was specially designed to do just that.

For example, as for the damage that occurred in the North Tower at the time of plane impact, the NIST Final Report had this to say:

[After plane impact] flash fires were also observed at other locations in the tower, including the ground-floor lobby, indicating that some fraction of the fuel was transported large distances, presumably via damaged ductwork and elevator shafts.[381]

The impact of the first aircraft into WTC 1 (North Tower) and the fires and overpressures that resulted created significant damage down to the building's basement.[382]

The report went on the state that a minute or two after plane impact, WTC security reported a fire on the 22nd floor and a lot of damage and debris there. They also reported that windows on the 44th floor had been blown out by a fireball.[383] After that, they received a report of burning jet fuel on the 51st floor.[384] Then the report continued, saying,

In addition, in first-person interviews PAPD personnel reported a huge fireball that came from the elevator shafts and filled the visible volume of the Concourse level (Main Lobby) between WTC 1 and the entrance to the Marriot Hotel. PAPD personnel reported that they observed numerous people being enveloped in flames as the fireball swept through the WTC Concourse level…The jet fuel had gone down the elevator shaft and had blown out the elevator doors and that is why the lobby windows were blown out and why interviewees had seen seriously burned people in the lobby.[385]

[And] a fire was started on the B4 level of WTC 1 when the first plane struck.[386]

Obviously, the institute had put some extra effort into their investigation of the damage done to the lower levels of the North Tower (WTC1). However, to say in one breath that there was "significant" damage done to the basement without specifying which level or exactly what kind of damage and then, in the next breath, to say that there was only a "fire" on B4, seems oddly out of sync with what the five maintenance workers on B4 said. The second explosion there leveled several walls and threw Hursley Lever so hard he sustained a broken ankle. And there was no fire.

Indeed, NIST's process for doing interviews was, by its very nature, limiting. They broke potential witnesses down into two major groups—"workers" and "first responders"—but they ended up contacting only a very tiny minority of them. None of whom would be from the subbasement levels.

The Worker Interviews

As for the North Tower workers: The NIST report says that there were 474 telephone interviews done with people who worked in the North Tower. But the report also says that there was a minimum of 7,470 workers who survived that tower's collapse.[387] This means NIST investigators only conducted telephone interviews with about 6.3 percent of the total number of North Tower workers who were available.

And did the group that was interviewed by phone in this phase of the investigation include any of the witnesses who were in the subbasement levels, like for example, the five maintenance workers on B4? No, it did not. The report notes that those North Tower workers who were contacted by telephone only came from the following floors:[388]

- **WTC 1 – floors 0-43**

- **WTC 1 – floors 44-76**

- **WTC 1 – floors 77 and above**

Worker Telephone Interviews
Source: NIST

As this accounting shows, the lowest level that the worker interviewees came from was floor "0," which refers to the main lobby.

NIST conducted another round of interviews with North Tower workers to study the effectiveness of the "evacuation" procedures available in the towers and any problems that might have been presented as far as "egress" from the building was concerned. But this section, called "Occupant Behavior, Egress, and Emergency Communications," did not include anyone who was in the subbasement levels, either.

The report says that in this phase of the investigation, the interviewees were "asked to relate their experience on September 11 from the time they first knew something was wrong to the time when they exited the building."[389] According to this, NIST would have gotten a complete view of what these particular survivors experienced in the towers after plane impact, including explosions, not just details about their difficulty evacuating.

Note the following graphic. It depicts the various conditions (fire, smoke, fallen ceiling tiles, etc.) that all those North Tower worker interviewees encountered on their individual floors before they started to evacuate.[390]

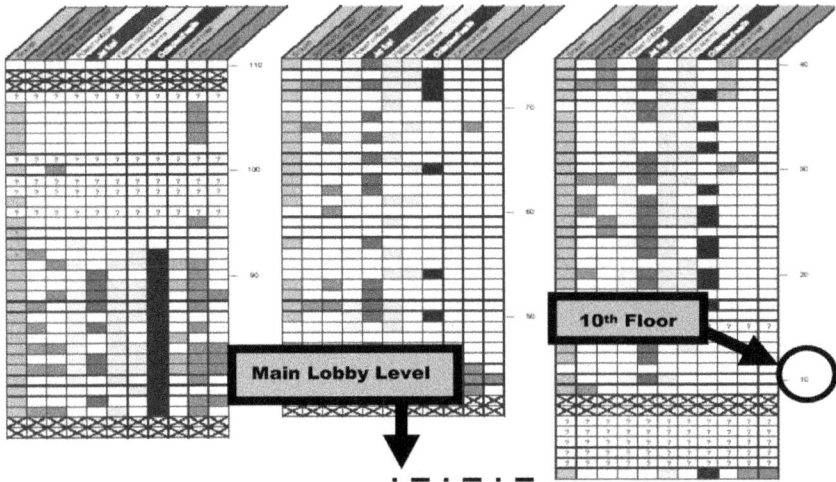

Figure 6-1. Observations of building damage after initial awareness but before beginning evacuation in WTC 1.

Observations in WTC 1

Source: NIST

But note that this illustration goes no lower than the main lobby. The six basement levels below ground are not even shown. This confirms that witnesses to explosions in the basement levels were not considered.

In addition to the five maintenance workers on B4, another of the basement witnesses excluded was stationary engineer **Mike Pecoraro.** After hearing explosions when the plane hit, he and a coworker made their way up through several basement levels of the North Tower, trying to get to the main lobby. The following is what they could have informed NIST about the explosions, if asked. (Please note that although the basement levels were formally designated as B1 thru B6, workers in the tower often referred to them by letters, descending alphabetically—where A meant B1, B meant B2, C meant B3, etc.)

We went up to the C level [B3], where there was a small machine shop, but there was nothing there but rubble. We're talking about a 50-ton hydraulic press—gone! [We then went] to the parking garage, and found that it, too, was gone. On the B level [B2], we found a steel-and-concrete fire door that weighed about 300 pounds wrinkled up like a piece of aluminum foil.[391]

This "egress" study by NIST also excluded North Tower maintenance supervisor, **Anthony Saltalamacchia**, who was previously mentioned as being on the B1 level. Again, this is what he could have told NIST investigators, if they were so inclined to ask:

We heard a massive explosion that was in the WTC about 8:46 a.m. in the morning. The explosion came from...I believe at first...We believed that it came from the mechanical room [one floor down]. And then we heard a series of other explosions that sounded up on the above levels of the building to where I then realized that there was something wrong. And that there was a major problem. And it literally sounded like...people setting off grenades. Picture just multiple grenades just going off. Like BAM, BOUND, BOOM! That's when I thought, "Is there, like, somebody in here, blowing up the place?"[392]

NIST compiled the information from the worker interviews in the following chart.[393]

Table 6–1. Observations of conditions in WTC 1 before beginning evacuation.

	At Awareness	During Interim Period
Smoke	10 %	35 %
Jet fuel	8 %	18 %
Fallen ceiling tiles	17 %	21 %
Power outage / flickering lights	17 %	17 %
Fire Alarms	8 %	14 %
Collapsed walls	6 %	10 %
Fire	3 %	5 %
Other events	45 %	48 %

Note: Total does not add up to 100 percent because respondents may have observed more than one event indicative of damage.
Source: NIST WTC Telephone Survey Data.

Source: NIST

But here, there is not even a category for explosions. Also, notice that 48 percent of the interviewees reported "Other events." It seems that if so many people reported other events, NIST should have also broken that category down. Did those other "events" include **Kim White**'s observations? She was a North Tower survivor, who said this: "We got down as far as the 74th floor...Then there was *another* explosion, so we left again by the stairwell"[394]

Or, did it include witnesses like North Tower office worker **Teresa Veliz**, who could have testified to experiencing explosions that appeared to be just like a controlled demolition? This is what she said:

There were explosions going off everywhere. I was convinced there were bombs planted all over the place and someone was sitting at a control panel pushing detonator buttons.[395]

And what about North Tower maintenance worker **William Rodriguez** who was in the B1 subbasement when the plane hit? As previously noted, he claimed that he experienced several initial explosions on the B1 level that do not fit the official story. He said they came from below, not from the plane impact zone. And one of them, he said, even happened before the plane hit. But there is no mention of him in the report.

He actually made himself physically available to NIST, and the institute ignored him. NIST prided itself on the fifteen public hearings it held around the country, the purpose of which, according to its report, was to "solicit input from the public." But, when people showed up who had things to say that did not fit the official story, they were ignored. Rodriquez was one of those. He tried contacting the institute on four separate occasions, but there was no response. Finally, he heard that NIST was going to hold a public hearing in his area, and he decided to go and tell his story.

But this is how he described the reaction of that panel of so-called "investigators" when he spoke up about the explosions:

Finally, I asked them before they came up with their conclusion... if they ever considered my statements or the statements of any of the other survivors who heard the explosions. They just stared at me with blank faces.[396]

It is also interesting to note that all those frustrating attempts by Rodriguez to get NIST to consider his story happened sometime after he had already become famous for the many heroic actions that he took in the North Tower that day. For example, in one such instance he saved the lives of twelve firefighters.[397] It was after the South Tower collapsed, and he was rushing down a North Tower stairwell from the 39th floor, trying to escape the building. Ignoring the obvious danger to his own life, as he was going down he took the time to stop at each floor to check for survivors. Coincidentally, the firemen had become lost and disoriented in the pitch darkness of a 4th-floor office area. Rodriguez found them and led them to a stairwell with his flashlight. They made it down to the main lobby and barely managed to escape the building just as it began to collapse. Rodriguez was actually the last person who made it out of the building.

The publicity surrounding his acts of heroism led to an invitation to the White House, where he was greeted by President Bush.

Rodriguez at the White House
Source: The White House

But his name does not appear anywhere in any report.

The First Responder Interviews

With respect to the first responders (firefighters, police, etc.), the NIST report says this:

> In October 2003, NIST entered into a three-party agreement between NIST, New York City (NYC), and the National Commission of Terrorist Attacks Upon the United States (the 9/11 Commission). The agreement provided procedures under which NIST and the 9/11 Commission would interview a maximum of 125 NYC emergency responders, 100 from the FDNY and 25 from the NYPD. ...In December 2003, NIST officially requested and the Port Authority agreed to interviews with twelve Port Authority personnel, including emergency responders, safety, security and management personnel.[398]

And the institute added that "in addition to the interviews conducted under the agreements described above, NIST interviewed eight people who contacted NIST directly and volunteered."

But who were those chosen eight? The report explains that the others interviewed included the following anonymous people: "A building security guard, dispatcher, firefighters, WTC building engineer and a fire safety director."[399]

Obvious questions arise from this process. In the first place, why should NIST, which was charged by the president of the United States to investigate the cause of the WTC collapses that led to the deaths of an estimated 2,100 people and whose investigation was funded by Congress to the tune of tens of millions of dollars of taxpayer money, have to negotiate with anybody to get access to witnesses? And secondly, why would the City of New York (i.e., Giuliani; the "benevolent dictator") and the New York Port Authority (under Governor Pataki) want to limit that access?

Furthermore, the report went on to say that the number of WTC first responders who were finally interviewed by NIST totaled up to be a meager 116. That number included only 68 of the over 5,000 firefighters who were at the WTC that day (1.36 percent), only 25 from the nearly 2,000 NYC police officers who were there (1.25 percent), and only 15 from the estimated 150 Port Authority of New York and New Jersey (PANYNJ/ PAPD) police officers who were there (10 percent).[400, 401]

In addition, the report also candidly admits that the paltry few interviewees were not selected based on the importance of the information they had to give, but rather, the report says, they were "randomly selected," which was another limiting factor.[402]

A Frequently Asked Question

The level of criticism that NIST's report received was to such an extent that a year later, in August of 2006, the institute was forced to issue a rebuttal in the form of a three-page document entitled "Answers to Frequently Asked Questions" (ATFAQ). In that document, one of the charges that NIST responded to was the question of why there was "a lack of consideration given to a controlled demolition hypothesis." The institute's answer was that after interviewing "more than 1,000 people," it found:

> no corroborating evidence for alternative hypotheses suggesting that the WTC towers were brought down by controlled demolition using explosives planted prior to Sept 11, 2001...There was no evidence (collected by NIST, or by the New York Police Department, the Port Authority Police Department of the Fire Department of New York) of any blast or explosions in the region *below the impact and fire floor as the top building sections* (including and above the 98th floor in WTC 1 and the 82nd floor in WTC 2) *began their downward movement* upon collapse initiation.[403] (Italics added)

Obviously, NIST was being transparently deceptive here when it said that the criteria for determining if explosives were planted in the building depended on whether there were any explosions below the impact and fire floor as the top of the building gave way. Why would it matter when the explosions occurred? That is immaterial to the question of whether they did occur.

FDNY Witnesses to Controlled Demolitions

As noted in the Introduction, the Fire Department of New York (FDNY) completed its own investigation within three months of the attacks. That so-called World Trade Center Task Force (WTCTF) collected recorded statements from 118 firefighters who said that they saw, heard and felt explosions going off at the WTC both before and during the collapses. One would think that those statements should have been made available to FEMA before its report was published, but Mayor Rudolph Giuliani did not allow it.

In fact, the City of New York successfully suppressed the WTCTF interviews from public view for nearly four years. It was not until the *New York Times* won a Freedom of Information Act (FOIA) lawsuit against the city that they were finally released on August 12, 2005.[404] However, they would have been easy for NIST to obtain because its final report was not released until two months later, on October 26. But the institute ignored them. Upon reading some of those statements, it is not hard to understand why.

The statements of FDNY heads Thomas Fitzpatrick, Dominick DeRubbio and Steven Gregory that were given in the Introduction are self-explanatory. But probably the most blatant example of this willful exclusion of eyewitness testimony is how the Bush investigations ignored some gripping dialogue that was presented in the award-winning film *9/11*.[405] Narrated by actor Robert DeNiro, this documentary on the WTC attack was broadcast to a nationwide audience in primetime by ABC-TV in March of 2002. That was two months *before* the release of the FEMA report and three years before the NIST report. In it, this is how FDNY Captain **Dennis Tardio** and Fireman **Patrick Zoda** described their dramatic escape from the collapsing North Tower:

Tardio:	What do we do? We made it outside. We made it about a block.
Zoda:	We made it at least two blocks.
Tardio:	Two blocks.
Zoda:	And we started runnin'.
Tardio:	Pop, pop, pop, pop, pop, pop, pop, pop.

Zoda:	Floor by floor, it started poppin' out.
Tardio:	It was like, it was if…It was as if they had detonators.
Zoda:	Yeah, detonators.
Tardio:	You know, as if they were planning to take down a building. Boom, boom, boom, boom, boom, boom, boom, boom, boom.
Zoda:	All the way down. I was watchin' it and runnin'.[406]

Other First Responders Outside the Towers

Other first responders had the same impression. Again, this is what Paramedic **Daniel Rivera** said about the collapse of one of the towers: "Do you ever see a professional demolition where they set the charges on certain floors and then you hear, "Pop, pop, pop, pop, pop?" I thought it was that."[407]

Richard Banaciski, another firefighter, described the collapse of one of the towers this way: "It seemed like on television [when] they blow up these buildings. It seemed like it was going all the way around like a belt—all these explosions."[408]

Firefighter **Kenneth Rogers**, who saw the South Tower come down, said this:

I kept watching. Floor after floor, after floor…One floor under another—after another. And when it hit about the fifth floor, I figured it was a bomb because it looked like a synchronized deliberate kind of thing.[409]

Many other WTCTF witnesses who observed the explosions from outside the towers could have also told NIST, if called, that they saw explosions going off *"below the impact and fire floor as the top building sections began their downward movement upon collapse initiation."*

One of those was firefighter **Edward Cachia**. He watched the South Tower come down. This is what he said:

As my officer and I were looking at the South Tower, it just gave. It actually gave at a lower floor, not the floor where the plane hit.

We originally had thought there was like an internal detonation. Explosives. Because it went in succession—boom, boom, boom, boom. And then the tower came down.[410]

Brian Dixon, a *battalion chief* with the FDNY, also saw the South Tower come down. This how he described it:

The lowest floor of fire in the South Tower actually looked like someone had planted explosives around it, because it just looked like that floor blew out. You could actually see everything blew out on the one floor. I said, 'Geez,' this looks like an explosion up there.[411]

Many others testified to seeing explosions *before* the collapse began. **William Wall**, a *lieutenant* with the FDNY, told the WTCTF this: "We heard an explosion. We looked up and the building was coming right down on top of us."[412]

And **Gregg Brady**, an emergency medical technician, said this: "I heard three explosions. I look up, and the North Tower is coming down now."[413]

Kevin Gorman, another firefighter, saw the North Tower when it began to collapse. He said, "I heard the explosion, looked up, and saw like three floors explode."[414]

Michael Ober was an Emergency Medical Technician who told the WTCTF this about the South Tower collapse: "I just heard like an explosion. And then a cracking type of noise. And then it sounded like a freight train rumbling and picking up speed. And I remember I looked up, and saw it coming down."[415]

Kevin Darnowski was a paramedic. This is what he told the task force: "I started walking back up towards Vesey Street. I heard three explosions. And then we heard like a groaning and grinding. And Tower Two started coming down."[416]

Thomas Turilli was another firefighter who saw the South Tower come down. This is what he said: "It almost sounded like bombs going off—like boom, boom, boom, boom—like 7 or 8."[417]

Craig Carlson was another firefighter who also heard explosions just before the South Tower came down. This is how he described it: "You just heard explosions coming from Building Two—the South Tower. It seemed like it took forever, but there were about 10 explosions...We then realized the building started to come down."[418]

John Coyle was a fire marshal with the City of New York. This is what he said about the collapse of the South Tower: "The tower was—it looked to me—I thought it was exploding, actually. That's what I thought for hours afterwards—that it had exploded."[419]

Frank Cruthers was a *chief* with the FDNY. This is how he described one of the towers coming down:

There was what appeared at first to be an explosion. It appeared at the very top. Simultaneously, from all four sides, materials shot out horizontally. And then there seemed to be a momentary delay before you could see the beginning of the collapse...I saw a large section of it blasting out, which led me to believe it was an explosion.[420]

First Responders Inside the Towers

Many first responders who survived were actually inside the towers when the explosions started. Because they had time to escape, those explosions must have happened a long time before the towers started to come down. Thus, they confirm the controlled demolition scenario, which is typically done in preparatory stages to first weaken the underlying structure.

One of those witnesses was firefighter **Stephen Viola**. He was in an upper floor of the South Tower when he said this happened:

You heard like loud booms. And then we got covered with rubble and dust. And I thought we'd actually fallen through the floor, because it was so dark you couldn't see anything.[421]

Sue Keane was a PAPD police officer who said she was trying to escape the North Tower when this happened:

There was another explosion that sent me and the two firefighters down the stairs…I can't tell you how many times I got banged around. Each one of those explosions picked me up and threw me. There was another explosion, and I got thrown with two firefighters out onto the street.[422]

Sal D'Agostino, a firefighter who had made it to the 10th floor of the North Tower, said this: "There were these huge explosions—I mean huge, gigantic explosions."[423]

Firefighter **Bill Butler** was with D'Agostino. He told the WTCTF this: "It was like a train going two inches away from your head: bang-bang, bang-bang, bang-bang."[424]

Firefighter **Lou Cacchioli** had just taken an elevator to the 24th floor of the North Tower when he said this happened: "(We) heard this huge explosion that sounded like a bomb (and) knocked off the lights and stalled the elevator." He and a fellow firefighter pried themselves out of the elevator, and then "another huge explosion like the first one hits. This one hits about two minutes later. I'm thinking, 'Oh my God, these bastards put bombs in here like they did in 1993!'"[425]

Brian Becker, a lieutenant in the FDNY, told the WTCTF that about thirty minutes after the plane hit, he and his firefighters from Engine 28 had climbed a North Tower stairwell to about the 31st floor when this happened:

A few of the guys were taking a break with their masks off and laying in the hallway when there was a very loud roaring sound and a very loud explosion…it felt like there was an explosion above us, and I had a momentary concern that our building was collapsing…It was a tremendous explosion and a tremendous shaking of our building.[426]

Then, there was firefighter **John Schroeder**. He was in a North Tower stairwell at about the 24th floor when there was a tremendously powerful explosion. This how he described it: "We got bounced around in the stairwell like pin balls."[427]

Conclusion

The evidence presented in this chapter clearly supports the contention that the Bush administration investigations were not honest searches for truth. Again, when NIST was asked why it had shown a total lack of consideration for the controlled demolition hypothesis and did not test the WTC steel for residues of explosives, the answer was that the institute found "no corroborating evidence for alternative hypotheses suggesting that the WTC towers were brought down by controlled demolition using explosives planted prior to Sept 11, 2001."[428] In actual point of fact, though, all the foregoing witnesses were available to NIST. But the institute willfully ignored them.

The next chapter presents a ton of hard evidence that was also ignored.

6

Further Evidence of Controlled Demolition

WHAT FOLLOWS IS FOURTEEN CATEGORIES of additional evidence that demonstrates to an overwhelming degree of certainty that explosives were used to bring down the WTC buildings.

Free-falling

One astonishing aspect of the WTC collapses is how incredibly fast the buildings came down. In the case of the North Tower, according to the official story, the top block of twenty floors above the plane impact zone crushed the lower, undamaged ninety floors below to the ground in about ten seconds.[429]

The North Tower Collapses
Copyright: Ray Stubblebine/Reuters

That is almost freefall speed. It was as if the lower ninety floors of the building offered no resistance to the falling, upper block. To the trained eye, the only way that could have happened is if the lower part of the structure was made to progressively disintegrate ahead of the collapse wave, which is a characteristic of controlled demolitions.

A panel of experts led by Dr. Steven Jones, PhD (mentioned previously as the professor of physics at BYU who released the North Tower blueprints) led a panel of experts that authored a paper for *The Open Civil Engineering Journal* arguing that the official explanation for that dramatic collapse process violates a fundamental law of physics called "Conservation of Momentum." That law dictates that the lower, undamaged section of the building should have slowed or even stopped the collapse and not allowed it to proceed in an accelerated manner as shown in the videos.

Dr. Jones's paper, called "Fourteen Points of Agreement with Official Government Reports on the World Trade Center Destruction," says the following:

...as documented in Section 6.14.4 of NIST NCSTAR 1, these collapse times show that: "...the structure below the level of collapse initiation offered minimal resistance to the falling building mass at and above the impact zone. The potential energy released by the downward movement of the large building mass far exceeded the capacity of the intact structure below to absorb that energy through energy of deformation. Since the stories below the level of collapse initiation provided little resistance to the tremendous energy released by the falling building mass, the building section came down essentially in free fall, as seen in videos."

We agree to some of this, that the building "came down essentially in free fall, as seen in videos." This is an important starting point... Further, we agree with NIST that "the stories below the level of collapse initiation provided little resistance" to the fall—but we ask—how could that be? NIST mentions "energy of deformation" which for the huge core columns in the Towers would be considerable, and they need to be quantitative about it (which they were not) in order to claim that the "intact structure" below would not significantly slow the motion.

Beyond that, NIST evidently neglects a fundamental law of physics in glibly treating the remarkable "free fall" collapse of each Tower, namely, the Law of Conservation of Momentum. This law of physics means that the hundreds of thousands of tons of material in the way must slow the upper part of the building because of its mass, independent of deformation which can only slow the fall even more. (Energy and Momentum must both be conserved.)

Published papers have argued that this negligence by NIST (leaving the near-free-fall speeds unexplained) is a major flaw in their analysis. ...NIST ignores the possibility of controlled demolitions, which achieve complete building collapses in near free-fall times by moving the material out of the way using explosives. So, there is an alternative explanation that fits the data without violating basic laws of physics. We should be able to agree from observing the near-free-fall destruction that this is characteristic of controlled demolitions and, therefore, that controlled demolitions is one way to achieve complete collapse at near free-fall speed. Then we are keen to look at NIST's calculations of how they explain near-free-fall collapse rates without explosives.[430]

NIST never did release any such calculations. But an independent study headed by mechanical engineer Tony Szamboti confirmed Dr. Jones's assessment that the NIST report's explanation for the collapse of the North Tower violated the law of Conservation of Momentum. In that impressively documented paper, his team considered NIST's contention that the top section of the building could have crushed the lower part of the building down to the ground and still maintained near free-fall speed. Their conclusion was as follows:

We have tracked the fall of the roof of the North Tower through 114.4 feet, (approximately 9 stories) and we have found that it did not suffer severe and sudden impact or abrupt deceleration. There was no jolt. Thus there could not have been any amplified load. In the absence of an amplified load there is no mechanism to explain the collapse of the lower portion of the building, which was undamaged by fire.[431]

The conclusion is that only very powerful explosives could have been the reason why the lower part of the building offered no resistance to the fall of the upper section and that there was no jolt.

Another independently produced study of the collapse of the North Tower was done by physics expert David Chandler. He studied the acceleration factor of the falling upper section of the tower, as seen in the videos, by utilizing a standard dictate governed by Newton's Third Law of Motion, which says that, for every action there is an equal and opposite reaction. He concluded that

the persistent acceleration of the top section of the building is strong confirmation that some other source of energy was used to remove the structure below it, allowing the upper block to fall with little resistance.

Having assumed the existence of an indestructible falling block, with or without accretion, we have demonstrated that, given the observed acceleration, such a block could not possibly have destroyed the lower section of the building.[432]

There is compelling seismic evidence that backs the opinions of Jones et al., Szamboti, and Chandler. It comes from Columbia University's Lamont-Doherty Earth Observatory (LDEO). LDEO, a facility that is located in Palisades, New York, about fifteen miles from New York City, keeps a constant around-the-clock vigil on the earthquake activity in the region. At the time of the 9/11 attacks, it picked up seismic waves coming from the WTC. LDEO later put together a report on its findings, which eventually became publicly available.

At one point, that report reveals that those at LDEO had calculated the total gravitational potential energy of the North Tower as being in the area of 100 billion joules (where one joule per second equals one watt of power, so that a 100-watt light bulb uses 100 joules per second of energy). Since the collapse of the tower was at nearly free-fall speed, essentially all of its 100 billion joules of energy should have been transferred to the ground. It should have acted in much the same way a brick would behave if it were dropped off the roof; all of its energy transferred to the ground.

Now, refer to the following table that summarizes LDEO's findings.[433]

Date	Origin Time (UTC)	Magnitude (Richter scale)	Time (EDT)	Dominant Period	Signal Duration	Remark
09/11/2001	12:46:26±1	0.9	08:46:26	0.8 sec	12 seconds	first impact
09/11/2001	13:02:54±2	0.7	09:02:54	0.6 sec	6 seconds	second impact
09/11/2001	13:59:04±1	2.1	09:59:04	0.8 sec	10 seconds	first collapse
09/11/2001	14:28:31±1	2.3	10:28:31	0.9 sec	8 seconds	second collapse
09/11/2001	21:20:33±2	0.6	17:20:33	0.7 sec	18 seconds	Building 7 collapse

LDEO Seismic Data for 9/11 Attack on the WTC

This shows that the collapse of the North Tower (second collapse) registered a magnitude reading on the Richter scale of 2.3 on LDEO's seismograph. This presents an important contradiction to the official account because LDEO also says a reading of 2.3 only corresponds to an energy level of *10 million* joules. So what happened to the other 99.99 billion joules of energy? The report attempts to explain it this way:

Hence, only a very small portion of the energy went into defor-mation of the buildings and the *formation of rubble and dust.*[434] (Italics added)

Here, LDEO is pushing the official explanation for the collapse by indicating that it was the crushing effect of the falling upper part of the building that consumed some 10 million joules of potential energy stored in the structure and produced the "rubble and dust." However, as Professor Jones noted, if some of the building's potential energy went into forming rubble and dust, another law of physics, namely the Law of Conservation of Energy, would require that the collapse would have to slow down; energy must also be conserved. But that did not happen. Instead of slowing down, the collapse accelerated. This means that the rubble and dust must have been created by some additional source of energy; like explosives.

In addition, the claim that there was "rubble" does not exactly fit the facts. It is apparent that, at the time the LDEO writers produced their report, they were unaware of the extent to which everything in the North Tower was *pulverized*. As will be detailed in the next section, practically everything except the tower's structural steel was turned to dust. There was precious little rubble. This indicates a massive *additional* force.

While LDEO does not attempt to detail in scientific terms the actual process by which 99.99 billion joules of potential energy that was stored in the building disappeared, the possibility that explosions were that additional massive force fits very well. Such an explanation would not, as Dr. Jones pointed out, violate the laws of Conservation of Momentum and Energy, or as David Chandler concluded, violate Newton's Laws of Motion—as the official scenario obviously does.

The Dust

Ironworkers Danny Doyle, Willey Quinlan and John Kirby spent months climbing around deep in the pit of the WTC debris pile, torching loose pieces of steel for the grappling cranes to pull out. In all that time, they never saw a desk, a chair, a filing cabinet, or anything else one would expect to find in the collapse of an office building.[435] The extent of that characteristic of the debris pile is truly startling. Practically everything except the structural steel had been completely turned to dust. It powdered the scene like snow.

North Tower Debris Pile

Copyright: Peter Morgan/Corbis/AP

In places, it was a foot deep.

The WTC Dust

Photo by Michael Rieger/FEMA

This is a close-up of it.

WTC Dust

Source: Environmental and Occupational Health Sciences of
New Jersey

The Environmental and Occupational Health Sciences of New Jersey (EHOS/NJ) analyzed the dust. This is what their report said: "The vast majority of the mass was *pulverized* building and construction materials, cement, cellulose and glass fibers."[436]

People who visited the site were amazed by what they saw. One was Greg Meeker. He was a research scientist and manager of the Electron Microbeam Laboratory at the United States Geological Survey (USGS) in Denver, Colorado and a principle investigator for the USGS study of the dust. This is what he said:

Six million sq ft of masonry, 5 million sq ft of painted surfaces, 7 million sq ft of flooring, 600,000 sq ft of window glass, 200 elevators, and everything inside came down as dust when the towers collapsed. The only thing that didn't get pulverized was the twin towers' 200,000 tons of structural steel.[437]

WTC Debris Pile
Photo by Michael Rieger/FEMA

No one had a better view of the pile than crane operator Bobby Gray, who said this:

I don't remember seeing carpeting or furniture. You'd think that a metal file cabinet would make it. But I don't remember seeing any. Or phones...Or computers...None of that stuff...Even in areas that never burned we didn't find anything. It was just so hard to comprehend that everything could have been pulverized to that extent. How do you pulverize carpet or filing cabinets?[438]

Many first responders echoed the same thing. Typical of them is firefighter Joe Casaliggi, who said this:

You have two, 110-story buildings. You don't find a desk. You don't find a chair. You don't find a telephone, a computer...The biggest piece of a telephone I found was one half of a keypad. And it was about this big (indicates a few inches).[439]

Veteran contractor Peter Tully, whose company helped clear some of the debris, was also stunned by the condition of the debris pile. This is how he described it: "Think of the thousands of file cabinets, computers and telephones in those towers. I never saw one. Everything was pulverized. Everything that was above grade...disintegrated."[440]

To put this absence of telephones in the debris pile in perspective: The North Tower alone had 25,000 of them.[441]

This astounding state of pulverization also extended to all of the concrete that was in the towers.[442] Tully, who specialized in concrete, was asked if he had ever seen it pulverized to such an extent. "No, never," he said.[443]

Considering how much concrete there was in the twin towers, Tully's statement is an eye-opener. For example, there was at least a four-inch-thick steel-reinforced slab at every one of their floors.

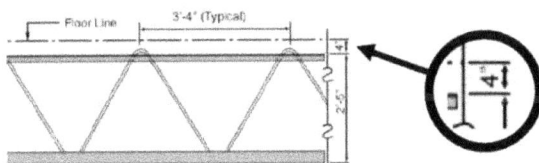

Typical North Tower Floor System
Source: NIST

Given the towers' interior dimensions, their 110 floors above ground, taken together, would have contained close to 138 million pounds of it.[444] There should have been big chunks of it all over the place. But it was almost totally pulverized to very fine dust.

Another witness to this was none other than New York governor, George Pataki. This is how he described it on a visit to the site:

And you look, and you see that there's no concrete. There's very little concrete. All you see is a little bit here and there. The concrete was pulverized. And I was down here Tuesday [the day of the attack], and it was like you were on a foreign planet. All of lower Manhattan, not just this site, from river to river, there was dust, powder, two to three inches thick. The concrete was just pulverized.[445]

A Mound of Pulverized Concrete
Photo by Michael Rieger/FEMA

The concrete used in the towers had a compressive strength of 3,000 psi. Each four-inch floor slab in the outer office areas was poured over a mesh of steel reinforcing bars. In the core areas, it was five inches thick. In addition, it was tied to the underlying steel floor trusses with a series of so-called shear studs, which protruded up from steel pan that it was poured onto. Thus, just getting that concrete out of its entrenchment had to have been a tremendous show of force. Added to that would be the energy required to then render it to powder, which would have another huge number.

But basic laws of physics dictate that expending that amount of potential energy in collapses that were allegedly gravity driven, as the official story claims, means that the tower collapses should have slowed down. But they did not. As the videos show (and the NIST report admits), they actually *accelerated* at the freefall speed of gravity. So, what could have pulverized the concrete, if not an additional force such as explosives?

Neither did the bodies of the victims escape this bizarre pulverization. New York Medical Examiner Charles Hirsch ended his forensic examination in early 2005. As of that time, the number of people believed to have been killed in the tower collapses was thought to be close to 2,500. But only 293 bodies were found intact.[446] In fact, it was found that one victim had been rendered into at least 200 pieces. In all, 20,000 pieces of human flesh and bones were found. 6,000 of those were small enough to put into a test tube. And 10,000 were left unidentified, which means that some victims—who were unknown to have been killed at the WTC—must have ended up in hundreds or even thousands of pieces.[447]

Most significantly, *no trace* was ever found of about 1,100 people who were known to have been killed by the collapses—not even small pieces of flesh or bone that could be used to identify their DNA. As one witness cryptically described it: The trade center area was "littered with hundreds of shoes," but "not a single corpse lay in sight."[448] In other words, more than half of the victims had been literally blown out of their shoes and completely vaporized.

The stunning fact of this vaporization was confirmed by Hirsch on November 12, 2001, during a meeting with family members of the victims.[449]

Harold Schapelhournan was also a witness to this bizarre phenomenon. He was a veteran member of the emergency rescue and recovery team that worked the Oklahoma City bombing site, but what he saw at the WTC was something altogether different. This is how he described it: "We went through decontamination one night, and one guy had a gold crown stuck in the sole of his shoe. I mean, that's the degree of what we found."[450]

This level of pulverization of physical objects and the complete vaporization of human beings had never been seen before in a building collapse. But neither FEMA nor NIST even mentioned it, never mind tried to explain it.

On the other hand, there is at least one scientific study of the dust problem that was done by an independent researcher named Jim Hoffman. He concluded that the potential energy stored in the North Tower was not sufficient to explain the volume of dust that was caused by its collapse and that, by implication, explosives had to be involved. In his study, Hoffman, who was experienced in mechanical engineering, analyzed a photograph taken of the North Tower as it was collapsing. Using standard formulas, he calculated the volume of the dust cloud that was created up to the point when the photograph was taken and then measured how much the building had collapsed down, which gave an indication of how much of the structure's potential energy had been expended up to that point. Comparing those two factors, he was able to determine that

the amount of energy required to expand the North Tower's dust cloud was many times the entire potential energy of the tower's elevated mass due to gravity. The over 10-fold disparity between the most conservative estimate and the gravitational energy is not easily dismissed as reflecting uncertainties in quantitative assessments.[451]

When hearing the evidence presented in this section, the first thing that comes to mind is very powerful explosives. But neither FEMA nor NIST ever tested anything from the WTC for traces of them. The report from FEMA does not mention doing it, and NIST freely admits that it did not do it.[452]

Flying Projectiles

Note the following photograph. It shows massively heavy perimeter column panels that were thrown in true spear-like fashion from the North Tower during its collapse that became impaled in the upper floors of a building known as "3 World Financial Center" (WFC 3).

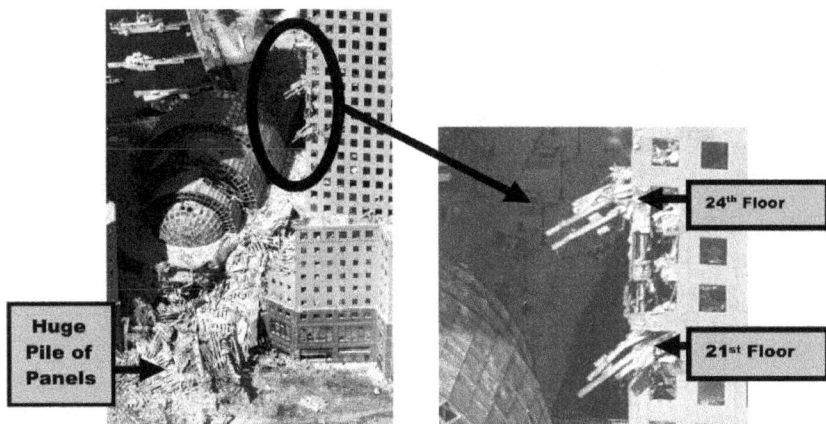

North Tower Perimeter Panels Embedded in WFC 3
Photo by Eric Tilford/United States Navy

Firefighter **Christopher Fenyo,** saw something like this happen. This is what he told the WTCTF: "There was this *explosion* at the top of the Trade Center, and a piece of Trade Center flew across the West Side Highway and hit the Financial Center."[453]

The following illustration taken from the FEMA report gives an idea of how far those panels traveled.[454]

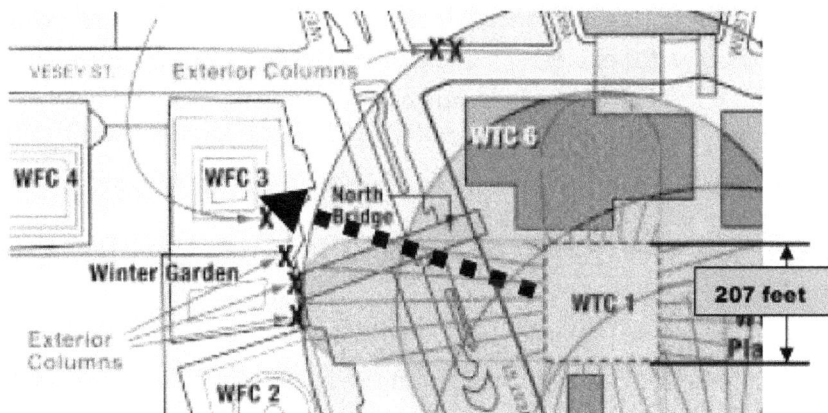

North Tower Debris Field
Source: FEMA

It is known that the footprint of the North Tower (WTC 1) was 207 feet square.[455] So the distance that the two panels seen protruding from WFC 3 were thrown can be scaled from this drawing. It turns out to be an incredible 500 feet. This is a massive show of force. If calculated out, just the force needed to dislodge one of those panels from the façade of the building turns out to be 11,189,040 pounds.[456] And the panels in the upper part of the tower weighed about 7,000 pounds, each.[457] So the force needed to then throw one of them 500 feet through the air had to be likewise enormous. It is hard to conceive of how this display of a massive horizontal force could have been the result of a straight downward, gravity-driven collapse caused by fire, as the official story claims. But the idea that very powerful explosions were involved fits very well.

In that same vein, it is also curious how 21,906 pieces of human remains were found scattered around the trade center, many as far away as two blocks.[458]

In addition, in September 2005, 783 small fragments of bone would be found on the roof of the Deutsche Bank Building, a 39-story skyscraper that was 400 feet south of the South Tower.[459] The medical examiner for the city speculated that they were possibly thrown there by the crash of Flight 11 into the North Tower.[460] But that is unlikely because the South Tower, which was still standing at that time, would have been directly blocking that path. It is more likely that either those victims were blown apart by powerful explosions going off in the collapsing North Tower after the South Tower had already come down and bits of them were thrown beyond it to the roof of the bank, or they were blown there by the demolition of the South Tower.

The Towers Were Designed to Survive the Plane Crash and Subsequent Fires

In 1964, when the builder of the WTC—the New York Port Authority (NYPA)—was still in the early planning stages for the project, the possibility that the towers might be hit by an airplane laden with jet fuel from one of the several airports in the area became a public safety issue. As a result, on February 3 of that year, the NYPA's chief engineer, Malcom

Levy, issued a white paper that said the structural designers from the firm of Worthington, Skilling, Helle, & Jackson (WSHJ), had taken that problem into consideration. Regarding the North Tower, his paper reads:

> The building was investigated and found to be safe in an assumed collision with a large jet airliner (Boeing 707-DC 8) traveling at 600 miles per hour. Analysis indicates that such collision would result in only local damage which could not cause collapse or substantial damage to the building and would not endanger the lives and safety of occupants not in the immediate area of impact.[461]

This statement indicates that the building should not have collapsed on 9/11 because Flight 11 was only going 443 mph when it hit, not 600 mph, and it was only carrying 8,684 gallons of jet fuel to feed any subsequent fire, versus the 23,000 gallons of a fully loaded 707.[462]

In addition, mostly due to that reduced amount of fuel, it also weighed less than 707 considered in Levy's study. In order to determine this weight factor, refer to the following illustration.[463]

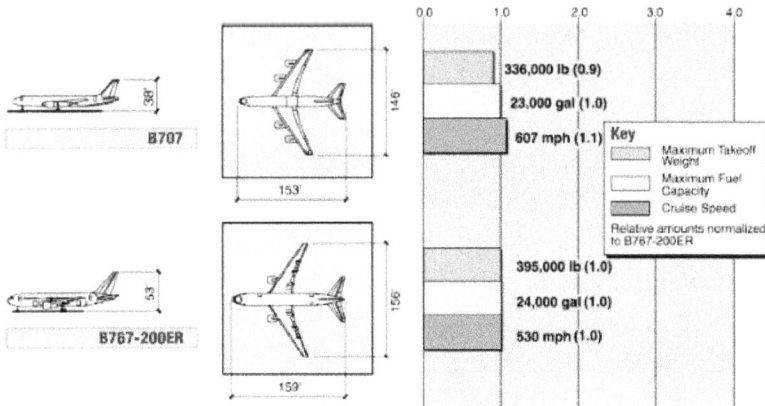

The 707 vs. the 767
Source: FEMA

Levy's statement indicates that when the designers did their calculations, they took into account that the 707 was fully loaded. That would have been the worst-case scenario. The maximum takeoff weight of a fully loaded 767 (395,000 lbs.) is, indeed, more than that of a fully loaded 707 (336,000 lbs.). But, if the 767 that hit the North Tower on 9/11 was only carrying 8,684 gallons of fuel instead of its full capacity of 24,000, the weight of the 707 that was considered in the design of the towers would have actually been more.

For instance, a gallon of jet fuel weighs 6.82 pounds. To get the actual weight of the 767, you would have to subtract about 104,455 pounds (6.82 lbs per gallon x 15,316 gallons) from its fully loaded weight. So the 767 that hit the North Tower on 9/11 had an actual weight of only 290,545 pounds, 45,455 pounds *less* than a fully loaded 707.

In fact, the weight of the 767 would have been even less than that because it was carrying only 92 people instead of its capacity of 169. Also, due to that, there would have been proportionately less luggage.

Since kinetic energy is a function of both speed and weight, the physical damage caused by the impact of the 767 that hit the North Tower would have been *less* than that done by the 707 that was considered in the design. And, since there was less fuel, there also would have been less fire damage. Accordingly, that building should not have collapsed on 9/11.

Both FEMA and NIST mentioned that the North Tower was designed to survive the crash of a 707, but they couched it in terms that were misleading. The FEMA report put it this way:

The Boeing 767-200ER aircraft that hit both towers were considerably larger with significantly higher weight, or mass, and traveling at substantially higher speeds. The Boeing 707 that was considered in the design of the towers was estimated to have a gross weight of *263,000* pounds and flight speed of *180* MPH as it approached an airport; the Boeing 767-200ER aircraft that were used to attack the towers had an estimated gross weight of *274,000* pounds and flight speeds of *470* and *590* mph upon impact.[464] (Italics added)

Practically everything in this statement is demonstrably false. In the first place, it appears that FEMA did not consider the fact that Flight

11 had less than half a tank of fuel and close to half the number of passengers and luggage it was designed to carry. It was, therefore, not of a "significantly higher weight" than the 707. Actually, it weighed less. And it would have caused less fire damage.

Secondly, the Levy white paper mentioned above specifically stated that the towers were designed to withstand the crash of a 707 going 600 mph, not 180 mph. Other expert testimony backs him up. For one instance, in 1984—some twenty years after Levy's paper appeared—John Dragonette, a Columbia University-educated architect who was a member of Levy's original team, released a statement of his own in which he specifically stated that the original design for the towers did, indeed, consider the impact of a 707 going 600 mph.[465]

It is not clear whether FEMA had Dragonette's statement, but NIST definitely did. In its report, that statement appears as an attachment to an obscure exhibit that is hidden in a footnote in a section entitled, "Aircraft Impact."[466]

The lead structural engineer for WSHJ on the WTC project, Leslie Robertson, gave that same impression at a conference held in Frankfurt, Germany only one week before the 9/11 attacks. At that time, he was asked if he had ever considered that the twin towers might be hit by a plane. His answer was rather succinct. Without elaborating, he stated, "I designed it for a 707 to smash into it."[467] This indicates that he must have followed normal engineering practice and designed the tower to withstand the worst-case scenario of a plane going at top cruising speed, which for a 707 is 600 mph. He would have also had to consider that the 707 was carrying 23,000 gallons of fuel. Given the situation, using anything less than these maximum numbers would have been irresponsible.

In addition, at another interview, Robertson was also quoted as saying that there was "…little likelihood of a collapse no matter how the building was attacked."[468] He could not have made that statement with any degree of confidence unless he had considered in his analysis the maximum numbers for speed and fuel load.

As for NIST, it simply dismissed the claim that the towers were designed to survive a worse plane crash than what happened on 9/11, by saying that the original calculations were lost and the study could not be verified. On the other side of that argument, however, is the fact that not only did NYPA head engineer Malcolm Levy stand by his white paper and the analysis done by WSHJ, but on February 14, 1964, two weeks after Levy's paper was released, another well-respected New York engineering firm, Emery Roth & Sons, issued its own statement in support of WSHJ's findings.[469] From this, one can reasonably assume that Emory Roth & Sons followed normal engineering protocol and double-checked the original calculations. This makes NIST's argument about the physical unavailability of the original calculations irrelevant.

Some supporters of the official explanation of the collapses say there is no proof that the designers actually did consider the effect that the fires would have in degrading the strength of the towers' steel structure. But that is countered by the fact that in normal practice, professional architects and engineers are responsible for taking into account the effect that a potential fire might have on the safety of the structure they are designing. This is especially true when their building will be so tall that it might be hit by an airplane laden with jet fuel.

In fact, John Skilling, an esteemed civil engineer and one of the partners of the WSHJ design firm, made a statement exactly addressing that point in a 1993 interview when he said, "Our analysis indicated that the biggest problem would be the fact that all the fuel would dump into the building. There would be a horrendous fire, [but] the building would still be there."[470] He could not have made such a statement unless he had actually addressed the effect that the subsequent fire temperatures would have on the strength of the building's steel framework.

Furthermore, aside from the foregoing argument about the speed, weight and fuel load of the 767s that hit the towers on 9/11, there is an additional factor that indicates that the damage they caused most likely would have been less than that caused by a 707. That has to do with the engines. While most of the lightweight aluminum body of either plane would be expected to be shredded upon impact with the buildings' perimeter columns, the engines would have survived to cause more damage to the inner core.

Note the following drawing. It shows the Pratt & Whitney PW4000 turbofan model used on the 767 that hit the WTC. It is typical of the construction used on all commercial airliners, including the 707. They are all made of hardened steel. Especially note the "spine." It is made of titanium, one of the hardest metals known to man. It is virtually indestructible.

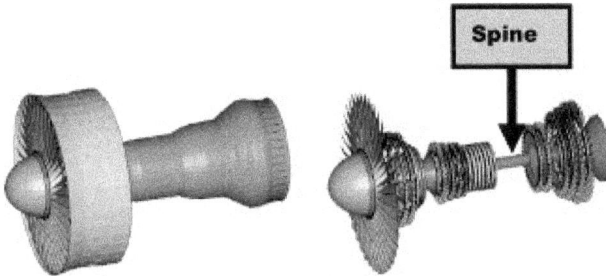

Figure E-17. Pratt & Whitney PW4000 turbofan engine model.

Engine for 767 Passenger Jet
Source: NIST

NIST itself took special note of the damage these engines would do to the inner core, saying, "The residual velocity and mass of the engine after penetration of the exterior wall was sufficient to fail a core column in a direct impact condition."[471] In this regard, the 707 would have caused more structural damage because it has four engines, whereas a 767 has only two.

All of the information in this section leads to one unassailable conclusion: The WTC towers were designed to withstand the damage done by the 767s that hit them on 9/11, including the subsequent fire damage. So what could have caused them to collapse, if not the plane crashes? Once again, explosives are the only alternative that fits.

There Was an Explosion Before the Plane Hit
The seismographic data from Columbia University's LDEO mentioned in Section 1 also provides evidence that backs up William Rodriguez's assertion that the very first explosion that he experienced in the B1 subbasement level of the North Tower occurred *before* the plane crash.

He said that that there was an initial explosion in the building coming from "below," and then, "When I went to verbalize it, we hear POW! An explosion all the way to the top of the building. And that was the plane hitting the top of the building. Two different events separated by almost 7 seconds."

Now, look again at the table of LDEO's findings.

Date	Origin Time (UTC)	Magnitude (Richter scale)	Time (EDT)	Dominant Period	Signal Duration	Remark
09/11/2001	12:46:26±1	0.9	08:46:26	0.8 sec	12 seconds	first impact
09/11/2001	13:02:54±2	0.7	09:02:54	0.6 sec	6 seconds	second impact
09/11/2001	13:59:04±1	2.1	09:59:04	0.8 sec	10 seconds	first collapse
09/11/2001	14:28:31±1	2.3	10:28:31	0.9 sec	8 seconds	second collapse
09/11/2001	21:20:33±2	0.6	17:20:33	0.7 sec	18 seconds	Building 7 collapse

LDEO Seismic Data for the 9/11 Attack on the WTC
Source: Columbia University

This represents LDEO's initial attempt to match up in sequential order the major events that they were aware of—the plane impacts and the collapses—with their seismographic data. However, it is apparent that the LDEO experts never considered the possibility that explosives were planted in the towers and that that could have been the cause of some of their seismic events. Once that possibility is figured into the scenario, a completely different picture emerges.

For instance, note that the first entry says that on 9/11/2001, their seismograph registered a tremor of the magnitude 0.9 on the Richter scale at 8:46:26 Eastern Daylight Time, which lasted for twelve seconds. They called that first reading the "impact" of Flight 11 on the North Tower. But that presents an important contradiction, because it is fourteen seconds sooner than the official time of plane impact given by the FAA's air traffic control software. That time was pegged exactly as 8:46:40.[472]

The FAA's time of impact is unassailably accurate; the plane was tracked via radar by the northeast Air Traffic Control Centers (ARTCC) of four cities—Boston, New York, Indianapolis, and Cleveland—and all the ARTCCs' times conform exactly to the world's atomic clock system, Coordinated Universal Time (UTC), which is regularly checked for accuracy.[473] In addition, the FAA impact times for the two planes that struck each of the towers was confirmed by the National Transportation Safety Board (NTSB).[474] So, what caused the early reading on LDEO's seismograph? It is very likely that it was the first powerful explosion that Rodriguez and the other witnesses experienced coming from the subbasement, not the impact of the plane. Although Rodriguez stated that the time difference between that explosion and the plane impact was seven seconds, not fourteen, given the startling nature of the circumstances, his estimate was remarkably close.

There is also an audio recording made of the crash of Flight 11 that appears to strongly confirm Rodriguez's account. It was made by a woman named Ginny Carr, who was working in a building across the street from the North Tower. On that tape, the first sound heard appears to be from an explosion. The second sound appears to come about nine seconds later and has a longer, grinding quality to it. After the first sound, a man is heard on the tape, asking, "What was that?" After the second sound, he says, "Sounds like a crash."[475]

With respect to the Carr tape, if the explosion took place nine seconds before the plane hit the tower (set by the FAA at 8:46:40) that would set the time of the basement explosion at 8:46:31, which is off the actual time set by LDEO (8:46:26) by five seconds. This discrepancy is hard to explain. Perhaps, having Carr's tape recorder available for testing or knowing more about the sub-surface strata that the sound waves passed through on the way to the lab would be helpful in clearing it up. But despite that, the information presented in this section, whether taken as a whole or in part, strongly indicates the distinct possibility that an explosion did occur in the subbasement of the North Tower *before* the impact of Flight 11.

One would think that either Rodriquez's statement—which he repeated to the 9/11 Commission before the release of the NIST report—or the information from Carr's tape, would have been more than enough to inspire NIST to at least test the steel from the subbasement of the North Tower for residues of explosives. But, even if their field investigators wanted to do that, due to Giuliani's ill-advised recycling effort and Cheney/ ONP's delaying tactics with the BPS engineers, it became impossible. By the time those investigations got started, the steel, for all practical purposes, was gone.

Pyroclastic Clouds

The official investigations also ignored the pyroclastic clouds of dust that resulted from the collapses. A pyroclastic cloud is a cauliflower-shaped, ground-hugging avalanche of hot gas, dust, and debris. Such clouds are typically seen in only two situations—volcanic eruptions and controlled demolitions.

The following photograph shows the dust created by the collapse of the North Tower as it moved through the surrounding buildings with the kind of turbulent fluidity that is characteristic of a pyroclastic cloud.

Pyroclastic Cloud from North Tower Collapse
Source: NYPD

One peculiar characteristic of a pyroclastic cloud is that it can move across a body of water like one less dense liquid poured over another. That phenomenon is demonstrated in this next photograph showing the WTC dust cloud as it floats onto the Hudson River.

Pyroclastic Cloud over the Hudson River
Source: NYPD

This is more compelling evidence pointing to the use of explosives that, once again, was ignored by the Bush administration investigations.

High Velocity Bursts

Another indication that explosives were at work in the towers is the several pointed, high velocity bursts of dust and debris that shot out of the middle of the sides of the buildings during their collapse. They occurred about twenty to thirty floors *ahead* of the collapse wave. Many were documented in photographs and videos.[476] Those bursts were very powerful. They were strong enough to break at least one or two of the exterior windows—which were typically made of high strength safety glass two to three inches thick—and still exit the building at a hurricane-force speed.

Note the following photograph of the North Tower.

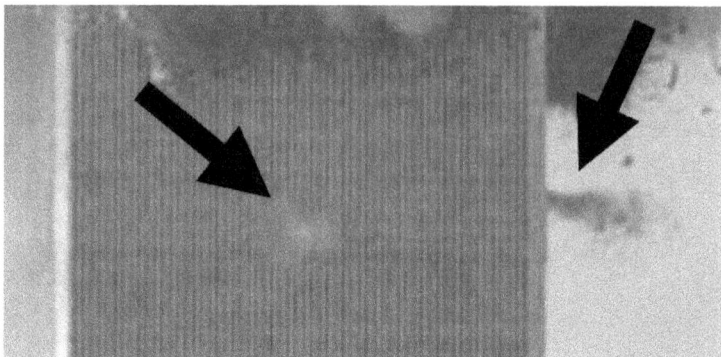

High Velocity Bursts
Source: 9/11 Truth.org

There were two studies done on the bursts to determine their velocity. One calculation was done by Dr. Crockett Grabbe, a professor of physics at the University of Iowa.[477] He utilized a video of the burst that was filmed by ABC-TV in order to measure the length of the plume and the average gravitational drop at its outer end. Dr. Grabbe observed that the plume, as compared to the known width of the building (207 feet), had traveled about 70 feet from the side of the building. He also measured that the end of the plume had dropped due to gravity about 3 feet. Using the formula for fall distance $S=0.5gt^2$, where S is fall distance of 3 feet and g is the constant for gravitational acceleration of 32 ft/sec/sec, Dr. Grabbe found the time for the plume to have a 3-foot fall distance to be 0.43 seconds. Knowing that the plume traveled outward from the face of the building 70 feet in those 0.43 seconds, he was able to determine that the plume exited the building at 163 feet/second, or 111 miles per hour.

The other calculation was done by Kevin Ryan, a scientist employed by Underwriter's Laboratory, Inc.[478] Ryan's approach was to use the known shutter speed of ABC's video camera. He knew the film speed in frames per second. He then counted the number of frames that it took for the end of the plume to travel what he observed to be 75 feet from the face of the building. Doing that, he determined a time of 0.45 seconds. That gave him a plume velocity of 170 feet/second, or 116 miles per hour; which confirmed Dr. Grabbe's work to within an acceptable margin of error.

The explanation of the mechanics of how these tremendously power-ful bursts occurred was a hard row to hoe for the official investigations. FEMA ignored the issue altogether, and NIST's attempt was weak. The institute claimed that it was due to the piston-like collapsing of floors inside the tower. According to NIST, when the top twenty floors above the plane impact zone fell as a block, that caused the floor truss seat connectors on certain lower floors to fail (at intervals of twenty to thirty floors ahead of the collapse wave), and those particular floors that were affected collapsed down inside the perimeter walls. Those floors that fell inside the perimeter walls caused a compression of air/dust against the next lower undamaged floor. That overpressure then forced a cloud of debris to break out of the sides of the building, causing the bursts.

The following illustration shows NIST's "Piston Theory."

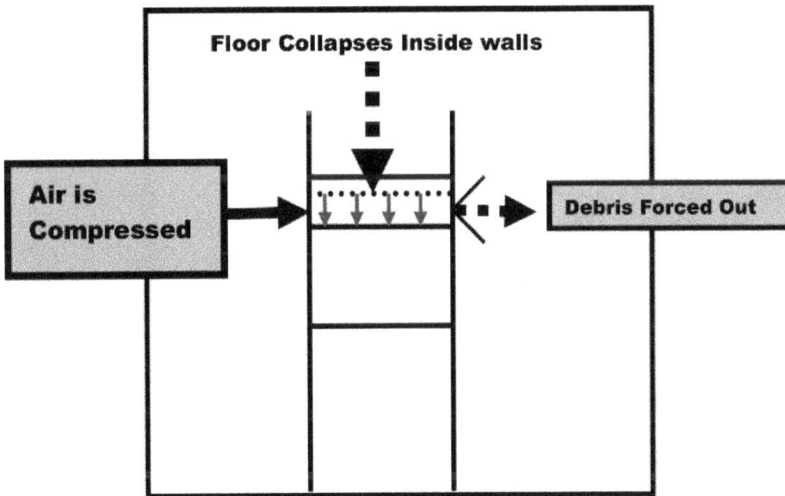

Floor Collapses Inside walls

Air is Compressed

Debris Forced Out

NIST's Piston Theory

However, a deeper study of the situation tells a different story. In the first place, it is obvious from the photograph shown above that the alleged action of floors collapsing had to have been occurring many floors above the bursts.

Secondly, the construction of the building makes NIST's theory virtually impossible. The North Tower drawings show that the actual strength of the connections of the ends of the floor trusses holding the floor system to the perimeter and core columns are not of the same strength.

Note the following plan. It shows the location of a floor truss in the outer office area of the North Tower at the 96[479] floor. This is typical for the rest of the building.[479]

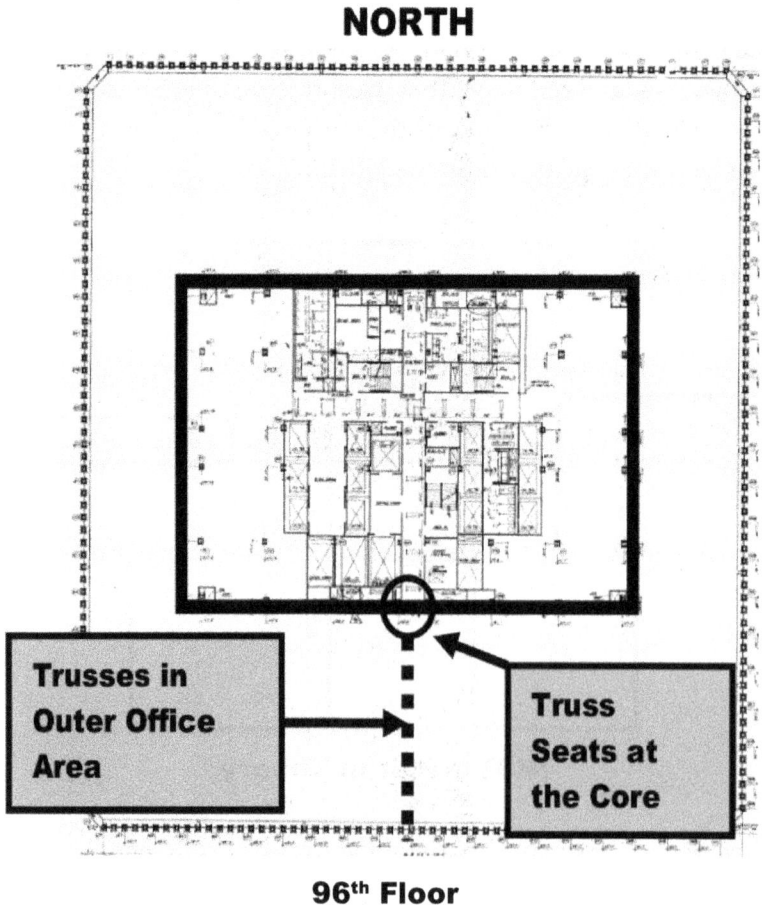

NORTH

Trusses in Outer Office Area

Truss Seats at the Core

96th Floor

Now, consider the illustration below which shows the number of connectors that held that floor truss in place at the perimeter columns.

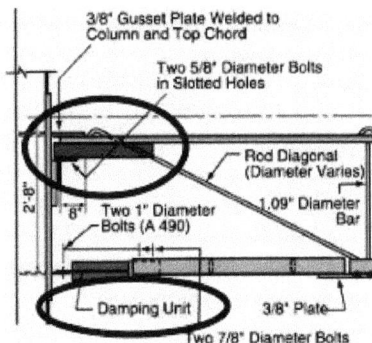

Truss Connections at the Perimeter Columns
Source: NIST

There is a welded-on gusset plate, two 5/8-inch A325 bolts at the truss seat angle, and a connection at the damper provided by two high strength, A490 bolts. In addition, not shown are two 1-inch wide steel bars called "diagonal bracing members" that were welded from the trusses to adjacent perimeter columns on either side of the main supporting column.

Now, for the other end of the floor trusses at the core, note the following drawing.

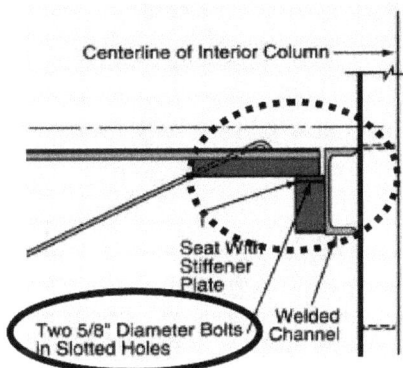

Truss Connections at the Core
Source: FEMA

There were only two 5/8-inch A325 bolts at this end, one for each truss on the seat angle.

It is clear from this that NIST's Piston Theory neglected to account for the difference between the greater *number* of floor truss connectors at the perimeter walls than at the core area. This makes it very unlikely that a single floor level could fall uniformly inside the perimeter columns, as the Piston Theory demands.

Under these conditions, the connectors at the core would have failed first and left the trusses hanging from the perimeter columns, at least for some period of time. That would have allowed any overpressures that might have occurred to be released past the edge of the falling floor near the core. No overpressure means there could be no pointed bursts.

Secondly, the core area consisted of 47 columns that were massive in size, which made it a super-strong structure capable of standing on its own. The NIST theory would have left the core structure standing inside the perimeter walls (that is, inside the so-called "cylinder") after the floors collapsed around it. By not mentioning this, the institute was conveniently able to ignore the entrances that lead to the core area from the outer office area. In the event that a floor did fall down between the perimeter walls and the core, those entrances would have acted as giant pressure relief valves. Thus, again, no pressure means no bursts.

Thirdly, in the unlikely event that the force of the falling upper block of twenty floors caused the interior core columns to collapse simultaneously with a falling floor inside the perimeter walls, all of the elevator shafts and the three stairwells that were located inside the core area would have been opened up. That would have also prevented any pressure from building up. Again, no pressure means no pointed, high-velocity bursts.

Fourthly, in the NIST's piston theory, there is no explanation of why the videos show that only a few windows in the center of the face of the building were blasted out. It seems more likely that the institute's explanation would require that a whole row of windows on a floor would have been blown out.

And finally, the high-velocity bursts seen on the outside face of the tower as it was collapsing were not random. There was a definite pattern associated with them, and that betrays the hand of man. This alone should have compelled NIST (or, for that matter, FEMA and the FBI, before it) to perform a simple test on nearby columns for residues of explosives.

But, as what happened so often with the Bush investigations, logic did not prevail. Again, the question is why did logic not prevail?

Evidence of Thermate at the WTC

The presence of molten steel at a demolition site is not surprising. But its presence at the WTC is alarming.[480] It is alarming because it indicates the strong possibility that devices containing thermate were planted there.

What is Thermate?

Thermate is a pyrotechnic compound which is sometimes used by dem-olition experts to cut steel supports of buildings. The first generation version of thermate was called thermite. It was discovered in 1893 by German chemist Dr. Hans Goldschmidt. Made very simply, thermite is a mixture of iron oxide and aluminum powders. Iron oxide is basically oxidized iron or, as it is more commonly referred to, rust.

An ordinary fuse does not burn hot enough to get the powders to react. In order for thermite to work, it must be ignited with a high temperature fuse, such as one made of magnesium.

The chemical reaction that thermite undergoes is according to the following formula:[481]

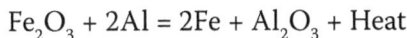

$$Fe_2O_3 + 2Al = 2Fe + Al_2O_3 + Heat$$

Once ignited, the aluminum powder of the mix (Al) pulls the 3 oxygen atoms (O_3) away from the iron oxide molecule (Fe_2O_3) and forms a new molecule of aluminum oxide (Al_2O_3), which is seen as a white gaseous by-product. This molecular exchange of the oxygen atoms results in the release of an enormous amount of energy, which causes the steel/iron (Fe) by-product to become molten. That by-product—called "slag"—has a working temperature of 2500°C and will easily turn solid steel into a liquid, since steel/iron melts at about 1538°C.

Thermite has many practical uses. One of Goldschmidt's first commercial applications was to use it to weld the ends of railroad tracks together. The military uses it by fashioning it into grenades and dropping them down enemy artillery barrels, welding them shut and rendering them useless. It was also used in World War II, in bombs, to set cities on fire during nighttime raids.

But when thermite is used for arson, it has a drawback. It leaves a big trail. Materials Engineering, Inc. (MEI), a company that investigates crimes of arson for various policing agencies, put it this way:

When thermite reactive compounds are used to ignite a fire, they produce a characteristic burn pattern and leave behind evidence [chemical elements]...While some of these elements are consumed in the fire; many are left behind in the residue...

MEI has conducted Energy Dispersive Spectroscopy (EDS) on minute traces of residue, identifying the presence of these chemical elements. The results, coupled with visual evidence at the scene, provide *absolute certainty* that thermite reaction compounds were present, indicating the fire was deliberately set, and not of natural causes...[482] (Italics added)

Ther*mate* became a new and improved version of thermite with the addition of sulfur. The presence of sulfur in the mix causes what is called a eutectic reaction in which the melting point of the steel to be cut is lowered from 1538° C to about 1000° C.[483] This lower melting temperature due to the sulfur, allows a column to get cut more quickly. And it occurs at lightning speed. Thermate can cut through an average-sized steel column in as little as a fraction of a second.[484]

If thermate is used, the presence of sulfur is easily detectable via electron microscopy due to a characteristic condition observed in the steel called "sulfidation." Sulfidation refers to the process by which the sulfur additive will quickly penetrate the melting steel that is being cut. Following behind this sulfur penetration, the molten iron slag formed by the thermate reaction attacks the column. This feature of the process is called "intergranular melting."

Worcester Polytechnic Institute and Thermate

A glaring example of FEMA's prejudice against considering explosives as a factor in the WTC collapses is the manner in which it handled crucial evidence uncovered by one of its own field investigative teams. That particular team was a learned group of scientists from Worcester Polytechnic Institute (WPI). It included Jonathon R. Barnett, a professor of fire protection engineering, and R.R. Biederman and R.D. Sisson, Jr., both professors of materials science. Shortly after the 9/11 attacks, they visited the scrap dealer sites in New Jersey where the steel from the World Trade Center site was being prepped for sale. There they were able to retain two samples that piqued their interest. One was a piece of A36 wide flange steel from Building 7. (The term "wide flange" refers to a beam that has an "H" shaped cross-section.) The other was a piece of high strength steel column from one of the towers.

In the opinion of the WPI professors, the "unexpected erosion" they observed in their samples "warranted a study of the microstructural changes that occurred in this steel."[485]

The following photograph shows the A36 steel sample from Building 7.[486]

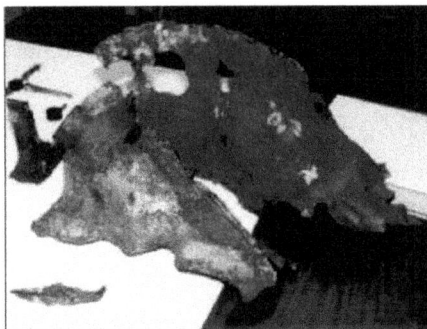

WPI Sample from Building 7
Source: FEMA

In December of 2001, a mere three months after the attacks, the preliminary results of their study on the Building 7 sample were presented to the Minerals, Metals & Materials Society and subsequently appeared in *Journal of Materials* (JOM), the society's magazine. Entitled "An Initial Microstructural Analysis of A36 Steel from WTC Building 7," that article, without directly stating any such charge, presents certain aspects of their findings that appear to be consistent with the use of thermate. In part, it reads as follows:

Rapid deterioration of the steel was a result of heating with oxidation in combination with *intergranular melting* due to the presence of *sulfur.* The formation of the *eutectic* mixture of iron oxide and iron sulfide lowers the temperature at which liquid can form in this steel. This strongly suggests that the temperatures in this region of the steel beam approached *~1,000 degrees Centigrade.*[487] (Italics added)

But 1000°C is far above the temperature that could have occurred in the towers, where there was a copious amount of black smoke, indicating that the fires were oxygen-starved. Except for occasional flashovers in isolated spots, such diffuse-flame fires, do not produce overall temperatures above about 650°C.[488] This fact, together with the sulfur finding, strongly indicates the presence of the pyrotechnic material thermate. Thermate being a material capable of undergoing a super high-temperature, self-contained and self-sustained exothermic chemical reaction that is capable of melting steel. It proceeds according the formula given above and, with the addition of sulfur, proceeds at lightening speed.

Note the following photo. It shows a section of that piece of A36 steel from Building 7 as observed under an electron microscope.[489] To an expert observer, the corrosive action that is a characteristic of the use of thermate is clearly visible.

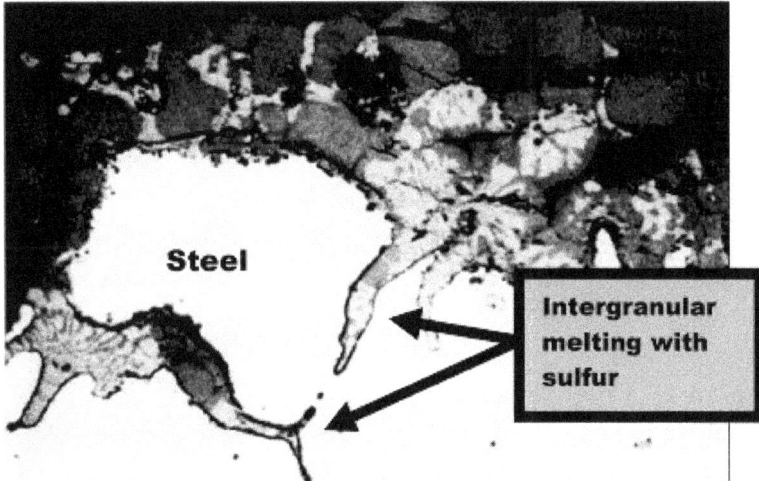

Micrograph
WPI Sample from Building 7
Source: FEMA

The white of the picture in the lower area is the steel. It is in the process of undergoing a slag attack at its boundary edge. The dark area at the top of the picture is the once molten iron slag of a possible thermate reaction. It is following behind the penetration of the sulfur, causing intergranular melting. The thinning veins seeping into the body of the steel are how the process proceeds—with sulfur penetration leading the slag attack.

The WPI team's surprising finding that sulfur was present in the WTC steel was revealed two months after the attack by the *New York Times*, which called it "perhaps the deepest mystery uncovered in the investigation."[490] But it went otherwise unreported by the rest of the mainstream media. Nor was it deemed important enough to spur the interest of any law enforcement investigative agency, including the FBI.

In the spring of 2002, the WPI team again went public when they published their surprising test results in the college's magazine, *Transformations*. This is how the writer of that article described the team's initial surprised reaction to the condition of their samples:

A one-inch column has been reduced to half-inch thickness. Its edges—which are curled like a paper scroll—have been thinned to almost razor sharpness. Gaping holes—some larger than a silver dollar—let light shine through a formerly solid steel flange. This Swiss cheese appearance *shocked* all of the fire-wise professors, who expected to see distortion and bending—but not holes. (Italics added)

The article also explained why the fire-wise professors were so shocked by the condition of the steel:

There is no indication that any of the fires in the World Trade Center buildings were hot enough to melt the steel framework. Jonathon Barnett, professor of fire protection engineering, has repeatedly reminded the public that steel—which has a melting point of 2,800 degrees Fahrenheit [1538°C]—may weaken and bend, but does not melt during an ordinary office fire. Yet metallurgical studies on WTC steel brought back to WPI reveal that a novel phenomenon—called a eutectic reaction—occurred at the surface, causing intergranular melting capable of turning a solid steel girder into Swiss cheese.[491]

Here again, we have the characteristic signature of a thermate reactive compound: "a eutectic reaction" followed by "intergranular melting" occurring at temperatures way above those found in an ordinary office fire that was "capable of turning a solid steel girder into Swiss cheese." And once again, this piqued no interest on the part of the FBI or any New York City or state governmental investigative agencies. They all simply ignored these astounding findings. In fact, the WPI results were merely published as Appendix C in the back of the FEMA report and summarily forgotten.

As if that was not enough, a year later, in August of 2003, Professor Biederman teamed with other scientists to present a third paper on the subject at a meeting of the National Metallographic Society in San Antonio, Texas, which echoed the results previously found by his WPI team. In that paper entitled, "Microstructural Analysis of the Steels from Buildings 7, 1 and 2 from the World Trade Center," they wrote:

An examination of the "slag" that formed on the surface of the steel found iron oxides and iron sulfides. It appeared that the "slag" was liquid at high temperature and easily attacked the grain boundaries. A eutectic microstructure was seen within the "slag" of iron oxides and iron sulfides. If these compounds were pure Wusite (FeO) and iron sulfide (FeS), the eutectic temperature is 940 degrees Centigrade. It appears that the severe "erosion" was due to the sulfidation and oxidation (i.e. hot corrosion) of the steel followed by the liquid "slag" attack of the grain boundaries...Evidence of grain boundary attack by sulfidation is clearly visible.[492]

Even after this third public announcement, which indicated that there was a strong likelihood that thermate had been used at the WTC coincident with the terrorist attack of 9/11, virtually no official eyebrows were raised.

The later NIST investigation would also completely ignore these findings.

The Location of a WPI Sample Confirms Photographic Record of Thermate

Note this photo. It is a frame from a video taken by a civilian named Luigi Cazzaniga. It shows liquid steel flowing from the 80th floor of the South Tower fifteen seconds before collapse.[493]

Molten Metal at the WTC
Copyright: Louis Cazzaniga

It is impossible to know the location in Building 7 where the sample of A36 steel came from, because Building 7 had that grade of steel in both the perimeter and core columns. However, a little more can be said about the piece of column from the towers. First, it was most likely from a perimeter column, because that was virtually the only place where high strength steel was used.[494]

And secondly, the approximate location in the structure where it came from can be determined. Note the following illustration:

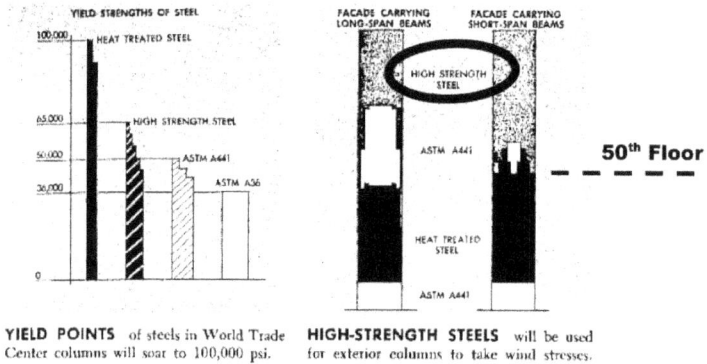

Strengths of Perimeter Columns

Source: PANYNJ

This graphic was obtained by the American Iron and Steel Institute in the early 1960s from the Port Authority of New York and New Jersey (PANYNJ) for an article entitled, "The World Trade Center in New York City," which appeared in their trade magazine, *Contemporary Steel Design* (CSD).[495] It depicts the arrangement of the different grades of steel used in the perimeter columns of the twin towers and shows that "high strength steel" was used in the upper half of the buildings. Calculating by proportions shown in the drawing, the WPI high-strength sample from one of the towers had to have come from above about the 50th floor.

Taken together with the Cazzaniga video, this can be considered strong evidence that a pyrotechnic compound such as thermate was planted in the upper reaches of the South Tower prior to 9/11. Of course, this leads to further speculation that there were many such devices that were planted in both towers as part of a demolition plan.

Thermate and Other WTC Samples

There were about 180,000 tons of steel in the debris pile of the twin towers, 99 percent of which was sold to Asian countries as scrap. Only a relatively tiny amount was saved by FEMA, and those samples were later turned over to NIST. A few of them piqued the interest of NIST field investigators, who photographed and performed metallurgical tests on them. A few of those photographs and micrographs of the tests later found their way into various sections of the institute's final report. What follows are two of those samples that show evidence of the use of thermate.

NIST Sample N-8: This is a floor truss seat angle from a recovered perimeter panel of the North Tower. It was located on the north face at column line 142 at the 99th floor.[496]

N-8, Floor Truss Seat
Source: NIST

There appears to be a considerable amount of iron slag on it (circle) accompanied by corrosion (arrow). Below is a look at the corroded area through an electron microscope.

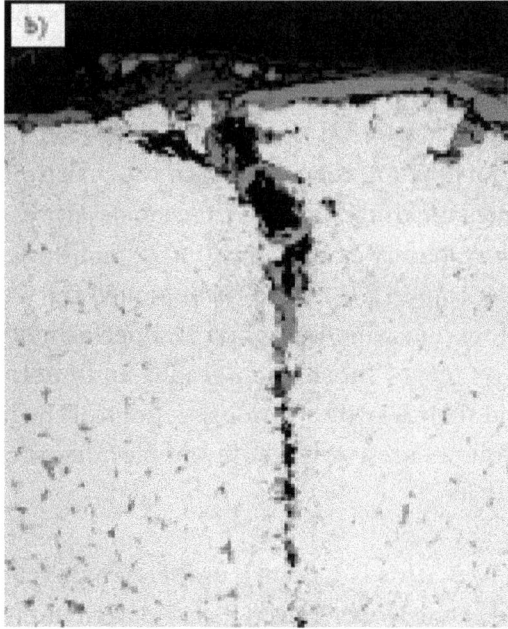

Micrograph of N-8
Source: NIST

The description given in the report under this micrograph describes what could very well be the results of a thermate-type reaction. It says that what you are looking at is an "iron oxide" (slag) penetration with internal "oxidation" accompanied by "decarburization" (dissolution of the carbon in the steel), which was "possibly due to elevated temperature exposure."[497]

Considering that the WPI evidence was available to NIST, it is incredible that this is the extent of their comments. Apparently, those who wrote the report did not puzzle over the fact that the temperature required for this to occur had to be 1538°C (or 1000°C, if thermate was used), which is a temperature level far above that which could be attained by the diffuse-flame, oxygen-starved, hydrocarbon-based fires that occurred in the towers.

Obviously, this was another great opportunity to test for thermate that was missed.

NIST Sample C-115: This is yet another sample that was seen as significant by the NIST field investigators who photographed it.[498] Notice how this piece of steel has been considerably thinned out at the left end due to melting.

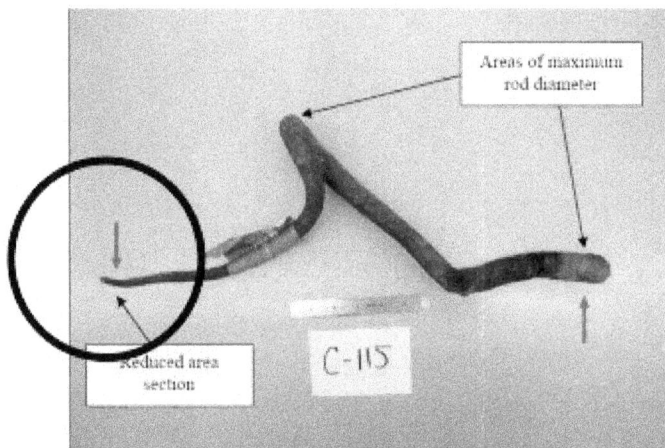

C-115, Steel Strut Rod
Source: NIST

C-115 is a piece of a one-inch diameter strut rod that formed the diagonal member of a floor truss. The following drawing shows its typical location.

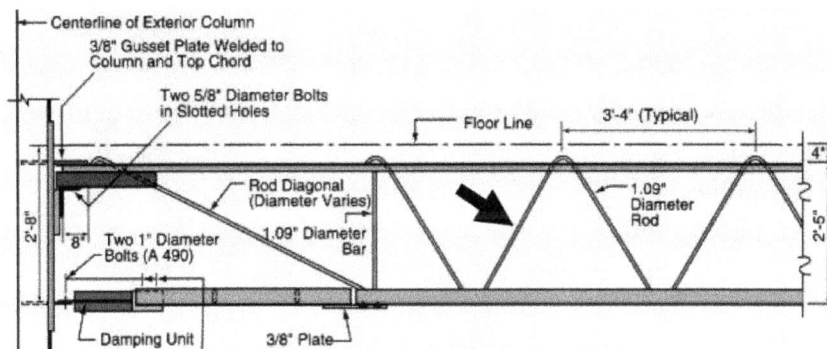

Typical Floor Truss Design
Source: NIST

Below is a micrograph of the thinned-out area as it appears in the NIST report.

Micrograph of C-115
Source: NIST

Again, this sample shows the deep penetration of a high-temperature slag attack that is characteristic of the use of thermate. But the comment in the report on this micrograph is, again, typically meagre. It uses words like "penetrating corrosion" and "internal oxidation." However, there is neither an explanation given of the possible cause of it nor a discussion of its significance.[499]

This is yet another example where testing for a pyrotechnic material such as thermate was obviously called for, but not done.

Other Photographic Evidence of Molten Steel

This piece of steel plate shows obvious signs of being melted and was still glowing yellow from what very well could have been a thermate reaction when FEMA field investigators photographed it. It is no surprise that they found it interesting, because the yellow color indicates a steel temperature of around 1200°C.[500] That is a level impossible to reach in an ordinary office fire that is accompanied by a copious amount of heat-smothering black smoke like what occurred in the towers.

Melted Spandrel Plate
Source: FEMA

This photograph also appeared in the NIST report, but it elicited absolutely no comment from the actual writers of the report.

Below is an extraordinary mass that was found at the WTC shortly after 9/11 by FEMA field investigators who it found of special interest and photographed it. It appears to be an amalgam of various pieces of debris—including concrete and steel rods—that have been welded together at what obviously had to have also been an extremely high temperature unattainable in the towers.

WTC Amalgam   Close-up
Source: NIST

This is a clear indication that something more was at work than the ordinary, diffuse-flame, oxygen-starved fires that occurred at the WTC. But, although this photo appeared in both the FEMA and NIST reports, there were no comments at all on what could have caused this condition.

As of November 2005, this historical specimen was being stored in a New York warehouse and remained uninvestigated, but this is what BYU physics professor Dr. Steven Jones said should have been done with it:

> X-ray energy dispersive spectrometry (XEDS) will yield the elemental composition, and electron energy-loss spectroscopy will tell us the elements found in very small amounts that were undetectable with XEDS. Electron-backscattered diffraction in the scanning electron microscope will give us phase information; the formation of certain precipitates can tell us a minimum temperature the melt must have reached.[501]

Below is a high-altitude photograph taken of the WTC by National Aeronautics and Space Administration (NASA) almost two weeks after the attacks, showing the many hot spots where molten steel still persisted.[502] It was publicized by the U S Geological Survey (USGS) in November 2001. But it received no mention in either the May 2002 FEMA report or the 2005 report from NIST.

Thermal image

SOUTH TOWER
NORTH TOWER
BUILDING 6
BUILDING 7

WTC Hot Spots

Source: NASA

Dr. Steven Jones, Molten Steel and Nano-thermite

In November 2005, Dr. Jones, while still at BYU, submitted his first 9/11-related paper. That led to his being presented with a sample of dust from the WTC site. It came from the apartment of Janette MacKinlay at 113 Cedar Street in Manhattan. The windows of MacKinlay's fourth floor apartment, which was about 100 yards from the WTC, had been blown in by the force of the collapse of one of the towers. The apartment was powdered with WTC dust. Before she cleaned it up, she saved a sample as a keepsake. After having learned of Dr. Jones via his website, she contacted him to see if he would be interested in having some of it. Jones was delighted, and she sent him some by mail.

Being of a practical mind, Dr. Jones predicted that, if thermate had indeed been used at the WTC, there should be particles of an iron-rich nature in the dust. So his first test was simply to pull a magnet across the sample. His hunch was correct, and he was able to collect particles of iron. This is how he described his discovery:

There was a surprising amount of this iron-rich material. I was surprised to find the abundance of spherical particles in this iron-rich component some of which were considerably larger than was previously reported. It was exciting to me to find for the first time iron-rich spheres up to about 1.5mm in diameter in a 32.1 gram sample of dust.

The iron-rich component of the WTC dust sample was analyzed in some detail by scanning electron microscopy (SEM) and x-ray energy dispersive spectroscopy (X-EDS). Using the scanning electron microscope, we found that much of the iron-rich dust was in fact composed of roughly spherical particles—microspheres. The presence of metallic microspheres implies that these metals were once molten, so that surface tension pulled the droplets into a roughly spherical shape. Then the molten droplets solidified in air, preserving the information that they were once molten in the spherical shape as well as chemical information.[503]

The presence of these iron-rich spheres implies a temperature of at least 1538°C, the melting point of steel (or 1000°C, if thermate was used). Again, this is way above the maximum temperature that could have occurred in the black smoke-laden WTC fires.

Also in 2005, the USGS's Greg Meeker, a geologist, cataloged particles that his own investigation found in the WTC dust. One of them is pictured below.[504] It is an iron-rich sphere of the same type that Dr. Jones discovered.

Iron-rich sphere

Source: USGS

Moreover, a further study of the dust by Dr. Jones revealed that it also contained an unusually high concentration of the chemical compound Barium Nitrate [$Ba(NO_3)_2$].[505] This is notable because Barium Nitrate is an ingredient found only in a version of thermate that was patented by the US military. This military aspect was confirmed when a further examination of the dust turned up what Jones determined to be unreacted chips of US military-grade, nano-engineered thermite. Often called "superthermite," this manmade material packs enormous power. When ignited, it can produce a shock wave on the order of Mach 3, which indicates a speed of 2,304 mph.[506]

Note the following photograph.

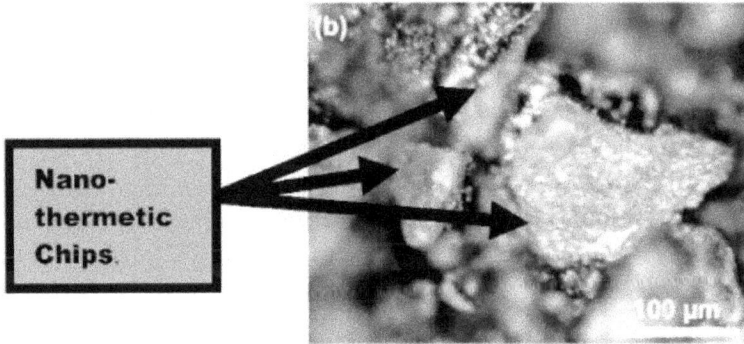

Source: 911Research.com

This discovery of the iron-rich spheres by Dr. Jones, together with the Barium Nitrate and thermetic chips, leaves little doubt that devices containing US military-grade thermate were planted at the WTC prior to the 9/11 attacks.[507]

Witnesses to Molten Steel

The Bush administration investigations downplayed the evidence of molten steel at the WTC, despite the fact that many eyewitnesses testified to its presence deep in the basement of the twin towers at the bottom of elevator shafts and at the foot of core columns. Some of this molten steel persisted for months after the attack. A couple of the witnesses were engineering professionals. One was none other than WTC structural designer **Leslie Robertson**, who was also part of the NIST investigation team, having been responsible for creating many of the computer simulations that appear in the report. During a speech in October of 2001, Robertson said, "As of 21 days after the attack, the fires are still burning and molten steel is still running."[508] Another was **Dr. Keith Eaton**, the chief executive of the Institution of Structural Engineers, who wrote about seeing "...molten metal that was still red-hot weeks after the event."[509]

Some of the witnesses ran companies involved in the cleanup. The previously mentioned Peter Tully talked of seeing "literally molten steel."[510] So did Controlled Demolition's **Mark Loizeaux**, who was consulted about debris removal. He talked of seeing "molten steel" at the bottom of elevator shafts for "four and five weeks" after the attack.[511] **Greg Fuchek**, vice president of Linkspoint, Inc., a company that supplied some of the computer equipment to help identify human remains, said, "Sometimes when a worker would pull a steel beam from wreckage, the end of the beam would be dripping molten steel."[512]

Some of the witnesses were involved in the debris removal. Construction supervisor **Charlie Vitchers** said that water could not cool the "blob" under the pile. Even after being hosed down, the heat increased. He said, "One day it would be hot here, it would be 1,400 degrees, and the next day it would be 2,000."[513] This is a strong indication of the use of thermate, which is its own supply of fuel and oxygen and cannot be put out by water. Even the head of the DDC, **Ken Holden**, testified to seeing liquid steel. Under oath, he told the 9/11 Commission that "underground, it was still so hot that molten metal dripped down the side of the wall from Building 6."[514]

Other witnesses were firefighters. Bronx firefighter **Joe O'Toole** said that some of the steel that was pulled out of the depths of the debris pile would be "dripping from the molten steel."[515] Likewise, FDNY Captain **Philip Ruvolo** said, "You'd get down below, and you'd see molten steel. Molten steel [was] running down the channel rails like you're in a foundry. Like lava."[516]

Still others were health professionals. **Dr. Alison Geyh** said that "in some pockets uncovered, they are finding molten steel."[517] And **Ron Burger** of the National Center for Environmental Health, Centers for Disease Control and Prevention, talked of "molten steel" that reminded him of the volcanic eruption of Mount St. Helens.[518]

Lee Turner was a member of the FEMA search and rescue team that arrived at the WTC site the day after the attack. He talked about there being five levels below ground where he saw "in the darkness a distant pinkish glow—molten metal dripping from a beam."[519]

Journalists were generally restricted from entering the site by the NYPD, on Mayor Giuliani's orders. But one of them, the previously mentioned **William Langewiesche**, was allowed unlimited access. He wrote that in lower areas "underground fires still burned and steel flowed in molten streams."[520] Another journalist, **Tom Arteburn**, wrote in *Waste Age* magazine that the New York Department of Sanitation removed "everything from molten steel to human remains" from the site for about "two and a half months."[521]

Both of the Bush investigations exhibited a distressing level of willful ignorance on the subject of molten steel at the WTC. It was as if they were determined to ignore the fact. For example, even in the face of all this eyewitness testimony, one NIST spokesman, Dr. John L Gross, PhD, who was a lead engineer for the investigation, actually had the audacity to deny that molten steel was ever seen at the WTC, by anybody. That happened during a public presentation he gave that was videotaped by an independent 9/11 researcher. It is obvious from the video that Gross was caught off guard when questioned about the subject. And he responded quite uneasily, saying,

Let's go back to your basic premise that there was a pool of molten steel. I know of absolutely nobody...no eyewitnesses who said so. Nobody's produced it. I was on the site. I was on the steel yard. I can't...I don't know that that's so. Steel melts at around 2600°F. I think it's probably difficult to get that kind of temperatures in a fire. So, I don't know the basis…I can't address your question, if I don't know the basis.[522]

The questioner then told Dr. Gross about the NASA thermal image shown above, which indicated that there were hot spots of molten steel that existed for weeks after the attack. Gross denied knowing about the photograph, and he asked the questioner to send it to him. But according to the questioner, when he approached Gross after the meeting to get his e-mail address, that so-called "investigator" for the Bush administration refused to give it to him.[523]

There is virtually no chance that this was merely a casual error by Gross. His education and experience belies that. He got his PhD in structural engineering from Cornell University and taught engineering at the University of Colorado in Boulder. In addition, he has a long professional resume on top of that.[524] For him to make up such an obvious lie like this on a topic so vital is a prime example of the level of deceit that permeates the NIST report. And it is a stark example of why he and every person who was involved in it needs to be thoroughly investigated.

Molten Steel Ignored

As mentioned, FEMA attached the WPI evidence as Appendix C at the back of its report. In the body of the report, however, this dramatic and very significant evidence—evidence that was so unexpected that the WPI professors were "shocked" by it—was barely mentioned. The sum total of FEMA's comments on the subject took up about a half of a page. The agency merely gave a quick overview of the WPI findings and then offered the following as part of its "Recommendations."

The severe corrosion and subsequent erosion of Sample 1 and 2 constitute an unusual event. No clear explanation for the source of the sulfur has been identified. The rate of corrosion is also unknown. It is possible that this was the result of long-term heating in the ground following the collapse of the buildings. It is also possible that the phenomenon started prior to collapse; and accelerated the weakening of the steel structure. A detailed study into the mechanisms of this phenomenon is needed to determine what risk, if any, is presented to existing steel structures exposed to severe and long-burning fires.[525]

That the severe corrosion seen in the WPI samples was caused by "severe and long-burning fires" clearly could not have been the case. In the first place, as has been adequately shown here, a kerosene/jet fuel fire does not burn that hot. Secondly, a hydrocarbon-based fire such as one fed by jet fuel and office furnishings would either have been smothered by the debris (which consisted mainly of pulverized concrete and office furnishings) or put out by the huge amount of water that was hosed onto the debris pile. On the other hand, a thermate-based fire cannot be put out by smothering or by water because it is its own source of fuel and oxygen.

Moreover, if the answer to the mystery was so obvious, then why were the WPI scientists so "shocked" by the condition of their samples?

Conversely, one might ask, why were those supervising the FEMA investigation not shocked?

FEMA opened the door to the possibility of the presence of a pyrotechnic material such as thermate at the WTC when their report said "It is also possible that the phenomenon started prior to collapse; and accelerated the weakening of the steel structure." But why did the institute stop there and not carry out that thought to its logical conclusion? Could it be that there was the presence of an ever-vigilant invisible hand standing over the investigation (read Cheney/ONP), ready to edit out any comments that might suggest that something other than the plane crashes and subsequent fires caused the collapses?

As for the NIST report, it stood with FEMA and rejected out of hand any evidence of the use of thermate. Due to that, it was hit with such severe criticism that it was forced to address the molten steel problem a year later in its 2006 supplement "Answers to Frequently Asked Questions."[526] Item 13 of that document asked, "Why did the NIST investigation not consider reports of molten steel in the wreckage from the WTC towers?"

NIST answered as follows:

NIST investigators and experts from the American Society of Civil Engineers (ASCE) and the Structural Engineers Association of New York (SEONY)—who inspected the WTC steel at the WTC site and the salvage yards—found no evidence that would support the melting of steel in a jet-fuel ignited fire in the towers prior to collapse. The condition of the steel in the wreckage of the WTC towers (i.e., whether it was in a molten state or not) was irrelevant to the investigation of the collapse since it does not provide any conclusive information on the condition of the steel when the WTC towers were standing.

But, as was adequately demonstrated in Chapter 1 of this book, the BPS team of investigators from the ASCE did not get to inspect the steel before it was destroyed by Giuliani. To say that they did is an outrageous lie. And the SEONY [sic] team's motives are suspect, due to their association with the City of New York—meaning Giuliani. Can there be any doubt that that relationship was the reason why they were selected over the ASCE's Dream Team of investigating engineers to handle the steel evidence when it would have been a simple matter to store all of it until the BPS team arrived? Recall the BPS team's ten steel samples which they collected and put aside for future analysis during their three-day walkthrough in the first week of October. Could it really be that all ten of them were "accidently" destroyed a few days later? If the BPS team had followed normal procedure, their samples would have been clearly marked with the word "SAVE" in big red letters.

Secondly, the reason that NIST did not find any evidence that the jet fuel-fed fire melted the steel was simply because a "jet fuel ignited fire" does not get hot enough to melt steel. So, if the steel did melt, it was not melted by that fire. It must have been melted by something else—something that gets much hotter—like thermate.

Thirdly, how could molten steel, no matter where it was found at the WTC site, be considered "irrelevant?" Again, FEMA's fire-wise professors from WPI were shocked at the condition of their samples. According to the dictionary, the term "shock" is defined as "an unexpected, intense, and distressing experience that has a sudden and powerful effect on somebody's emotions or physical reactions." This is not a description of something that is irrelevant.

The presence of molten steel at the WTC is beyond dispute. And NIST's own metallurgic tests on samples N-8 and C-115 indicated that the likely cause of it was thermate. Despite that, though, neither of the Bush investigations showed any interest in testing for it.

Another of the "Frequently Asked Questions" directly addressed that issue, asking,

Did the NIST investigation look for evidence of the WTC towers being brought down by controlled demolition? Was the steel tested for explosives or thermite residues? The combination of thermite and sulfur (called thermate) "slices through steel like a hot knife through butter."

NIST's answer was blunt: "NIST did not test for the residue of these compounds in the steel." As for why the steel was not tested, NIST said,

Analysis of the WTC steel for the elements in thermite/thermate would not necessarily have been conclusive. The metal compounds also would have been present in the construction materials making up the WTC towers, and sulfur is present in the gypsum wallboard that was prevalent in the interior partitions.

But this is a compete distortion of the situation. Again, here's what the experts at Materials Engineering, Inc. had to say on the subject:

MEI has conducted Energy Dispersive Spectroscopy (EDS) on minute traces of residue, identifying the presence of these chemical elements. The results, coupled with visual evidence at the scene, provide *absolute certainty* that thermite reaction compounds were present. (Italics added)

Were the writers of the NIST report implying that the scientists from MEI are unaware that minuscule amounts of sulfur and metal compounds are present in some construction materials?

A panel of professional engineers, architects, and scientists headed by Dr. Jones was strongly critical of NIST's admitted failure to test WTC steel samples for residues of explosives and pyrotechnic compounds. That failure by the official investigations was, the panel's members charged, against accepted protocol for investigations of suspicious fires. Their paper explains the issue this way:

We agree: there is no evidence that NIST tested for residues of thermite or explosives. This is another remarkable admission. Probing for residues from pyrotechnic materials including thermite in particular, is specified in fire and explosion investigations by the NFPA (National Fire Protection Agency) 921 code:

Unusual residues might remain from the initial fuel. Those residues *could arise from thermite*, magnesium, or other pyrotechnic materials.

Traces of thermite in residues (solidified slag, dust, etc.) would tell us a great deal about the crime and the cause of thousands of injuries and deaths. This is standard procedure for fire and explosion investigations. Perhaps NIST will explain why they have not looked for these residues? The code specifies that fire-scene investigators must be prepared to justify an exclusion.

NIST has been asked about this important issue recently, by investigative reporter Jennifer Abel:

Abel: What about the letter where NIST said it didn't look for evidence [residues] of explosives?

Newman: [Spokesperson at NIST, listed on the WTC report]: Right, because there was no evidence of that.

Abel: But how can you know there's no evidence if you don't look for it first?

Newman: If you're looking for something that isn't there, you're wasting your time...and the taxpayer's money.

The evident evasiveness of this answer might be humorous if not for the fact that NIST's approach here affects the lives of so many innocent people. We do not think that looking for thermite or other residues specified in the NFPA 921 code is "wasting your time."

High Factor of Safety Points to the Use of Explosives

NIST said the initiating factor for the collapse of the North Tower was that high fire temperatures led to large deflections (sagging) of particular floor trusses in the south side area of the plane impact zone, which pulled their perimeter columns inward. Those columns, being unsupported horizontally for several floors due to the failure of 20 percent of the floor truss connectors on the south side of floors 97 and 98 and weakened by the fire themselves, became critically out of vertical alignment and unable to support the weight of the block of the 20 or so floors above. At that point, all the columns at that level quickly buckled in succession, causing that upper block to fall with such force that it crushed the close to 90 undamaged floors below straight down to the ground at free fall speed.

The information presented in this section, however, contradicts that hypothesis in these very important ways: (1) The high degree of factor of safety that was designed into the tower's support columns dictates that the structural integrity of the building was not affected significantly by the plane crash; (2) due to that high factor of safety, the fires in the tower's plane impact zone were not nearly hot enough nor uniform enough across one whole floor area to cause the straight downward collapse as seen in the videos; and (3) the pulling force that the sagging south side floor trusses exerted on their perimeter columns, as calculated by NIST, was wholly inadequate to initiate collapse.

1. The High Factor of Safety

NIST admitted that the *overall* factor of safety of the North Tower's design was about 3. Therefore, on the day of the 9/11 attacks, since there was no wind, the building was utilizing only 1/3 of its load bearing capacity. This means that, in order to justify its collapse theory, NIST had to prove that fire temperatures in the plane impact zone were way above the maximum for an ordinary diffuse-flame, oxygen-starved office fire of 650°C, a temperature at which the tower's steel framework would lose only half its strength.

NIST attempted to do that by fire-testing real life models, in combination with the use of that computer model for predicting fire development that was mentioned earlier—the so-called Fire Dynamics Simulator (FDS). From that FDS model, NIST determined that fire temperatures in the North Tower impact zone approached 1000°C, which weakened the steel enough to cause collapse.[527]

However, there were problems with NIST's approach. One is that the real life models it constructed and fire-tested were of small compartmentalized rooms, not the wide-open spaces that existed in the office areas of the North Tower.[528] Secondly, the Fire Dynamics Simulator that NIST used was originally designed for predicting fire development in "industrial fires," not an office fire in a huge building like the North Tower.[529] As a result, according to NIST's own report, "the [FDS] model had to be re-written," and that new model would be used for the first time in this analysis.[530] Thirdly, fire-testing of real-life mockups of the composite floor system of the towers were only done on the 18-foot east/west spans, not the 60-foot southside ones that NIST said sagged.[531] And they failed to replicate the institute's theory for collapse. Finally, the copious amount of black smoke present indicates that the fires were most likely burning at less than 650°C, where steel loses half its strength. With the building designed with a factor of safety of 3, that would have no effect on the integrity of its steel framework.[532]

Due to all of this, NIST's slight-of-hand "finding" that there were extraordinarily high fire temperatures in the North Tower can be discounted as being an unproven red herring; as noted previously, that could only have been proven by metallurgical testing of the steel, which was never done.

As for the physical damage, this is how NIST described the effect that the plane crash had on the North Tower's support columns: "The impact of the aircraft into WTC 1 substantially degraded the strength of the structure to withstand additional loading and also made the building more susceptible to fire-induced failure."[533] But a deeper look at the actual design of the tower reveals that this statement is an exaggeration. Even if one accepts NIST's own estimate of the number of columns destroyed by the plane crash, it can be shown that due to the high factor of safety built into the tower's design, the load bearing capacity of the remaining support columns was still very substantial, and they could easily withstand the temperatures that are normal to an ordinary diffuse-flame office fire.

To begin with, as noted in the Introduction, the North Tower had a factor of safety of at least 5.40 in the perimeter columns and at least 1.80 in the core columns.[534] This means that its perimeter and core columns could handle 540 percent and 180 percent of their actual gravity load, respectively.[535] And by NIST's own reckoning, there was a very low percentage of both perimeter and core columns lost due to the plane crash.

The number of perimeter columns lost was determined by visually examining the many photographs that were taken of the plane impact hole. By overlaying a plane damage photo over the design of the north face of the tower, one can see exactly which perimeter columns had been compromised. In the case of NIST, that process resulted in the following illustration.

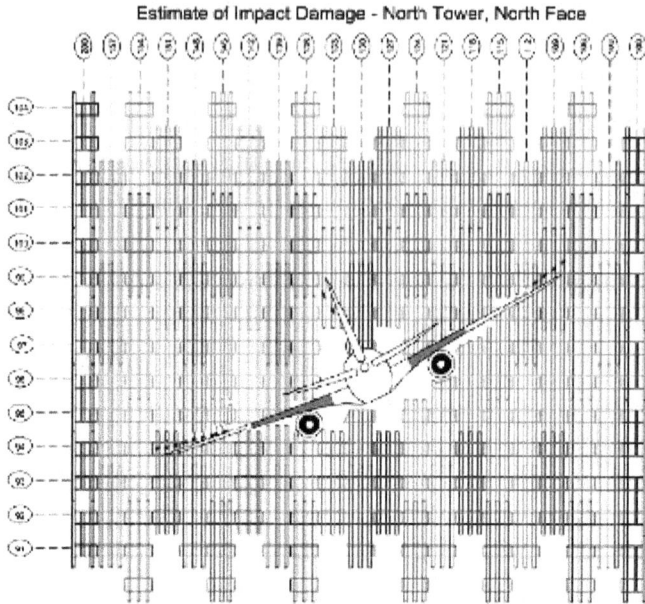

Estimate of Impact Damage - North Tower, North Face

Figure E–1. A scaled outline of a Boeing 767-200ER is superimposed on the damage diagram for the north face of WTC 1. The position of the aircraft has been adjusted to best match the damage pattern and marks showing where the wing tips and vertical stabilizer struck. The red areas correspond to the approximate locations of fuel on the aircraft based on an analysis reported elsewhere (NCSTAR 1-2B).

Actual Impact Damage
Source: NIST

In this way, NIST deduced that there were "35 exterior columns severed. 2 heavily damaged."[536] How much of the two heavily damaged columns remained is not noted, but if we consider them damaged beyond any useful load bearing capacity, that would give 37 perimeter columns incapable of bearing a load. And that would result in a conservative figure for a calculation of the reserve load bearing capacity of the columns that survived.

Including the 4 corner columns, there were 240 perimeter columns at any one floor level of the tower. So, if there were 37 missing, that would represent about a 15 percent loss of their total load bearing capacity. If the original factor of safety of the perimeter columns was 5.4, then the factor of safety after the crash would have been [5.40 − (.15 x 5.40)] or 4.59, which is still a very comfortable number.

Even if the temperature of the perimeter columns in the plane impact zone that survived the plane crash reached the maximum of 650°C that could be expected in the black smoke-laden, hydrocarbon-based fires that occurred in the towers, the columns' structural integrity would not have been fatally affected. That is because, again, when steel reaches 650°C, it only loses about half its strength. And that still would have left the surviving perimeter columns with a remaining factor of safety 4.59/2, or 2.30, which means that they still would have been able to carry more than twice the actual gravity load. So, as far as the integrity of the overall structure goes, the damage done to the perimeter columns was not substantial.

Determining how many of the core columns were lost due to the crash presented a more difficult problem because the inner columns were obscured by smoke and debris and could not be seen from the outside of the building.

North Tower Impact Hole
Copyright: Robert Robanne/Corbis/AP

So NIST turned to computer simulations. Note the following plan. It shows the results of the final simulation for the plane crash on the North Tower's 96th floor—the floor where the most severe damage occurred.

NORTH

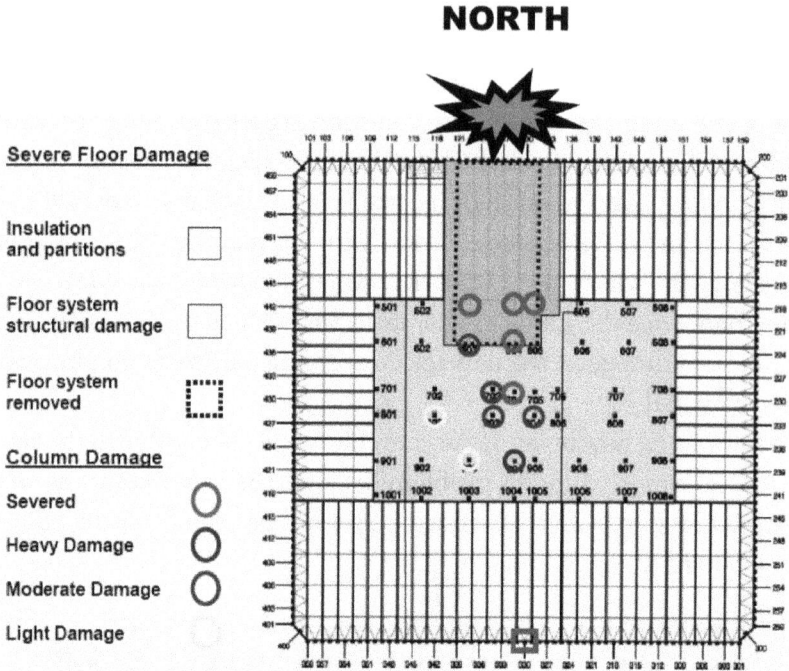

Figure 2–4. Simulation of aircraft impact damage to the 96th floor in WTC 1.

Case B Impact Damage
Source: NIST

NIST called this "Case B," which, according to the report, was "an account that is believed to be close to what actually occurred." In actual fact, however, a close reading of the report reveals that the data fed into this model for plane impact—speed of the plane, its weight and angle of approach, etc.—were, by NIST's own reckoning, exaggerated and overestimated. (This is discussed more fully in the next section.) But using the result of this simulation in the present analysis will yield an extremely conservative estimate for the reduced factor of safety after the plane crash.

According to this simulation, 5 core columns would have been completely severed by the plane crash. The wording in the report, however, presents a contradiction that needs to be noted. At one point, the report says there were "6 core columns severed." At other times, the number is reported as "5 or 6." To further stay on the conservative side, the number 6 will be used here.

The NIST report also notes that, in this Case B analysis, 9 other core columns on floors 93 to 98 suffered heavy to moderate damage. To be even more conservative, consider that all of those were damaged beyond any load bearing capacity. So, considering that there were a total of 47 original core columns, and 15 of them were fatally damaged by plane impact and unable to carry any load, that would mean that about 32 percent of the total combined load bearing capacity of the core columns was eliminated due to the plane crash. Therefore, the overall factor of safety of the core area support columns that remained after the crash would be [1.80 – (.32 x 1.80)], or 1.23, which is still a comfortable number. They could still hold 123 percent of the actual gravity load. Therefore, just as was the case with the perimeter columns, the loss of core columns due to the plane crash was not significant, and, *absent any extraordinary fire conditions,* the building would be expected to remain standing, indefinitely.

2. The Low Fire Temperatures

In the case of those core columns noted above that survived the plane crash, if the temperature of the oxygen-starved, hydrocarbon-based office fire in the tower reached its potential high mark in the area of 650°C, that could have caused a problem, because, at that point, those core columns would have lost about half their strength, leaving them with a factor of safety below parity of 1.23/2, or 0.62, which would make them susceptible to failure. However, the following four categories of evidence say that did not happen.

The Paint-cracking Study

The results of a so-called "paint-cracking study" done by NIST field investigators indicated that the temperature of the core columns in the plane impact zone of the North Tower never exceeded even 250°C, a temperature level which has no effect on the strength of steel.

This method of arriving at probable steel temperatures did not involve intricate computer simulations or complicated engineering calculations.

It simply involved observing the cracking patterns in the factory-applied primer paint on the 16 perimeter panels and 2 pieces of core columns that NIST said were saved from the North Tower's plane impact zone. The following photographs show the results of that study.

No burn
faint cracks from drying of paint   1 mm

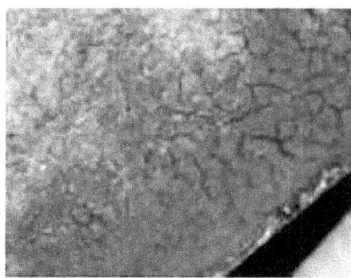

250 °C for an hour
mud cracks much more visible

The Paint-Cracking Study
Source: NIST

NIST's investigators observed the following:

Of the more than 170 areas examined on (the) 16 perimeter column panels, only three columns had evidence that the steel reached temperatures above 250°C...Only two core column specimens had sufficient paint remaining to make such an analysis, and their temperatures did not reach 250°C.[537]

Regarding the three columns that had evidence of temperatures above 250°C, the report said the high temperatures were only found in isolated spots on those columns—one spot for each column. Thus, they were insignificant as evidence of what might have caused the building to collapse.[538]

As for the core columns: The paint-cracking tests showed that their temperatures also did not reach the 300°C threshold where they would begin to lose strength.[539] Accordingly, it is reasonable to assume that after the plane crash, the factor of safety of the core columns in the area of the plane impact zone would remain at about 1.23. And that should have been sufficient to keep them from failing, because they still should have been able to carry at least 123 percent of their actual gravity load.

So, as was the case with the perimeter columns, the damage done to the core columns was not substantial.

As for the temperature that the steel floor trusses in the plane impact zone reached which caused them to sag, that cannot be definitively determined because none of those were specifically noted as being saved or tested by either FEMA or NIST before they were destroyed by Giuliani's recycling program. However, one can logically assume that, if the two pieces of core columns in the plane impact zone and the perimeter columns around the impact hole showed no sign of fatal steel temperatures, then the floor trusses located in that same area most likely would not, either. Also, due to the high factor of safety designed into the floor trusses, even if their temperature reached the maximum 650°C for a diffuse-flame, oxygen-starved office fire and they lost half their strength, they would not have sagged, at all. (This will be discussed more fully shortly.) So NIST's theory which says that it was the sagging of the south side floor trusses that initiated the collapse of the North Tower by pulling their perimeter columns inward cannot be correct.

Apparently, the paint-cracking study did not agree with NIST's preconceived notion of what caused the towers to collapse, because, oddly enough, it attempted to counter its own findings. The institute next said that the steel that was saved from around the North Tower's impact hole only represented less than 1 percent of the steel from that area and that it was, therefore, insufficient to make a general conclusion as to the overall level of the heat to which the total steel framework in the plane impact zone was subjected.

But that is a false argument and only serves as a counterproductive diversion. Whether or not the results of the paint-cracking test truly give a general idea of the temperatures of the fires that were widespread in the building is not the point. The point is that the results of the paint-cracking study should have been enough to spur NIST on to at least consider an alternative cause of the collapse and test the steel it inherited from FEMA for residues of explosives. Instead, the institute hastily ruled out the possibility that explosives might have been involved. The question is, why?

The Cardington Tests

A series of tests performed by British Steel (BS)—well-known in the civil engineering community as the Cardington Tests—directly refutes NIST's collapse sequence hypothesis.

Starting in 1994, BS began conducting fire stress tests at a facility in Cardington, England on a mock-up of a steel-framed structure with a concrete and steel composite floor system comparable to that of the twin towers. Their tests were conducted at temperatures that ranged upwards to 650°C, which would be expected as the upper limit for a normal, everyday hydrocarbon-fed office fire. The tests ran for two hours, which most building codes specify for fire resistance tests. While the steel was observed to have lost 50 percent of its strength under those conditions, and there was buckling (sagging) of the concrete/steel floor slab system, it did not lead to total collapse of the structure.

The Cardington results were publicized in a book, *Structural Performance of Redundant Structures under Local Fires*, which said,

In structures such as the composite steel frame at Cardington, the [floor] slab strongly restrains the thermal expansion strains and thus consequently develops large membrane compression and tension forces in the composite steel-concrete floor system. The membrane compressions can be limited by the large downward deflections which occur through thermo-mechanical post-buckling effects and thermal bowing (these are nonlinearly additive). The resulting behavior is then a combination of displacement and other responses. The heated steel part of this composite [floor] system, if unprotected, rapidly reaches its axial capacity (through local buckling and strength degradation), and produces a beneficial effect by limiting and then reducing the total membrane compression, so by allowing increased expansion of the steel through softening and ductility. This is clearly a desirable behavior here, as it reduces the force imposed on the structure by the expansion forces and allows the damage to be localized.

Simply put, this report says that that the sagging of a concrete and steel composite floor system under stress from a fire actually is a good thing, as far as the survivability of the structure goes. It says nothing about the initial axial compressions due to expansion in the floor system turning into a tension-type effect that might pull a column inward, as NIST says happened in the North Tower.

A PhD thesis by Susan Lamont at the University of Edinburgh confirmed these results. Her paper, entitled, "The Behavior of Multi-story Composite Steel Framed Structures in Response to Compartment Fires" says,

In composite floor slabs, buckling [sagging] of the steel beams as a result of large compressions induced by restrained thermal expansion was a positive event. The buckle allows the increase in length, as a result of thermal expansion, to be accommodated in downward deflections relieving axial compressions.[540]

The University of Edinburgh's School of Civil and Environmental Engineering took specific note of the Cardington experiments in their paper, "Behavior of Steel Framed Structures under Fire Conditions," which concludes that "despite deflections of structural members affected by fire, runaway type failures did not occur in real frame structures when subjected to realistic fires."[541]

The lead investigators for the two Bush administration studies of the WTC collapses—Gene Corley, in the case of FEMA, and Sivaraj Shyam-Sunder, in the case of NIST—both had PhDs in structural engineering, and it is impossible to believe that they were unaware of these well-known tests which directly contradict their theories for the unprecedented collapses at the WTC.

Historical Examples

Just as the Cardington tests predicted would be the case, there are many real-life examples that support the claim that a steel-framed structure such as the North Tower is entirely capable of enduring fiercely burning fires for several hours without collapsing.

1. The North Tower itself had a fire in 1975.[542] That fire burned for three hours and sent sixteen people to the hospital for smoke inhalation. It involved six floors and was fought by 132 firefighters. A *New York Times* article on the event said that "flames could be seen pouring out of the 11ᵗʰ floor windows" on the east side of the building. And although the fire spread to the core, the only damage "was confined to electrical wiring." There was no damage to the steel structure from this fire, and, obviously, the building did not collapse.

2. One Meridian Plaza in Philadelphia had a fire in 1991.[543] It gutted nine floors of a 38-story skyscraper and killed three firefighters. It was fought for eleven hours before the fire department gave up trying to put it out. Philadelphia officials called it "the most significant fire in this century." There was $100 million in property damage, but no collapse.

3. The First Interstate Bank Building in Los Angeles had a fire in 1988.[544] It was called the worst high-rise fire in the city's history. A total of sixty-four fire companies fought it for three and a half hours. It gutted five floors. Property damage was estimated at $200 million. But again, there was no collapse.

4. There was a fire at the Beijing Mandarin Oriental Hotel, in Beijing, China, on February 9, 2009.[545] That building had an atrium that went up the center of the building for its full 520-foot height. Basically, it had a hollow shell interior, like a fireplace chimney. But despite being fully engulfed in fire from top to bottom, it did not collapse.

Some supporters of the official story say that the examples given of fires in other tall buildings are not analogous to the WTC collapses because they did not suffer any structural loss due to being hit by an airplane. But as has been shown, it is also true that the structural damage sustained by the towers as a result of the plane crashes was insignificant due to their uncommonly-high factor of safety.

Dr. Jonathon Barnett, PhD—the professor of fire engineering at WPI who was the lead investigator for the FEMA team that discovered the possibility of thermate at the WTC that was recorded as Appendix C of the report—said this about the WTC collapses:

> We have a long history of successful steel construction in this country, and, in fact, the world. And one of the great successes is that, under normal fire conditions, we don't have building collapse. In fact, until 9/11, I was unaware of any protected steel structure that had collapsed, anywhere in the world.[546]

The Photographic and Audio Record of Witnesses

A couple key photographs taken of the North Tower on 9/11 and at least one audio recording of a conversation that occurred between firefighters who were high up in the South Tower strongly indicate that the fires in both of those buildings were not uniform across any one floor level, nor were they hot enough to affect the strength of steel. Accordingly, the collapse of those buildings should not have occurred. Furthermore, even if fire was the cause of the collapses (which is highly unlikely), they should have been asymmetric and not straight downward, as seen in the videos.

The North Tower: NIST's explanation for the collapse of the North Tower says that, due to an unusually intense fire that was fed by jet fuel, part of the composite concrete/steel floor truss system on the south side, between floors 95 and 99, sagged to such an extent that they pulled their perimeter support columns inward and that is what began the sequence of structural failures in the plane impact zone that resulted in the top block of twenty floors crushing the ninety floors below it straight downward, at freefall speed.

In the first place, however, according to NIST's own "most reasonable" estimate of the plane impact damage, the fires on the south side of the North Tower were not fed by jet fuel to any significant extent. When describing what happened after Flight 11 hit the north side of the building, the report says:

The aircraft fuel cloud began to spread out after impact but remained relatively dense until the leading edge of the fuel reached the tower core. The aircraft fuel and debris cloud eventually penetrated most of the distance through the core before their motions were halted.[547]

What the report is saying here is that jet fuel was not a significant factor in feeding the south side fires because the "aircraft fuel and debris cloud" was "halted" while still in the building's core area. And if jet fuel that was dispersed in the form of a cloud—in other words, in gaseous state—did not make it through the core, it is hard to see how liquid jet fuel could. Thus, right off the bat, NIST's other claim which says that the fires on the south side of the North Tower after plane impact were abnormally high due to being fed by large amounts of jet fuel is suspect.

Secondly, visual evidence shows that the fires between the 95th and 99th floors were not uniform, and thus, even if by some peculiar twist of fate fire was the cause of the collapse, the tower should have come down unevenly or asymmetrically.

That is substantiated by the following illustrations that were presented in NIST's own report.[548] In them, the "fire" bars indicate the positions where flames could be seen in the hundreds of various photographs and videos taken during the indicated time periods, while the tower stood.

This first set is for the "North Face."

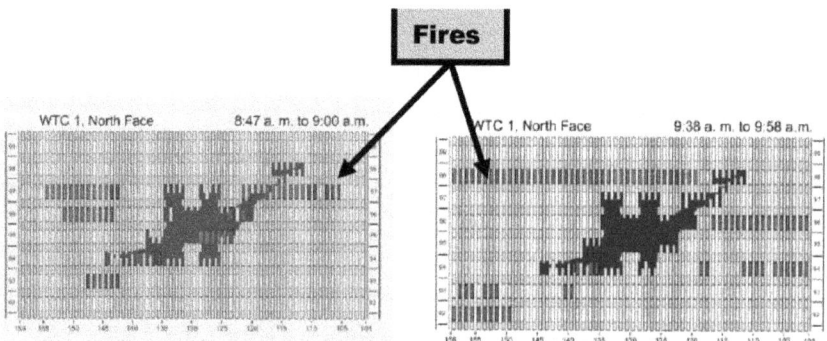

North Tower Plane Impact Zone Fires

Source: NIST

These show that in the one-hour period after the plane crash—from 8:47 to 9:58 a.m.—the fires were spotty. They were flaring up and burning down, just as any fire would normally be expected to do; consuming fuel wherever it could find it.

The following illustrations show basically the same thing on the east, south and west faces.

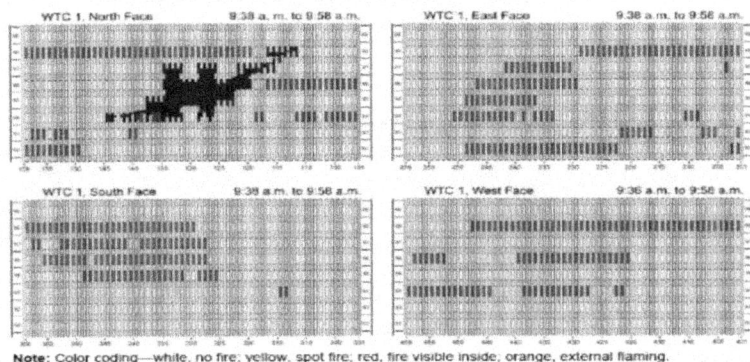

Note: Color coding—white, no fire; yellow, spot fire; red, fire visible inside; orange, external flaming.

Figure 2–7. Representation of exterior views of the fires on the four faces of WTC 1 from about 9:38 a.m. to 9:58 a.m.

North Tower Fires: All Faces
Source: NIST

The notion that the fires in the plane impact zone were uniformly spread across a whole floor area is also contradicted by the following photographs that were taken that day. First, note the following one. It was taken at 10:28 a.m., just before the collapse. It shows that the south side of the 96th floor was, indeed, substantially engulfed in flames, at that point.[549]

249

North Tower: 10:28 a.m.
Copyright: Ray Stubblebine/Corbis/AP

But the following photograph, which was taken at about that same time, shows that fires in the plane impact zone on the north side of the building—where the huge fireballs occurred upon plane impact—had actually died out. In fact, while the fires were raging on the south side of the 96th floor, the plane impact hole on the north side had cooled to the point where a woman was able to walk right up to it and stand there.

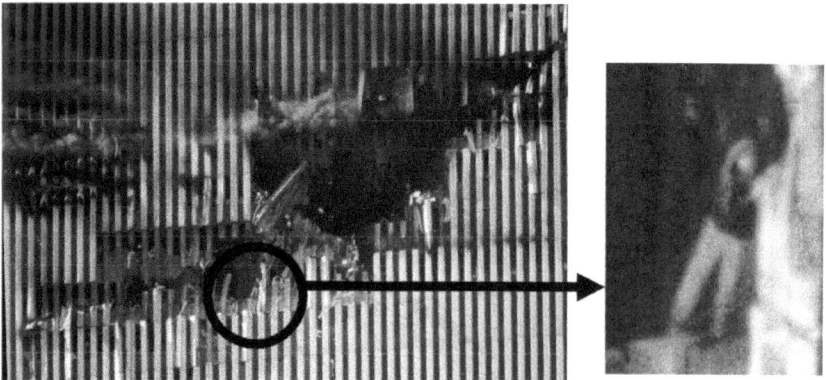

North Tower Plane Impact Hole
Copyright: Roberto Robanne/Corbis/AP

She is standing at the 94th floor. And above her, the 96th floor also shows no sign of fire. So how could the whole 96th floor have been completely and uniformly involved in fire? Clearly, it never was. This shows that the fires in the plane impact zone actually died down in one area after having burnt up their fuel supply of office materials and then flared up in another area. Just as one would expect from an ordinary office fire, it was consuming fuel wherever it could find it. Thus, the steel support columns in the plane impact zone could not all have been subjected to the same degree of heat at the same time and could not uniformly have lost the same amount of strength, all at once.

The conclusion is that there had to be some other forces acting on the structure that conditioned it to go straight downward. And that leads to the strong possibility that explosives were expertly planted in the building.

The South Tower: As mentioned in the Introduction, FDNY Battalion Chief Orio J. Palmer was one of the true heroes of 9/11.

**FDNY Battalion Chief
Orio J. Palmer**
Source: FDNY

A tape recording of his firsthand reports from the plane impact zone of the South Tower proves that the fires there were not hot enough to affect the strength of steel, nor were they uniform enough across any one floor area to have caused the straight downward collapse of that building, either.[550]

Affectionately described by friends as health nut, Palmer was a marathon runner in terrific shape. He first took an elevator to the 40th floor and then started hiking up stairwells, trying to reach the plane impact zone, which began at the 78th floor.[551] The following part of the transcript of the tape starts at 9:48 a.m., when he reached the 74th floor. There were a couple of other groups of firefighters making their way up to him. One of those was Ladder Company 15.

> Ladder 15: What do ya got up there, Chief?
> Palmer: I'm standing in Boy stairway on the 74th floor. No smoke or fire problem. The walls are breached so be careful.
> Ladder 15: Yea, 10-4. I saw that on 68. We're on 71. We're coming up behind ya.
> Palmer: OK...six more to go.
> Ladder 15: Let me know when you see fire.
> *9:51:03*
>
> Ladder 15: One Five to Battalion 7.
> Palmer: Battalion 7.
> Ladder 15: What floor you on, Orio?
> Palmer: Stairway on 75. Go to the south stairway and continue up.

The south stairway was the A Stairway.

> Ladder 15: 10-4.
> *9:52:43*

When Palmer reached the plane impact zone at the 78th floor and exited the A stairwell, his voice suddenly turned frantic.

Palmer: Battalion...We got...Ladder One Five, we've got two
            to three pockets of fire. We should be able to knock it down
            with two lines. Rad...Radi...Radio that. 78th floor, numerous
            10-45 Code Ones.

"10-45 Code Ones" means dead and injured civilians.

Ladder 15: What floor you on, Orio?
Palmer: (No response)
Ladder 15: One Five to Battalion 7.
Palmer: Go ahead One Five.
Ladder 15: Chief, what stair you in?
Palmer: South stairway, Adam. South Tower.
Ladder 15: Floor 78?
Palmer: 10-4. Numerous civilians injured. Two engines up here.
Ladder 15: 10-4. We're on our way up.

7-Alpha was a part of Palmer's battalion. They were on a lower floor.

7 Alpha to Lobby Command Post: Chief Palmer on the 78th floor.
    Numerous 10-45 Code Ones. We got an isolated pocket of
    fire and need at least two hand lines up there, K.
9:54:40

Palmer: Battalion 7 to Ladder One Five.
Ladder 15: One Five.
Palmer: I'm gonna need your firefighters, Adam stairway, to
            knock down two fires. Get a... house line stretched.
            We can get some water on it and knock it down. K?

The "house lines" were water standpipes located in the stairwells on
each floor and equipped with 145-foot long hoses.[552]

Ladder 15: Alright. 10-4. We're coming up the stairs. We're on 77
now, on the B stairs. We'll be right to ya.
9:55:06

Palmer: One Five OV. One Five.

According to the transcript, at 9:57:51, about five minutes after Palmer said he encountered "two to three pockets of fire" that were manageable, the amplitude on his radio channel suddenly "drops to zero."[553] In other words, the signal of the channel on which all of the foregoing conversations were heard was suddenly lost. It was as if someone had just turned off the system.

One minute and nine seconds later—at 9:59—the South Tower collapsed, killing Palmer and everyone else inside.

There are a couple of conclusions that can be drawn from Chief Palmer's account. In the first place, photographs taken that day (which were later printed in the NIST report) agree with his observations. They show that the fires in the South Tower's plane impact zone, in the time period leading up to the collapse, were not uniform.[554] They were spotty, at best, indicating that, if fire caused the collapse, it should have been asymmetric. But that stands in stark contradiction to the videos, which show the building coming uniformly straight downward.

Secondly, Palmer's reports indicate that he was near the area where the plane went through the building, and that the fires there were not as hot as NIST would like to think they were. The blueprints of the North Tower show that the A Stairwell at the 78th floor was located in the east end of the rectangular-shaped core area.[555] It is also known that the South Tower had, for all practical purposes, that same design, except that, at the WTC site, its footprint was rotated 90° counterclockwise with respect to the North Tower.[556] This means that when Palmer exited the A stairwell of the South Tower at the 78th floor, he was in the north end of the core, furthest away from where the plane hit, which was at the southeast corner, but close to where it came out— the northeast corner.[557] This confirms that the fires in the plane impact zone were not uniform across the whole floor area and not nearly hot enough to uniformly weaken the steel framework of the building to cause a straight-downward, gravity-driven collapse. Otherwise, Palmer could not have stayed in that area, and the victims he encountered that were alive would not have been merely "injured." They would have been fried.

And thirdly, there is an air of mystery about Palmer's death that is yet to be adequately explained. The official account is that the steel framework of the towers was fatally weakened over time by intensely burning fires, and that is what precipitated their collapse. According to that, one would expect that the North Tower would come down first, because it was hit first and burned longer. Yet the South Tower was first to go. That development is puzzling unless you consider the possibility of controlled demolition.

Some go so far as to say that Palmer wrote his own death warrant by reporting back that the fires in the South Tower were manageable. For instance, imagine yourself as the conspirator who had his or her finger on the computer control console and was supposed to start the series of explosions that was going to collapse the North Tower first, which would have been the original plan since it was hit first. You would, of course, have your radio tuned to listen to the reports coming over Palmer's frequency, which was the fire department's main channel for communicating with firefighters who were high up in the buildings. Palmer's reports, however, would have made you increasingly anxious that he and his firefighters might be able to extinguish the fires. If that was allowed to happen, your cover story would be blown, because how could fires cause a collapse, if there were no fires? So you would have been more or less forced to alter the original plan and prematurely demolish the South Tower first.

This lends a conspiratorial aspect to Palmer's death that has never been investigated.

In summary, as noted in the Introduction, the fires in the plane impact zone were dying down when Palmer radioed back that they were manageable. This supports the charge that fire did not initiate the series of structural failures that resulted in the collapse of the South Tower. There had to be some other force involved. And the most likely cause of that additional force was explosives.

3. The Inadequate Pulling Force

NIST determined the amount of pulling force that it said the North Tower's south side floor trusses exerted on their perimeter columns. But when that force is compared to the actual load on each of those columns, it appears to be wholly inadequate to have displaced a column to any degree, at all. Additionally, when one considers the very high factor of safety built into the floor trusses, even if their temperature reached the 650°C maximum for the oxygen-starved WTC fires and they lost half their strength, they still would not have buckled. Thus, no extraordinary pulling force could have developed, as NIST claims.

Instead of building a life-like test model of the south side 60-foot long floor system and testing that model under realistic conditions to determine the amount of the pulling force, which would have been the preferred method, NIST resorted to the use of a series of computer simulations. [558] Those simulations had this as one of its results:

The sagging of [south side] trusses resulted in approximately 14 kips of inward pull per truss seat on the attached perimeter column.[559]

(Note: In another section of the final report the exact figure for this force was pinpointed as being 14.8 kips, or 14,800 pounds, since one kip equals 1,000 pounds). To stay on the conservative side, the higher figure will be used in this analysis)

First, the only physical evidence that NIST ever presented to confirm that columns were actually pulled inward was a photograph taken of the south face of the building minutes before collapse.[560] When it measured the amount of inward deflections of the perimeter columns as seen in that picture, NIST came up with figures that ranged upwards to a maximum of 55 inches.[561] But this determination stands in distinct contradiction to a finding of the FEMA investigation. At one point in that investigation, FEMA engineers calculated that a perimeter column would become unstable and buckle if it was brought only 4½ inches out of alignment at its end splice connection.[562] According to that, none of the columns on the south side of the building should have been able to deflect the 55 inches that NIST said one of them did.

In fact, many skeptics say that the image in the photograph is merely an optical illusion due to light being refracted by the heat coming off the building and the angle that photo was taken from, and that it is not a true representation of what really happened.

Secondly, it is known that the perimeter columns of the tower were uniformly stressed at 15,000 psi (psi means pounds per square inch).[563] It is also known that above the 89th floor all the perimeter columns were box-shaped, 14 inches square and were fabricated from 1/4 inch steel plate.[564] That gave them a steel cross-sectional area of 13.25 square inches. This means that each of the perimeter columns at the south side floor area was carrying an actual gravity load of 199 kips (15 x 13.25) or 199,000 pounds. Therefore, the 14.8 kip pulling force on the column would amount to only 7.4 % of the actual gravity load on that column. On its face, it doesn't seem possible that a relatively small pulling force like that could have any success in even budging a perimeter column.

Even if the temperature of the steel column reached the 650°C maximum for diffuse-flame fires and it lost half of its strength that would not make it more vulnerable to the pulling force. This is due to the fact that the tower's perimeter columns were made of 12 grades of high strength steel, ranging from 45 ksi to 100 ksi.[565] This means that their minimum ultimate load bearing *capacity* was 596 kips (45 x 13.25). Even a 50% loss of strength due to a 650°C fire (like in the towers) would leave them with a load bearing capacity of about 298 kips, and they only had to carry 199.

Thirdly, NIST tried to buttress its argument by saying that 20% of the south side floor truss to perimeter column connections on floors 97 and 98 failed, which effectively increased the length of the columns due to the loss of horizontal support, causing them to become unstable. But by saying that, NIST conveniently ignored a couple of important factors having to do with the high factor of safety of the floor trusses and their bolted connections to the perimeter columns. It is known from the NIST report itself that the floor trusses had a factor of safety of at least 2.0, and the bolts that fastened them to their respective perimeter columns were "much stronger" than required.[566] In the case of the floor trusses, the factor of safety was further increased due to the additional fact that their manufacturer, Laclede Steel, fabricated them out of high strength 50 ksi steel instead of the 36 ksi steel that was called for by the designers.[567] This means that even if the fire reached the 650°C maximum for a hydrocarbon-based, black smoke-laden, diffuse fire and the floor trusses on floors 97 and 98 lost half their strength, they would still be able to carry their actual predicted load without sagging to a degree that would cause their bolted connections to the perimeter columns to fail.

Fourthly, NIST's collapse theory conveniently ignores the additional structural element of the tower's design that was provided by the spandrel plates. The spandrel plates attached all of the perimeter columns together around the total perimeter of the building in the horizontal direction, at every floor level.[568] Those plates, which were 52 inches wide, formed what is called a Vierendeel truss with the columns. A Vierendeel truss is one that is simply supported at both ends and does not have diagonals. They were specifically designed into the tower as a redundancy should the tower be hit by a plane. One of their functions was to transfer the vertical loads of columns that might be destroyed by a plane crash to other surviving columns surrounding the defect that would be made in the wall. Taking that into consideration, if some columns were pulled inward by the sagging floor trusses to the point where they could not support a load, their loads would have been taken up by the columns that survived on both sides of the affected area, as the spandrels transferred the loads out to them.

And the extra load put on those surviving columns would have been well within their load bearing capacity to withstand due to the high factor of safety of their design. In fact, it has been calculated that, even if all of the perimeter columns on one side of the building at one floor level and several others on the adjacent sides were completely removed, it would have no effect on the structural integrity of the building.[569]

As was shown previously, NIST's estimate of the number of perimeter columns "severed" by the crash of Flight 11 into the North Tower was only 37 of the 59 that were on the north face. According to the calculations, this should have had no effect on the structural integrity of the building.

258

And, indeed, it did not, as is evidenced by the fact that the building remained standing for 102 minutes after the crash.

This would also hold for the perimeter columns that were allegedly pulled inward on the south side. Assuming for the moment that the photograph NIST used to prove that column deflection is not an optical illusion, it clearly shows that not all of the south-side perimeter columns were bent inward. There appears to be 4 on the east side of the affected area that remained straight and 9 on the west side.[570] Since there were 59 columns on each side of the tower, that means 46 were bowed inward and in danger of failing (59 − 13). But the loads carried by those missing columns could have easily been transferred out to the surviving columns halfway on east and west faces through Vierendeel action.

For instance, consider that there were 59 perimeter columns on each of the four sides of the tower. As previously mentioned, the set gravity load on each of those columns was 199 kips, or 199,000 pounds. So, if you are looking down on those columns from the top, you find that the total gravity load on all of those columns that were on the southern *half* of the tower was no more than about 199 x (29 (east face) + 59 (south face) + 29 (west face)), or 23,283 kips. The perimeter columns were all high strength and rated from 45 ksi up to 100 ksi. To be conservative here, consider that they were all of the lower strength. But stressing 45 ksi steel columns to only 15 ksi (or, 15,000 psi) gives them a huge factor of safety of 5.4, which means that the load bearing *capacity* of those columns on the southern half would have been 5.4 x 23,283, or 125,728 kips. The capacity of the 46 columns which appear to be bent inward on the south side in the photograph would have been only 5.4 x 199 x 46, or 49,431 kips. If they were lost, that would still leave a *reserve* load bearing capacity of the remaining perimeter columns on the southern half of 125,728−49,431, or 76,297 kips.

Even if their temperature did reach the uniformly distributed maximum of 650°C and they lost half their strength, the resulting load bearing capacity of those perimeter columns on the southern half that survived would have been 76,297/2, or 38,148 kips, which would still have been way above the 23,283 total kips of actual gravity load. This would have mitigated the possibility of collapse.

The same logic would hold for the northern half of the tower. It is clear from the photos that the plane crash took out less perimeter columns than what was claimed to have been bent inward on the south side. Therefore, the net reserve capacity of those columns that survived on the northern half would have been even more than on the southern half. This would also have mitigated the possibility of collapse.

But what about the core columns? Were they weakened enough by the plane crash and subsequent fires that the core could not hold up its share of the load? It is known that the core columns were also stressed at 15 ksi, but there is not enough information in the plans that have been released to determine their plate thickness or their shapes at the North Tower's 96th floor plane impact zone. So, it is not possible to calculate the net reserve capacity of the core, after the crash. But the results of the paint-cracking study and the amount of black smoke coming from the tower are both very strong indicators that those columns never reached 300°C, the temperature at which steel starts to lose strength. These have to be considered determining factors since neither of the Bush investigations ever presented any reliable hard evidence to the contrary.

Accordingly, the overall factor of safety of the total core area after the crash most likely would have remained at 1.23, as previously calculated. Thus, they should not have collapsed because they would have been able to carry 123 percent of their actual gravity load. Taken together with the perimeter column study, this strongly indicates that the North Tower could not have collapsed without the use of explosives.

In summary, this brief overview gives the impression that NIST was desperate to grasp on to anything that might convince the casual reader of its report that the tower could collapse without the use of explosives. If the institute had built and tested a realistic model of the 60-foot south side floor truss system and demonstrated how a comparatively measly 14.8 kip pulling force on a perimeter column could initiate a series of structural failures fatal to the whole building, its case might have some legs. But the likely reason why NIST did not attempt to do such a simple thing was because it knew its theory for collapse was bogus.

Manipulated Computer Simulations

With the paint-cracking study failing to confirm the official explanation for the North Tower collapse, one would think that NIST, if it was being honest, would have begun to look for some other cause that more reasonably fits the totality of the evidence, such as, for instance, explosives. But instead, the institute took a drastic tack. It went off in search of a hypothetical computer simulation of the North Tower plane crash that might establish the "fact" that it was, indeed, extremely high steel temperatures that initiated the tower's collapse. It was at this point that the investigation began to take on the unmistakable characteristics of a cover-up.

A standard principle of fire engineering dictates that the fire temperature levels in the WTC towers would have been directly proportional to the amount of interior structural damage that occurred due to the plane crashes. This is so because the intensity of the fire depended largely on the free flow of air/oxygen through the openings in the interior of the buildings. So the first step in this kind of analysis would be then to establish how much interior damage was caused by the impact of the planes. But the actual, real-life interior damage was obscured by smoke and debris and could not be observed. So, NIST turned to computer modeling in an attempt to approximate it.

But from the start of this phase of their investigation, its approach was fraught with uncertainties. NIST's report admits as much, saying,

> The analysis of aircraft impacts into the WTC towers was subject to uncertainties in the input parameters such as...aircraft speed, horizontal and vertical angles of incidence, orientation and locations of impact...high strain rate material constitutive behavior and failure criteria for the towers and aircraft...aircraft mass and stiffness properties and the jet fuel distribution...[as well as] tower parameters: structural strength and mass distribution, connection and joint positions relative to impact and joint failure behavior... [and] nonstructural building contents that may share in absorbing energy by the aircraft impact.[571]

261

Therefore:

Because of the complexity of the problem and the limited number of parameters that could be varied in the global analyses, it was necessary to down-select a refined list of uncertainty parameters from all of the possible parameters.[572]

In other words, this phase of the investigation was going to have results that were highly uncertain due to the subjective nature of selecting parameters to input into the models.

But that did not stop this process. The report went on to describe the method NIST used to search for an internal structural damage estimate for later use in its so-called Fire Dynamics Simulator (FDS) model for determining resulting steel temperatures. The goal was to prove its theory that severe damage from the plane crash led to severe fires and extraordinarily high steel temperatures, which, in turn, weakened the building's steel frame and led to total collapse. In a search for that justification, the report says that several computer analyses were run:

The object of these analyses was to estimate the condition of the two WTC towers immediately following the aircraft impacts... The global impact simulations provided, for each tower, a range of damage estimates. These included a **base case** based on *reasonable* initial estimates of all input parameters, along with a **less severe** and **more severe** damage scenario.[573] (Italics/Highlights added)

Of course, one person's reasonableness is very often another person's annoyance. Moreover, if the base case parameters were "reasonable" estimates, doesn't that imply that the other two cases were not reasonable? Then, what could possibly have been the motive for even considering the "less" and "more" severe cases? This approach by NIST illustrates how desperate it was to find a set of conditions—no matter how unreasonable—that would support its preordained conclusion that the collapse of the tower did not need to involve explosives.

NIST began building its model for computer simulations by assessing the exterior damage to the North Tower as seen in photographs. According to NIST, "Matching the projected impact points of the wings, fuselage, engines and vertical stabilizer onto the exterior wall of each tower to the observed damage pattern was an important constraint in the determination of impact conditions."[574]

From photos of the impact hole in the tower, NIST developed the following illustration.

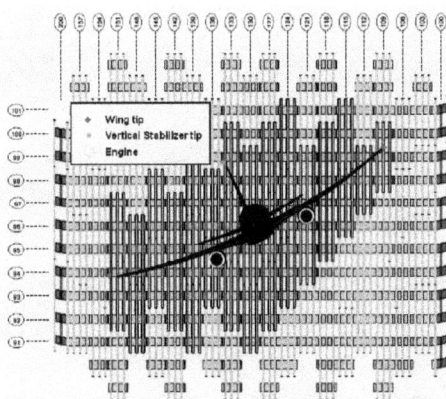

Flight 11 Orientation upon Impact
Source: NIST

In order to simulate what NIST called "global collapse" in the computer, NIST had to first develop digital models depicting the structural system of the building and the plane. They would then crash the digitalized model of the plane into the building model to arrive at an interior damage estimate. Their FDS program, would then use the resulting data from that as its parameters to get an estimate for fire development and resulting steel temperatures.

With respect to the North Tower, the only video showing the crash of Flight 11 was captured by Jules Naudet, an independent filmmaker who happened to be making a documentary in the area. His film provided the plane's vertical approach angle. The plane's speed was known from the FAA. And the attitude of the impact hole in tower provided the rest of the needed information. NIST Table E-8, below shows the results of all of those evaluations. It contains the values for the parameters that would be used to estimate the amount of interior damage caused by plane impact in the three computer models: The Base Case, the Less Severe Case, and the More Severe Case.[575]

Table E-8. Summary of refined aircraft impact conditions.

	AA 11 (WTC 1)	UAL 175 (WTC 2)
Impact Speed (mph)	443 ± 30	542 ± 24
Vertical Approach Angle (Velocity vector)	10.6° ± 3° below horizontal (heading downward)	6° ± 2° below horizontal (heading downward)
Lateral Approach Angle (Velocity vector)	180.3° ± 4° clockwise from Structure North	15° ± 2° clockwise from Structure North
Vertical Fuselage Orientation Relative to Trajectory	2° nose-up from the vertical approach angle	1° nose-up from the vertical approach angle
Lateral Fuselage Orientation Relative to Trajectory	0° clockwise from lateral approach angle	-3° clockwise from lateral approach angle
Roll Angle (left wing downward)	25° ± 2°	38° ± 2°

Aircraft Impact Conditions
Source: NIST

The Base Case model (the "reasonable" one), for example, used the impact speed of 443 mph, and the vertical approach angle was taken as 10.6° from the horizontal.

The values for the parameters of the More Severe case for plane impact were made relative to the Base Case. The report explained,

For the more severe case, the impact speed was increased to the upper bound obtained from analysis of aircraft impact conditions, while the aircraft vertical trajectory angle was reduced to impart more impact energy inward toward the core. A 5 percent increase in the total aircraft weight was considered for the more severe case, while failure strain was varied to be 125 percent of the baseline value *to inflict more damage on the towers.*[576] (Italics added)

NIST also manipulated the tower model for the More Severe Case. As the report explains,

For the tower model, the failure strains of the tower steels were reduced to 80 percent of the baseline value, and the mass of the building contents was reduced. These variations contributed to more severe damage to the tower structure, by *making the tower structure weaker and the aircraft structure stronger.*[577] (Italics added)

The parameters for all three impact conditions were fed into the respective computer models for impact simulations, to see what kind of interior structural damage would result from each. In all three cases, the results of the computer simulations showed that the predicted interior structural damage done by the plane impact was dramatic. In describing the Base Case simulation, the report reads as follows:

The aircraft impact response was dominated by the impact, penetration, and fragmentation of the airframe structures. The entire aircraft fully penetrated the tower at approximately 0.25 s [seconds]. The fuselage structures were severely damaged both from the penetration through the exterior columns and the penetration of the 96th floor slab that sliced the fuselage in half.

The downward trajectory of the aircraft structures caused the airframe to collapse against the floor, and the subsequent debris motion was redirected inward along a more horizontal trajectory parallel to the floor. The downward trajectory of the aircraft structures transferred sufficient vertical load such that the truss floor structures on the 95th and 96th floors collapsed in the impact zone.

The wing structures were completely fragmented by the exterior wall. The aircraft fuel cloud began to spread out after impact but remained relatively dense until the leading edge of the fuel reached the tower core. The aircraft fuel and debris cloud eventually penetrated most of the distance through the core before their motions were halted.

The aircraft was severely broken into debris as a result of the impact with the tower. At the end of the impact analysis, the aircraft was broken in thousands of debris fragments of various sizes and masses. Larger fragments still existed for specific components, such as the engines. At the end of the simulations, the port engine was still inside the core, and the starboard engine was roughly one third of the distance from the core to the south exterior wall. Each had a speed of less than 50 mph.[578]

So far, so good. However, at this point, NIST starts weaving questionable assertions into the narrative. These are so transparently meant to deceive that one might justifiably describe them as *"bald-faced lies."*

The Bald-faced Lies

These are highlighted in italics in the passage that follows:

The damage to the towers reached a steady state and *the motion of the debris was reduced to a level that was not expected to produce any significant increase in the impact damage.*

The exterior wall was the one structural system for which direct visual evidence of the impact damage was available. Therefore the comparison of the calculated and observed exterior wall damage provided a partial validation of the analysis methodologies used in the global impact analyses…*The comparison of the calculated and observed damage indicated that the geometry and location of the impact damage zone were in good agreement.*

The estimation of the damage to the core columns and core beams was important in determining the residual strength of the subsequent analyses of structural stability and collapse. The core had significant damage in the region close to the impact point. The columns in line with the aircraft fuselage failed on the impact side and several of the core beams were also severely damaged or failed in the impact zone.

A total of three columns failed, and four columns were heavily damaged...*Figure E-34 presents the cumulative damage on all affected floors and columns.*

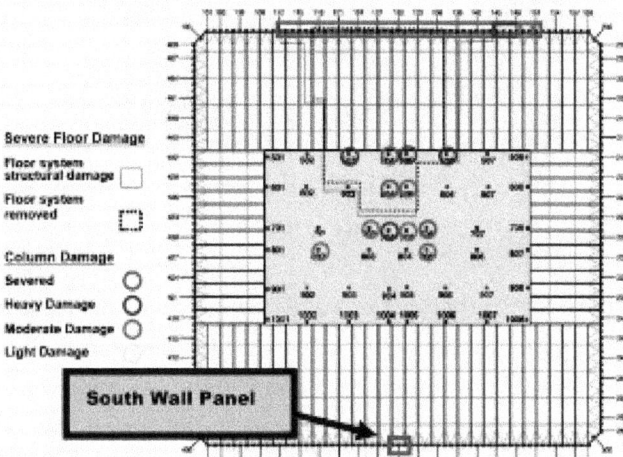

Figure E-34. Cumulative structural damage to the floors and columns of WTC 1 (base case).

Base Case
Source: NIST

These were used to identify slab openings in the fire dynamics simulations. Note the panel that was severed in the south wall of the tower. While *analysis did not capture the failure of the connections at the ends of this panel due to the coarse mesh of the south wall,* photographic evidence showed that this panel was knocked down by the impact.[579] (Italics added)

What NIST is referring to is this photograph of that *south wall panel* taken by the NYPD, proving that it was actually knocked out of the building.

South Wall Panel
Source: NYPD

The institute claims that this was due to being hit by the piece of landing gear from the plane that is seen lodged in the fallen panel. But, as NIST admits, their Base Case simulation did *not* show this occurring. The only proof they present that it did occur is the photo, which was taken after the fact. However, a deeper analysis of the situation indicates that it had to have been a very powerful explosive force that dislodged this panel, not the landing gear. (This will be explained shortly.)

What follows is a step-by-step analysis of the misleading statements in this passage.

Bald-faced Lie #1: *"...the motion of the debris was reduced to a level that was not expected to produce any significant increase in the impact damage."*

This statement is not true. The simulation was stopped 0.50 seconds after the plane impacted the building. At that point, according to the report, "the starboard engine was roughly one third of the distance from the core to the south exterior wall" and "had a speed of less than 50 mph." According to this, the engine was very close to the south wall and also had a lot of speed. NIST claims that a piece of landing gear knocked out the south wall panel, so could it be correct that this engine would not be "expected to produce any significant increase in the impact damage" even though it appears to be well on its way to hitting the south wall and presumably also knocking a panel out of the building?

This appears to present an important contradiction. It deserves further investigation because it indicates that the parameters fed into this Base Case simulation for plane impact damage were exaggerated (not "reasonable") and that one of the reasons NIST prematurely stopped this simulation was to hide that.

This is the reason NIST gave for stopping the Base Case simulation:

At 0.25 s, the aircraft completely penetrated the building and retained approximately 30 percent of its initial momentum. Beyond this time, the rate of load transfer steadily decreased with very little load transfer after approximately 0.5 s.[580]

While it may be true that there was proportionately less load transfer after 0.5 seconds, still, this statement is misleading in a very key way. Refer to the following plan view taken from the NIST report. It shows what the Base Case plane impact simulation would have looked like if it was frozen in time at the 0.50 second mark. Note how close the fast-moving starboard engine would have been to the south wall.

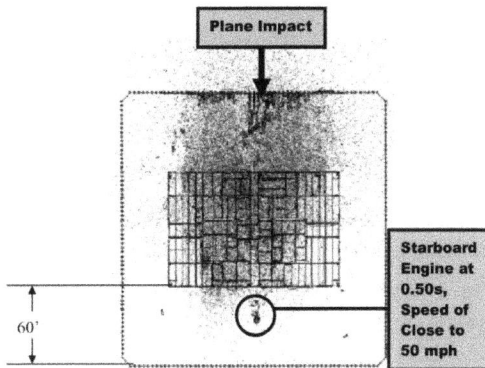

Base Case for Plane Impact
Source: NIST

This engine, made by Pratt & Whitney for the Boeing 767-200ER, has a total weight of about 9,500 pounds (4.75 tons). Since kinetic energy is directly proportional to an object's velocity and its mass, according to NIST's Base Case analysis, at 0.50 seconds after plane impact, the engine most likely had a significant amount of kinetic energy because it could have been going as much as 49.9 mph ("less than 50 mph").

To that point, note the following illustration. It is from a separate simulation that NIST did for just the engine.

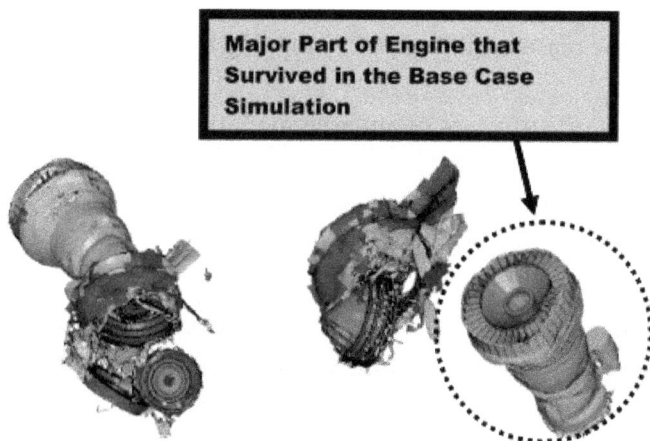

Major Part of Engine that Survived in the Base Case Simulation

Calculated Condition
of Engine at 0.715 Seconds
Source: NIST

This shows the configuration of what NIST calculated would be the condition of the starboard engine at 0.715 seconds after plane impact (which would be 0.215 seconds after the Base Case plane impact simulation was terminated). According to NIST's own estimate, therefore, there is a considerable amount of the engine that survived up to this point. In fact, the condition of the engine at the end of this simulation is remarkably similar to the condition of the mystery engine that was found at Fresh Kills.

Engine Found at Fresh Kills
Photo by Andrea Booher/FEMA

If the Base Case simulation had been allowed to continue, at the 0.715 second mark after plane impact, this heavy chunk of metal would have been about 31 feet from the south wall.[581] If it was going close to 50 mph, can there be any doubt that it would have hit the wall with a tremendous force, more so than the lighter remnant of the landing gear?

This conclusion is backed up by the real-life situation depicted in the NYPD photo of the dislodged panel. Again, *if* a piece of landing gear could hit this panel and knock it out of the building, as NIST claims, should not a more massive remnant of the engine also be able to do that?

North Tower Panel and Landing Gear
Source: NYPD

271

It appears that NIST made an error by terminating Base Case simulation for plane impact when it did. But was that a calculated error? If it had allowed that particular simulation to continue, logic dictates that it likely would have shown the starboard engine also coming out of the building and landing on the street south of the tower, just as the landing gear with less kinetic energy upon plane impact is alleged to have done. But if this particular Base Case simulation—which was supposed to be the most "reasonable" case—showed that happening, it would have put NIST in a tight spot, because, in the real-life situation, the starboard engine from the plane did not exit the building.

Note the following illustration taken from the FEMA report. It shows the major airplane parts that were recovered at the WTC.

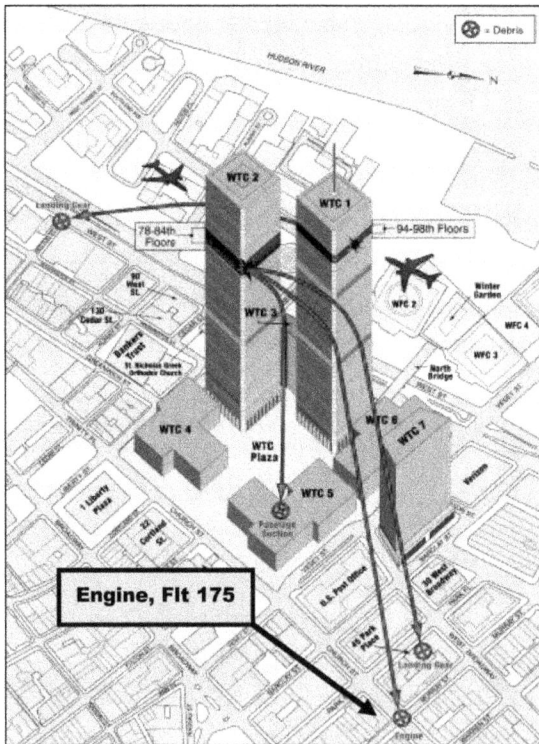

Major Plane Parts Found at the WTC
Source: FEMA

The only engine found on the streets was the one from the plane that hit the South Tower. No engine was found in the area south of the North Tower.

So, it appears that, in the real-life situation, the engine shown in the Base Case simulation could not have been going anywhere close to 50 mph and/or could not have been as close to the south wall as the Base Case simulation results indicated. This leads to the conclusion that the parameters that NIST fed into the Base Case simulation were overestimated and not "reasonable."

As for the what really knocked the panel out of the building, the NYPD photo gives a clue. This panel, which NIST claimed was knocked out of the building by the landing gear, was found 700 feet south of the tower at the intersection of Cedar and West Streets.[582] That is a tremendous show of horizontal force. Just the force needed to break all of that panel's connections to the wall calculates out to be more than 11 million pounds.[583] And a panel at that level of the tower weighed about 7,000 pounds, so the force needed to then throw it 700 feet had to be likewise astronomical.[584]

But, as the photo shows, the panel remained essentially straight and was not distorted as one would expect if it was hit that hard by a projectile, like the landing gear. This suggests that the landing gear is not what severed the south wall panel from the building. It is more likely that a tremendously powerful explosive force acting uniformly across the whole breadth of the panel did that. And the landing gear, which had already been stuck in the wall when that secondary explosion hit, went along for the ride.

As for the starboard engine: In real-life, either it did not make it out of the core, or, if it did, it was moving at a much lower velocity than NIST said when the explosion hit and, therefore, did not make it out of the building.

Accordingly, it becomes apparent from all of the above that NIST prematurely stopped this simulation at the 0.50 second mark for two reasons: (1) to hide the fact that even the Base Case—the simulation that was supposed to be the most reasonable—was, in fact, an overestimation; and (2) to also hide the fact that the landing gear is not what knocked the panel out of the building.

These were huge problems for NIST, because, according to its report, even this Base Case simulation with its overestimated parameters "did not result in the collapse of the tower."[585] And, if it was found that the landing gear did not knock the panel out of the south wall, that would bring up the question, what did? The only possible answer to which would be: an explosion.

Bald-faced Lie #2: *"The comparison of the calculated and observed damage indicated that the geometry and location of the impact damage zone were in good agreement."*

NIST published illustrations meant to prove this point. But that "evidence" leads to quite a different conclusion. Just as the dynamics of the path of the starboard engine in its simulation indicates that the Base Case model for the plane crash was an overestimation, so do the illustrations showing the calculated exterior damage to the tower that was predicted by that simulation.

The following illustration shows the total calculated exterior structural damage to the North Tower that resulted from the computer simulation using the so-called "reasonable" Base Case parameters. The calculated damage areas in question are encircled and noted as areas 1, 2, and 3.

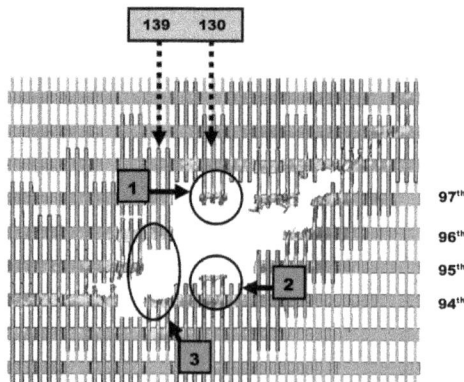

Base Case Calculated Damage
Source: NIST

Area 1: Column line 130 at the 97th floor. This panel was labeled NIST sample *M-2*. Note that there is much more damage to the columns and the spandrel plate calculated by the computer than what actually happened.

274

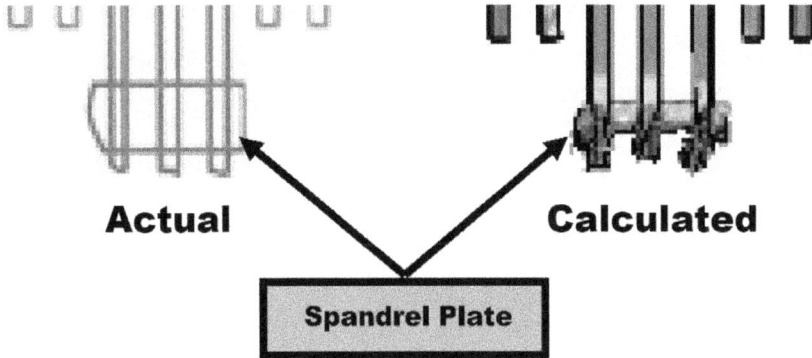

Actual   **Calculated**

Spandrel Plate

In the graphic of the actual damage that was presented on page 238, the spandrel has its full width. It is ripped on the left end and had simple bolt-hole tear-out on the right end. But for Base Case parameters, it was calculated not only to have been ripped on the left end but also ripped on the right end as well as torn horizontally in half for a distance of about 2½ times its depth—about seven to eight feet.

It appears from simple visual inspection that the calculated damage is more than two times the actual. That is not "good agreement."

Area 2: Column line 130 at the 95th floor. Now drop down two floors to the 95th floor level in the same column line.

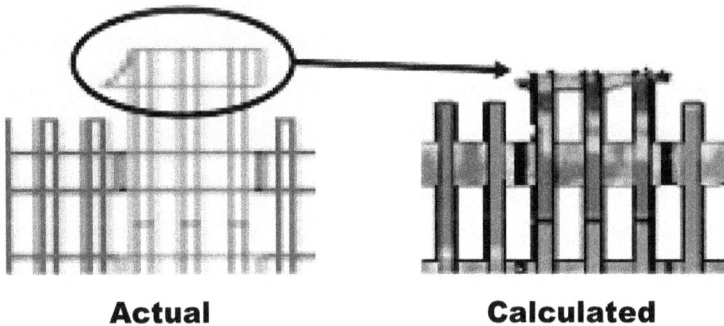

Actual   **Calculated**

This is about the same situation. This spandrel, as predicted by the computer, has been ripped in half horizontally and at the right end, while the graphic of actual damage shows that it was not. Again, this is not good agreement.

Area 3: Column line 139 at the 94th floor. Now look at column line 139 at the 94th floor in the actual damage graphic and compare it to the computer calculated damage for the Base Case. Practically a whole panel and a spandrel have been removed by the computer, using the "reasonable" Base Case parameters, where the actual damage graphic shows that that level of damage was not the case.

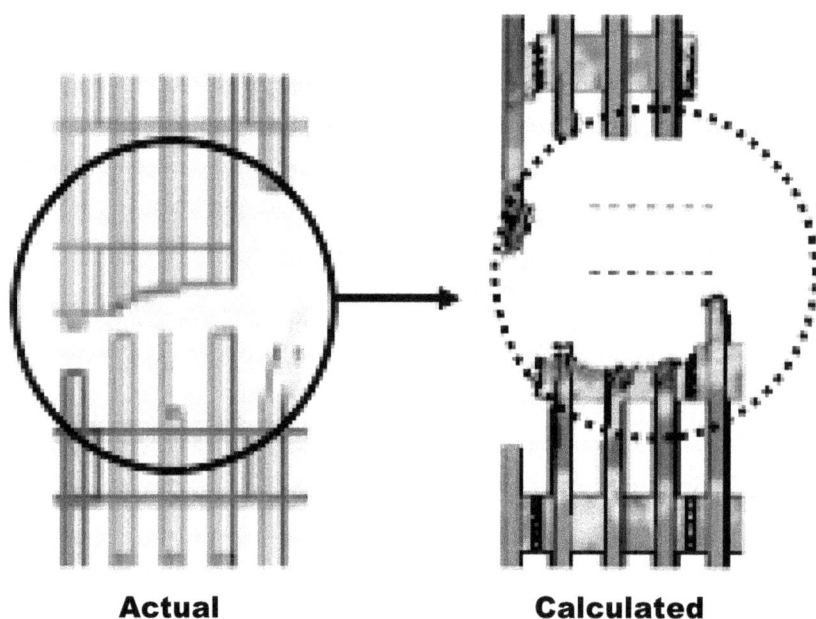

Actual   **Calculated**

These are only three of the most glaring examples of areas in the actual damage illustration that do not match the computer predictions. And there are more. The sum total of all the differences appears to show that the calculated damage to the exterior of the building, using Base Case parameters, was at least fifty percent more than the actual damage; again, not "good agreement."

Bald-faced Lie #3: *"Figure E-34 presents the cumulative damage on all affected floors and columns."*

It follows that, if the parameters for the simulated Base Case plane impact model were overestimations, then any damage predicted by that simulation could not be accurate. Figure E-34 says that three core columns were severed and four were severely damaged. But that has to be an overestimation. A more accurate description of the predicted damage would have been something like this: "There were most likely fewer than 3 core columns severed and fewer than 4 severely damaged." And that is all that can be accurately said about the damage done in this simulation.

Bald-faced Lie #4: *"Analysis did not capture the failure of the connections at the ends of this panel due to the coarse mesh of the south wall."*

This statement is also disingenuous. As discussed in Lie #1, the Base Case simulation for plane impact damage was stopped when the starboard engine was going close to 50 mph and was about 40 feet from the south wall and poised to hit it. The failure of the simulation to show the perimeter panel being dislodged was not due to the south wall model being of a "coarse mesh." It was because NIST terminated the simulation prematurely to hide the fact that the starboard engine was going to hit the wall and possibly knock a panel out of the building, just as the institute claimed the landing gear did in real life.

In other words, the "reasonable" Base Case simulation, was stopped before it could show either (1) that its parameters were exaggerated, or (2) that explosives were what likely dislodged the NYPD panel, or (3) both.

The More Severe Case Renamed Case B

At a certain point, without explanation, the final report rejects its "reasonable" Base Case model and creates a so-called "Case B" simulation for plane impact damage. The report gets tricky at this point, and it requires some careful reading to follow this sudden development. But suffice it to say that the parameters for Case B were exactly the same as for the More Severe Case.[586]

Despite the fact that the Base Case simulation showed that Case B (or as it was previously called: the More Severe Case) was likely an overestimation,

NIST would end up using this renamed model for its final simulation for predicting plane impact damage. And why was it used? It was used as the final simulation precisely because a "preliminary examination" of this simulation showed that it would make the tower collapse.[587]

It is also remarkable that, in this later Case B simulation, NIST suddenly and inexplicably decided to ignore the starboard engine factor completely and instead concentrated solely on the landing gear. About the disposition of the landing gear, the report says, "The Case B prediction showed landing gear penetrating the building core, but stopping before reaching the south exterior wall."[588]

NIST did not give the exact speed or position of the landing gear. But they seem to indicate that it had exited the core and was approaching the south wall when the simulation was stopped. This indicates that the Case B simulation—the parameters of which were more trumped-up than the Base Case—was also stopped prematurely, because it did not even show the landing gear reaching the south wall and hitting the panel, an event that the NYPD photograph indicates did occur.

This brings up an essential question, which is: What happened to the starboard engine? Was that Case B engine even more poised to bust out of the south wall? Case B was more exaggerated than the Base Case so, according to NIST's theory, that should have been true since the engine, being heavier than the landing gear, would have had more kinetic energy upon plane impact. But, if its complete flight was shown in this Case B simulation, that would have clearly exposed the Case B model to also be an exaggeration of the true facts of the North Tower crash because, again, there was no Flight 11 engine found south of the North Tower, only the landing gear.

The essential takeaway from this examination of NIST's Base Case and Case B plane impact simulations is that they were not, in any way, accurate representations of the true crash of Flight 11. The institute insists that only the landing gear broke out of the south wall of the building. But the results of both of those simulations clearly indicate something different. They suggest that the starboard engine likely would have also broken out of the building and been found in the streets below. In real life, though, that did not happen.

The Less Severe Case

The manner in which NIST handled the Less Severe Case is especially revealing. It shows how much the institute's predetermined theory for the cause of the collapse of the North Tower corrupted its investigation and how it ignored any evidence to the contrary.

The report notes that this case was tossed from consideration very early on. This is how that decision was explained:

> The less severe damage case did not meet two key observables: (1) *no aircraft debris was calculated to exit the side opposite to impact* and most of the debris was stopped prior to reaching that side, in contradiction to what was observed in photographs and videos of the impact event and (2) The subsequent structural response analyses of the damaged towers indicated that *the towers would not have collapsed had the less severe damage results been used.*[589] (Italics added)

The first reason given here for rejecting the Less Severe Case is another obvious contradiction. Neither the Base Case nor Case B showed any objects exiting the south side of the tower, either. So there was no reason to reject the Less Severe Case on that basis.

The second reason is even more revealing. The reasoning of the writers of the report was that the less severe case did not lead to tower collapse, so it had to be rejected. But why is that a reason for rejecting it? Well, because NIST had already predetermined that the collapse of the North Tower was due to the fires caused by the plane crash to the exclusion of all other possibilities, including explosives.

It is apparent that, in their single-minded search for higher steel temperatures that could justify their unlikely theory for collapse, NIST's investigators started with the most "reasonable" Base Case. But, when a complete study of that model did not result in collapse, they moved up to the More Severe Case, which did result in collapse. But they did not stop there. They renamed the More Severe Case "Case B" and then ran its simulation without showing the disposition of the starboard engine, which was so prominently featured in the Base Case. In order to appear diligent, they then added the Less Severe Case to make it appear that they had studied a full range of possibilities. Why they renamed the More Severe Case and then decided to concentrate on the landing gear in the newly named Case B simulation instead of the starboard engine is not explained in the report. But it all feels like a shell game of misdirection meant to confuse the reader.

They then fed the overestimated plane impact damage from the Case B simulation into their final FDS fire simulation model. And voila! Using those trumped up Case B parameters, the tower model collapsed—and without the use of explosives.

As noted previously, the writers of NIST's final report were well-aware that an "important source of uncertainty" in their investigative method of relying exclusively on computer simulations was "the inaccuracy associated with mathematical or numerical models." But what else could they do? Giuliani and Cheney had made sure that the steel from the North Tower's plane impact zone—the *only* evidence that could have been used to prove the official explanation for the collapse—was destroyed before the investigating engineers could examine it. So, NIST was "forced" to go to computer simulations to prove its theory that explosives need not be involved. The problem with that reasoning, though, is that NIST's Case B findings could never rise above being just that—a theory. Yet, the institute cynically continued to state it as fact.

High Strain Rates and WTC Steel

As of this writing, virtually none of the WTC steel is left to study.[590] By the time the BPS engineers began their investigation in January of 2002, ninety-nine percent of it had already been shipped off and recycled. Later, the remaining one percent, including the perimeter panels from around the plane impact hole, which the paint-cracking study found showed very low temperatures for the North Tower fires, was cut up into souvenir-sized pieces and given out as mementos to various cities and museums around the country.

However, the reports from both NIST and FEMA present photographs taken by their field investigators of various steel connectors found in the debris pile that they considered unusual. To the trained eye, those exhibits show failure patterns that are consistent with the use of explosives. What is baffling is the fact that the FEMA report, in particular, mentions the phenomenon but fails to point out how those samples were prime examples of it.

For instance, the report says this:

High strain rates tend to increase the observed yield strength and tensile strength of steel...There is a greater influence on the yield point than on the tensile strength. Figure B4 compares the effect of a very high strain rate (100 in/in/sec) for a mild carbon steel with a more usual test speed of 850 micro in/in/sec. In this sample, the yield point more than doubled, whereas the tensile strength was increased about 27 percent, and the Y/T ratio approached unity.[591]

What FEMA is explaining here is that steel exhibits a peculiar characteristic that has to do with the relationship between its shear (yield) strength and its tensile strength when a force is applied extremely quickly—as is the case of an explosion.

To further explain the phenomenon, refer to the following illustration.

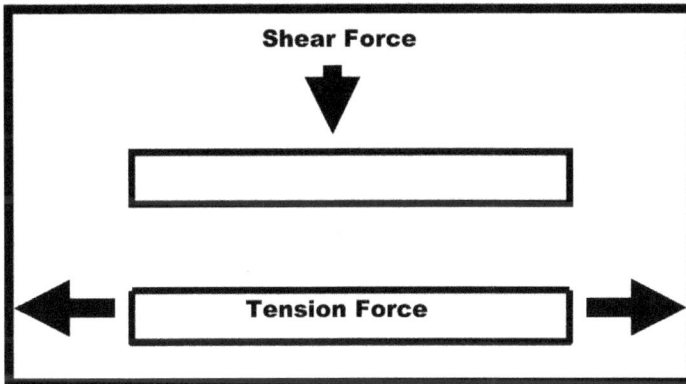

Shear vs Tension

Shear strength is the resisting force of the sample that tends to prevent it from being cut, and tensile strength is its resisting force that tends to prevent it from being torn. Under normal circumstances, where the force on a steel sample is applied gradually, its shear strength is equal to only about 62 percent of its tensile strength. That relationship becomes dramatically reversed, however, when the force is applied at a high rate of speed. When a piece of steel is hit with the high-speed force of an explosion, for example, its strength in shear increases exponentially while its strength in tension is only marginally increased.

What follows is three examples of high strain rates in WTC steel samples that piqued the interest of FEMA field investigators enough to want to document them in photographs.

FEMA Figure B-9(B)

This is a floor truss seat from one of the towers. It connected a floor truss in the outer office area to a perimeter column.[592] The critical aspect of this sample is the way the left-hand connecting bolt tore out the seat angle.

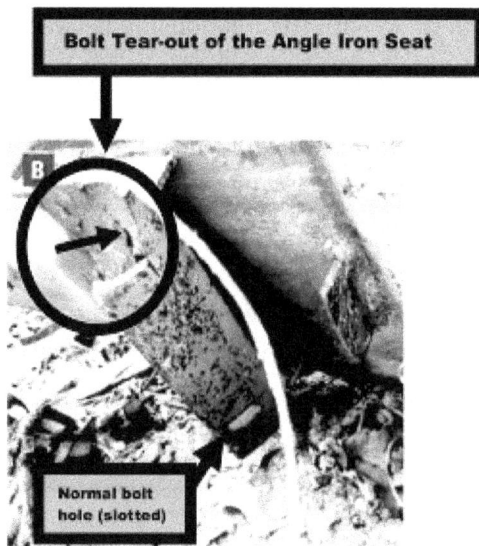

Figure B-9(B)
Source: FEMA

Floor Truss Seats—Where, What and How

The following plan shows the layout of the floor truss system for the North Tower.

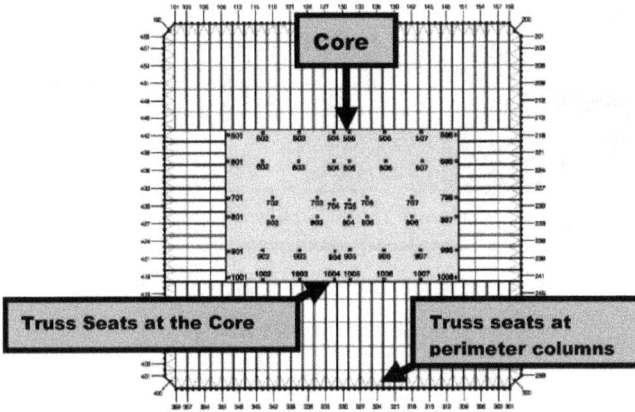

Floor Truss Layout for the North Tower
Source: FEMA

The floor panels were delivered to the site already assembled and then were welded together in place. The following drawing shows how three sections went together in a typical floor area. Their trusses were doubled up at every other perimeter column.

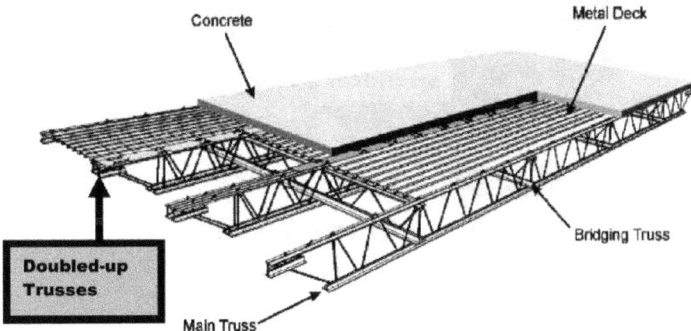

Figure 1–6. Schematic of composite floor truss system

Three Floor Truss Panels Joined
Source: FEMA

The seats for the trusses were pieces of angle iron that were welded to the interior faces of the perimeter columns at one end and to channel beams that were welded across the outer rows of the core columns at the other end.

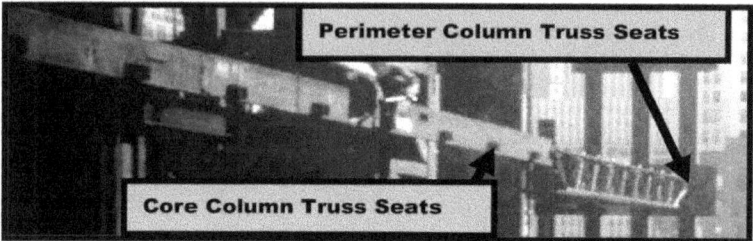

Truss Seat During Construction
Source: PSNYNJ

It was on those truss seat angles that the floor system was hung. The following photograph shows floor truss seats welded to the perimeter columns. (Note: There is an error in the notation of this photo. The middle seat pointed out is not a truss seat. Note the absence of bolt holes.)

Floor Truss Seats
Source: PANYNJ

When set in place next to each other, the floor panels ended up having two trusses per seat angle on every other perimeter column. The trusses were then bolted to the seat angles with two 5/8-inch high strength steel bolts. Thus the need for the two slotted bolt-holes in each seat angle—one for each truss. The following drawing details the truss seats at the perimeter columns and the core columns.

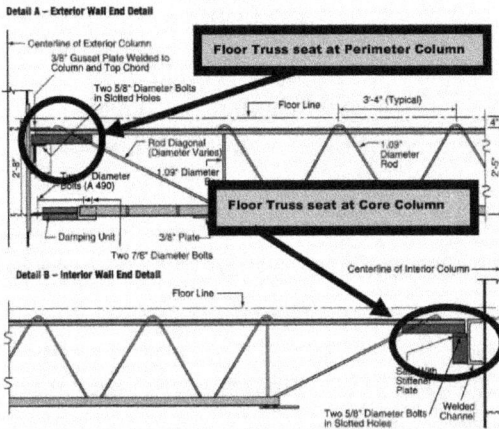

Typical North Tower Floor Truss

Source: NIST

The following close-up shows the seat angle tear-out of Sample B-9(B) in more detail.

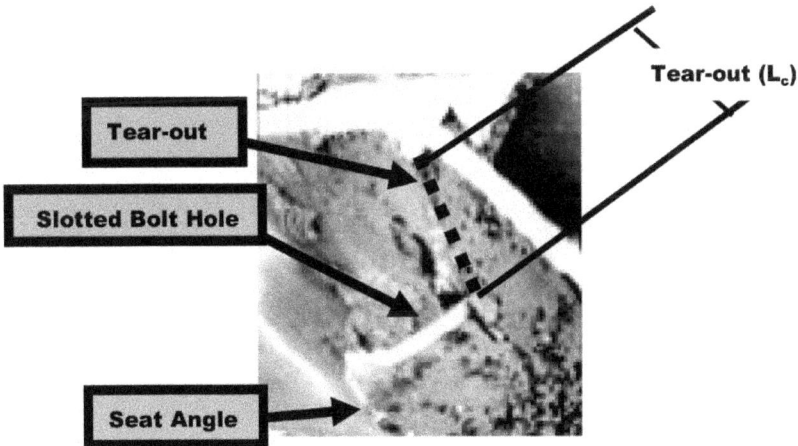

Detail

Here, FEMA admitted that the type of failure seen in this sample was unusual:

> It is probable that, once the 3/8-inch gusset plate fractures, the next lower bound resistance is provided by the bearing capacity of the two 5/8-inch bolts on the beam seat angle. This failure also tore off the end[s] of the angle even though the tensile capacity of those segments was predicted to be higher.[593]

In other words, normally, the tensile strength of the torn out portion of the truss seat was higher than the shear strength of the bolt, so the bolt should have been sheared off (been cut) instead of tearing out the angle iron. The fact that the bolt tore out the angle iron is an indication that the bolt flew against the truss seat angle at such a high rate of speed (high strain rate) that its strength in shear was increased many times over.

The following calculations illustrate this phenomenon.

The Left-hand Bolt Hole

The bolt used to fasten a floor truss to its angle iron seat was a high strength type, designated as A325. The relevant formula for calculating shear capacity of one A325 high strength bolt is the following:[594]

$$R_v = (.62 F_v A_x)\, 1.18$$

F_v is 120 ksi, the tensile capacity of an A325 bolt. And .62 is the coefficient for converting tensile strength to shear strength (steel is stronger in tension than in shear). ksi designates 1000 pounds of force (k) per square inch (si), so that 120 ksi would equal 120,000 pounds of force per square inch of surface area where the force is applied. A_x is 0.307 square inches, the effective cross-sectional area of one 5/8-inch bolt. And 1.18 represents the fact that testing has found that high strength bolts normally exceed their calculated tensile strength by 18 percent.

Solving for R_v:

$$R_v = .62 \times 120 \times .307 \times 1.18$$
$$R_v = 26.95 \text{ kips}$$

The shear capacity of one 5/8-inch bolt is 26.95 kips, or 26,950 pounds (1 kip equals 1,000 pounds). That's how much force it would have taken to cut the bolt in half.

Now, compare that to the bearing capacity of the seat angle. That is the force in tension at the seat angle plate that was created by the bolt slamming against it and tearing it out, the way it appears in the photograph. The relevant equation for bearing capacity, R_u, of the seat is the following:[595]

$$R_u = L_c t F_u$$

L_c is the length of the fracture of the seat angle. Referring to the previous photograph, by proportions, the edge of that fracture appears to be about 4.5 times the width of the slotted hole, which is slightly larger than the diameter of the 5/8-inch bolt, which is 0.63 inches. Using $L_c = 2.84$ inches (.63 x 4.5) will, therefore, give a conservative figure for R_u. The thickness of the seat, t, was 3/8-inch (or 0.375 inches). The seat was made of A36 steel, which has a tensile strength, F_u, of 60 ksi.

Solving for R_u:

$$R_u = 2.84 \times .375 \times 60$$
$$R_u = 63.9 \text{ kips}$$

Under normal conditions, the force that it would take to tear the seat angle the way it appears in the photo is 63.9 kips, which is close to 2.4 times the normal shear capacity of the bolt. Therefore, the bolt should have failed first. But it did not. This indicates that the bolt was energized by a high-speed force that increased its shear strength many times over, while the effect on the tensile strength of the seat angle was minimal. This is a phenomenon common to explosions.

And that is exactly why FEMA field inspectors took special note of this sample. But for some inexplicable reason, the actual writers of the report did not share that curiosity enough to test it for residues of explosives.

FEMA Figure B-9(A)

This next photograph is of a second truss seat angle failure that FEMA's field investigators also found suspicious enough to document.[596] It shows evidence of high strain rate in an even more dramatic fashion.

Figure B-9(A) **Detail**

Source: FEMA

Both sides of this seat angle have been torn out by bolts exiting at a high rate of speed. Like the previous example, the bolts should have sheared off first. But that did not happen. They tore out the seat angle, instead.

Also, here there appears to have been at least two forces acting on the seat angle simultaneously, in different directions. This also indicates the use of explosives, since explosions blast out in all directions simultaneously.

Even though the condition of this truss seat angle was judged to be extraordinary by FEMA field investigators, and though the writers of the FEMA report made note of it, there was no effort in the report to explain its possible significance with respect to the collapses.

At the very least, the condition of this sample should have prompted FEMA supervisors to have it tested for residues of explosives. But they failed to have that done. Again, the question arises, why did the Bush investigations neglect the obvious?

FEMA Figure B-11

This third truss seat failure pattern on a perimeter column was also considered to be worthy of further study by the FEMA field investigators who photographed it.[597]

Figure B-11
Source: FEMA

All of the welds that held the various floor truss connectors to the perimeter column in this sample have been completely sheared off. This indicates the strong possibility that explosives were involved. But the comments on this phenomenon in FEMA's report are, again, typically meager:

Many of the bearing brackets and the damper angle connections on the column/spandrel beam plate were completely sheared off. Only the weld segments remained on the face of the column/spandrel beam plate (Figure B-11). This mode of failure appears to be due to excessive vertical overloads on the floor system.[598]

Perhaps a tremendously powerful force could have randomly caused the condition exhibited by sample B-11 a few times as the building was collapsing, but the report says that there were "many" instances of this type of failure.

Of course, having all of the steel from the debris pile would have been immensely helpful in discovering the actual frequency of this type of failure pattern. But due to Giuliani's destruction of the evidence, that is now impossible to do. At this point in time, the only way to get a general idea of how frequently this failure pattern might have occurred throughout the whole building is to look at the area where FEMA's engineers from the SEAoNY did manage to recover a high percentage of perimeter panels. That was from the area around the plane impact hole in the North Tower.

The following illustration, NIST Figure 3-51b, documents the results of a study of the condition of the truss seats on those panels.[599]

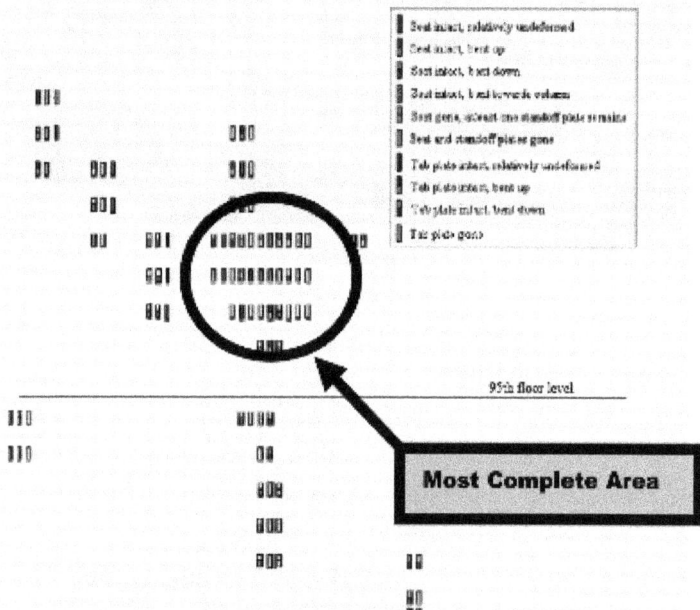

Figure 3–51b. WTC 1, damage of connectors. At or below the 95th floor, all connectors are either bent down or missing.

North Tower Truss Seats

Source: NIST

Here is a close-up of the most complete area:

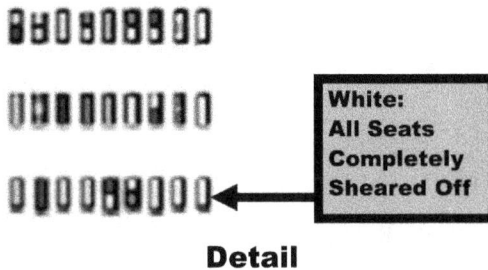

Detail

This particular area contains 27 total floor truss to perimeter column connection patterns like that of sample B-11. Of that number, 13 had all welds completely missing. That means that 48 percent of them (13/27 x 100%) in this area showed that type of extraordinary damage. If this pattern held throughout the entire exterior of the building, of the close to 13,200 total number of perimeter column to floor truss connections that were in the 110 stories above ground, 13,200 x .48, or 6,720, would have shown this extraordinary condition.

Of course, there is a lot of uncertainty in this number. But it should have been intriguing enough for FEMA and/or NIST to see the need for more study, because it doesn't seem likely that this type of damage to that many truss connections can be explained by a completely random, gravity-driven collapse. On the other hand, powerful enough explosive devices attached to columns at the floor truss to column connections could have blown away all of those connectors just as easily as a strong gust of wind can blow dust off a table top.

Once again, a simple test for residues of explosives was called for here. But, also once again, that was not done.

Fractured Steel

In fire-damaged, steel-framed structures, where temperatures are very high, it is typical to find structural members that have become bent and distorted. At times, that can be extremely pronounced without the sample actually being torn or fractured. Below are photographs from the NIST report that show that kind of damage found at the WTC.[600]

WTC Bent Steel
Source: NIST

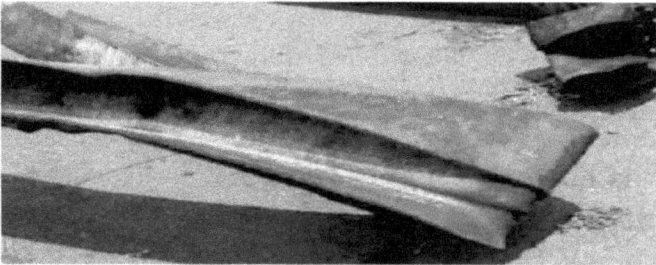

WTC Bent Steel
Source: NIST

The next photo shows a complete exterior panel saved from around the impact hole in the North Tower that actually took a direct hit by Flight 11.[601] Notice just how much stress it took without fracturing.

Source: NIST

WTC 1 Exterior Panel Hit by
the Fuselage of the Aircraft
Source: NIST

On the other hand, note the following steel samples that were also rescued from Giuliani's recycling program. Presented in a section of a 2005 "Draft" NIST report entitled "Metallurgical Analysis of Structural Steel," they exhibit fracture patterns consistent with the use of explosives. And it is not surprising that NIST's field investigators found them interesting enough to document in photographs.

NIST Sample HH
This is part of a core column that was located in the fire floors of the North Tower.

Source: NIST

Figure 4-5. Core column HH (605A: 98-101) from the fire floors of WTC 1. a) Failure at both ends and b) separation between flange and web in the 99th floor region.

Sample HH
Source: NIST

Note that the fractures of HH at its midsection and at one end are not clean breaks. Also, the edges of the flanges and vertical web appear to be exploded outward in all directions, as opposed to being crushed. That is a strong indication of an explosive force.

HH could not have been hit by the plane. During construction, each of the structural steel elements (columns, beams, trusses, etc) that went into the twin towers were delivered to the site with a code number either painted on it or stamped into it. This told the workers where it was to be located in the structure. Due to this, after the collapses it was easy for investigators to figure out where the pieces of steel in the debris pile came from. In this way, it was determined that HH was a section of column line number 605 in the core area. It is circled in the following plan view.[602]

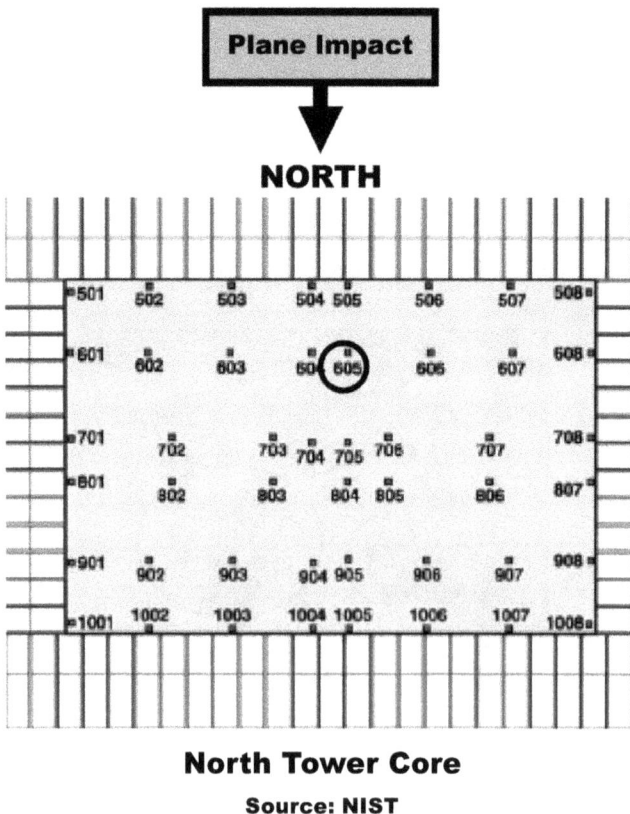

North Tower Core
Source: NIST

Typically, the vertical core columns were made up of sections that were 44 feet long and spanned 4 floors. Core column sections were stacked one on top of the other as the tower was erected. And column sections such as HH were bolted and/or welded together at the column ends with splice plates like that seen in the photograph: "splice in the 98th floor."

From the plan view above, one might think that HH was in the direct line of the plane. But the following elevation drawing shows that it was not. The item circled represents the vertical position of sample HH relative to the plane impact zone.

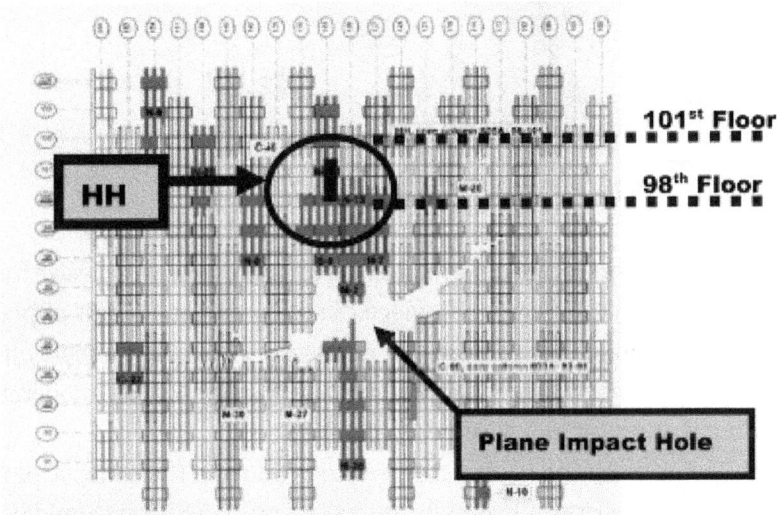

"HH" and the North Tower Impact Zone
Source: NIST

The original full length of HH spanned between the 98th and the 101st floors. The illustration shows that the bottom end-splice of column section HH was well above the plane's impact hole and could not have been affected by the plane crash.

Additionally, note that HH was right behind perimeter panel "N-13," which was not damaged by the plane crash and was recovered in its complete condition from the debris pile.

Yet, HH was chopped off at its middle at the 100th floor level by an enormous force. Calculations show that it had to be close to 1.4 million pounds.[603]

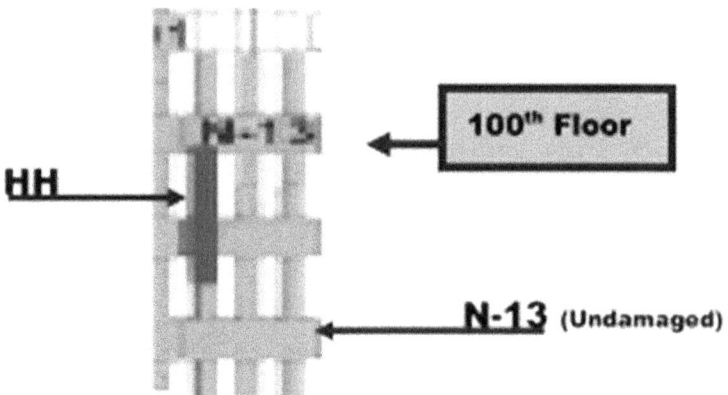

NIST Panel N-13

The NIST report itself admits that the extremely violent explosive force that damaged this super-strong piece of steel was not a result of plane impact. In its modeling of the impact damage of Flight 11, the report lists the probable damage due to the impact of the plane on HH as "moderate," meaning that it was "not severed on impact."

While it is true that asymmetric collisions during the collapse of the tower could have ripped this column, its curious condition should have prompted testing for explosives; certainly, the photographer thought so. But it did not.

NIST Sample C-46

This is a perimeter panel from the South Tower that NIST field investigators also found interesting.[604] The photograph of this sample shows how the column section on the left side of this three-column panel appears to have been completely blasted off just above the middle spandrel plate—which would have been just above the 70th floor level. Other than that, the panel is not significantly distorted.

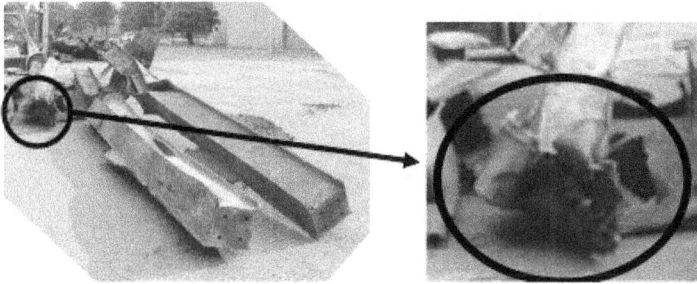

Sample C-46
Source: NIST

There is no chance that this sample was hit by the plane, either. Note the following plan view. C-46 was part of perimeter column line 156, located at the northwest corner of the building, putting it far away from the plane impact area.

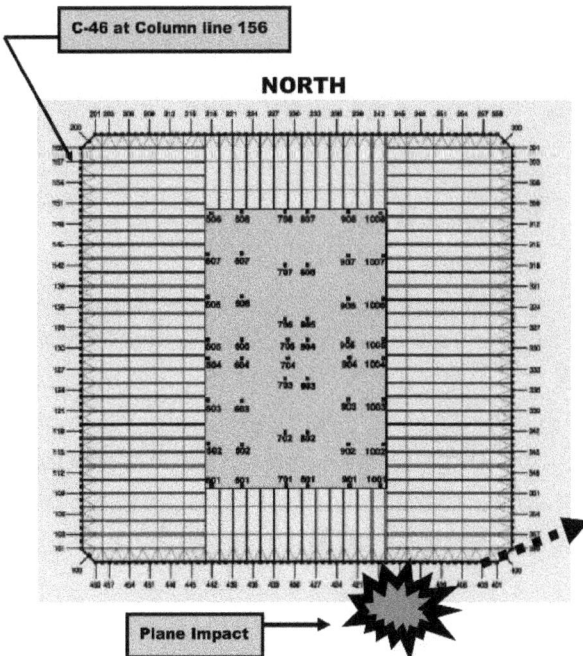

South Tower Plan
Source: NIST

The following graphic is from the NIST Report. The shaded part is the piece that was sheared off of sample C-46.

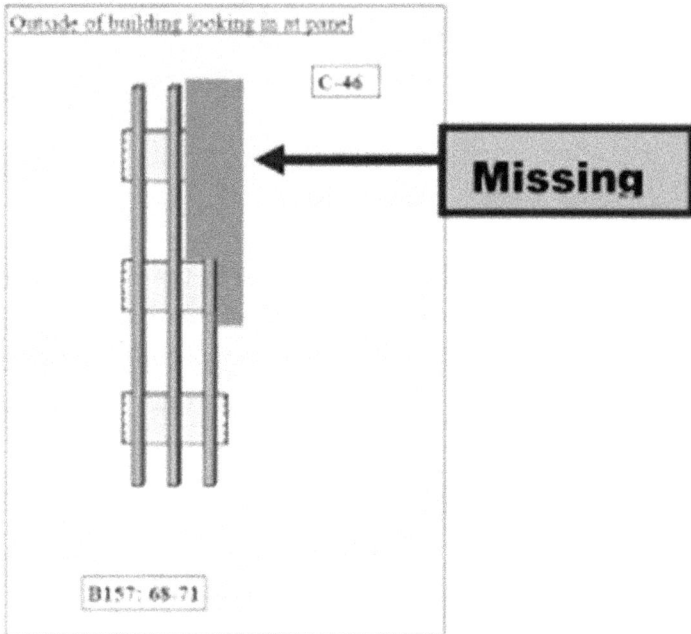

Sample C-46
Source: NIST

Because of the tremendous strength in shear of the perimeter columns at this level of the tower—1,376,667 pounds—and the fact that the column in question on this panel appears to be not just severed but blown outward, the use of explosives becomes a distinct possibility.[605] Again, this is another sample that presented a great opportunity that was missed for the testing for residues of explosives.

NIST Sample C-24

This sample is a perimeter panel section from the South Tower.[606] It was located in about the middle of the north face at perimeter column line 203. It spanned from the 74th up to the 77th floor.

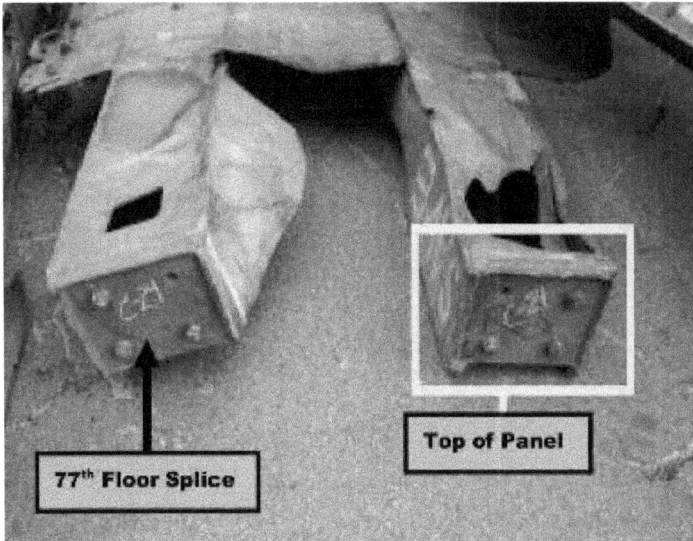

Sample C-24
Source: NIST

This NIST photograph, however, does not show the most interesting aspect of this sample. For that, you have to go to another section of the report that details how this panel was cleanly chopped off at the seventy-sixth floor. Note the following graphic.

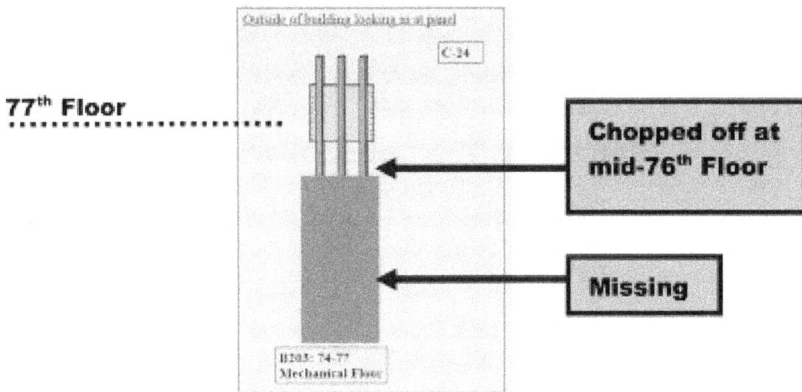

NIST Illustration C-24

Stress calculations show that the force needed to accomplish this was an incredible 4,132,000 pounds.[607]

This next illustration shows that C-24 was nowhere near the crash site and also could not have been fractured by plane impact.

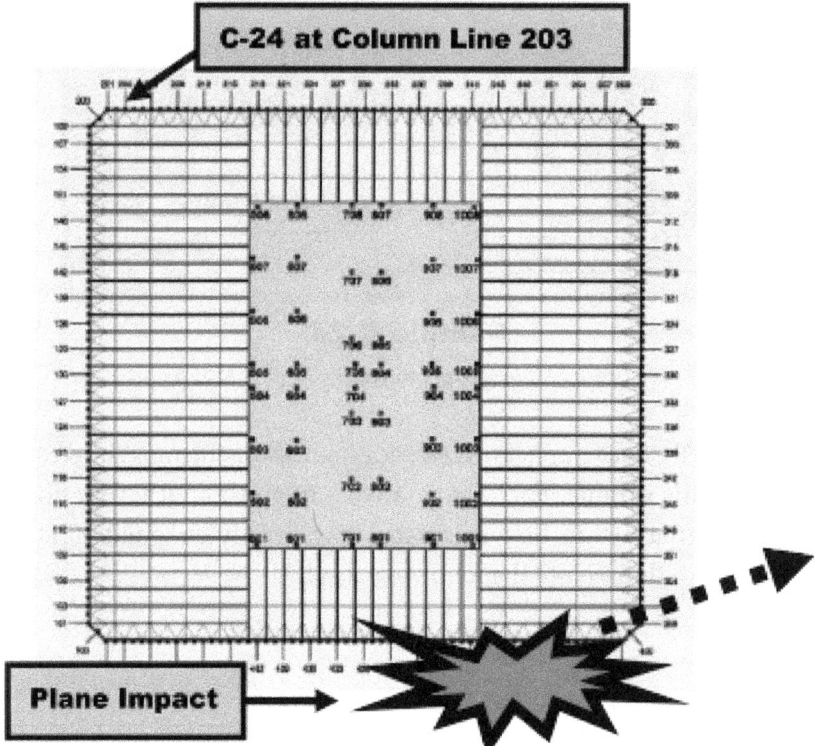

C-24 at Column Line 203

Plane Impact

Plan View: The South Tower
Source: NIST

The NIST photograph gives another clue that indicates that C-24 could have been hit by an explosion. Note that the bolt access hole for the splice plate in the right side column has been noticeably enlarged by some kind of impact.

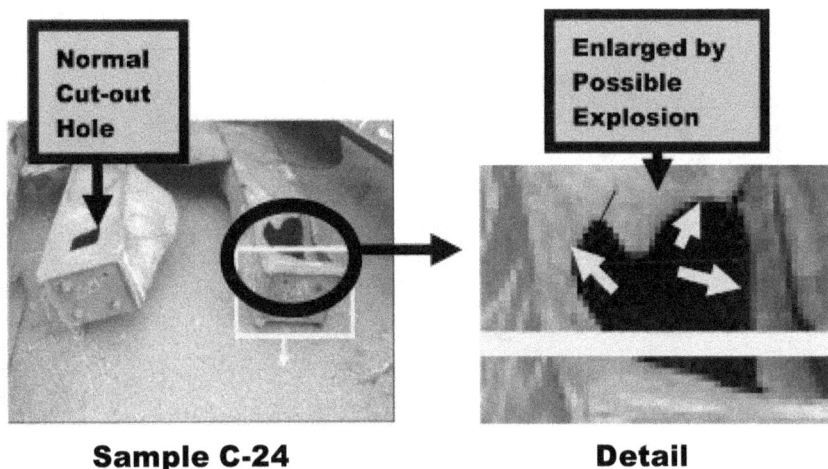

Sample C-24   **Detail**

The arrows point out the irregular edge of the fracture. The steel has not just been bent in; it is missing, having been completely torn out around the edge of the hole. In the report, the caption under this photo says, "Damage of this type may be due to any one of the extreme loading events." And that is entirely true. However, it is unlikely that it could have been caused by asymmetric collisions during collapse. That would not have *removed* material. It is more likely that the "extreme loading event" was an explosion.

Unfortunately, this sample, too, was never tested for residues of explosives.

NIST Sample C-14

This is the lower part of a perimeter box column that also escaped Giuliani's recycling program. FEMA field investigators found it interesting enough to save, and NIST field investigators found it intriguing enough to photograph. It was part of corner panel number 300 of the South Tower, located between the 85th and 87th floors.[608]

Sample C-14

Source: NIST

Notice how the steel plates that made up this column appear to be peeled back like a banana at its midpoint. This is a strong indication that it was hit by an explosion.

The NIST graphic below shows that C-14 was the only part of this perimeter panel that was recovered.

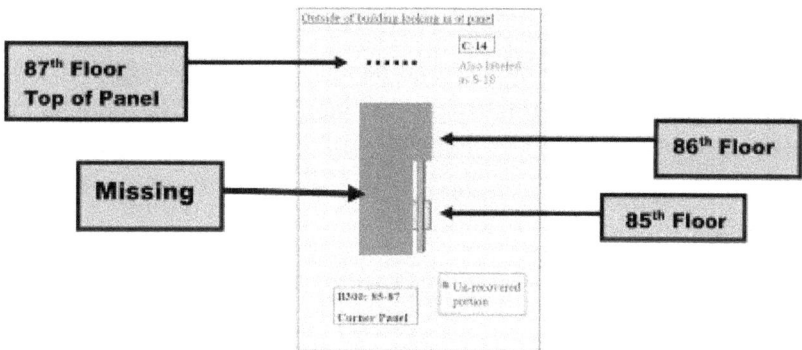

Outside of building looking in at panel

C-14

Also labeled in S-18

87th Floor Top of Panel

86th Floor

Missing

85th Floor

B308: 85-87 Corner Panel

* Un-recovered portion

NIST Illustration C-14

This column sample is only 16 feet of its original 34-foot length. It had been literally torn out of its panel—chopped off at just below the 86th floor, and the lower spandrel plate at the 85th floor has been torn vertically to the left of the column. This indicates an explosive force. Additionally, all of the spandrel's 5/8-inch splice bolts on the right side have been either sheared off, or they tore out the plate. If torn out, that could indicate that the bolts had been subjected to a high strain rate—another indication of an explosion.[609]

The plan view below shows the location of this sample in relation to the plane impact zone. It was part of perimeter column line 259, located at the chamfered northeast corner of the South Tower.

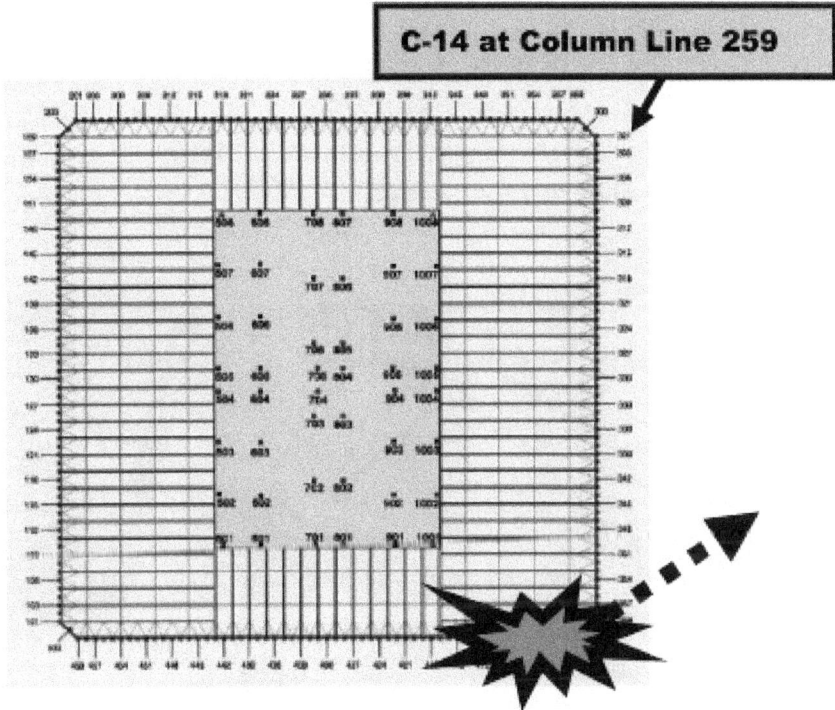

South Tower Plan
Source: NIST

Obviously, the dramatic damage done to C-14 was not caused by the impact of the plane.

This was yet another excellent opportunity to test for traces of explosives that was missed.

FEMA Figure B-6

This is another example of how the leaders of the official investigations avoided studying steel samples that field investigators found suspicious enough to save and document in photographs.[610]

The FEMA report used this sample to discuss the way that core columns were stacked and secured end to end with fillet welds. But it ignored the obvious defect (a hole) in its side. This column, the report said, failed at the welded joint from overloading due to some unknown cause. But it neglected to mention that the hole in the column's side looks suspiciously like it was caused by an explosion, and that that could very well have been the cause of the failure of the end-welds.

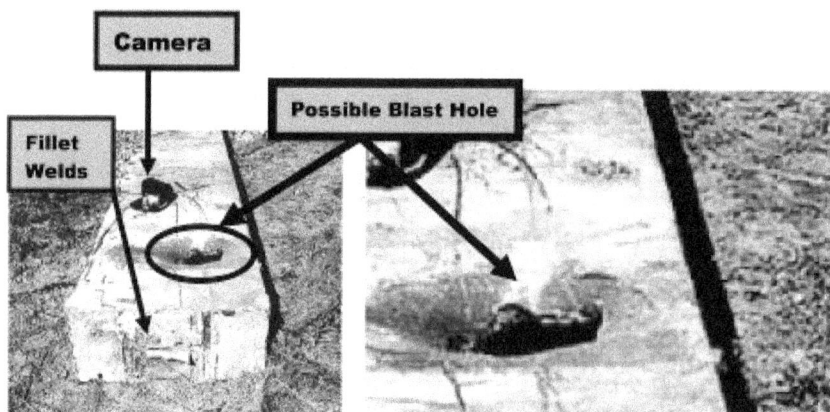

Figure B-6   **Detail**

Source: FEMA

Note the concave shape of the large depression surrounding the hole and the jagged edge of its inside rim.

Did the writers of the NIST report wonder why their field investigators put a camera on the column before photographing it? Most likely it was put there to give a scale to the photograph for estimating the size of the hole.

This was yet another excellent candidate for testing for residues of explosives that was ignored by the Bush administration investigations.

NIST Sample B-1011

Columns that are cut at an angle can be a tip-off that controlled demolition has taken place. In controlled demolitions, a column is cut at an angle so that the upper part will more easily slide off its support. The following sample—B-1011—appears to be a prime example of that.

Sample B-1011
Source: NIST

This was a segment of North Tower core column line 508.[611] Note the following plan.

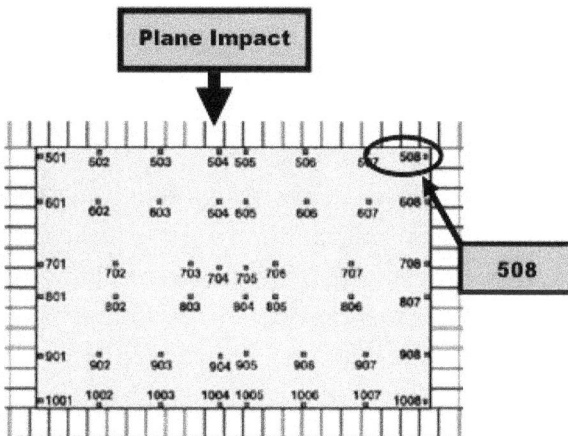

North Tower Core
Source: FEMA

This part of B-1011 was located between the 51st and 54th floors—some 40 floors below the plane impact zone, so damage by plane impact was impossible.

There are a couple of aspects to this curious piece of metal that indicate the use of explosives. In the first place, notice the absence of slag and that there are no torch marks on it. That is strong evidence that traditional explosives were used on this sample. If B-1011 was torch cut by workers at the scene or was cut by thermate, slag would be spread around the cut surface, and there would be jagged burn marks along the length of the cut. Neither of those is present. It is a clean cut.

Secondly, any plan for the controlled demolition of the North Tower would have to pay special attention to this particular column because it was one of the four corners of the core area, and, as such, it played a major part in tying the whole core structure together.

Despite its potential importance, however, the photograph of this incredible piece of evidence was presented in the NIST report without comment. But it should have prompted the testing for residues of explosives. Unfortunately, it did not.

Were the Planes Modified to Fire a Missile?

Many critics of the official story of the 9/11 attacks have pointed out startling anomalies that can be seen in the photographs and videos of the plane that hit the South Tower, which indicate that it might not have been the real United Airlines Flight 175 that took off from Logan International Airport that morning.

Interestingly, all of those strange images appear in the NIST report's repository of photographic material, but the startling contradiction they present was not mentioned in the actual report.[612] It is also important to note that NIST attempted to keep this photographic material from becoming public, and that it took a Freedom of Information Act (FOIA) lawsuit brought by the International Center for 9/11 Studies to get them released.[613]

The Photographic Evidence

First, note the following photograph. It shows a standard Boeing 767-200ER, the model of the planes that allegedly struck the WTC. Note how its underbelly normally has a uniformly smooth, aerodynamically efficient surface.

Boeing 767-200ER
Source: Corbis/AP

This next photo shows a 767 from the starboard side.

Boeing 767-200ER
Copyright: Jean-Philippe Boulet

Now look at this next photograph, showing the Boeing 767-200ER that hit the South Tower. There has been an odd tubular section that has been added along the starboard side of its belly.

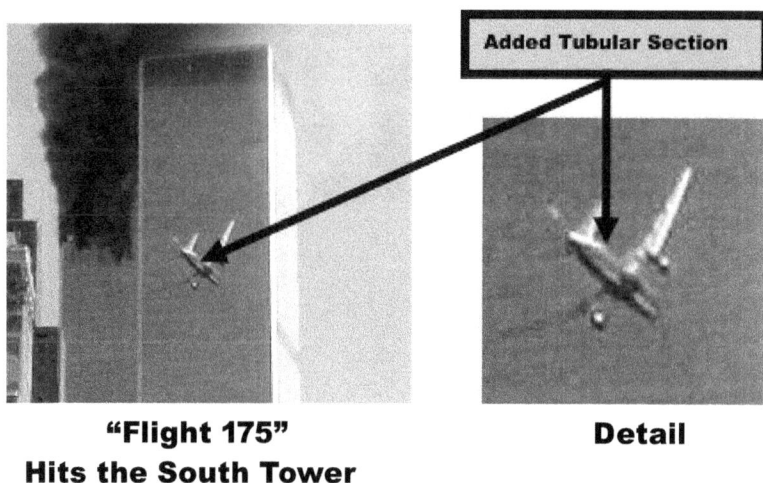

"Flight 175"
Hits the South Tower

Detail

Copyright: Carmen Taylor/AP

Also, the videos of the plane impact, when run in slow motion, reveal the flash of what looks suspiciously like an explosion an instant before the nose of the plane touches the building. The best still picture of this was taken from a video shot by CNN.[614] Unfortunately, it could not be accessed for this publication. However, that flash can be seen in the film *Loose Change, Second Edition,* which can be viewed for free online.[615]

Others also caught this unusual occurrence on film. Another video of it was taken by Spiegel TV.[616] And a bystander named Evan Fairbanks photographed it.[617] Both a frame taken from the video and the photograph were published in the NIST report, but without comment.

In addition, Jules Naudet's video of the plane that hit the North Tower shows a similar flash just before impact.[618]

Calculations Indicate Possible Missile

Some say that the flash before impact is evidence that a missile was fired from the tubular addition to the plane. And a certain aspect of a study done at the Massachusetts Institute of Technology (MIT) seems to bear that out.[619] At one point, that study determined that the amount of energy required to produce the fireballs that occurred upon plane impact with the South Tower was equal to the energy contained in 4,375 gallons of jet fuel. But FEMA and NIST concluded that the fireballs consumed only a maximum of 3,000 gallons.[620] So, either both FEMA and NIST were off in their estimates for the amount of fuel that was consumed by the initial fireballs, or the MIT calculations indicate that there had to have been some other source of energy present. That other source would have provided the amount of energy contained in 1,375 gallons of jet fuel (4375 – 3000). And that could very well have been due to a missile that the videos apparently show exploding on the face of the building a fraction of a second before the plane hit.

Of course, if all of this is truly the case, then the planes that hit the WTC were probably not the ones that took off from Boston that morning. And that brings up the question of what happened to the real planes and all the people on them. This is a mystery that is beyond the abilities of any independent investigator to solve. Only the federal government, with the vast resources it has at its disposal, can do that, if it has the will. All that an independent researcher can do is to point out facts such as those presented here that stand in stark contradiction to the official story and hope that the government takes them to heart.

In any case, as far-out as this theory may seem, with nearly 3,000 innocent people murdered on 9/11, it does not seem unreasonable to expect that Bush administration investigators should have considered *all* of the evidence available to them, including this. Unfortunately, they did not. The question is why?

Missing Airplane Parts

Even though nearly 2,600 people were murdered at the WTC, practically no airplane parts from the two huge jetliners that hit the twin towers were saved by the FBI for further investigation. This is another strong indication that the Bush administration had a plan in place to cover up the true nature of the attacks. Some of those lost parts—most obviously the engines—had serial numbers that could have been checked to see if the planes that hit the towers were, indeed, the actual planes that took off from Logan that morning.

At one point, the fact of the missing airplane parts had become public knowledge, and independent researchers started asking questions. On February

23, 2002, FBI spokesman Joseph Valiquette responded with this: "So little [airplane] debris has been recovered that there's really no way to quantify it."[621]

But that is hard to fathom, since a lot of substantial plane parts had been seen on the streets around the WTC, and photographs of them had appeared in various news articles as well as in FEMA's report, which came out the following May. Here are two of those pictures. They show the only engines that were recovered from the WTC site:

Engine at Fresh Kills

Photo by Andrea Booher/FEMA

Flight 175 Engine Found at WTC

Copyright: Chris Kline/AP

The man on the left in the photo taken at Fresh Kills is an FBI agent. The man with the hard hat is FEMA coordinating officer Ted Monette.[622] As mentioned in Chapter 1, on September 11, 2001—the exact day of the attack on the WTC—President Bush personally appointed Monette to serve as the Federal Coordinating Officer (FCO) for FEMA at the WTC. As such, he was the senior federal official who was

> responsible for establishing the immediate federal presence on the scene, establishing command and control of federal resources, and coordinating all federal assets deployed for the response and initial recovery efforts supporting the City and State of New York.[623]

One might expect that Mr. Monette and the FBI agent would both be extremely interested in knowing if the serial numbers on the engine in front of them matched the maintenance records for either of the planes that were alleged to have hit the twin towers. But they neglected to check that.

As for Monette, his failure to do that could very well have been due to the fact that he was operating under the direct supervision of Vice President Cheney's Office of National Preparedness (ONP). As for the FBI's negligence in not checking the serial numbers of this engine, that is simply inexplicable unless one considers the possibility that it was being directly influenced by the Bush White House.

The other photo is of one of the engines from the plane that hit the South Tower. This engine was found a few blocks away from the WTC, at the intersection of Murray and Recker Streets.[624] There is no record showing that its serial numbers were ever checked, either.

The planes that hit the towers on 9/11 had a total of four engines between them (two each). They were made of high strength steel with a titanium core, some of the hardest metals known to man. They could not have been melted or totally blown apart. Just like the steel columns and beams from the towers, they should have survived in the debris pile. Yet the Bush administration investigators say they never recovered the other two engines. But how could that be? Even the WTC debris at Fresh

Kills was put through a screening process so intense that even very small fragments of bone and pieces of human flesh were sifted out. So, what happened to the other engines?

Also, contrary to what Valiquette said, there were a great many pieces of plane parts found at the WTC. The FBI collected them in this dumpster.

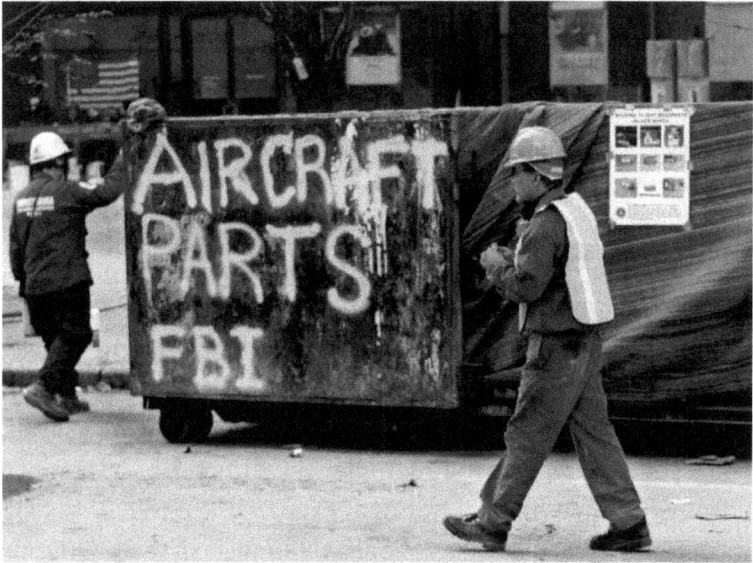

FBI Plane Parts
Copyright: Ryan Remiorz/AP

Unfortunately, like the missing steel from the towers, all of those plane parts, including the engines, were hauled off to God-knows-where, never to be seen again.

The Question of Access

Even in the face of this overwhelming evidence, many defenders of the official story of the attacks continue to dismiss it all in one fell swoop by claiming that it would have been an impossible task to rig either of the WTC towers with explosives without being detected. That, however, is not necessarily so. Getting access to the towers could have been done with the cooperation of Securacom, the company that handled security for the WTC. Or it could have been done with the cooperation of the owners of the complex. Once either (or both) of those was assured, planting the explosives could easily have been done during the nighttime, or other hours of low occupancy.

The notion that security could have been compromised is given considerable weight by the striking coincidence that the company doing security upgrades at the WTC during the year before the attacks, Securacom, was intimately tied to President Bush, with his brother, Marvin, and his first cousin, Wirt Walker, being top leaders of that company.[625]

As to the possibility that the conspirators also had connections to the owners: that was given substantial credibility by a self-incriminating statement made by **Larry Silverstein** of Silverstein Properties (the company that held the lease on the WTC) in the Public Broadcasting System's film "America Rebuilds."[626]

Silverstein in "American Rebuilds"

In that film, this is how he described the moment when he first became aware that Building 7 was going to be intentionally demolished:

I remember getting a call from the fire department commander, telling me that they were not sure they were gonna be able to contain the fire. And I said, "We've had such a terrible loss of life, maybe the smartest thing to do is pull it." And they made the decision to pull, and we watched the building collapse.[627]

By the time he made this statement, Silverstein was a highly successful real estate developer and had years of experience with large-scale inner city projects, going back to 1957.[628] There can be little doubt about what he was referring to by the use of the term "pull." It is technical lingo used by experts in the business of controlled demolitions. It means to bring a building down through the use of explosives. This presents a big problem for him, because it takes weeks to rig a building for demolition, not the few hours that he implied the "fire department commander" took.

Although some time later, Silverstein made an effort to backpedal from this stunning admission of complicity, it was clumsy and not convincing. In June of 2005, he was asked by *New York Post* reporter Sam Smith what he had meant by use of the term "pull it", and Silverstein was evasive. He simply responded that he "meant something else" by it.[629] And that was it.

A few months later, on September 9, 2005, the Bush administration's State Department, no less, took up the torch in support of Silverstein.[630] It released a statement by Silverstein Properties spokesperson, Dara McQuillan, in which McQuillan stated that Silverstein, by saying "pull it," was referring to the withdrawal of firemen who were inside Building 7, trying to put out fires. But this assertion would make his original statement rather incorrect grammatically. If that is truly what he meant, he should have more properly said pull "them," not pull "it." Moreover, it has been documented by several sources that there were no firemen fighting fires in Building 7 at the time he made the "pull it" comment to the "fire department commander."[631]

Furthermore, in the days after the attacks, several Port Authority (PA) officials came forward to say that Silverstein had recently taken over command of the safety systems in place at the WTC. According to the *New York Times*:

[Port Authority] executives like Alan L. Reiss, the director of the World Trade Center, had been working on a transition team with

Silverstein Properties that was to last for three months. But in recent weeks, agency executives said, Silverstein Properties asked Reiss to let it more fully operate everything from safety systems to tenant relations.[632]

This issue surfaced when it was learned that after the North Tower was hit, several security people with bullhorns appeared at lower levels of the South Tower, urging workers trying to get out of the building to go back to their offices. They were being told that the building was "secure."[633] Most did not listen to this nonsense. But many of those who did added to the death toll when Flight 175 struck the building, minutes later.

One of those was Shimmy Biegeleisen. He was working on the 97th floor of the South Tower when the North Tower was hit. Subsequently, he called his family to say that he was okay. During that call, his family members could hear an announcement in the background being given over the PA system, telling people to stay in their offices and that the building was "secure."[634] Being a responsible employee, Biegeleisen obeyed. When his building was hit minutes later, thinking he was trapped, he ended up being killed in the collapse. Evidence would later show that the A Stairway in that building was clear up to his floor.[635] But he was never given that information.

Also, evidence shows that Silverstein was scheduled to have a breakfast meeting with some tenants in the Window on the World restaurant on the 106th floor of the North Tower early on the morning of the attack, something that was a regular routine of his. But he had called it off. His excuse was that his wife had, unbeknownst to him, already made a doctor's appointment for him.[636] If that is the truth, given what happened that day, he was an extremely fortunate man. But he has never revealed the names of the people he was supposed to meet with, nor has he explained how, or even if, he had called them early (the building was hit at 8:47 a.m.), or if any of them had shown up for the meeting and were, therefore, killed in the collapse.

In summary, Silverstein's motives before, during, and after 9/11 are suspect.

Also, as to the question of access to the towers for the planting of explosives, a few witnesses who worked at the WTC came forward to describe several unusual occurrences that took place in the days prior to the attack, which could have provided opportunities for conspirators to enter the buildings unmolested. One of these witnesses was Scott Forbes. He was an information technology specialist for Fiduciary Trust, which occupied floors 90 and 94 through 97 of the South Tower. On April 9, 2004, prompted by an internet posting entitled, "The Official Version of 9/11 is a Hoax," he sent the writer, John Kaminski, a letter, saying this:

> On the weekend of 9/8, 9/9 there was a 'power-down' condition in WTC tower 2, the South Tower. This power down condition meant there was no electrical supply for approx 36hrs from floor 50 up. I am aware of this situation since all systems were cleanly shutdown beforehand…And then brought back up afterwards. The reason given by the WTC for the power down was that cabling in the tower was being upgraded…Of course without power there were no security cameras, no security locks on doors and many, many 'engineers' coming in and out of the tower.[637]

His account was corroborated by a coworker, Gary Corbett, who said there was a "complete breakdown of security that weekend because of the power-down."[638] According to him, the power-down started on Friday night, at the close of business, and only came back up on Sunday afternoon.

Another witness was Ben Fountain, who also worked in the South Tower. He was a financial analyst for Fireman's Fund and had his office on the 47th floor. That was three floors below the block of upper floors that Forbes and Corbett said had the power cutoff. The day after the attack, he told *People Magazine* that, in the weeks before 9/11, his company had been evacuated several times for security drills.[639] He thought the evacuations were very unusual and had the suspicion that "they (presumably meaning the owners of the building and/or Securacom) knew something was going on."

Granted, a weekend window of opportunity seems a very tight time slot to plant the thousands of explosive devices that it would take to bring down a 110-story building. But it could have been last-minute final touches to devices already planted that were behind this final rush of "engineers" into the building.

Perhaps the most important witness of all concerning the question of access is Daria Coard, a former security guard who worked in the North Tower. She recounted to *Newsday* how bomb-sniffing dogs, which had had a presence at the WTC since the 1993 bombing, a period of some eight years, were abruptly removed on Thursday, September 6.[640] That was just two days before the many "engineers" started working on the "cabling" in the South Tower.

Rigging the Buildings

As for the actual process of planting explosives in the towers, that would have taken a considerable amount of time, but it would not have been difficult. Planting either traditional explosive charges or thermate devices on the core columns could have been done via the elevator shafts.

Refer to the typical core area plan that follows. The larger boxes marked with an "X" are elevators. Notice how many columns are located in their shafts.

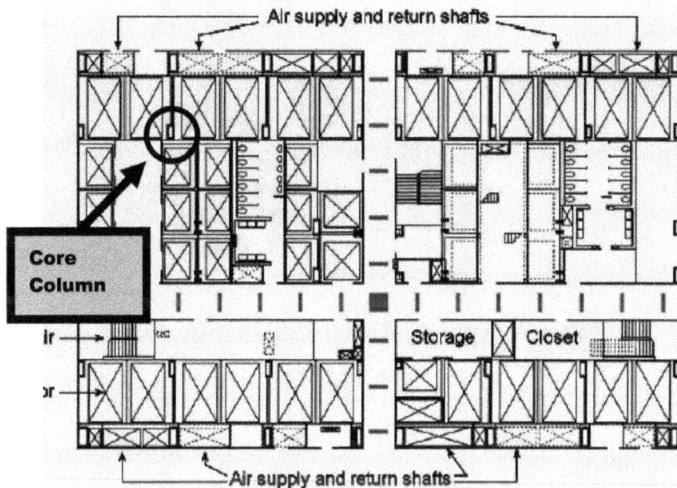

Typical Core Area

Remotely controlled devices could be attached to these columns simply by riding the top of an elevator car and planting them along the way.

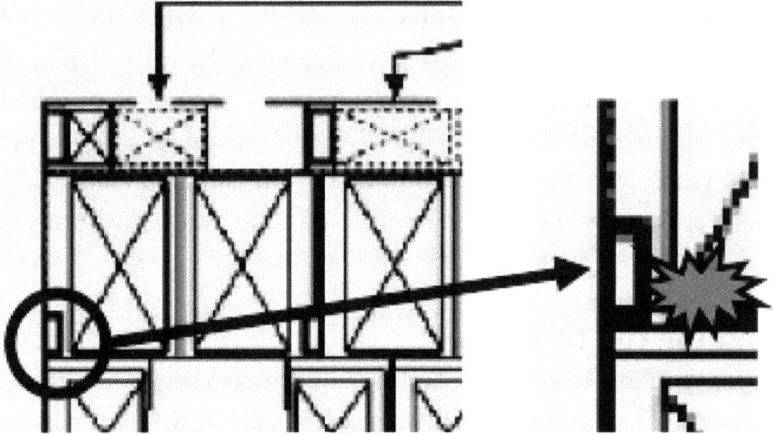

Core Column Details

The planting of explosive devices on the floor trusses and at their end connections could also have been easily done. In the office areas, the ceiling was a simple dropped acoustic tile system. Note the following drawing, showing its construction.

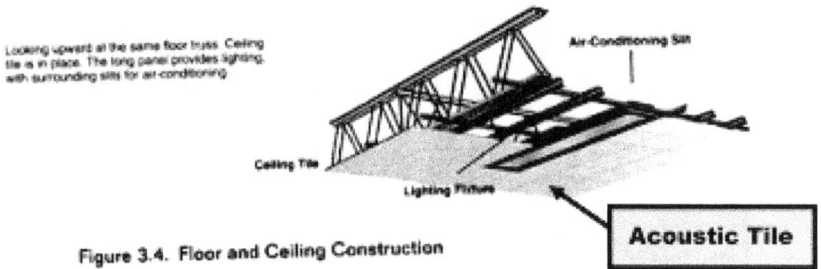

Figure 3.4. Floor and Ceiling Construction

Floor and Ceiling Construction
Source: FEMA

All one had to do was remove some of the tiles, attach more remotely controlled explosive devices to the trusses and their column end connections where needed, and replace the tiles.

Note the following drawing.

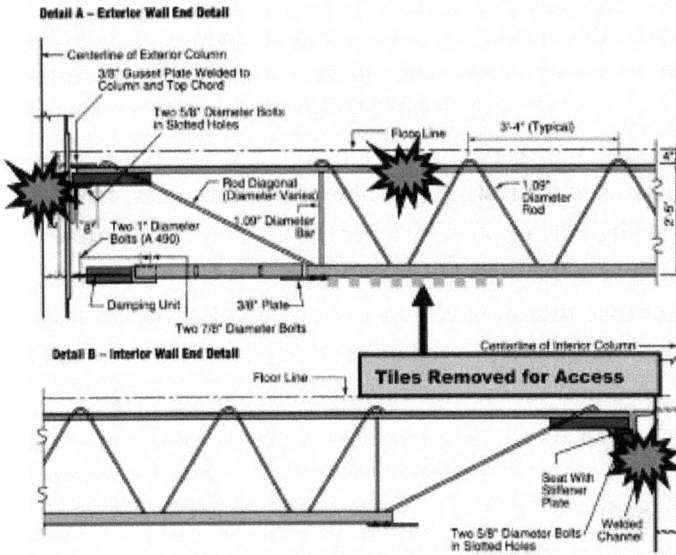

Planting Explosive Devices on Floor Trusses and Columns
(Original Drawing) Source: NIST

With this, the buildings would be ready for demolition.

Detonating the thousands of devices that would have been involved in this kind of complex demolition plan could have been handled remotely through the use of a modern, computerized, and highly portable control panel that is typically no larger than a small suitcase. Its operator could have been conveniently located in any nearby building that had a good view of the planes coming in, so that he or she could time the first explosions to coincide with the crashes in order to make it appear that jet fuel caused secondary explosions in the towers.

That scenario is given a lot of weight by the fact of the fire at the SCC control center that was described in Chapter 4, "More Explosions." That fire could not have been caused by jet fuel coming down a shaft. That fact, combined with the fact that it flamed up at precisely the time of plane impact, is a strong indication that it was caused by an incendiary device that was remotely detonated by a person observing Flight 11's approach.

Of course, the structural steel in the debris pile of any building brought down this way would be loaded with residues of explosives and very possibly with various trace elements characteristic of the thermate reaction. The BPS team of investigators sent by the ASCE certainly had access to procedures used for testing for them. But then again, any such testing was made virtually impossible after the Cheney cabal banned the team from the site for the three months that it took Giuliani to have a critical amount of that vital steel evidence shipped out of the country as scrap.

As NIST candidly admitted in its 2006 paper, "Answers to Frequently Asked Questions," no such testing was ever done; not even on one, single, solitary piece of steel.

Conclusion

The evidence presented in this chapter makes it perfectly clear that the North Tower—and, by implication, the South Tower and Building 7, as well—was brought down by explosives in the manner of an inside job of controlled demolition. It also shows that, although the plane crashes could have very well been the work of terrorists, the actual collapses had nothing to do with Osama bin Laden or al Qaeda.

Clearly, the Bush administration's official investigations were charades meant to ignore or destroy key evidence of that.

*   *   *

Who actually placed the explosives in the WTC buildings, and when and how that was done, remains a mystery. But let there be no illusion that it could have been bin Laden's terrorists, acting independently. For several reasons, that would have been impossible. In the first place, designing a demolition plan sufficient to cause the almost total disintegration of three tall buildings could not have been done without first having an extensive technical understanding of how they were built. Thus, getting possession of their construction drawings was an imperative. However, to get those plans, bin Laden would have needed some significant amount of influence with either the Port Authority of New York and New Jersey (PANYNJ), the agency that built the trade center, or Silverstein Properties, the company that had acquired the lease on the buildings, because those drawings were tightly held and never released to the public.[641] This practicality rules out al Qaeda.

Secondly, the number of explosive devices required to bring all three buildings down had to be enormous, and it is impossible to think that bin Laden's terrorists could have acquired them anywhere in the US without raising suspicion. For example, the tallest building ever demolished up to 9/11 was the 344-foot tall 500 Wood Street in Pittsburgh.[642] It was done by Controlled Demolition, Inc. of New Jersey. That job required 1,590 explosive charges, weighing 595 pounds.[643] Judging by that, in order to demolish the twin towers, which were almost four times as high at 1,370 feet, and Building 7, which was about half the height of the towers, it would have likely taken altogether about 16,000 explosive charges, weighing close to 6,000 pounds.[644] No doubt, demolition experts could have found a way to reduce that number somewhat, but it still would have been huge.

Thirdly, assuming that bin Laden could have gotten possession of those explosives, it is impossible to think that his disciples could have gotten the freedom of access required to plant them without being detected. All those bombs would have had to have been trucked into various underground parking areas, hand-carried into the three buildings, and placed at critical points throughout their entire steel frameworks. Then, if they were not set to be exploded remotely, detonation cords would have to have been run throughout the buildings, from top to bottom.

Adding to the difficulty of that task, is the fact that security at the WTC was extremely tight. After the '93 bombing, it was upgraded to the tune of about $100 million.[645] Under a new protocol, in order to enter the twin towers, either in the main lobbies or in one of the underground parking areas, a visitor first had to be interviewed, photographed, entered into a computer, and given a plastic picture ID card.[646] In addition, video surveillance cameras were installed virtually everywhere, from the outside perimeter of the roofs to the six subbasement levels, and they were constantly being monitored from a security office on the 22nd floor of the North Tower and a second, backup office in the B1 subbasement level of the South Tower.[647] Perhaps most important is that security guards were expected to be always patrolling, often with bomb-sniffing dogs.[648]

Finally, the complexity of the twin towers' design most certainly would have required a very complex demolition plan. In actual practice, the timing of the thousands of explosions would have required the use of a programmable, computerized control panel. But that requires a rare, specialized skill-set to operate, which is something that only a handful of companies in the world and the US military possess. In all likelihood, it also well beyond the capabilities of al Qaeda.

*　*　*

All of this points to the collapses being an inside job. But, if so, who could have facilitated it? For an answer to that, one must, as normal police practice also dictates, look at who was involved in the cover-up. Ultimately, since it was Bush's May 2001 directive to FEMA that created the ONP and put Cheney as its head and in a position to affect the cover-up, that brings us back, once again, to the White House.

Some may argue that President Bush was personally unaware that the WTC buildings were going to be brought down by explosives, that his May 2001 order to Allbaugh to create the ONP was done innocently and that Cheney was the real evil-doer who took advantage of the leverage that gave him to further his own agenda. But on the other hand, it is highly likely that had a proper investigation of the collapses been done, it very well would have revealed the intimate family ties that the president could have had to a controlled demolition plot. As mentioned previously, this stems from the fact that his brother, Marvin Bush, and his cousin, Wirt Walker, had strong connections to Securacom, a company that had been upgrading the security system at the WTC since 1996.[649]

Per Securities and Exchange Commission filings, Marvin Bush was a director of that company up to the fiscal year 2000, and Wirt was its

Chief Executive Officer (CEO) on the day of the 9/11 attacks and remained so until sometime in 2002.[650] And according to Barry McDaniel, who succeeded Wirt as CEO, their WTC contract was "ongoing" when the "center went down."[651] This would have given Wirt and Marvin supervisory control over Securacom's job for several years leading up to the attacks. With that, they would have been in a perfect position to ensure that their workers doing the "security upgrades" got extensive private access to every nook and cranny of all three buildings to plant the thousands of explosives.

Another remarkable connection that would have proven embarrassing to the White House, had the official explanation for the collapses been undermined, is the fact that in the year 2000 Marvin joined the board of one of the insurance carriers for the WTC, HCC Insurance.[652] After the WTC was destroyed, HCC was one of the companies that paid the owners of the WTC, real estate magnate Larry Silverstein and his partners, $4.5 billion for their loss.

Marvin would subsequently resign his directorship sometime in 2002. The reason was never made public.

Epilogue

AS TO THE QUESTION OF MOTIVE for such a heinous crime as engineering the WTC collapses and knowingly snuffing out the lives of thousands of innocent people, that requires a deeper look. For an answer to that burning question, following normal police procedure is, again, helpful. It dictates that we look for who *benefited* from the crime.

The most obvious answer is the corporate war machine that supplied the armed conflicts that resulted; billions of taxpayer dollars were transferred into its coffers in Afghanistan and Iraq. For a prime example of that take Haliburton, a company for which V.P. Cheney was a former CEO. It was tipping on the verge of bankruptcy before the administration awarded it several no-bid contracts to supply war materials to those military campaigns. That not only saved Haliburton from possibly being thrown on the junk heap of history, but it also made it possible for Cheney to personally profit to the tune of $8 million on stock he still owned in the company.[653]

But then, the question becomes: Why the collapses? Would not the plane crashes have been enough to spur the country on to war? Apparently, the cabal of insiders responsible did not think so. It is quite possible that they took their cue from the so-called *Project for a New American Century* (PNAC), a neoconservative think tank that was manned by several powerful people associated with the Bush administration.[654] PNAC's membership included Cheney, President Bush's brother, Jeb, Donald Rumsfeld (Bush's Secretary of Defense), Paul Wolfowitz (Bush's Undersecretary of Defense), Richard Perle (a former Assistant Secretary of Defense), James Woolsey (a former Director of the CIA), John Bolton (Bush's Ambassador to the UN), Elliot Abrams (a former Assistant Secretary of State), Robert Zoellick (a former President of the World Bank), Lewis "Scooter" Libby (Cheney's chief of staff) and Dan Quayle (a former vice-president under George H W Bush).

About a year before 9/11, PNAC published an unabashed warmongering manifesto entitled "Rebuilding America's Defenses: Strategies, Forces, and Resources for a New Century." It espoused the theory that, in order to establish American hegemony in a post-Cold War world, the specter of US military would need to be increased exponentially.[655] But to accomplish that would take a long time, unless something spectacularly catalyzing happened that could gain the support of the public for such a huge build-up. Something was needed that was, they said, "like a new Pearl Harbor." Pearl Harbor, being that history-altering event that launched America into WWII.

Of course, there is no proof that that is the way the plot for WTC demolitions came down. But however it happened, those collapses did the job. It was, in fact, exactly like a new Pearl Harbor; the stunning nature of seeing those two iconic towers fall raised the 9/11 attacks to mythic proportions and galvanized a cry for revenge against the Middle East.

Upon reflection, the fog of cognitive dissonance created in the mind of the public by the startling nature of the collapses is impressive. Even though the unorthodox official explanation for them defies the basic laws of physics taught in every high school in the country, the inertia toward war they set in motion could not be stopped. Those immutable laws of science that were born of an apple falling on the head of Sir Isaac Newton all those hundreds of years ago—laws which had made it possible to put a man on the moon—suddenly became no longer valid. Somehow, it became accepted that the impossible could happen—that a massive, expertly engineered, steel-framed building could collapse like a house of cards due to fire, alone. And three in the same day, no less.

No one has ever better understood how this suspension of rational thinking can come to infect the consciousness of a nation than did that charismatic, evil genius, Adolph Hitler. From somewhere in the darker reaches of his blighted soul, he conjured up a practical method for manipulating a country into war that works. He called it the "Big Lie" technique. This is how he described it his 1925 book *Mein Kampf* ("My Struggle"):

[In] the big lie, there is always a certain force of credibility; because the broad masses of a nation are always more easily corrupted in the deeper strata of their emotional nature than consciously or voluntarily; and thus, in the primitive simplicity of their minds they more readily fall victims to the big lie than the small lie, since they themselves often tell small lies in little matters but would be ashamed to resort to large-scale falsehoods. It would never come into their heads to fabricate colossal untruths, and they would not believe that others could have the impudence to distort the truth so infamously. Even though the facts which prove this to be so may be brought clearly to their minds, they will still doubt and waver and will continue to think that there may be some other explanation. For the grossly impudent lie always leaves traces behind it, even after it has been nailed down, a fact which is known to all expert liars in this world and to all who conspire together in the art of lying.[656]

In other words, on matters of great consequence, we do not expect our government to lie, so we assume the official story is the truth. The Big Lie in Hitler's time was how, in order to militarize the German populace and lay the groundwork for WWII, he secretly engineered the torching of the Reichstag Building, the home of Parliament and a symbol of democracy, and blamed it on communist terrorists. On 9/11, the Big Lie was that the WTC collapses were caused by al Qaeda plane crashes.

And just as Hitler predicted, those spectacular collapses caused a kind of mass psychosis in a significant segment of the population. Blind, widespread belief in the unlikely official explanation for the collapses allowed for the Bush administration to make things happen that would have previously been unthinkable. When the quick passage by Congress of the 342-page Patriot Act—without so much as a reading—took a huge bite out of traditional American civil liberties in the name of the newly-minted "War on Terror," there was hardly a whimper of protest. Nor was there much concern expressed for the massive loss of innocent civilian lives that occurred when—just four weeks after 9/11—the US invasion of Afghanistan commenced with the indiscriminate bombing of Kandahar. Even to this day, it continues; few people seem to mind that in 2014 the National Defense Authorization Act (NDAA) gave the US military the power to snatch any American citizen off the street who is merely *suspected* of ties to a terrorist group and secretly hold him or her indefinitely without trial.[657]

Such was the power of the "Big Lie" of the WTC collapses. In the immediacy of the 9/11 attacks, it gave birth to a mythology that became burned into the consciousness of far too many patriotic, yet tragically uninformed, people.

*　*　*

As to the entire scope of what happened at the WTC on 9/11, the fact that the controlled demolitions could only have been the result of an inside job leads to only two possibilities; either the collapses were piggybacked onto an existing al Qaeda plot to crash planes, or they were part of a wider inside job that encompassed the entirety of the 9/11 events, including the plane crashes. The former possibility seems the more likely of the two. But, as the information in Appendix F shows, the latter cannot be entirely ruled out.

In any case, polling has consistently shown that a majority of Americans are deeply troubled by the multitude of inconsistencies that have been uncovered in the Bush administration's account the attacks.[658] As mentioned, a 2007 Zogby poll showed that more than 106.6 million adult members of the public (51%) held that view.[659, 660] They wanted Bush and Cheney "investigated regarding the 9/11 attacks."

No doubt, what is also hugely troubling to an enormous segment of the country is the intensity with which the president who succeeded Bush, Barack Obama, persisted in refusing to address the controversy. Just after taking office, he basically put his arm around Bush and Cheney and admonished their critics to "look forward as opposed to looking backwards."[661]Taking his own advice, he did so himself—and with a vigor uncharacteristic of the liberal-minded façade he had run on.

And that was not done without his first having access to the facts. In early 2008, a group backing author David Ray Griffin and working though his publisher, delivered a copy of his book, *9/11 Contradictions; An Open Letter to Congress and the Press*, to the offices of every Democratic member of Congress, including Obama, who was then a senator.[662] That book covers twenty-five major contradictions in the official story of the 9/11 attacks and presents a forceful argument for a complete reinvestigation.

There can be little doubt that it was brought to Obama's attention. At the time, his office was staffed by sixty people, many of whose job it was to carefully read and respond to incoming mail.[663, 664] One would think that a book by someone of Griffin's credibility would have provoked some serious discussion; he was, after all, a Claremont Graduate University professor of theology and the author of some thirty books on other subjects. But, despite having direct access to the provocative information contained in Griffin's book that touches on virtually every controversial aspect of the 9/11 attacks, President Obama never acknowledged, even in the slightest degree, that a legitimate argument exists.

Nor did he ever intend to. He made that clear in a May 5, 2011 statement to the country concerning the death of Osama bin Laden. (Bin Laden had been shot dead three days earlier by US Navy Seals during a nighttime raid on his compound in Pakistan.) In the course of his statement, Obama said that anyone who would even so much as question that "justice" had been done when bin Laden was killed "needs to have their head examined."[665]

But that statement should be troubling to any fair-minded person. Before saying that, did the president take into consideration the tens of millions of Americans the Zogby poll indicated had serious doubts about the official account of the 9/11 attacks? Was he insinuating that all those millions of people are insane?

Or, did he consider the findings of his own Justice Department? He must have been aware that the reason the FBI had never listed the 9/11 attacks on bin Laden's Most Wanted page was because, as bureau spokesman Rex Tomb candidly admitted in a 2006 interview, "The FBI has *no* hard evidence connecting bin Laden to 9/11."[666,667]

Moreover, since when is it justice to declare a man guilty of a crime before giving him due process. As a former constitutional law professor, Obama must have been keenly aware that, under our system, even a mass murderer gets a fair trial before he is executed.

Perhaps the most revealing example of the kind of painfully un-American stance Obama has taken on this issue is what rightwing columnist and leading Bush administration apologist Charles Krauthammer wrote regarding the firing of White House aide Van Jones. Jones had become the object of an intense campaign of hate mongering in the mainstream media after he signed a petition asking for a reinvestigation of the 9/11 attacks, which had as part of its premise that the Bush administration may have been somehow involved. After Obama fired Jones, Krauthammer defended the president, saying this:

> [Van Jones] is gone for one reason and one reason only. You can't sign a petition demanding…investigations of the charge that the Bush administration deliberately allowed Sept. 11, 2001—i.e., collaborated in the worst massacre ever perpetrated on American soil—and be permitted in polite society, let alone have a high-level job in the White House. Unlike the other stuff…, this is no trivial matter. It's beyond radicalism, beyond partisanship. It takes us into the realm of political psychosis, a malignant paranoia that, unlike the Marxist posturing, is not amusing. It's dangerous…You can no more have a truther in the White House than you can have a Holocaust denier—a person who creates a hallucinatory alternative reality in the service of a fathomless malice.[668]

Just the hyperbolic, over-the-top nature of this tirade is enough to indicate that Krauthammer was also not dealing with a full deck. Most significant in this piece is the fact that he mirrors Obama exactly by studiously avoiding a frank discussion of the facts of the case. Instead, also like Obama, he resorts to name-calling, saying that anyone who questions the official account is crazy. There are only two possibilities that can explain the odd coupling of these two unlikely allies from opposing poles of the political spectrum: Either they were both ignorant of the vast amount of inconsistencies surrounding the 9/11 attacks that the majority of Americans find disconcerting and were shooting from the hip (not likely), or they were acting as shills who were recruited to keep up the ruse that the official story has legs (very likely).

Furthermore, since when, in this day and age, is having an opinion based on science a sign of a mental disorder? The 2,900 professional architects and engineers who have petitioned Congress for a reinvestigation of the WTC collapses base their findings on sound scientific principles, not on a "hallucinatory alternative reality." Nor do they need their heads "examined." That massive group of technical experts, many of whom have PhDs in structural engineering, insist that there is so much solid evidence that so strongly supports the claim that it was explosives that caused the deaths of so many people at the WTC that having a reinvestigation of the collapses is not only the reasonable thing to do, but that there is an underlying moral obligation that demands it.

Whether Congress ever musters the courage to heed that call remains to be seen. But one thing is certain: Failure to have such an honest, open reinvestigation will ensure that the complete story of what happened at the WTC on 9/11 will forever join the victims of the collapses in the grave, eternally pushing up daisies of regret for those tens of millions of people who do not believe the official account but feel powerless to do anything about it. The truth, if Obama, Krauthammer, and others of their ilk get their way, simply will not be told in any official forum, not ever.

Appendix A:

The Force Needed to Displace a Perimeter Panel

IN THE NORTH TOWER, there were two floor trusses bolted to every other perimeter column. The top chords of the trusses were connected to a seat angle, and the bottom chord was connected with a so-called "damping unit." See the detail, below.

Detail A – Exterior Wall End Detail

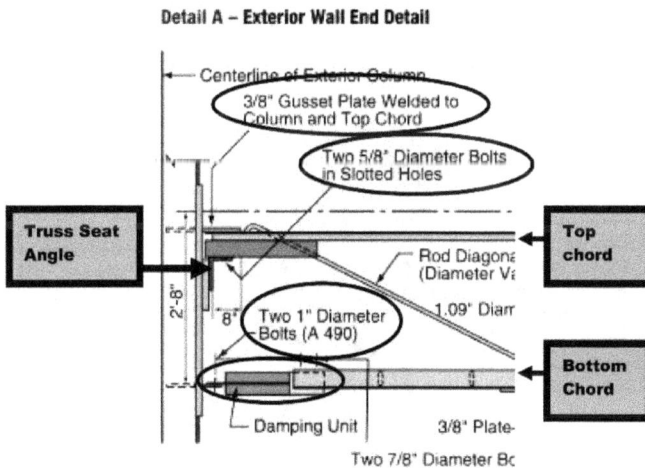

- Centerline of Exterior Column
- 3/8" Gusset Plate Welded to Column and Top Chord
- Two 5/8" Diameter Bolts in Slotted Holes

Truss Seat Angle

Top chord

Rod Diagona (Diameter Va

2'-8"   8"   Two 1" Diameter Bolts (A 490)

1.09" Diarr

Bottom Chord

Damping Unit   3/8" Plate

Two 7/8" Diameter Bc

Perimeter Column to Floor Truss Connections
Source: FEMA

There was one other connection involved here that was called a diagonal brace member. It is shown in the following drawing of the tower's floor grid system.

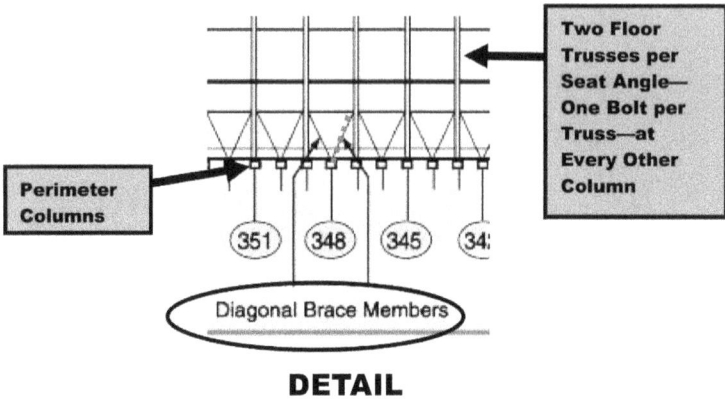

DETAIL

These braces were welded at the top chord of the floor trusses and to their own seat angles at the spandrel plate. The purpose of the braces was to provide an additional stabilizing factor for the trusses at the perimeter columns.

Below, the previous photograph has been annotated to show the locations of all of the connections that held a perimeter panel in place.

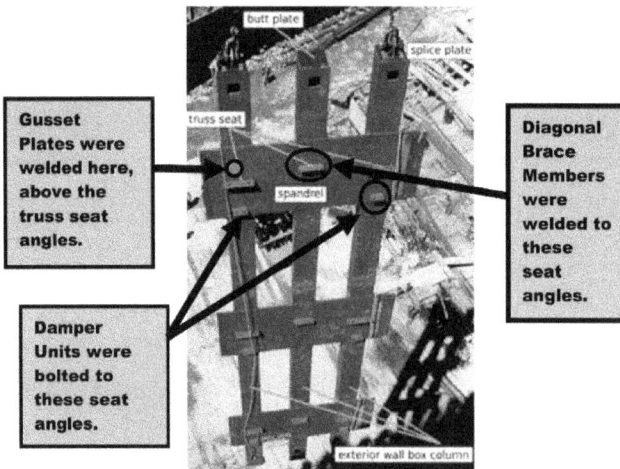

Source: PANY/NJ

What follows is an accounting of the forces needed to overcome all of those connections. (Note: If explosives inside the building are assumed as the cause

332

of dislodging a panel, then all of the connectors holding the panel in place in the building would have failed in shear except the gusset plates and the diagonal bracing members, which would most likely have failed in tension.)

1. Floor Truss Bolts. Refer to the above photograph and drawing for the locations of these bolts. The relevant formula for calculating shear capacity of one 5/8-inch, A325 high strength bolt is

$$R_v = .62F_v \, A_x \, (1.18)$$

where F_v is 120 ksi, the tensile capacity of an A325 bolt.[669] The factor .62 is the coefficient for converting tensile strength of A325 steel to shear strength (steel is stronger in tension than in shear). A_x is 0.307 square inches, the effective cross-sectional area of one 5/8-inch bolt. And 1.18 represents the fact that testing has found that high strength bolts normally exceed their calculated tensile strength by 18 percent.

Solving for R_v:

$$Rv = .62 \text{ x } 120 \text{ x } .307 \text{ x } 1.18$$
$$RV = 26.95 \text{ kips}$$

Each panel had 12 of these bolts. The total resistive force of the truss seat bolts was thus **323.40 kips** (26.95 x 12), in shear, or 323,400 pounds.

2. Gusset Plates. The relevant formula for tensile capacity of one 3/8-inch by 4-inch A36 steel gusset plate is

Ru = Ag Fu

where A_g is 1.5 square inches (.375 x 4) and F_u is the tensile strength of A36 steel, 60 ksi.[670]

Solving for R_u:

$$Ru = 1.5 \times 60$$
$$Ru = 90 \text{ kips}$$

There were 6 gusset plates in a panel. The total resistive force of the gusset plates was therefore **540 kips** (90 x 6), in tension, or 540,000 pounds.

3. Damper Units. The damping units connected the bottom chords of the floor trusses to the perimeter columns. Their purpose was to dampen the effects of the natural side to side sway of the building—which was several feet in either direction—to make it less noticeable to the occupants. See the above for their location.

The weakest link in this unit was the four 1/4-inch bolts that held the damper together internally.

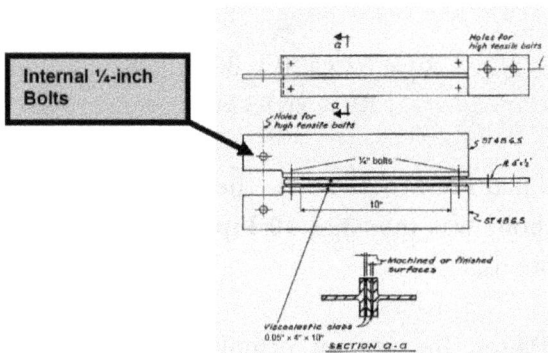

Damping Unit – Floors 7 to 107
Source: NIST

They are not noted as being "high strength," which means they were made of ordinary A36 steel. The equation for finding the shear capacity (R_v) of one of the 1/4-inch bolts is

RV = (Fv Ax)

where A_x is 0.06 in^2, the cross-sectional area of the shank of a 1/4-inch bolt. A36 steel has a shear capacity, F_v, of 36 ksi.[671]

Solving for R_v:

$$Rv = 36 \times .06$$
$$RV = 2.16 \text{ kips}$$

There were 12 of these bolts. So their total resistive force would be **25.92 kips** (2.16 x 12), in shear, or 25,920 pounds.

4. Diagonal Brace Members. These steel straps measured 1-inch wide by 3/8 of an inch thick. They were made of ordinary A36 steel. And they failed in tension. The relevant formula for calculating the resistive force in tension for one brace is

$$Ru = Ag Fu$$

where A_g equals .375 (1 x .375). And F_u is the approximate tensile strength for A36 steel, 60 ksi.[672]

Solving for R_u:

$$Ru = .375 \times 60$$
$$Ru = 22.50 \text{ kips}$$

There were 12 brace members attached to each panel. The total resistive force of the brace members was then **270 kips** (22.50 x 12), or 270,000 pounds in tension.

5. Spandrel Splice Plate Bolts. Note the photograph of a perimeter panel above. The spandrel plates of adjoining perimeter panels overlapped with splice plates and were bolted. See the illustration below.

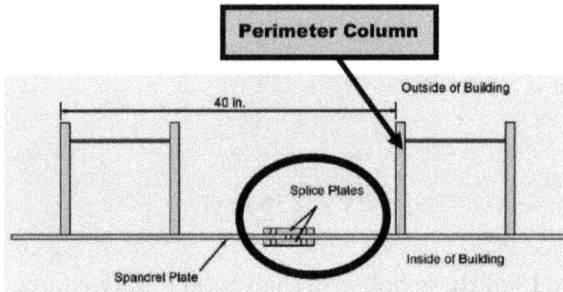

Spandrel Plate Splice Connection
Source: NIST

The splice bolts were 7/8-inch, high strength A325 bolts. The relevant formula for calculating the resistive shear strength for one bolt is

$$Ru = .62 \ As \ Fv \ (1.18)$$

where A_s equals .6013 square inches, the cross-sectional area of the bolt. F_v is 120 ksi, the tensile strength of high strength A325 steel.[673] The factor .62 refers to the fact that shear strength of A325 steel equals 62 percent of tensile strength. And the 1.18 factor, as in case 1, represents the fact that lab testing has shown that the actual tensile strength of the high strength steel exceeds its calculated strength by 18 percent.

Solving for R_u:

$$Ru = .6013 \ x \ 120 \ x \ .62 \ x \ 1.18$$
$$Ru = 52.8 \ kips$$

The number of bolts per spandrel splice varied depending upon how high up they were located in the tower. It is likely that the perimeter panels that were thrown into the upper floors of WFC

3 came from upper levels. And the NIST report says that on floors 68 through 71, there were ten bolts per spandrel connection. Using that number would give a good approximation for the panels that were thrown toward WFC 3. One complete exterior panel would have six total spandrel splices for a total of sixty bolts. Their total resistive capacity in shear would have been **3,168 kips** (52.8 kips x 60 bolts), or 3,168,000 pounds.

6. Butt Splice Plate Bolts. The perimeter columns were butted together with butt splice plates. The photograph below shows what they typically looked like.

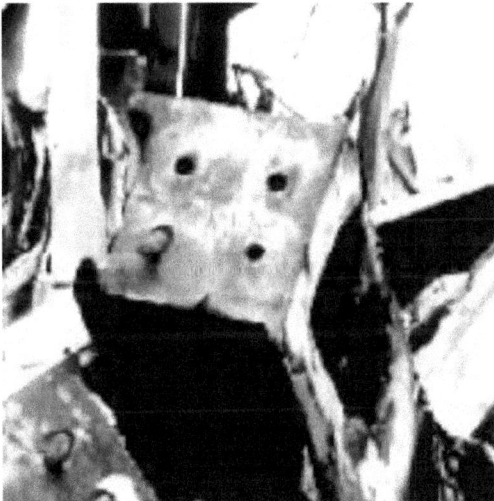

Source: FEMA

In the lower levels of the tower, there were six per column. In the upper levels, where the column spears that hit WFC 3 most likely came from, there were only 4.[674]

These bolts were also 7/8-inch and made of A325 steel. There were 24 of them altogether (4 per plate x 6 plates per panel). Their resistive strength in shear can be calculated from item 5. Their total resistive force would have been 52.8 kips x 24 bolts, or **1,267.20 kips** in shear—which is equal to 1,267,200 pounds.

Therefore, excluding factor of safety, the total minimum amount of force needed just to break all of a panel's connections that held it in place in the façade of the building and free it up so that it could then be thrown toward WFC 3 calculates out to be 5,954.52 kips, or 5,594,520 pounds (add items 1 thru 6). Normal engineering practice requires a factor of safety of 2 in connectors such as this.[675] Therefore, the actual resisting force needed to overcome the connectors in this case would have been an incredible **11,189,040 pounds**.

Appendix B:

The Force Needed to Shear NIST Samples C-46 and C-24

NOTE THE DETAIL below. It shows a typical perimeter column design for the twin towers.

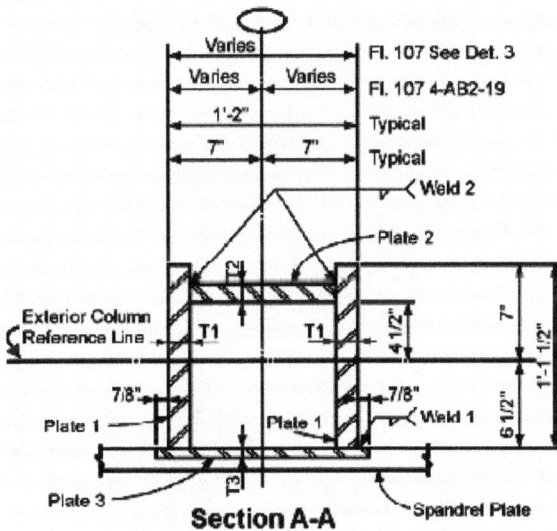

Perimeter Column Design

Source: NIST

The only missing variable in this drawing is the actual thickness of the plate at the seventy-sixth floor. But it is known that the thinnest plate thickness was ¼ inch, and that was at the upper levels, so using that figure for plate thickness would give a conservative estimate for the strength of the column in shear. The relevant formula is:

$$Fv = 3(Fs \ A)$$

F_v is the shear force needed to fracture the three columns. F_s is the shear strength of the high strength steel that was used at this level of the tower, which was 65 ksi (65,000 pounds per square inch).[676] And A is the cross-sectional area of the columns assuming a 1/4-inch plate thickness, which calculates to be 21.19 square inches.

Solving for total Fv:

$$Fv = 3 \ (65) \ 21.19$$
$$Fv = 4{,}132.05 \ kips$$

The minimum total force needed to shear the three columns of C-24 was an incredible **4,132,000 pounds**.

Appendix C:
The 50-, 6- and 7-Shafts

WHAT FOLLOWS IS AN in-depth examination of the North Tower elevator system, which explains the importance of the 50-, 6-, and 7-shafts to the charge that the explosions many witnesses observed in the lower levels of the building prior to its collapse could only have been due to a plan of controlled demolition.[677]

All Shafts Were Sealed Vertically

In order to understand why most of the 99 elevator shafts above ground in the tower did not provide a direct conduit to the lowest levels from the plane impact zone, it is important to note that each of the elevator cars was required to have its own lift motor at the top of its shaft. Those motors, which could be quite heavy, needed to occupy a level above the top floor serviced by that car. It is also important to know that each elevator car had to have its own return mechanism in the pit (its bottom). And that return mechanism had to occupy a level below the first floor serviced.

In many instances, the floor area over a lift motor room was reclaimed as additional rentable floor space if another elevator for the floors above it was not required. Or at other times, that reclaimed space above a motor room became the bottom pit for another elevator car that serviced an upper zone, if it was in the same vertical alignment. The North Tower blueprint below illustrates this aspect of the design.

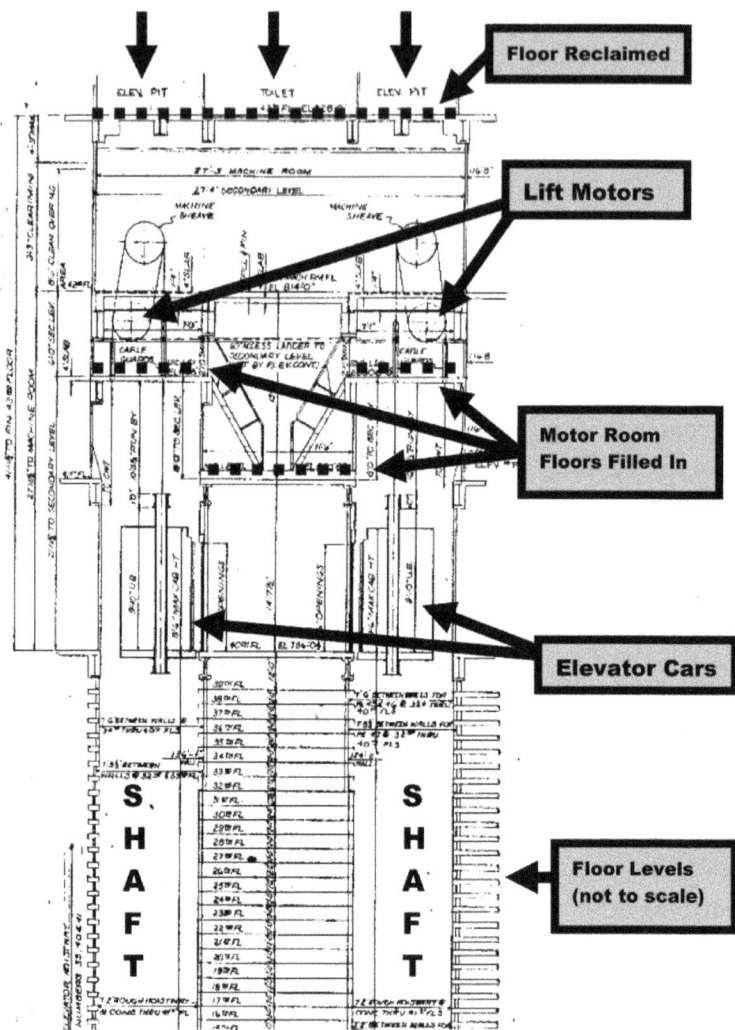

Upper Motor Rooms

Note that a lift motor room was created at the 41th floor in Zone 1 and how the 43rd floor above the lift motor room was reclaimed for a restroom and for the bottom pits of two other local elevators that serviced upper floors in Zone 2.

The following drawing shows the extension of the same shafts down to the B1 level, where their bottom pits were located.

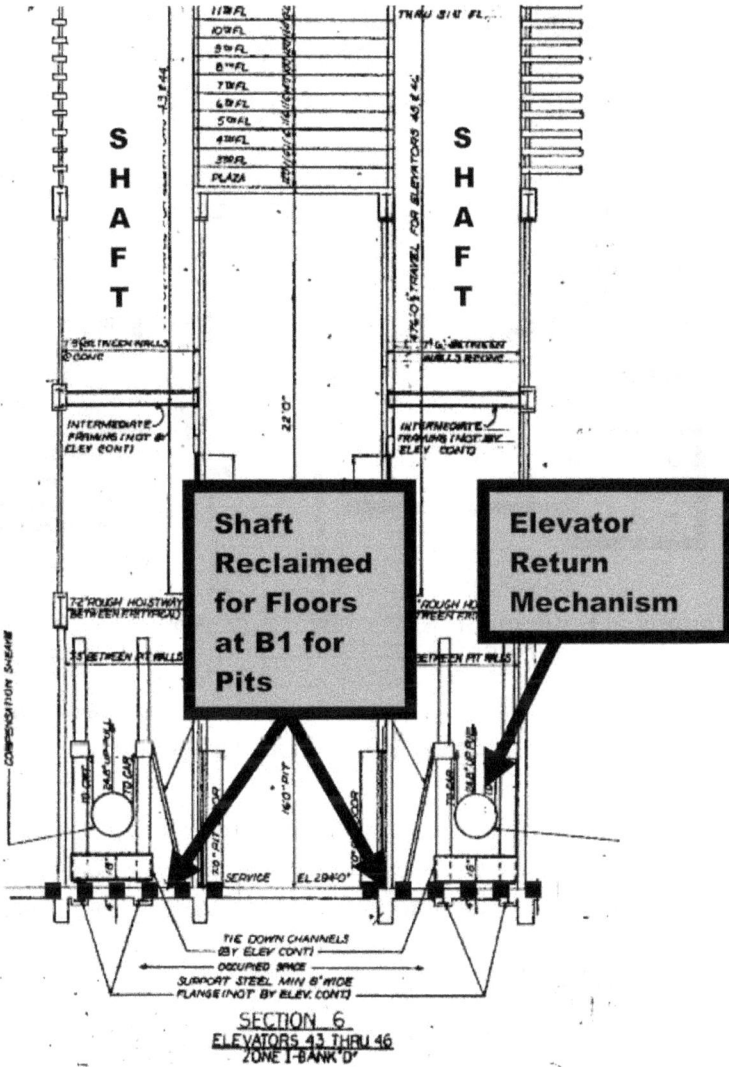

Shaft Reclaimed for Floors at B1 for Pits

Elevator Return Mechanism

SECTION 6
ELEVATORS 43 THRU 46
ZONE I BANK "D"

Bottom Pits at B1

Here, the B1 level has been filled in for pits to accommodate the return mechanism for these particular elevator cars.

In cases like these, the floors that were laid were substantial. They consisted of a 5-inch thick concrete slab with a compressive strength of

3,000 pounds per square inch (psi) that was poured onto a corrugated steel bed and a grid of steel reinforcing rods (rebar).

Next, note the illustration below. It shows the path of the 9/11 Commission's alleged fireball superimposed over the drawing for Zone 3.

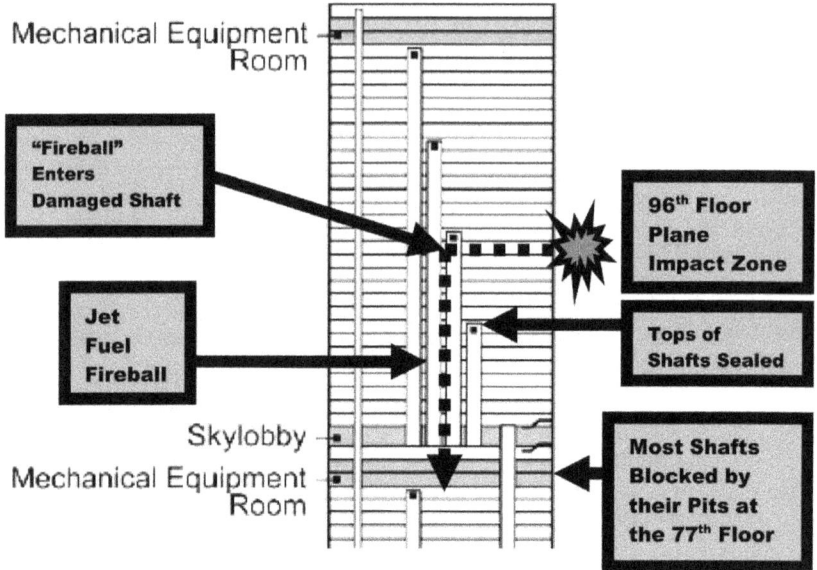

Zone 3 – North Tower

This shows that the tops of most of the elevator shafts below the plane impact zone would have been sealed, preventing any jet fuel or fireball from entering them. It also shows that should a shaft be damaged at the level of the plane impact and a fireball was able to enter it, in most cases it could go down no further than the pit which was—except for rare exceptions—located at the 77th floor.

The Shafts Were Also Sealed Horizontally

It is also important to note that all of the elevators in the tower were also hermetically sealed off from each other horizontally. The following drawings show the construction of the walls of the shafts.

Elevator Car

Gypsum Wall Construction in
Elevator Shafts and Office Spaces
Source: NIST

The detail "L/209" is a side view of the elevator shaft wall system. It shows that the wall was made of custom-made gypsum planks 2 inches thick for floors with 10-foot ceilings (it was 2½ inches thick on floors with 16-foot ceilings) and that it was 16 inches wide. On the office side of the shaft, the wall was finished off with two layers of ½-inch thick standard sheetrock, making a total wall thickness of 3 inches.

The drawing above on the right shows how the walls were constructed with a specially designed metal tongue-and-groove interlocking edge method. The planks were placed into metal L channels at the bottom of the walls, with channels of various shapes at the top, depending on the construction element with which they needed to interface. They were then screwed into place. The middle of the sheetrock planks had mesh reinforcement that increased their sturdiness. The thickness of all the gypsum walls in the tower was influenced by New York City fire regulations. They had to provide 2 hours of fire resistance.

Each elevator shaft in the tower was boxed in with this type of construction, so it would be unlikely that a fireball would blow horizontally into an adjacent shaft rather than taking the path of least resistance, straight down or back up the shaft after it hit the bottom pit.

And if a fireball did manage to cross over into another shaft, it would have to expend most, if not all, of its energy doing so. For example, if a fireball did come down a shaft in this manner and it did not hit the elevator car on the way down and explode there, it would have to hit the bottom pit of the shaft at the 77th floor. The fireball would then explode—but without a shock wave, since we are talking about kerosene. And it would blow out in all directions, like explosions do. Most of its energy would be redirected back up the vacant shaft—the path of least resistance. Therefore, only a small fraction of its original energy would be directed horizontally to the walls of any other shafts that might be adjacent to it. It therefore seems unlikely, if not impossible, that such a fireball could make it through one shaft wall and then enter another shaft and still have enough energy left to get down to the B4 level—about ¼ of a mile below—and cause all of the damage observed there.

The 50-, 6-, and 7-Shafts

From the plans, it is obvious that the vast majority of the elevator shafts in the tower were not continuous from the plane impact zone down to B4, and they could not have acted as a conduit for a jet fuel-fed fireball to reach down to that level of the tower. None of the passenger local elevator shafts that serviced floors in Zone 3 (above the 78th floor sky lobby) could have acted as conduits, because their pits were located at the 77th floor. And those passenger express elevators that serviced the 78th floor sky lobby couldn't either, because their lift motors were located at or above the 79th floor.

The NIST report's illustration of the sky lobby system, however, denotes a rare exception to this arrangement. It is labeled as an "Express Elevator" that goes all the way to the top of the building. Here is that drawing again, with the shaft in question circled.

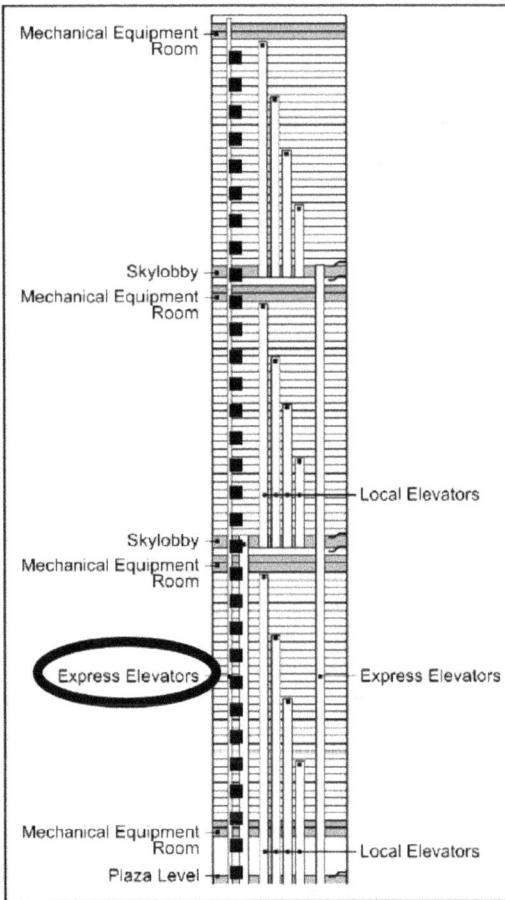

Specifically, what a close examination of the blueprints shows is that of the 99 total number of elevators that serviced the upper 110 floors of the North Tower, only three of them were continuous in this manner from the plane impact zone down to the B4 subbasement level. These were the 50-, 6-, and 7-shafts. Because of that, it was only those 3 key shafts that could have acted as conduits for jet fuel from the plane—in any form, fireball, liquid, or vapor cloud—to get to the B4 subbasement level.

It is on these 3 shafts, therefore, that the viability of the official explanation for the lower level blasts stands. The next series of blueprints bears that out.

This first drawing is of the 96th floor core area, the floor level that sustained the most damage from the plane crash.[678] This plan shows all the elevator shafts on this level of the North Tower. If the 9/11 Commission was correct, this is where most of the damage to the elevator shafts would have occurred and where a jet fuel fireball from the plane would have shot down any shaft that was compromised.

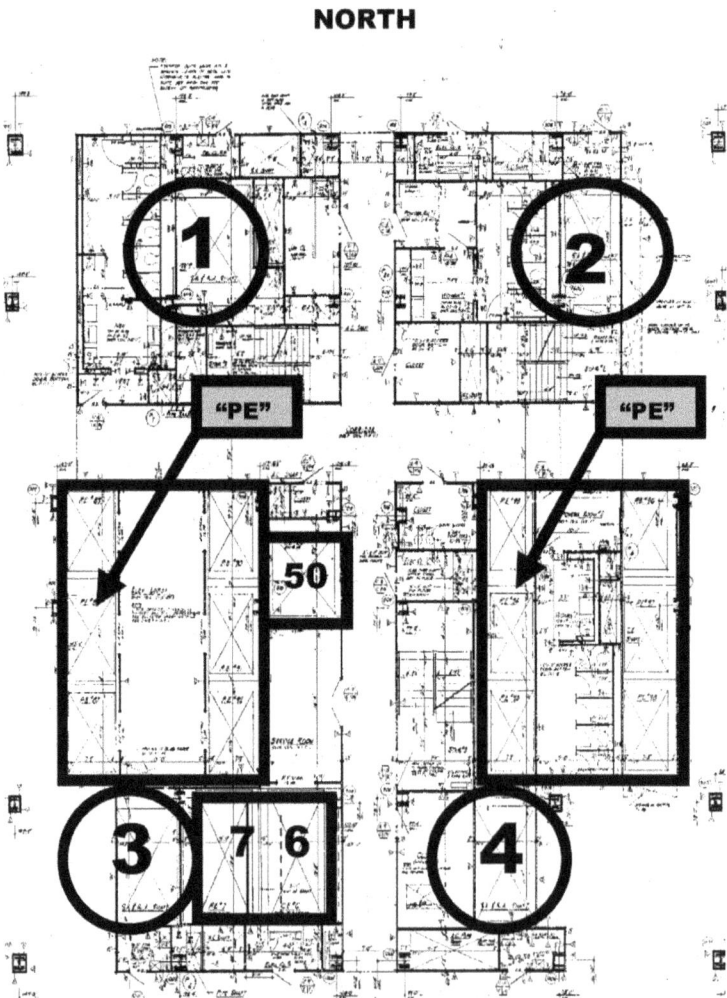

The 96th Floor Core – Elevator Plan

Note the 6 elevators in each of the two big boxes that are labeled "P.E."

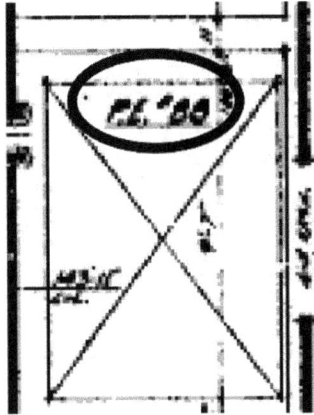

Detail

This indicates that they are **passenger local** elevators that serve only the floors in Zone 3. These elevator shafts had their pits on the 77th floor and could not have been conduits for a jet fuel fireball to get to the lower levels of the tower.

The elevator shafts in the circles—numbered as positions 1 through 4—are all labeled "S.A. & R.A."

Detail

This indicates that they are service elevators, not passenger elevators. Now look at the locations of all of these particular elevators at the 78th floor sky lobby.

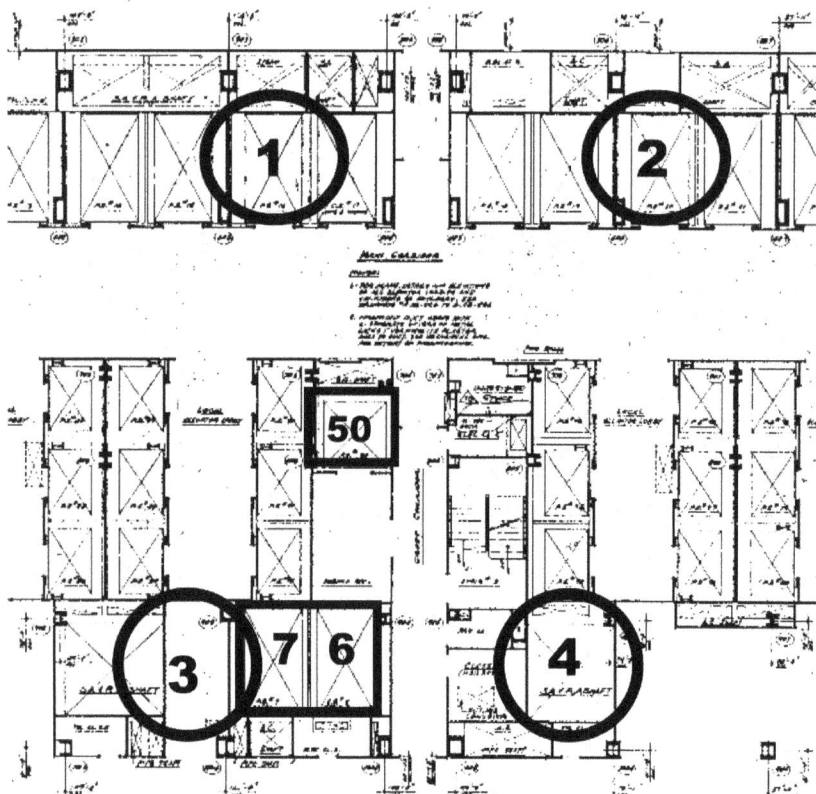

78th Floor Sky Lobby – Core Area Elevators

The 50-, 6-, and 7-shafts are still there and have not changed, indicating that they were continuous down to this level. But the service elevators are not the same. Note that the elevator in position 1 is now labeled as being passenger express elevator #14.

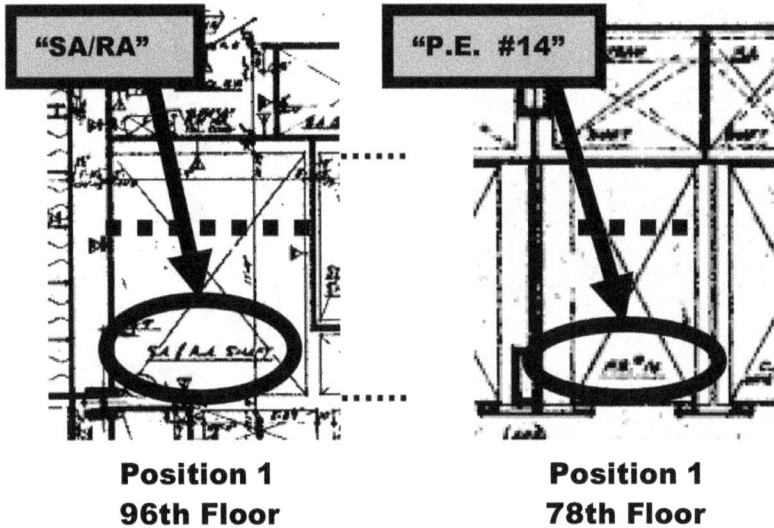

Position 1
96th Floor

Position 1
78th Floor

Note also that, at the 96th floor, it was noticeably wider. What was more of a square shape at the 96th floor is now clearly a rectangular shape at the 78th floor. This indicates different car sizes. That means that this particular shaft at the 78th floor had to be in vertical alignment with another shaft that went to the 96th floor. The change in cars took place at some point between the two floors. So there had to be a motor room for the lower elevator and a pit for the upper elevator located at the point where the cars changed. Therefore, this particular shaft alignment could not have been continuous down to the 78th floor from the plane impact zone, and it could not have been a conduit for a jet fuel fireball to get down to the lower levels of the tower.

The elevator in position 2 is also different at the 78th floor. Where it was previously labeled a service elevator (S.A. & R.A.) at the 96th floor, it is now labeled as being passenger elevator #22.

Position 2
96th Floor

Position 2
78th Floor

Therefore, there must also have been a change in cars for two different shafts that were in this vertical alignment. At some point between the 78th and 96th floors, there had to be a motor room for the lower elevator and a pit for the higher of the two cars. So this shaft also could not have been a conduit for a fireball from the plane impact zone to reach the lower levels, including B4.

The elevator in position 3 is the most obvious. It is not even there at the 78th floor. The area where it once was, at the 96th floor area, is now blank at this level—meaning that the floor area has been reclaimed for other uses.

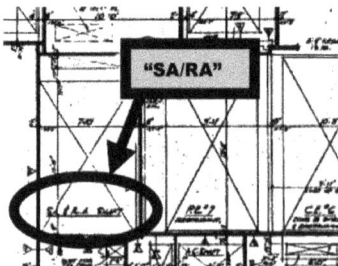

Position 3
96th Floor

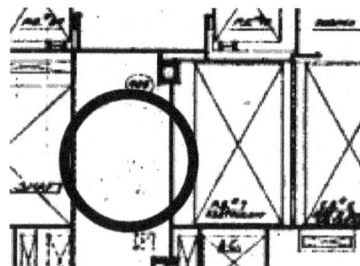

Position 3
78th Floor

Obviously, this shaft also could not have been a conduit for the fireball that hit on B4 or any of the other lower levels.

Finally, elevator position 4 at the 96th floor—which was labeled as a service elevator—is still labeled as a service elevator at the 78th floor. But, as was the case with elevator position 1, it is also a different shape at the 78th.

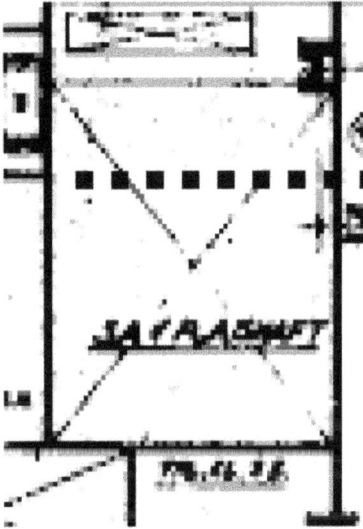

Position 4
96th Floor

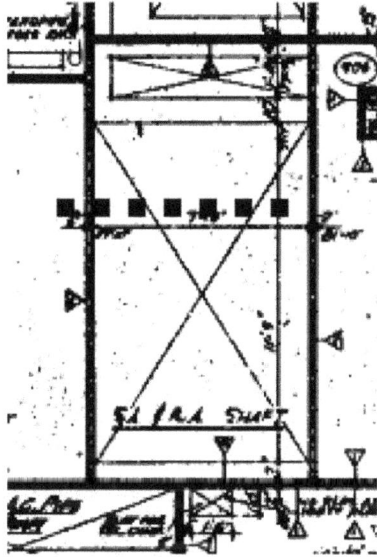

Position 4
78th Floor

This indicates that there was also a change in cars in this shaft somewhere between the 78th floor sky lobby and the 96th floor plane impact zone. This shaft, therefore, could not have been a conduit for a fireball that hit the lower levels.

The next blueprint shows the elevator arrangement at the main lobby.

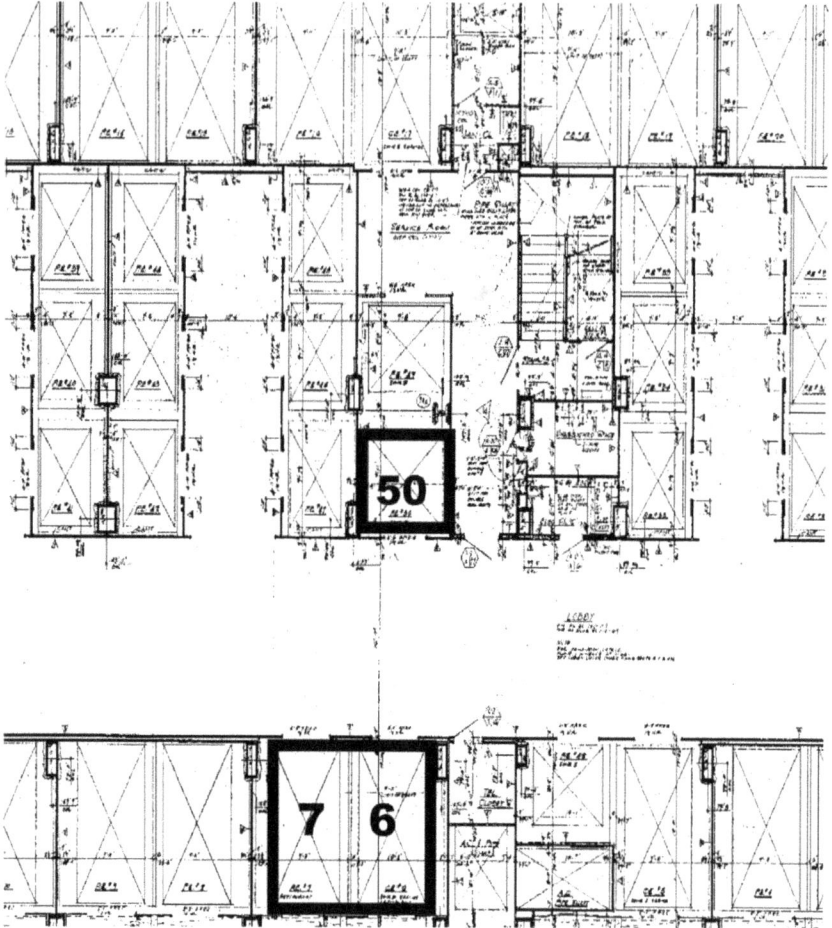

The Main Lobby

The plan shows that the 50-, 6-, and 7-shafts were still continuous down to this level. Since none of the other shafts that existed at the 96th floor level made it past the 77th floor, only these three shafts could have acted as conduits for a fireball from the plane impact zone to reach the main lobby.

Now take a look at the plan for the B4 Subbasement level:

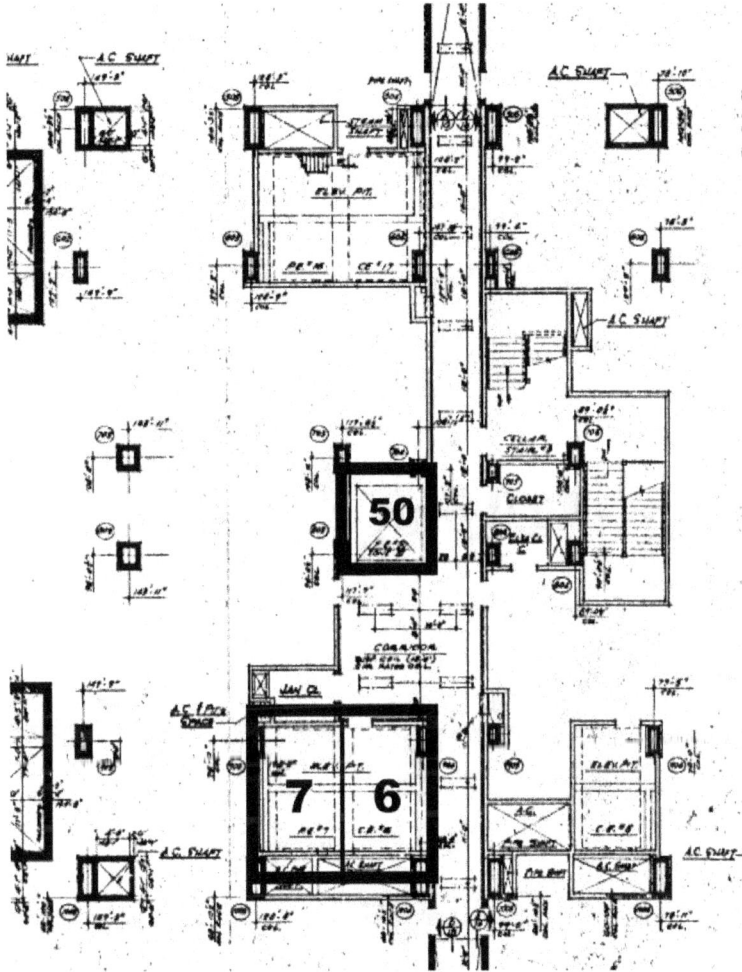

B4 Level

Note that there is only one elevator car coming from the upper floors that actually serviced this level—the 50-car. That is indicated by the "X" in its box. The other elevator shafts shown, including the 6- and 7-shafts, do not have an "X," which means that there was no car moving in those shafts at this level. Also note that the walls for the 6- and 7-shafts are shown by dotted lines. That means that although their cars did not actually service this floor, their shafts went down to this level.

If you look at the plans for levels B1 through B6, you can see that the lowest level that the 6- and 7-cars actually serviced was the B1 level—one floor below the main lobby.

The following plan shows the B1 level.

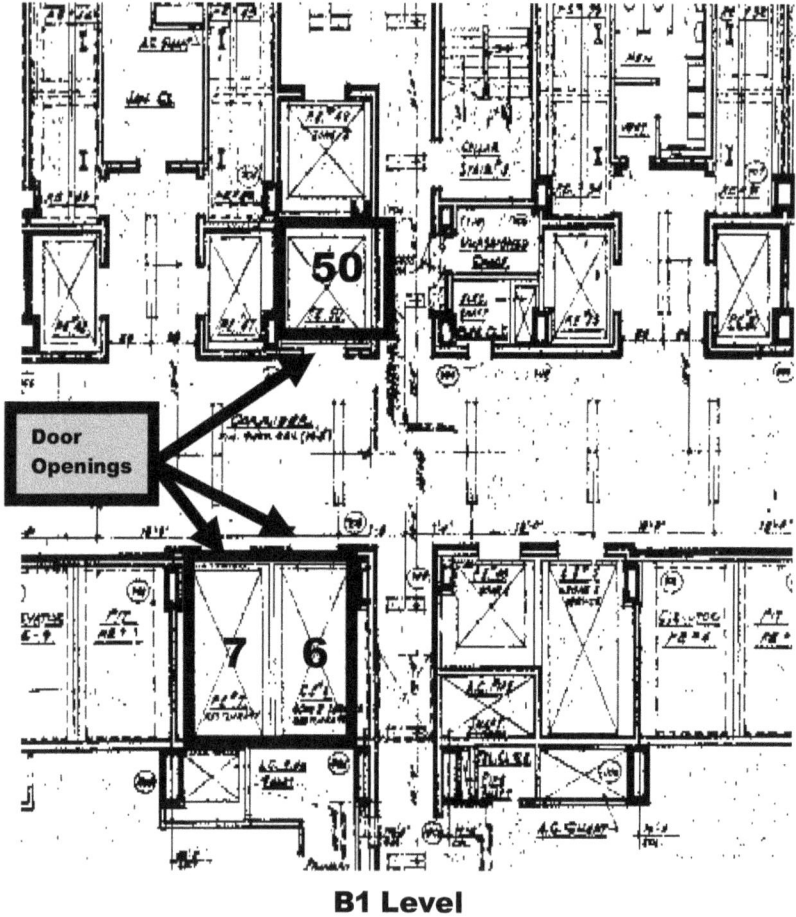

B1 Level

The 6- and 7-shafts have door openings and X's in their boxes. That indicates that those elevator cars actually serviced the B1 level.

Now look at the following plans for B2 through B4. There is a small access door in the 6-shaft at the B4 level, but there are no normal elevator door openings shown for either the 6-shaft or the 7-shaft at these levels.

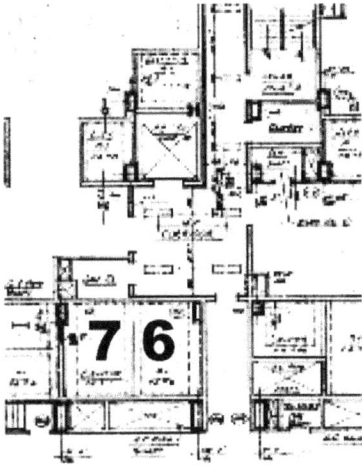

B2 Level

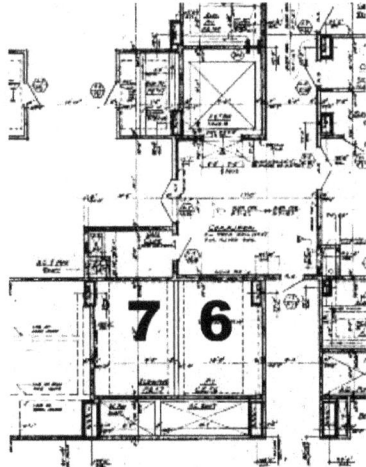

B3 Level

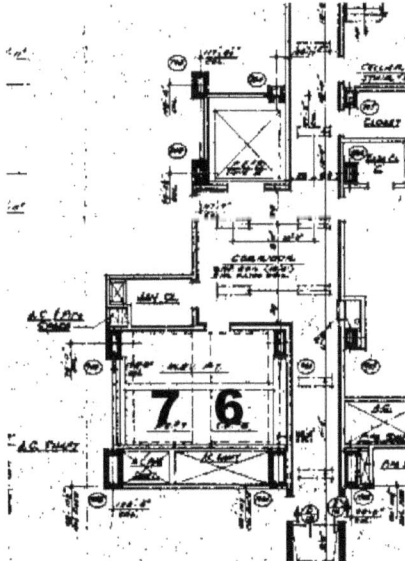

B4 Level

Now, look at the plan for B5.

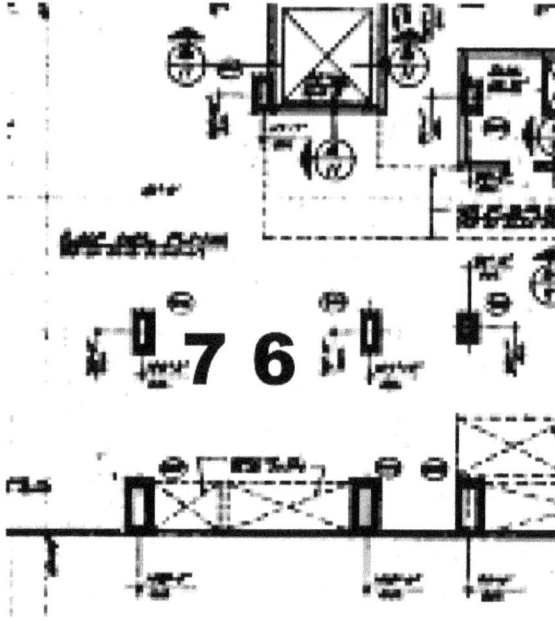

B5 Level

The drawings for the B2, B3, and B4 do show walls for the 6- and 7-shafts (dotted lines), which indicates that the shafts went down to B4, although their cars did not service those levels. But the absence of walls on B5 indicates that the 6- and 7-shafts bottomed out on B4.

Given all of the above, one thing is clear. If the official story is to be believed, a jet fuel fireball from the plane impact zone could only have reached the B4 level by coming down the 50-shaft (which served that level) or down the 6- and 7-shafts (both of which had shafts that went down to B4).

Appendix D:

The Factor of Safety

WHEN THE PLANNING for the WTC project was still in its infancy in the early 1960s, the wisdom of building such tall buildings became a public safety issue that was widely debated in the local press. In reaction to that public pressure, the architects and engineers involved in the project made pronouncements in various news media in an attempt to allay those fears. One of those outlets was a 1964 article in *Contemporary Steel Design* (CSD), an industry periodical put out by the American Iron and Steel Institute.[679] In that piece, the engineers revealed an interesting aspect of the tower's design that resulted in the vertical support columns having a very high factor of safety. When analyzing whether or not the damage caused by the plane crash and the intensity of the fires that resulted from it were sufficient to cause the North Tower to collapse, that factor of safety becomes vitally important.

The design of the North and South Towers was essentially the same. They had an outer tube of perimeter box-shaped steel columns and an interior tube of core columns. The CSD article explained that if normal strength steel (designated as A36) was used for both perimeter and core columns, due to the ¼-mile height of the building, the 1400-foot length of the columns would be such that the compressive loads on them would have resulted in the floors of the office areas at the top of the building being uncomfortably sloped by as much as 16 inches.

The engineers came up with a two-fold solution to the problem. First, they employed various grades of high strength steels in the perimeter columns. And secondly, they maintained a uniform unit stress of 15 ksi (15,000 pounds per square inch of cross-sectional area) on all of the columns throughout the building. They ended up using twelve grades of steel in the perimeter columns, which varied in strength from 45 ksi to 100 ksi. The core columns remained fabricated of ordinary grade A36 steel, which has a strength of 36 ksi.

This is how the article explained the beneficial effect this technique had on the strength of the structure:

> Proportioning the columns to produce the same unit stress due to gravity loads also achieved the built-in increase in safety factor... *This reserve strength can be drawn upon should the structure suffer severe damage for any reason.*[680] (Italics added)

When this increased factor of safety of the support columns is considered, it is clear that the building could not have collapsed due to the plane crashes that occurred on 9/11.

The Perimeter Columns

To be very conservative in their analysis, the engineers considered the strength of the lowest grade of high strength steel that was used, 45 ksi, as their basis. This is how the CSD article explained the effect on the factor of safety of the tower design which was made possible by fabricating the perimeter columns of high strength 45 ksi steel, while maintaining a unit stress of only 15 ksi (15,000 psi):

> (A) heat treated high alloy steel column stressed at 15,000 psi rather than its allowable of 45,000 psi has an effective factor of safety of 5.4.[681]

This means that the perimeter columns were capable of handling a load 540% of the actual gravity load, a very comfortable figure.

The Core Columns

Maintaining a uniform 15 ksi stress resulted in an excess load capacity for the core columns in the same way it did for the perimeter columns, except that the core columns were all made of the standard strength A36 steel plate. The CSD article noted that stressing A36 steel to 15 ksi instead of its allowable of 36 ksi results in a factor of safety of 1.8.

The core was capable of handling 180% of the actual gravity load, which is likewise a very comfortable factor of safety.

Based on yield strength and the assumed standard gravity load distribution of 80% dead load (DL) and 20% live load (LL), the maximum *live load increase*, as a multiplier, (X), at ultimate strength may be found as :

For A36 Steel Core Columns
DL + LL + Reserve LL = 1.8P
.8P + .2P + X (.2P) = 1.8P
           X = 4

For High Strength Steel Perimeter Columns
.8P + .2P + X (.2P) = 5.4P
           X = 22

Where P equals the total calculated axial load in the columns (DL + LL), this results in a 400% reserve live load in the 36 ksi core columns and a reserve live load of 2200% for the 45 ksi, high strength perimeter columns.

This made the twin towers tremendously safe from an engineering standpoint, far beyond what was needed.

Appendix E:

The Strange Case of Building 7

THE PECULIAR CIRCUMSTANCES surrounding the collapse of Building 7 are so astonishing and go so deeply to the heart of the question of whether the WTC collapses were the result of an inside job of controlled demolition that they deserve serious consideration.

The following plan shows Building 7's location at the WTC.

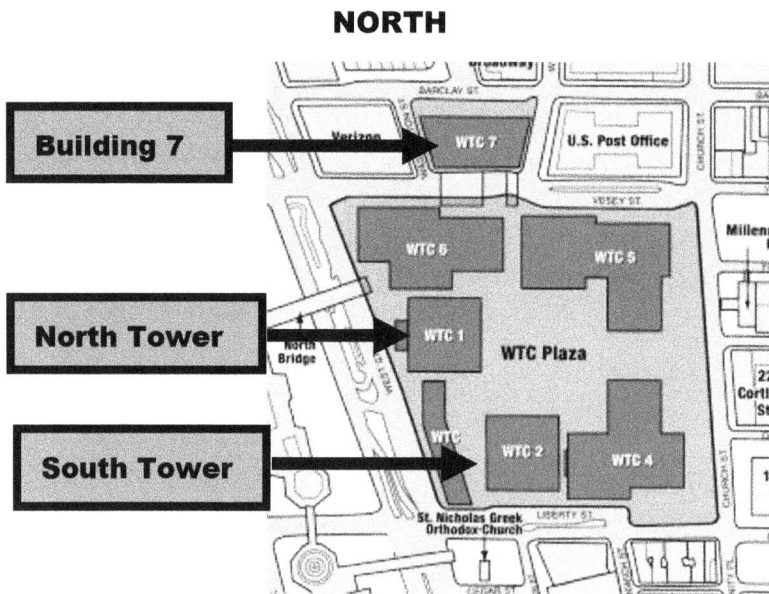

WTC Plan
Source: FEMA

Building 7 was also known as the Salomon Brothers Building. At forty-seven stories, it would have been called a skyscraper in any city. Its collapse was notable for the fact that it was not hit by an airplane and that the fires it had were scattered and manageable. The fires were considered so minor, in fact, that the fire department didn't even bother fighting them that whole day.[682]

But, suddenly, later in the afternoon, word of its possible collapse began to spread like wildfire. And, strangely enough, the reports of its demise seemed to have even overtaken the event itself.

The BBC Report:

At 4:54 p.m. EST (New York time) on the afternoon of the attacks, a news anchor at the BBC's London station reported the following:

> We've got some news just coming in, actually, that the Salomon Brothers Building in New York, right in the heart of Manhattan, has also collapsed. This does fit in with a warning from the British Foreign Office a couple of hours ago to British Citizens that there is a real risk—ah, let me get the exact words—the British Foreign Office—the foreign part of the British government—said it was a strong risk of further atrocities in the United States, and it does seem as if there now is another one with the Salomon Brothers Building collapsing. We've got no word yet on causalities. One assumes that the building would have been virtually deserted.[683]

They cut to a commercial. It is about 4:57 when they come back. The anchorman continues:

> Now, more on the latest building collapse in New York. You might have heard a few moments ago I was talking about the Salomon Building collapsing. And, indeed, it has. Apparently, it was only few hundred yards away from where the World Trade Center towers were. And it seems that this was not the result of a new attack. It was because the building had been weakened during this morning's attack. We'll probably find out more about that from our correspondent Jane Standley. Jane, what more can you tell us?

The picture on a monitor shows reporter Jane Standley on location near the WTC. The caption on the screen reads, "Live. The 47 story Salomon Brothers building close to the World Trade Center has also collapsed." But, oddly enough, Building 7 can be seen in the background, still standing.

Standley starts her live report:

> Well, only really what you already know. But this isn't the first building that has suffered as a result. We know that part of the Marriott Hotel next to the World Trade Center also collapsed as a result of this huge amount of falling debris from the 110 floors of the two twin towers of the World Trade Center.

If all of this is not strange enough, what happens next is positively spooky. At about 5:14, as Standley continues with her story, the TV image begins to break-up. In seconds, it is completely lost. The anchorman seems bewildered, saying:

> Unfortunately, I think we've lost the line with Jane Standley in Manhattan.

About five minutes later, at 5:20 p.m. in New York, Building 7 does, indeed, collapse. In a manner strikingly similar to a controlled demolition, it goes straight down into its own footprint at the freefall speed of about 6.5 seconds. If the picture of Standley had not broken up, the collapse would have been seen behind her occurring in real time, twenty-six minutes *after* she had already reported on it.

The Fox News Report:

There was also a premature report of Building 7's collapse that was aired on a Fox News affiliate in Washington, DC.[684] First, the screen shows two anchors, a man and a woman. The woman says:

I want to tell you that we are getting word from New York right now that another building has collapsed, and we understand this is a 47-story building. Do we have pictures of it?

The screen switches to a live shot of the WTC with a lot of smoke billowing into the sky. But Building 7 can clearly be seen, still standing. The woman anchor continues:

Correct me if I am wrong, in the control room, but is that smoke coming from this third collapse? Okay, that is what we are under-standing, which makes sense because the sun is going down.

Seconds later, Building 7 can be seen collapsing on the screen. The startled male announcer says, "Take a look at that. Right hand side of the screen." The woman announcer replies, "It's going down, right now." The male announcer then says, "There it is. It went down, right there.

They have just seen Building 7 collapse *after* they had already reported on it. But neither one of them seems to grasp the import of what they have just witnessed, and they continue on as if nothing strange has happened.

The Official Reports:

The official reports on the collapse were suspiciously vague. As noted in the Introduction, the first one came from FEMA. It was released rather quickly in May of 2002. That report admitted that the cause of the collapse of Building 7 was a mystery, saying that even their "best hypothesis has only a low probability of occurrence" and that "the specifics of the fires in WTC7 and how they caused the building to collapse remain unknown at this time." And it called for further research.[685]

The 9/11 Commission Report came out next in July of 2004. It boasted of reviewing 2.5 million pages of documents and interviewing 1200 people, but in its 571 pages not one word is said about Building 7.[686]

Up next was the NIST report, which came out in September of 2005. After more than three years of study, which consumed somewhere in the area of $20 million, it said that its study of Building 7 was incomplete and required more work.

It wasn't until August of 2008, some seven years after the fact, that the institute's report on the collapse of Building 7 was finally released. At a news conference presented on the C-Span cable network, lead investigator Dr. Shyam Sunder, PhD, reported that Building 7 collapsed due to structural damage caused by the collapse of the North Tower and "fires that raged out of control."[687]

Sunder's presentation included a computer simulation of the collapse which keyed in on the failure of a particular steel girder at the 13th floor that had been weakened by the intense fires, which lead to a series of other structural failures, and then complete collapse. However, his "analysis" was lacking in the kind of detail that one would expect from a person of his impressive academic credentials and experience. For example, there were no numbers given for fire temperature, for the temperature of the steel, or the amount of stress put on the failed girder and the rest of the building's support structure that would support his theory for collapse.

When asked by an independent investigator in the audience why explosives were not considered as a possible cause of the collapse of Building 7, Sunder said that explosives had been ruled out very early on in the investigation because no one in the vicinity of Building 7 reported hearing a loud "BOOM" sound.[688] But that statement was patently false, as Sunder should well have known. Several witnesses did come forward in very public ways and gave statements indicating that they heard explosions. Moreover, many said the collapse appeared to be just like a timed demolition. And it is hard to believe that Sunder and his investigators did not become aware of them.

The Witnesses

The most important witness to the WTC 7 explosions is **Barry Jennings**. As noted in Chapter 1, he was the deputy director of the City of New York's Emergency Services Department and worked in close liaison with Giuliani's Office of Emergency Management (OEM). After Flight 11 hit the North Tower, his supervisor called him and told him to go to the

OEM office, which was located on the 23rd floor of Building 7. When he arrived there, a security guard and a police officer eventually brought him and another city official, Michael Hess, up to the OEM offices via a freight elevator. This is what Jennings said happened next:

> Upon arriving into the OEM/EOC, we noticed that everybody was gone. I saw coffee that was on the desk. Smoke was still coming off the coffee. I saw half-eaten sandwiches. And only me and Mr. Hess was up there. After I called several individuals, one individual told me that we need to leave right away. Mr. Hess came running back in and said we were the only ones in there and he found a stairwell. So, we subsequently went to the stairwell, and we were going to the stairs. When we reached the sixth floor, the landing that we were standing on gave way. There was an explosion, and the landing gave way. And I was left there hanging. I had to climb back up and now had to walk back up to the eighth floor...When I made it back to the eight floor, both buildings [the twin towers] were still standing.
>
> After getting to the eighth floor, everything was dark. It was dark and it was very, very hot. Very Hot. I asked Mr. Hess to test the phone, as I took a fire extinguisher and broke out the windows. The firefighters came, they came up to the window cause I was gonna [climb] out with the fire hose. It was too hot. They came to the windows, and they said do not do that. It won't hold you. And then, they ran away. You see, I didn't know what was going on. That's when the first tower [South Tower] fell [at 9:58 a.m.]. When they started running, the first tower was coming down. I had no way of knowing that.
>
> Then I saw them come back. Now, I saw them come back with more concern on their faces. Then, they ran away again. The second tower [North Tower] fell [at 10:29 a.m.]. So, as they turned and ran the second time, the guys said, "Don't worry, we'll be back." And they did come back. This time, they came back with ten firefighters. And

they kept asking where are you. We don't know where you are. I said, "I'm on the north side of the building...All this time, I'm hearing all kinds of explosions. All this time, I'm hearing explosions.

When they finally got to us, they took us down to what they called the lobby. Cause I asked them when we got down there, I asked them, "Where are we?" They said, "This was the lobby." And I said, "You gotta be kidding me." Total Ruins, total ruins. Keep in mind, when I came in there, the lobby had nice escalators. It was a huge lobby. And for me to see what I saw, was unbelievable. And the firefighter that took us down, said, "Don't look down." And I kept saying why. He said, "Do not look down." And we were stepping over [dead] people. And you can tell when you're stepping over people. And they took us out through this hole. I don't know who made this hole in the wall. That's how they got us out.

So, they [the 9/11 Commission] called me down...I didn't give it much thought. I thought they were just doing an investigation as to what happened. I gave them my point of view. And I hadn't heard anything more from them.[689]

Even after hearing this dramatic testimony, the 9/11 Commission did not even mention Jenning's name in their report, never mind said what he told them. He was totally expunged from the record.

Jennings, who, by all accounts, was in good health, suddenly fell ill and died in August 2008, at the age of 53. That happened just two days before NIST released its report on Building 7. Jennings was not mentioned in that report, either.

Another witness to explosions in Building 7 is **Kevin McPadden**. He was a former member of the Air Force's Special Operations for Search and Rescue team. He came to Ground Zero as a private citizen to volunteer in the rescue effort, and he was standing near some firefighters a short distance away from Building 7 when he said the following took place:

There was a whole lot of commotion. The firefighters were picking up, starting to roll out and go follow these buses that go downtown. And the Red Cross rep, he goes over and he says, "You gotta stay behind this line because they're thinking about bringing the building down. They didn't say what building. They just said, 'Bringing a building down.'"

So, we're like, okay, we'll take their word for it. We'll stay behind the line. And he goes over and—through all the commotion—he went over and talked to one of the firefighters [about] what was going on, I guess...I don't know if he got an answer or not. He came back over with his hand over [his] radio, and with what sounded like a countdown. And, at the last few seconds, he took his hand off. And you heard, "three, two, one." And he said just, "Run for your life!"

And then, it was, like, another two [or] three seconds, you heard explosions. Like, BA-BOOOM! It was, like, a distinct sound. It's not, like, BOOM, BOOM, BOOM, BOOM—like, floors that were dropping and collapsing. This was, like, BA-BOOOOM! You felt a rumble in the ground—almost like you wanted to grab onto something. To me, I knew that was an explosion. There was no doubt in my mind.[690]

Indira Singh, a volunteer emergency medical technician, substantially backed up McPadden's story. Note the following excerpt from a 2007 interview she gave on Berkeley, California radio station WKPFA:

Singh: All I can attest to is that by noon or one o'clock, they told us we had to move from that triage site up to Pace University, a little further away, because Building 7 was going to come down, or being brought down.

WKPFA: Did they actually use the word "brought" down, and who was it that was telling you this?

Singh: The fire department... The fire department, and They did use the word "we're going to have to bring it down."[691]

What Singh apparently did not know is that Building 7 could not have been rigged for demolition in just a few hours. If the collapse of Building 7 was a planned demolition, it would have taken at least a couple of weeks to accomplish that.

Also, there was a New York City police officer named **Craig Bartmer.** He was in the immediate vicinity of Building 7 before it collapsed. This is his full description of that event:

I was real close to the building when it fell. It didn't sound like just a building falling down to me while I was running away from it. There's a lot of eyewitness testimony down there of hearing explosions. I didn't see any reason for that building to fall down the way it did—and a lot of guys should be saying the same thing. I don't know what the fear is coming out and talking about it? I don't know. But it's the truth.

I walked around it. I saw a hole. I didn't see a hole bad enough to knock a building down, though. Yeah, there was definitely fire in the building, but I didn't hear any...I didn't hear any creaking. Or I didn't hear any indication that it was going to come down. And, all of a sudden, the radios exploded and everyone started screaming, "Get away! Get away! Get away from it!"

It was at that moment, I looked up, and it was nothing I would ever imagine seeing in my life. The thing started pealing in on itself. Somebody grabbed my shoulder, and I started running. And the shit's hitting the ground behind me. And the whole time you're hearing, "boom, boom, boom, boom, boom." I think I know an explosion when I hear it.[692]

Larry Silverstein's company, Silverstein Properties, Inc., held the lease on the WTC, but he actually owned Building 7 outright. As noted previously in Chapter 6, in an interview he gave for PBS's film *America Rebuilds*, he said the following:

> I remember getting a call from the fire department commander telling me that they were not sure they were going to be able to contain the fire. And I said, "We've had such a terrible loss of life, maybe the smartest thing to do is pull it." And they made the decision to pull, and we watched the building collapse.[693]

Again, the term "pull" is used by experts involved in the business of controlled demolitions. It means to bring a building down through the use of explosives, which would have taken at least a couple of weeks to prepare.

Conclusion

Given the witness statements presented here, does Sunder's claim that nobody heard a loud "BOOM" sound when Building 7 collapsed seem credible?

As to question of complicity, the question Sunder should have been asking is: Who or what organization has enough power over media broadcasts that they can monitor live international news reports like the one from the BBC and cut off the signal at will?

Also, note that a contributing factor to the collapse, as described in the BBC report, is remarkably close to what the official story would eventually say: that the building was severely damaged by falling debris from the collapsing towers. Apparently, somebody already knew what the official story would be before it became the official story.

So, who gave the BBC and FOX the heads-up? Who cut the BBC feed? What about the countdown? What about the explosions? And why did Sunder and the other Bush administration lead investigators ignore all of this?

Appendix F:

9/11 Contradictions

THE CONTRADICTIONS found in the official story of the 9/11 attacks that are presented here are not necessarily germane to the subject of this book. This work is primarily meant to illuminate the evidence which proves that the collapse of the North Tower was due to an inside job of controlled demolition and who was likely involved in the cover-up. But the striking inconsistencies that follow are pertinent to the question of whether the Bush White House had foreknowledge of the attack on the WTC, knew the buildings were going to be brought down by explosives and that they let happen. They also explore the wider question of whether the totality of the 9/11 attacks could have been a homegrown scheme of domestic terror that was planned and perpetrated with the complete complicity of the Bush administration.

The Movement for Truth

In the months and years that followed 9/11, a majority of the American public became painfully aware that the enormous consequences of the 9/11 attacks were going to include extended military operations in Afghanistan and Iraq as well as an eternal war on terrorism, and they were demanding a more satisfying explanation to justify that than the account of the attacks that the Bush administration had given. As mentioned, in 2007, some six years after the fact, the Zogby poll reported that "51% of Americans Want Congress to Probe Bush/Cheney Regarding 9/11 Attack."[694] If conservatively based on the 2000 Census—which found that there were 209,096,476 people in the United States over the age of eighteen—that majority of 51% figures to be about 106.6 million adult Americans who had, and presumably still do have, serious doubts about what really happened that day.[695]

In fact, also as noted previously, a later 2013 YouGov poll had this headline: "Most Americans Open to 9/11 Truth."[696]

The Question of White House Complicity

Not surprisingly, much of that movement's energy was/is focused on White House lies. To begin with, as incredible as it may seem, there are two self-incriminating statements that President Bush himself made in speeches he gave shortly after 9/11, in which he basically admitted that he had foreknowledge of the attack on the WTC. The official version says that he first learned that Flight 11 had crashed into the North Tower when he was *informed* of it by his aides about eight minutes after it happened, when his motorcade arrived for a photo op at the Booker Elementary School in Sarasota, Florida. However, during the course of speeches he gave within a few months of the attacks—first in December 2001 in Florida and then in January 2002 in California—he said that he actually *saw* the first plane fly into the WTC in real time, on a TV inside the school.[697]

In the Florida speech, he was asked by a child named Jordan what his first reaction was to the WTC attack. This is what he said:

> Well, Jordan, you're not going to believe what state I was in when I heard about the terrorist attack. I was in Florida. And my chief of Staff, Andy Card... Actually, I was in a classroom talking about a reading program that works! And I was sitting outside the classroom waiting to go in, and I saw an airplane hit the tower of and...you know, the TV was obviously on. And I used to fly myself and I said, well, there's one terrible pilot. I said it must have been a horrible accident. But I was whisked off there. I didn't have much time to think about it.

> And I was sitting in a classroom, and Andy Card, my Chief of Staff, who is sitting over here, walked in and said, "A *second* plane has hit the tower. America is under attack."[698] (Italics added)

But this was physically impossible. Flight 11 hit the North Tower at just before 8:47 a.m., but, at that exact time, Bush's motorcade from his hotel on Longboat Key was still on its way to the school.[699] According to the many reporters and witnesses who were waiting for him, Bush did not reach his destination until a few minutes before 9:00 or 8:55, at the earliest.[700] So, contrary to his claim, he could not have seen the first crash at the WTC on a normal TV broadcast, in real time, at the school.

Moreover, also as noted, the only actual video of Flight 11 hitting the North Tower was captured by Jules Naudet, an independent filmmaker who was working in the streets in the area making a documentary film on the FDNY. He heard the plane go overhead and panned his camera up to catch it hitting the building. But that film was not made immediately available. It was shown for the first time on TV news programs later that evening. So Bush could not have even seen a replay of it on a TV when he was at the school.

But Bush repeated his absurd claim in the later California speech, saying this:

> Well, I was sitting in schoolhouse in Florida. I was sitting there, and my Chief of Staff—well, first of all, when we walked into the classroom, I had seen this plane fly into the first building. There was a TV set on. And, you know, I thought it was pilot error, and I was amazed that anybody could make such a terrible mistake. And something was wrong with the plane, or...anyway, I'm sitting there, listening to the briefing and Andy Card came and said, "America is under attack." And, in the meantime, this teacher was going on about the curriculum, and I was thinking about what it meant for America to be under attack. It was an amazing thought.[701]

Again, this was impossible. It is clear that the only way Bush could have actually seen the North Tower get hit on a TV—either in real time or in a quick replay—is if he knew the attack was going to happen and he had arranged for a video feed of it to be sent from the WTC to a monitor in his limo, while he was on the way to the school.

This opens up a new avenue for investigation of Bush administration complicity. If Bush did have foreknowledge of the attack on the WTC, it is not out of bounds to pose the question of whether that extended back to May 8, 2001 when he ordered the creation of the ONP inside of FEMA, which put Cheney in a position to corrupt the investigations. If so, it would also not be unreasonable to further suspect that he knew that the WTC buildings were rigged with explosives, knew that people were going to die by the thousands in the demolitions after the planes hit, and that he created the ONP specifically to stall the investigation of the collapses while Giuliani got rid of the steel.

Did Bush Watch the WTC Attack Live?

So, is it possible that Bush received a video image of Flight 11 hitting the North Tower while in his limo was on the way to Booker? The answer is yes. Note the following photograph. This is called a Phased Array Satellite System. It is capable of receiving live digital video signals from anywhere in the world. It is very likely that a receiver of this type was part of the vast communications equipment that was known to be inside the presidential limousine.

TracVision A7 Car Mount
Source: KVH Industries

Put this together with a Department of Defense (DoD) office known as the Defense Information Systems Agency (DISA), and, presto, you've got live video signals from any place in the world that could have been beamed right into Bush's limo. DISA's mission prospectus reads:

The Defense Information Systems Agency is a combat support agency responsible for planning, engineering, acquiring, fielding, and supporting Global Net-Centric Solutions and operating the Defense Information System Network to serve the needs of the President, Vice President, the Secretary of Defense, and the other DoD Components, under all conditions of peace and war.[702]

If Bush had ordered DISA to transmit images of the WTC on the morning of 9/11 to his presidential limousine, that agency would have no grounds to refuse to do so. Indeed, it would have been required to do it. And there is compelling evidence, independently gathered by associates of the group *911 Blimp.net*, that indicates that there were, indeed, video images being sent by DISA to the presidential limousine at the time Flight 11 hit the North Tower.[703]

A Freedom of Information Act (FOIA) request to the Pentagon filed by those independent researchers on September 20, 2005, asked for documents and visual information in the possession of DoD that was transmitted to the presidential motorcade between the hours of 7:00 and 9:00 a.m. on the day of the attack. The request was denied. A letter explaining that denial was sent by DISA General Counsel Carl Wayne Smith. It said, in part:

Please be informed that the information you are requesting is not Information Act and DOD Regulation 5400.7A, Department of Defense Freedom of Information Act. Please be further advised that these records belong to the White House Office. The Executive Office of the President, White House Office is exempt from the provisions of the Freedom of Information Act...[704]

This letter seems to confirm that visual information *was* sent to Bush's limo on the morning of the WTC attack, and that they *do* exist. The request was denied, the letter says, not because they do not exist, but because the records are not in the possession of the DoD. "These records," the letter says, "belong to the White House." According to DISA, not only do the records exist, but they were also transferred into the possession of the Bush White House, which, it says, "is exempt from the provisions of the Freedom of Information Act."

Their curiosity no doubt piqued by this response, the independent researchers from *Blimp* appealed the denial, and a second letter, dated October 11, 2006, was generated by DISA Major General Marilyn A. Quagliotti. It reads:

> You requested a copy of records pertaining to the visual information that [was] made available to the U.S. Presidential limousine motorcade on 11 September 2001, between 7:00 a.m. and 9:00 a.m., when the motorcade was located in Florida, as well as information pertaining to the Defense Information Systems Agency's network operations related to the acquiring and delivery of such specific visual information between 7:00 a.m. and 9:00 a.m. on 11 September 2001.
>
> The records you have requested are not located within the Defense Information Systems Agency, nor do we have control of the records. Per the White House Military Office (WHMO), these records are in the possession and control of the White House Office. This Agency suggests that you contact the WHMO to get further clarification on the release of the records you are requesting.[705]

In this letter, DISA basically admits that "visual information" does exist that was made available to the "U.S. Presidential limousine motorcade" during the time of Flight 11 hit the North Tower, and that the visual images in question "are" in the possession and control of the White House.

So what kind of special "battlefield" satellite broadcast from DISA was being beamed into Bush's limo during the time he said that he saw a video image of "this plane fly into the first building" on a TV? It very possibly could have been just that—American Airlines Flight 11, hitting the North Tower—which would be strong evidence that Bush had fore-knowledge of the attack.

A Carefully Scripted Stage Play

Further damaging to Bush is his odd behavior that morning in a class-room at the school. Indeed, his performance during that period of time seems as if he was acting out a part in a carefully scripted stage play. For one thing, despite learning about the first WTC plane crash, he did not alter his schedule one iota. With a horde of newsmen in the back of the classroom recording his every move, he entered at about 9:00 a.m., almost exactly as scheduled. There is no doubt that by that time he was aware of the first plane crash, but he smilingly posed for the cameras as though it was just another day. Then, he sat quietly while the teacher, Sandra Kay Daniels, demonstrated the success of her reading program by running the children through their paces, reading from the book *My Pet Goat.*

In the fall of 2002, about a year after the attack, Bush was asked about his thoughts at this time. He said, "I was concentrating on the program at this point, thinking about what I was going to say. Obviously, I thought it [the first WTC plane crash] was an accident. I was concerned about it, but there were no alarm bells."[706]

But then, after his aide, Andrew Card, stepped into the room a few minutes later and (according to the official story) whispered in his ear the devastating news that a second plane had hit the South Tower and that "America was under attack," Bush remained peculiarly unresponsive. He did not say anything back to Card, and he continued to sit there.[707]

Adding to this intrigue is the fact that at the exact moment when Card entered, White House Press Secretary Ari Fleischer was seen in the back of the room, holding up a sign directed at Bush. Handwritten in big block letters were the words "DON'T SAY ANYTHING, YET."[708] Apparently, the President of the United States was being ordered to sit there, do nothing, and shut up. Someone, somewhere else, was calling the shots, and it was not George W. Bush.

Meanwhile, Mrs. Daniels resumed thumping a cadence, and the children chanted,

A...girl...got...a...pet...goat...but...the...goat...did...some...things... that...made...the...girl's...dad...mad.

As much as nine minutes went by like that. Then, at approximately 9:15, Bush joked with the children, saying,

Hoo! These are great readers. Very impressive! Thank you all so very much for showing me your reading skills. I bet they practice, too. Don't you? Reading more than they watch TV? Anybody do that? Read more than you watch TV? (hands go up) Oh, that's great! Very good. Very important to practice! Thanks for having me. Very impressed.[709]

As the video of the event clearly shows, even for the next several minutes after this, Bush continued to do nothing with regard to the threat that America was under attack.

Nor did he seem the least bit concerned about what was happening in New York. By this time, many helpless victims had already jumped from the North Tower to escape the fires that were raging in its upper floors. According to *USA Today*, "The jumping started shortly after the first jet hit at 8:46 a.m. People jumped continuously during the 102 minutes that the north tower stood."[710] Most of those victims jumped alone. But at least one couple was seen holding hands. Others jumped clutching their briefcases. Estimates are that up to 200 people died this way.[711]

Moreover, while in the classroom, Bush seemed to be unduly confident that he was not putting himself in danger by staying at the school. His trip to Booker had been well-publicized. And, with Bradenton International Airport being only a few miles away, there were many planes up in the air over the region, any one of which could have been another hijack, homing in on him. Despite that, though, according to author Bill Sammon, who was standing nearby, after the photo op, Bush continued to linger in the classroom, smiling and chatting with the children "as if he did not have a care in the world." This carefree milling about continued even after the news crews left. In fact, in his book on the Bush presidency, which was ironically entitled *Fighting Back*, Sammon referred to Bush during this period as acting more like a "Dawdler-in-Chief" than the President of the United States facing a crisis.[712]

For many, the blasé attitude Bush displayed during this episode basically confirms that he had some secret insider knowledge about what was going on that morning and he knew very well that he was not a target of another hijacked plane. In fact, White House aide Karen Hughes witnessed a rather bizarre moment that occurred with Bush at this time, which basically confirms not only that he was not concerned at all about staying at the school, but that it was also his personal decision to stay there, despite the apparent danger that that presented to himself, the children, or any of the other people who were also there. She said that when the subject of his leaving for security reasons came up, Bush "insisted" on staying. "I'll never forget," she recalled, "he said, 'In fact, I'm hungry. I want a hamburger.'"[713]

Then, at 9:30 a.m.—again, exactly as scheduled—Bush stepped in front of a microphone in the school library and addressed a national TV audience. But his speech was not as planned. Instead of talking about Mrs. Daniels' successful reading program, he read this short, prepared statement in a grave voice:

Ladies and gentlemen, this is a difficult moment for America...Today, we've had a national tragedy. Two airplanes have crashed into the World Trade Center in an apparent terrorist attack on our country. I have spoken to the vice-president, to the governor of New York, to the director of the FBI. And I have ordered that the full resources of the federal government go to help the victims and their families and to conduct a full-scale investigation to hunt down and to find those folks who committed this act. Terrorism against our nation will not stand.[714]

Of course, the apparent solemnity of his delivery of this statement is belied by the lack of concern that he had displayed in the classroom only minutes before, which was clearly documented in the video of the event, as well as by Sammon and Hughes.

Bush Lies to the American Public

Later that night, at 8:30 p.m., President Bush looked straight into the camera from his desk in the Oval Office of the White House and, with an expression of great sincerity, lied to the American people about his reaction to the first plane crash.

Bush Addresses the Nation
Source: The White House

Apparently, he and whoever wrote his speech forgot that there was a video of his movements in the classroom, as well as witnesses who were present, because he said, "Immediately following the first attack, I implemented our government's emergency response plans."[715] But the video does not show that. Neither did Sammon report anything resembling that. According to him, even after the second crash, Bush continued to dawdle there even until after the news crews left "as if he did not have a care in the world." And then, there is the stunning statement from Hughes, who said that he was more interested in getting something to eat than people dying in New York.

Moreover, for years after 9/11, the official story remained that Bush thought that the first crash was an accident, not an attack. For example, in a 2007 interview with CBS News for their program *60 Minutes*, he said, "I thought it was an accident. I thought it was a pilot error. I thought that some foolish soul had gotten lost and made a terrible mistake."[716]

The August 2001 PDB

What unquestionably became the most famous issue concerning possible Bush administration complicity in the 9/11 attack on the WTC surrounded a President's Daily Brief (PDB) titled, "Bin Laden determined to strike in US."[717] This document, which was produced mainly by the CIA, was delivered to Bush on August 6, 2001, about one month before the attack, but was kept secret until 2004, when it was finally obtained by the 9/11 Commission.

The PDB turned out to be surprisingly prophetic. It specifically warned that bin Laden "wanted to hijack a US aircraft" and possibly crash it into a building in the US mainland. And one of the targets, it said, could be in New York City. But Bush did not inform the American public about the danger that was possibly looming. And he neglected to order the airlines to beef up security. And then, 9/11 happened, almost as scripted in the PDB.

The fact of this document is intriguing. For those who would accuse the Bush administration and the CIA of having foreknowledge of the WTC attack or, indeed, of conspiring to perpetrate the totality of the 9/11 attacks, it is a quandary. For instance, if the administration and the CIA were in some way complicit in the attack(s), why would the agency ever mention the fact that it had foreknowledge by creating the PDB and then delivering it to Bush?

On the other hand, it is possible that the PDB was delivered to Bush by elements of the CIA who were not part of the impending attack but had knowledge of it and also knew that the Bush Administration was going to let it happen. And they wanted to go on record that they warned Bush about the attack in order to cover themselves. Whether this was the case is, of course, not known to a certainty. But this angle is given a great deal of credence by what Bush reportedly said to the agent who delivered the PDB to him. It is alleged that he told the agent, "Now that you've covered your ass, you can go."

Then again, the PDB could have been what is called in intelligence circles a "limited hangout." This is a propaganda technique of misdirection used in false flag operations.[718] It is where a plot is formulated, and then certain details of it, but not enough to expose it, are revealed to the public. This is done for two reasons: first, to give the operation's false premise credibility, and secondly, to lay the groundwork for setting up a patsy to take the blame. In the case of a supposed administration engineered 9/11 conspiracy, the PDB's notion that planes are going to be hijacked and flown into buildings in the US would have given the false "9/11 terrorist attacks" premise credibility. And the idea presented in the PDB that bin Laden was behind that attack would lay the groundwork for him later taking the blame for the false flag operation.

The Mineta Testimony

Pertinent to that wider question of whether the Bush White House was complicit in the entirety of the 9/11 attacks is the startling sworn 9/11 Commission testimony given by the administration's secretary of transportation, Norman Mineta. In his statement, he gave the strong impression that Vice President Cheney actually facilitated the attack on the Pentagon.

Norman Mineta
Source: The White House

In May of 2003, while under oath, Mineta told the commission how he watched as Vice President Cheney monitored Flight 77 from a White House basement bunker known as the President's Emergency Operations Center (PEOC).

The PEOC Bunker on 9/11
Source: The White House

In his testimony, Mineta said that he arrived at the PEOC at 9:20 a.m.

Mineta and Cheney in the PEOC
Source: The White House

Subsequently, at about 9:26, he said a "young man" came into the bunker and informed Cheney that "the plane" (Flight 77) was "fifty miles out." Mineta said that, minutes later, he heard Cheney reaffirm to the young man what, by all appearances, seems to have been a stand-down order that he (Cheney) had previously given to the military not to interfere with it. If so, the office of the military that Cheney had to have been in communication with would have been the National Military Command Center (NMCC) at the Pentagon, the office in the military chain of command which had the final responsibility for ordering up interceptor jets or defensive missiles.

As Mineta testified:

> During the time that the airplane was coming in to the Pentagon, there was a young man who would come in and say to the Vice-President, "The plane is fifty miles out." "The plane is thirty miles out." And when it got down to "the plane is ten miles out," the young man also said to the Vice-President, "Do the orders still stand?" And the Vice-President turned and whipped his neck around and said, "Of course, the orders still stand. Have you heard anything to the contrary?"[719]

Then, a few minutes later, the Pentagon was hit, killing 130 people in the building.[720] Of those, 75 were civilians and 55 were from the military.[721] The loss of military leadership was staggering. The Army lost a Lt. General, eight Lt. Colonels, and six Majors. The Navy lost four Captains, four Commanders, and six Lt. Commanders.[722]

When asked by the 9/11 Commission about his activities that morning, Cheney denied all culpability by claiming that he was not even in the bunker at 9:37 when the Pentagon was hit. In other words, Cheney claimed that the conversation that Mineta said he overheard between him and the young man never occurred. On the other hand, though, it seems unlikely that Mineta, who had an unblemished reputation, would have committed perjury, or that he would have intentionally made up such a damaging accusation against the man who was, essentially, his boss.

The level of seriousness of the implications that Mineta's testimony had for Cheney was reflected in the extremes to which the 9/11 Commission, under its director, Philip Zelikow, went in an attempt to virtually eliminate it from the public record. He neglected to ensure that Mineta's testimony was included in the commission's final report. And later, the video of it would mysteriously turn up missing from the commission's archives.[723]

Many critics explain this mysterious loss of critical evidence by pointing out that Zelikow was not exactly the right person to head up that supposed unbiased investigation. He was, they charge, in fact, exactly the wrong person due to his strong connection to the Bush administration. Previous to becoming director of the commission, Zelikow was a member of the White House staff and was considered a faithful "Bushie."

In addition, he was a longtime confident of Bush's National Security Advisor, Condoleezza Rice. Zelikow and Rice worked together on the National Security Council staff in the administration of the first President Bush, George H.W. Bush, beginning on the same day in 1989 and leaving within twenty-four hours of each other in 1991. They then co-wrote the book *Germany Unified and Europe Transformed; A Study in Statecraft*, an academic book on U.S. policy during the tumultuous period of German reunification. In fact, it was on Rice's recommendation that Zelikow was brought to the second Bush White House.

Fortunately, though, the video of Mineta's testimony is still available on *C-Span.com*, as well as other websites. In it, Mineta can be clearly heard saying that he arrived at the PEOC by 9:20 and that Cheney was there. But, instead of presenting Mineta's timeline, which would have placed Cheney in the PEOC before 9:20, the commission concluded that Cheney was being truthful when he testified that he did not enter the PEOC until just before 10:00. The commission explained its decision this way:

There is conflicting evidence about when the Vice President arrived in the shelter conference room. We have concluded, from the available evidence, that the Vice President arrived in the room shortly before 10:00, perhaps at 9:58.[724]

Zelikow's commission never explained what the "conflicting evidence" was that troubled it so, but it apparently had no problem accepting Cheney's claim that he arrived at the PEOC proper at close to 10:00 a.m. Cheney told the commission that he entered a tunnel that led to the actual PEOC bunker before the Pentagon crash, but that he remained in that tunnel while watching news reports of it on a TV that was there, and that he did not actually enter the PEOC bunker proper until about a half hour later.

However, under close examination, the evidence that the commission cited for its justification for the arrival time of Cheney in the PEOC leaves a lot to be desired. In making its claim, it did not produce one source that was not potentially tainted in one way or another by a personal bias in favor of Cheney.

The following is the list of evidence that the commission cited for its time of Cheney's arrival at the PEOC:

1. White House record, PEOC shelter log September 11, 2001.
2. Secret Service memo, OVP 9/11 Timeline, November 17, 2001.
3. White House notes of Lynn Cheney.
4. Lynn Cheney interview with *Newsweek*, November 9, 2001.
5. Vice President Cheney interview with *Newsweek*, November 19, 2001.
6. Carl Truscott interview with commission, April 15, 2004.
7. Vice President Cheney interview with commission, April 29, 2004.
8. White House transcript of Condoleezza Rice interview with Evan Thomas, November 1, 2001.[725]

The most glaring example of the commission's bias in favor of Cheney is that they named him as being a witness for himself. And, as incredible as it seems, Cheney's statement to the commission was not even given under oath. One of the conditions Cheney and Bush both insisted upon in finally consenting to an interview, and which the commission agreed to, was that they would not be put under oath as one would normally do in a legal proceeding.[726]

Furthermore, Cheney's *Newsweek* interview obviously was also not given under oath, either, and should not have been considered by the commission as "testimony." Citing Lynn Cheney as a witness for her husband is almost as absurd. Did the commissioners really think that she would say anything that might potentially put her husband in jail and impoverish her family by opening the door to the very real possibility of any number of liability lawsuits? Additionally, her interview with *Newsweek* was not taken under oath, either.

And Condoleezza Rice's statement was also unreliable. Evan Thomas, who apparently interviewed her, was the assistant managing editor of *Newsweek*, at the time.[727] Why the commission did not make a point of revealing that fact is odd. Were they hoping that unsuspecting readers might naturally assume that he was an attorney for the commission and that, therefore, her interview was taken under oath? Obviously, it was not.

The rest of the 9/11 Commission's evidence that Cheney was not in the PEOC when the Pentagon was hit pertained to the Secret Service, which also could very well be unreliable. The Secret Service agents who are assigned to the White House are basically personal bodyguards of the president and vice-president. As such, it is not unreasonable to suspect that they might be motivated to protect the "Boss." In furtherance of that objective, they very well could have doctored the PEOC log book, which was in their custody. Likewise, they could have falsified their "Timeline" to keep Cheney out of harm's way.

Was that kind of Secret Service corruption possible? The one remaining item left to be examined on the list that was offered by the commission as proof that Cheney did not arrive at the PEOC until close to 10:00—the commission's interview with Secret Service Agent Carl Truscott—gives a lot of weight to that possibility. It appears that Truscott might have benefited from his testimony in favor of Cheney because his career took a significant upward swing just before his appearance before the commission. On April 1, 2004, just days before he testified, he was promoted by Bush to be the head the Bureau of Alcohol, Tobacco, and Firearms (ATF).[728]

The Missing Alarm Data

Truscott's name also surfaces in another regard to the charge that the Secret Service helped to establish Cheney's alibi. That concerns an alarm that was wired to the door of the underground tunnel leading to the PEOC. The data from that alarm would have proved beyond any reasonable doubt when Cheney went to the PEOC on the morning of the attacks. However, that evidence mysteriously disappeared while it was apparently in Truscott's custody.

The existence of this alarm data was *not* a subject of discussion by the 9/11 Commission and was only revealed in a tagline to a footnote that was buried in the back of its 2004 report. That notation reads:

> Secret Service personnel told us that the 9:37 entry (to the tunnel that leads to the PEOC) in their timeline was based on alarm data, which is no longer retrievable.[729]

Many years after 9/11, in a May 2009 speech to the American Enterprise Institute (AEI), Cheney gave an account of his activities on the morning of the attacks that is in distinct contradiction to what he told the 9/11 Commission, and the missing alarm data from the entrance door to the tunnel leading to the PEOC would have been very helpful in clearing up those discrepancies. In that speech, Cheney seems to indicate that he was in the PEOC during the time the WTC was being attacked and that he watched it in real time, as it was happening. If so, it proves his complicity with Bush in having foreknowledge of the attack because, as has been shown, Bush also very well may have been watching that attack live from inside his limo via a DISA satellite broadcast while on the way to Booker.

In that 2009 speech, this is how Cheney described what happened after he first learned that Flight 77 was fast approaching:

> As you might recall, I was in my office in that first hour, when radar caught sight of an airliner heading toward the White House at 500 miles an hour. That was Flight 77, the one that ended up hitting the Pentagon. With the plane *still inbound*, Secret Service agents came into my office and said we had to leave, now. A few *moments* later I found myself *in* a fortified White House command post somewhere down below.

There *in* the bunker came the reports and *images* that so many Americans remember from that day—word of the crash in Pennsylvania, the *final phone calls* from hijacked planes, the final horror for those who jumped to their death to escape being burned alive. In the years since, I've heard occasional speculation that I'm a different man after 9/11. I wouldn't say that. But I'll freely admit that *watching* a *coordinated*, devastating attack on our country from an underground bunker at the White House can affect how you view your responsibilities. [730]Italics added)

In the first place, here Cheney says that Secret Service agents ushered him into the command post (the PEOC) only "moments" after learning that Flight 77 was "still inbound," indicating that he was in the bunker when that plane hit the Pentagon. But Flight 77 hit the Pentagon at 9:37 a.m., which means he was not being truthful when he told the 9/11 Commission that he was not in the bunker until just before 10:00.

Moreover, if Cheney heard the "final phone calls from hijacked planes" in real time while in the PEOC, that means he must have been in the bunker even earlier than the 9:20 a.m. arrival of Norman Mineta. The official story is that there were two calls made by crew members from Flight 11 before it hit the North Tower. One was made by flight attendant, Betty Ong. Using a seatback Airfone, she called the American Airlines Reservations Center to report that the plane had been hijacked. That call began at 8:18 a.m.[731] It lasted for twenty-five minutes and ended a few minutes before the crash.[732] So, if Cheney heard that call, he must have been in the bunker *before* 8:47, the time of that crash.

The other "final" call from the planes that Cheney could have been referring to was alleged to have been made by another flight attendant on Flight 11 named Amy Sweeney. Calling from a seatback phone to American Airlines Operations Center, she also talked for twenty-five minutes until the plane crashed. If Cheney heard that call, it would be another strong indication that he was in the bunker well before 8:47.[733]

In addition, what "images" of a "coordinated attack" could Cheney have been "watching" while "in" the bunker? The use of the word "coordinated" implies that he saw more than one plane attacking in an organized sequence. He could not have been watching the crash of Flight 93 because he said that he only had "word" of that crash, not images. And according to Mineta's testimony, images of the Pentagon crash were not beamed into the PEOC. So the only images of a coordinated attack that Cheney could have been referring to were the two planes that hit the WTC. But in order to be watching that, he had to be in the PEOC from at least about 8:47 to 9:03, the times of those two crashes.

Presumably, the alarm data recorded at the tunnel entrance leading to the PEOC would have confirmed when Cheney actually entered the tunnel to the PEOC bunker that morning. Apparently, the 9/11 Commission didn't think it important enough to find out what happened to that data, but somehow that unique and vital piece of evidence that had been in the possession the Secret Service was mysteriously lost.

This brings us back to Carl Truscott and the prospect of Secret Service corruption. Specifically, with regards to that missing alarm data, on January 12, 2003, nearly a year and a half *before* Truscott's appointment to head ATF and his 9/11 Commission testimony, he was appointed by President Bush to be assistant director of the Secret Service Office of Protective Research.[734] That is the office which is responsible for "technical security" and "information technology" at the White House. Presumably, that job involved the collection of exactly the type of electronic alarm data that was at the entrance to the PEOC tunnel; the alarm data that was "no longer retrievable."

Richard Clarke Confirms the Mineta Testimony

Bush administration advisor Richard Clarke provides some vital insight into to Cheney's movements on the morning of 9/11, basically confirming Mineta's testimony that Cheney was in the PEOC bunker during the attack on the Pentagon and that he actually facilitated it.

Richard Clarke
Source: The White House

Clarke was the administration's foremost expert on terrorism. And it was he who ended up commanding the vitally important Situation Room conference in the White House on the morning of the attacks.

The Situation Room
Source: The White House

Clarke's Situation Room conference had all the available heads of departments on video screens, including the FBI, CIA, FAA, DoD, etc. He had a direct telephone line to Cheney's desk in the PEOC bunker that was supposed to stay open. It was Clarke's job to gather information about what was going on with the hijackings and transmit that immediately to Cheney via that open line, along with suggestions for actions to take. Cheney was supposed to then contact Bush in Florida for approval.

Clarke wrote a book on the 9/11 attacks entitled *Against All Enemies*. In it, he said that he first met Cheney in the Vice President's office a few minutes after the second crash at the WTC. From what he wrote about his route to the White House and then to Cheney's office, that figures to have been about 9:07.[735] But Cheney's AEI speech brings up the question of whether he (Cheney) went down to the PEOC before Clarke's arrival, watched the WTC attacks on DISA satellite TV—just like Bush may have done in his limo—and then, anticipating a meeting with Clarke, he went back up to his office.

This is where the alarm data at the entrance to the PEOC tunnel becomes so vital. It would not only show when Cheney first entered the tunnel to the PEOC on the morning of the attacks, but it would also show how many *times* he entered the tunnel.

Was it possible for Cheney to make it back to his office in the four minutes he had before Clarke's arrival after having watched the second WTC crash from the PEOC? For an answer to that question, note the following plan of the White House. Cheney's office was on the first floor of the West Wing.[736] The PEOC bunker is located in the basement under the East Wing.[737]

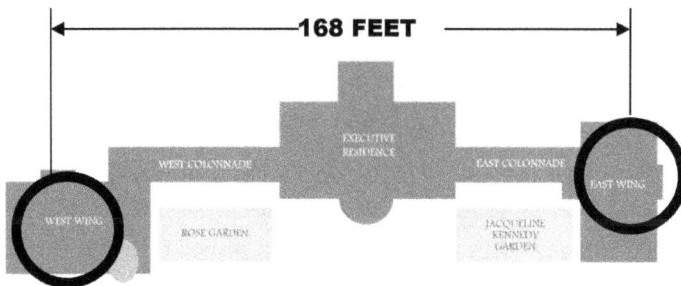

White House Floor Plan
Source: Wikipedia

The White House has a main first floor corridor.[738] The distance from the PEOC to Cheney's office was about 168 feet.[739] A normal walking pace is about three miles per hour, or 264 feet per minute. Thus, it was very possible for Cheney to make it back to his office from the PEOC after the 9:03 South Tower crash in less than one minute by going down the main corridor. That would put him in his office well before Clarke's 9:07 arrival.

Also, recall that in his AEI speech Cheney said that it took only "moments" for the Secret Service agents to get him to the PEOC from his office when Flight 77 was approaching. Presumably, the trip back could be made just as quickly.

Clarke wrote that after their approximately two-minute meeting in Cheney's office, Cheney began gathering up papers and indicated that he was going immediately to the PEOC. That would have been at about 9:09.[740] Theoretically, Cheney easily could have made it back there as soon as about ten minutes before Mineta's 9:20 arrival.

Also to that point, recall that in his commission testimony, Mineta said that the first thing he heard the young man say to Cheney was, "The plane is fifty miles out." That was at about 9:26. But at that time, Mineta did not hear the young man say anything of an introductory nature regarding the aircraft. He simply stated that "the" plane was fifty miles out. Yet, it is clear that Cheney understood what plane the young man was referring to. This indicates that Cheney and the young man had to have had an exchange about the incoming plane before Mineta entered the bunker at 9:20.

According to this, Cheney had at least seventeen minutes (9:20 to 9:37), at a very minimum, to do something. If he wanted to, he could have called the NMCC and ordered the evacuation of the Pentagon. Or, interceptor jets could have been scrambled from Andrews Air Force, which was only ten miles away. That would have taken only a minute. Without any problem, interceptor jets could have been in the air a couple of minutes later, or by about 9:23. And, in two or three minutes, they would be in a position to shoot. Theoretically, the air threat to the Pentagon could have been eliminated by 9:26. The sixty-four people who were said to be on that plane would have died due to this horrendous decision that had to be made, but 125 people in the building would still be alive.

All of this could have been accomplished, if Cheney had wanted it to happen. But apparently, he did not. In fact, the evidence shows that he did exactly the opposite. It indicates that he paved the way for that plane to hit the Pentagon. Mineta's testimony is devastating to Cheney in this regard. His statement indicates that by at least 9:20 a.m., Cheney, instead of issuing a shoot-down order, had issued stand-down "orders" to the NMCC not to interfere with the attacking plane. Obviously, the NMCC had obeyed those orders, because Flight 77 was not shot down.

The office of the Vice President does not have any legal authority in the military chain-of-command, certainly not to order the military to deal with any domestic, commercial aircraft that was threatening. So, Mineta's testimony also indicates that by at least 9:20, the time of his (Mineta's) entrance to the bunker, Cheney must have been given that authority by Bush, the Commander-in-Chief. It also indicates that the commanding officer at the NMCC, who at the time was Captain Charles Liedig, had been sufficiently impressed that Bush had done so. Otherwise, Liedig would not have been legally able to obey any order coming from Cheney.

Clarke's book adds even more intrigue to this scenario. He wrote that from when he first met with Cheney in his office at about 9:07 a.m., up to the time Flight 77 hit the Pentagon thirty minutes later, Cheney never informed him that the hijacked Flight 77 was approaching. As was mentioned, the most direct method of communication that Clarke had to reach Cheney from the Situation Room was a direct, open phone line to Cheney's desk in the bunker. Barring that, the only other way was the more time-consuming method of going through the regular White House switchboard. Clarke assumed that Cheney would be monitoring the proceedings in the Situation Room via the bunker's closed circuit TV system and that if Cheney had anything to add, he would pick up the direct line and alert him to it. But in his book, Clarke indicates that Cheney never did that.

Essentially, this means that in addition to Cheney issuing a stand-down order to the military, he was, at the same time, cutting Clarke out of the action. In effect, he was preventing Clarke from being able to take any independent action of his own in the Situation Room that might have interfered with the attack on the Pentagon.

In his book, Clarke gives further proof of that. He wrote that, on his own initiative, he realized that the Air Force would need shoot-down authority from Bush should additional hijacks be out there. And the one person he had to go through to get that authorization from Bush was Dick Cheney, whom he presumed was in the PEOC bunker. But, when the occasion finally did arise when Clarke had the opportunity to try to get Cheney's assistance in that regard, he found that his open line to Cheney had been tampered with, and he could not get through to the bunker.

Clarke wrote that this first attempt to contact Cheney via the open line was made at exactly 9:30—about seven minutes before the Pentagon was hit. That was when Bush stepped to the podium in the library at Booker Elementary School to address the nation about the WTC attacks. Clarke said that the Situation Room paused at that time to listen to Bush and that he took that opportunity to contact Cheney via his open line in order to ask him to contact Bush in Florida so that he (Clarke) could get shoot-down authority for the Air Force. But, when Clarke tried to do that, this is what he said happened: "I picked up the phone to the PEOC. I got a dial tone. Someone had hung up on the other end."[741]

With the hot line unavailable, Clarke had to go through the regular White House switchboard. But, when he finally did get through to the PEOC, he still could not get Cheney on the phone. One of Clarke's own aides, Army Major Mike Fenzel, whom he had sent to the PEOC earlier as his representative, answered the phone. Clarke told Fenzel, "We need to authorize the Air Force to shoot down any aircraft—including a hijacked passenger flight—that looks like it is threatening to attack and cause large-scale death on the ground. Got it?"[742]

Considering what was going on in the bunker at that time, Fenzel's response was odd. He merely said, "Roger that, Dick. I'll get right back to you."[743] And he hung up.

This puts a cloud over Fenzel because, according to Mineta's commission testimony, this 9:30 call by Clarke occurred only about four minutes after 9:26, the time of the young man's report to Cheney that Flight 77 was fifty miles out. So Fenzel, who was in the bunker and must have heard that announcement, had to be aware that Flight 77 posed a threat. It is very likely that he also heard the earliest mention of "orders" in the conversation that Cheney previously had with the young man, which should have indicated to him that Cheney already had shoot-down authority from Bush. Yet he never mentioned these facts to Clarke.

Furthermore, according to Clarke, Fenzel never got "right back" to him about anything before Flight 77 hit the Pentagon.

In his book, Clarke picks up his narrative again at about 9:35—two minutes before the Pentagon was hit. He said that was when Brian Stafford, the head of the Secret Service, who was in the White House that morning (presumably in the Secret Service office), entered the Situation Room and "slipped" him a note.[744]

Brian Stafford
Source: The White House

The note said, "Radar shows aircraft headed this way."[745] This short and sweet message referred to Flight 77, and it was the first time that Clarke became aware of that threat. But by this time, it was too late for him to do anything about it, because he had only two minutes to react.

This puts a cloud of suspicion over Stafford, as well. He must have known about the approach of Flight 77 all along—even if he was not actually in the bunker with Cheney—because Cheney was always accompanied by his Secret Service detail, and they would have kept Stafford appraised of what was going on. In addition, it is known from Clarke's book that the Secret Service office in the White House had a radar system that mirrored that of the FAA, and so Stafford must have known about the approach of Flight 77, which was declared a hijack at 8:56 a.m., some 39 minutes earlier.[746, 747]

So, if Stafford's true intention was to inform Clarke about the danger presented by Flight 77, why did he wait so long to do it? And why did he walk the note to the Situation Room instead of phoning it in, which would have been the quicker method?

For those who accuse the Bush White House of having direct involvement in the 9/11 attacks, the answer to these questions is two-fold. In the first place, by Stafford delivering the note, it gave Cheney plausible deniability that he was in the PEOC and monitoring Flight 77 before it hit the Pentagon. Cheney's alibi would be that he was not in the bunker during that time, and that is why he did not inform Clarke, himself. Secondly, this would also coincide with Clarke's statement that his open line to Cheney had been hung up. With the line "accidentally" closed, Clarke could not actually talk to Cheney personally and thereby confirm that he was in the PEOC at 9:30, as Mineta would later testify.

Cheney's professed absence from the bunker during the Pentagon crash would have also been supported by the fact that Clarke had to have Fenzel transfer the message to Cheney when he finally got through to the PEOC at 9:30. Again, Cheney was not able to take calls himself, his alibi would say, because he was not in the bunker at that time.

And, barring any damaging commission testimony from anyone else who was in the bunker, which Zelikow presumably would be more than willing to guarantee, it would then be Cheney's word against that of Mineta as to whether Cheney had any such interactions with the "young man" about Flight 77. Which is finally what actually occurred with Zelikow's commission, in the end, siding with Cheney and saying he was not in the bunker until shortly before 10:00.

If all of the above is not enough to convince even the most timid among us of Cheney's complicity in the attack on the Pentagon, in his book, Clarke reveals further proof. He picks up this part of his narrative at about 9:45 to 9:55 a.m. At that time, he said this occurred:

> I picked up the open line to the Presidential Emergency Operations Center only to find that, once again, it was a dial tone. When I punched the PEOC button [on the White House phone system], the person answering the phone grunted and passed the phone to Major Fenzel.
>
> "Who is the asshole answering the phone for you, Mike?" I asked. Fenzel answered. "That would be the Vice President, Dick."[748]

Cheney's behavior here is nothing short of bizarre. One would think that after what had just transpired that morning that he should have been more than a little interested in knowing what the Bush administration's foremost expert on terrorism had to say about it. But he brushed Clarke off like a bug.

After this strange encounter, Clarke decided to make a personal appearance at the PEOC.[749] He said he was finally able to do that by about 12:30 p.m.[750] By then, the attacks were over. But Fenzel was still there, and a few TV monitors were on. This is how Clarke described what happened next:

> On one screen, I could see the Situation Room. I grabbed Mike Fenzel. "How's it going over here?" I asked. "It's fine," Major Fenzel whispered. "But I can't hear the [Situation Room] crisis conference because Mrs. Cheney keeps turning down the volume on you so she can hear CNN. And the *Vice President keeps hanging up the open line* to you."[751] (Italics added)

By revealing to Clarke that it was Cheney himself who had been hanging up the open line to the Situation Room all along, Fenzel had confirmed that Cheney was, indeed, in the PEOC at 9:30, the time of Clarke's first attempt to contact him. This also provides proof that it was Cheney himself who was intentionally cutting Clarke out of the action regarding the attack of Flight 77, and, in effect, preventing Clarke from being able to take any action that might have interfered with it.

What is also peculiar is what Fenzel revealed to Clarke about the Vice President's wife, Lynn Cheney. Fenzel said that she was taking an active role in the bunker by turning down the volume of the Situation Room proceedings and drowning it out with the cable news channel CNN. By doing that, she was, in effect, controlling the outside, first-hand information that was coming into the bunker. This could be an indication that both she and her husband were well aware that there were other people with them in the bunker that were not a part of their scheme.

The fact that the information coming into the PEOC was tightly controlled is also indicated by this photograph taken by White House photographer David Bohrer. It shows how Cheney did not use a speaker phone while in the bunker. All of his calls were conducted using a private landline. Notice in this photo how the others in the room are seen hovering, waiting for him to tell them what was going on.

White House photo by David Bohrer

Cheney in the PEOC on 9/11
Source: The White House

As for Lynn Cheney, it would be interesting to know what qualified her to be inside the White House bunker during a national security crisis. It is doubtful that she has a top secret security clearance that would allow it. Or that she would have anything substantive to add to the discussions that would make her presence an imperative. But there she was, nonetheless, taking an active part in the proceedings.

In addition, according to at least one source, she was seen taking copious notes all during this period.[752]

The 9/11 Commission and Vice President Cheney said that Mrs. Cheney arrived at the PEOC *after* the Pentagon was hit. They said she had been a hair salon in Washington when her Secret Service detail learned of the WTC attack, and, for some reason that has yet to be explained, they saw fit to bring her to the White House. Once there, they ushered her to the tunnel leading to the PEOC where she met up with her husband. They both told the 9/11 Commission that they stayed in the tunnel until after the Pentagon was hit. And only after that did they enter the PEOC together at 9:58 a.m.

However, in a June of 2007 videotaped interview with an independent researcher, Mineta said that Mrs. Cheney was already in the bunker with the Vice President when he (Mineta) arrived at 9:20.[753] This indicates that the Vice President and his wife conspired to concoct a false account of their movements that morning. The question remains, why?

Also, note the following photograph. It shows that Vice President Cheney and his wife had at least one confidential conversation while in the bunker.

Cheney and his Wife in the PEOC
Source: The White House

What were they whispering about? Apparently, Zelikow's commission did not care enough to ask. But one would think that at least the FBI should have been interested. The bureau could have shed some light on that question—as well as on the question of Dick Cheney's odd movements and questionable behavior during the attacks—by interviewing other people who were photographed as being in the bunker.[754] Those included Condoleezza Rice; Cheney's lawyer, David Addington; aides Mary Matalin and Karen Hughes; White House photographer David Bohrer; and others. It could have also located and interviewed the "young man" who Mineta said kept coming into the room to inform Cheney of Flight 77's progress. But, for reasons unknown, the FBI, under its new director, Robert Mueller, chose not to do that.

In light of Mineta's public commission testimony, Director Mueller's negligence in not having his FBI investigate Cheney's suspicious activities while in the PEOC bunker on the morning of the attacks speaks volumes. Here you have 125 people in the Pentagon murdered and absolutely no questions asked. And that unconscionable fit of inactivity lines up exactly with the fact of the FBI's failure to do any forensic investigation of the WTC collapses; there you had 2,100 people murdered, and despite the accounts of hundreds of eyewitnesses to the explosions, not one piece of structural steel was ever tested for residues.

Many critics of the official story of 9/11 link the two by pointing out that Mueller was appointed by Bush to be FBI director just two months prior to the attacks, which was at nearly the same time that he put the plan in place to use Cheney/ONP to cover-up the WTC demolitions.

Problems with the Hijacks

As to the question of whether the entirety of the 9/11 attacks was a homegrown plot of domestic terrorism, many find the official scenario of the hijackings far-fetched.

Flight 77: "Knives and Box Cutters"

In the first place, there are bothersome problems with the explanation of how the hijackers took control of the planes. The official story is that the only weapons the hijackers had used were "knives and box cutters." The fact of these weapons was said to have been established by a series of cell phone calls that were alleged to have been made by a passenger on Flight 77, Barbara Olsen, to her husband, Bush administration Solicitor General Ted Olson, several minutes before that plane hit the Pentagon.[755]

Ted Olsen
Source: The White House

But when Mr. Olsen's account of those calls is examined closely, one is forced to question whether he was being truthful. In the first place, his account of the calls from his wife has been questioned because it is a known fact that such cell phone calls from Flight 77 would have been virtually impossible to make; by September 2001, planes were not equipped with the technology to do that.[756, 757] At one point, Olsen changed the method of the call, saying that his wife was using an onboard, seatback Airfone. But, according to American Airlines, the Boeing 757 she was on did not have Airphones at the time she supposedly made the calls.

Moreover, at the later 2006 trial of Zacharias Moussaoui, whom the FBI believed would have been the 20th hijacker if not for a few miscues on his part, a report was entered into evidence that confirmed that only one call came from Mrs. Olsen's cell phone to her husband's office that morning, not the several described by Mr. Olsen. Furthermore, the report also states that the call lasted "0" seconds.[758] According to this, the conversations that Mr. Olsen said he had with his wife did not happen.

This begs the question of why the Bush administration's top lawyer would tell a material lie in an attempt to substantiate the official story of the 9/11 attacks.

Flight 175: The Impossible Cell Phone Calls

Two calls were made from Flight 175, both by passengers also allegedly using cell phones. However, as was the case with Barbara Olsen's call to her husband, Ted Olsen, that was impossible to do at the time of the 9/11 attacks. United Airlines Flight 175, under normal conditions, was not equipped with technology to do that. It was at cruising altitude of about 30,000 feet. But after about 8,000 feet of altitude cell phones calls could not lock on to a transmission tower long enough to connect.[759] But passenger Peter Hanson's father confirmed that he did talk to his son at 9:00 a.m. The logistics of how this was arranged is a mystery, because it certainly could not have been done without the plane being on the ground.

Another discrepancy is that Hanson told his father, "I think they intend to go to Chicago or someplace and fly into a building." This also is a mystery, because how could he know about hijacked planes flying into buildings? Hanson and his father did not talk about Flight 11 hitting the North Tower. And it is not believable that one of the hijackers came to the back of the plane and told Hanson what they were going to do. Even if that did occur, most likely Hanson would have also related that to his father, but he did not.

At 8:59, the other Flight 175 passenger, Brian Sweeney, also using his cellphone, called his wife and left a message on their home answering machine. Then he called his mother and they had a conversation. These calls, which also should have been impossible to make, were confirmed. But like the Hanson call, how they were accomplished remains a mystery.

Flight 93: The Impossible Call of Cee Cee Lyles

Another impossible call was made by Cee Cee Lyles, a flight attendant on United Flight 93, the plane which allegedly crashed in Pennsylvania. Her husband, Lorne, a police officer, was still in bed sleeping when she called at about 9:30 a.m., so she left message on their home answering machine. In a flat, plain-speaking, unemotional manner, she said the following:

> Hi, baby. I'm... Baby, you have to listen to me carefully. I'm on a plane that's been hijacked. I'm on the plane. I'm calling from the plane. I want to tell you I love you. Please tell my children that I love them very much. And I'm so sorry, babe. Um... I don't know what to say. There's three guys. They've hijacked the plane. I'm trying to be calm. We've turned around, and I've heard that there's planes that's been, been flown into the World Trade Center. I hope to able to see your face again, baby. (voice cracking) I love you. Goodbye.[760]

Notice how she repeats three times that she is on the "plane." It is as if she is trying to give him the message that she is not on the plane. Also, before she hung up, she said something under her breath that is absolutely chilling. She whispered into the phone, "It's a frame."[761]

It later became obvious to Lorne that his wife could not have been on the plane. He said she called back a second time about a half hour later, woke him up and they had a short conversation of the same nature. After she hung up, he wondered if it all was just a bad dream, saying,

> I looked at the caller ID. And it was a call. And it was from her cell phone. And I'm like, okay, wait a minute. How could she call me from the plane from her cell phone, because cell phones don't work on a plane.

Confounding this is a report presented by the FBI at the trial of Zacarias Moussaoui, the would-be fifteenth hijacker who did not make it on the planes. That report also states that despite "an exhaustive study ... of the cell phone records" no such call was found on Cee Cee Lyles' cell phone bill.[762]

All of this begs a lot of questions. In the first place, if she did make the call, as her husband insists she did, why is there no record of it? Or, was his wife really on a plane when she made this call? How was that call made? Was she told what to say? Was it really Flight 93 that crashed in Pennsylvania? If not, what happened to that plane and all the people on it? Most importantly, the vital question of what she meant by "frame" has never been asked in any official forum.

Flight 11: The Betty Ong and Amy Sweeney Calls

As mentioned, two calls were made from Flight 11 before it hit the North Tower. They were made simultaneously by flight attendants Betty Ong and Amy Sweeney, using onboard Airfones. Their calls were made at about 8:20 a.m., some twenty minutes after takeoff. But a close examination of them brings into question whether they were legitimate, because the details of the hijacking given by Ong do not agree with what Sweeney said.

With regard to the Ong call, it was first received by Vanessa Minter at the American Airlines (AA) Southeast Reservation Center in Cary, North Carolina.[763] Realizing the importance of what Ong was saying and unable to locate the button on her console needed to record the call, Minter handed it off to Winston Sadler who was manning the "Help Desk." Sadler hit his emergency button, which started the recording and also opened up a line to Nydia Gonzalez at AA Operations Center in Dallas, Texas. Sadler and Gonzalez proceeded to jointly question Ong, who related that a hijacking was taking place.[764]

The AA recording system was only capable of recording about the first four minutes of Ong's twenty-five-minute call. That recording, which was on a CD, was played over the telephone to the FBI on the afternoon of the attacks.[765] A poorly transcribed version of the CD was taken down by an FBI agent on the other end. The actual AA CD was then given to the FBI later on that same day. The FBI re-recorded the CD onto a digital audio tape for transcription purposes.[766] But the day after the attacks, after the audio recording of the Ong conversation had been transcribed a second time by the FBI, it differed considerably from transcribed version done the day before over the phone. Under close inspection, it is obvious that the first FBI transcription was terribly flawed. The second FBI transcription made from the actual AA CD on the 12th thus became the official version of the call that is used in virtually all of the reports.

The other flight attendant, Amy Sweeney, made a series of three calls to AA Flight Services in Boston. They were not recorded, but the two AA employees who took the calls, Evey Nunez and Flight Services Manager Michael Woodward, made written notes of what she said. However, the details of what Evy remembered disagreed with what Woodward wrote down, and they both disagree in several respects to what Ong said on the AA CD. And none of those accounts agree with the FBI's final official version of the hijacking.

For example, Ong at first referred to two hijackers who had forced their way into the cockpit.[767] But later, she said three. Sweeney told Woodward that there was three or four.[768] The FBI says that there were five.

Secondly, Ong said two hijackers had been seated in 2A and 2B. She later said that there was a third one that came from seat 10B.[769] In Sweeney's first call, she told AA employee Evy Nunez that there were three hijackers who had been seated in 10B, 9C and 9G.[770] Sweeney's second or third call was taken by Woodward. He later told his boss, AA Vice President of Flight Services Jane Allen, that Sweeney said there were four hijackers who had been seated in 10C, 9B, 9E and 9G.[771] In a later interview with the FBI, Woodward contradicted that, saying that Sweeney said there were three hijackers who were seated in 10B, 9C and 9G, or 9D and 9G.[772] The FBI says that five were seated in 2A, 2B, 8D, 10B and 9G.[773] Also, neither Ong nor Sweeney said that there was a hijacker in seat 8D. This is significant because the FBI would later determine that that was where lead hijacker Mohammad Atta was supposed to be seated. Atta, it is said, was the one who allegedly piloted the plane into the North Tower after he and his al Qaeda terrorists took control of the cockpit.

Thirdly, Ong mentioned only knives as hijacker weapons.[774] But Sweeney said the hijackers also had a bomb, which, she said, was two boxes connected together with yellow and red wires.[775] The FBI, based on the statement of Ted Olsen, said they were armed with only knives *and* box cutters.

Fourthly, Ong said that she was seated in the very rear of the plane in her jumpseat, 3R.[776] And she did not mention Sweeney, who, at that time, was talking on another Airfone. But Sweeney told Woodward that she and Ong were seated together in back of the coach section.[777]

Fifthly, Sweeney said that the two injured flight attendants who had been stabbed were being cared for by a doctor and a nurse who were onboard the plane.[778] But according to Craig Marquis, AA System Operation Control, there was no doctor on the plane.[779] Apparently, this was known to Ong because the last thing she said before the recording stopped was that "someone" was "calling medical," presumably to talk to a doctor because there was *not* one on the plane.[780]

Sixthly, another item in the official story that does not fit reality is when Ong and Sweeney both described how the hijackers had sprayed something up front in the business section of the cabin that forced them and the passengers to the rear coach section. They said it smelled like mace.[781,782] But the inside of the plane would have been pressurized at high altitude, which means that the air was being recirculated. In which case, the mace would have been spread throughout the whole cabin, and they, as well as all the passengers *and the terrorists*, should have been gaging on it. But not once during their twenty-five-minute calls did they or any of the passengers (who were packed in the rear coach section of the plane near them) show signs of being affected by it. The logical conclusion is, therefore, that there was no mace and Ong and Sweeney were being told what to say.

There are several other aspects to the Ong recording which indicate it might have been staged. Although Ong sounds decidedly calm and collected before the plane's final dive, there is a halting manner to her responses when she is first asked what was happening. One of the first things she says on the FBI tape is, "I *think* we're being hijacked."[783] But by this time, there should be no doubt in her mind that the plane was being hijacked; she knew that two flight attendants and a passenger had been stabbed, mace had allegedly been sprayed, and it was her impression that two of the hijackers had forced their way into the cockpit. Additionally, she has to be asked four times where she is seated before she gave the answer, "3R."[784] Also, there is absolutely none of the kind of background noise of panicky, screaming passengers that would be expected from a hijack situation, not even when the plane went into its fast and final decent which apparently prompted Ong herself to cry out.

In summary, all of these discrepancies leave open the possibility that the hijacking of Flight 11 was staged and that the Ong and Sweeney calls did not occur while the plane was in the air.

This hypothetical would also explain the impossible cell phone calls that were allegedly made from the other planes that were supposedly flying at high altitudes. But again, how such a scenario was accomplished remains a mystery.

The Novice Hijackers

Another reason why many question the official account of the attacks is because it relies heavily on the incredible claim that the novice hijackers allegedly flew the four airliners themselves manually without any assistance at all from ground control. The reports on the hijackings done by the Federal Aviation Administration (FAA) say that the hijackers turned off the planes' automatic pilots, manually veered the planes off of their planned routes, flew them for several hundreds of zigzagging miles at altitudes exceeding 20,000 feet, and then hit three out of their four targets with pinpoint accuracy.[785]

However, doing all of that without assistance from ground control would have been an extremely difficult task even for a professional pilot to accomplish, never mind the amateurs who were said to be flying those planes. That is because maintaining contact with ground control is essential during such maneuvers. First, to avoid a possible midair collision, the air traffic controller tracking the plane must clear the air of any other aircraft that might be in the new flight path. Then, due to the limited visibility that the pilot has through the cockpit window at such altitudes, he or she needs to be told such things as when to turn, what heading to maintain, what air speed to fly at, and when to start descending toward the target.

The need for ground control help with this scenario is especially confounding in the case of the Flight 77, which allegedly hit the Pentagon. According to officials at Freeway Airport in Bowie, Maryland, the piloting skills of the hijacker who was said to have flown that plane, Hani Hanjour, were so poor that, after going up with him one time in a single-engine Cessna 174, they refused to rent him a plane.[786]

In addition, according to the *New York Times*, Pan AM International, the flight school Hanjour attended in Phoenix to learn how to fly big jet airliners, reported him to the Federal Aviation Administration (FAA) in February 2001 after his instructors "had found his piloting skills so shoddy and his grasp of English so inadequate that they questioned whether his pilot's license was genuine."[787]

Said one former employee of the school, "I am still amazed to this day that he could have flown into the Pentagon. He could not fly at all."[788]

Yet the FAA reported that Hanjour's final approach to the Pentagon included piloting a highly sophisticated Boeing 757 commercial airliner flawlessly through a 330-degree downward spiral from 7,000 feet in the space of less than four minutes, and then leveling it off only a few feet above the ground in order to hit the first floor of the building.[789]

This extremely difficult maneuver could only have been performed by a highly experienced professional, if at all. In fact, it was executed so nimbly that those air traffic controllers who were monitoring it on their screens at Dulles International Airport thought they were tracking a military fighter jet.[790]

The War Games

Many also find it unbelievable that the hijackers could have single-handedly defeated the highly sophisticated air defense system of the US. It is said that the four renegade aircraft flew unmolested for an unprecedented amount of time through two of the most heavily defended airspaces in the world—that of the northeast sector of the country and over the Pentagon. But this is oddly out of sync with reality. It is a matter of record that the Air Force routinely intercepts troubled flights. On average, that happens about 100 times a year.[791] In actual point of fact, according to the FAA, in the period between September 2000 and June 2001, there were 67 such encounters.[792] If normal protocol for the interception of troubled flights had been followed on 9/11, indications are that all four hijacked planes should have been intercepted before they crashed. The fact that none of them were is an indication to many that there must have been an extraordinary circumstance involved that delayed a more normal response.

And there was. Michael Ruppert, in his book, *Crossing the Rubicon*, summed it up this way:

As it turns out, on September 11th, various agencies, including NORAD [North American Aerospace Defense Command], the FAA, the Canadian Air Force, the National Reconnaissance Office and possibly the Pentagon were conducting as many as five wargame drills—in some cases involving hijacked airliners; in some cases involving blips deliberately inserted onto FAA and military radar screens, which were present during (at least) the first attacks; and which in some cases had pulled significant fighter resources away from the northeast US on September 11th...all of this as the real attacks began."[793]

Due to these exercises, most of the military jet aircraft of the northeast sector of the US had been flown out of the country into Canada, some as far away as Alaska, leaving only four fighter jets to protect against the real attacks. In addition, it has been reported that as many as twenty-two false blips appeared on air traffic controllers radar screens on the northeast sector, making it extremely difficult to pick up the real hijacks when reports started coming in.

This raises the question of whether the timing of the terrorist hijackings was merely serendipitous, or whether there was some collusion involved at a high level of the US military chain of command.

The Military Stand-Down

In support of the latter, consider what happened to the four Air Force interceptor jets that day.

In the New England area, standard protocol for hijacks is for the air traffic controller to immediately contact the Northeast Air Defense Sector (NEADS) and the FAA once he senses a plane he is tracking is in trouble and/or if he thinks it presents a danger to other aircraft in the area.[794] NEADS can take immediate action in exigent circumstances, if, in its judgment, the situation requires it. If not, the FAA is then to immediately contact the National Military Command Center (NMCC) at the Pentagon, which would then contact NORAD, which would, in turn, order up interceptor jets.

If NEADS does not take independent action, historically, FAA to the NMCC and then the NMCC to NORAD would be the normal chain of command when dealing with hijacked planes.

There is conflicting testimony as to whether it was NEADS or NORAD that took action on 9/11, but, in either case, the responding interceptor jets, F-15s, can go from scramble order to 29,000 feet in 2½ minutes and then fly toward the target at 1,650 mph.[795] But, due to the lack of jets available, the scramble order for New York had to be sent to Otis Air Force Base on Cape Cod in Massachusetts, which was 155 miles away.[796]

Even at that, if standard protocol for hijacks had been followed, and presuming that it was NORAD which gave the final order, those Otis jets still should have been able to reach the World Trade Center (WTC) well before the hijacked planes crashed. As noted previously, the hijack of Flight 11 was confirmed by 8:24 a.m., and the abrupt change in the flight paths of the two planes, which was due south from up-state New York, was a strong indication that they were heading toward the City of New York.

The calls from the air traffic controller to the FAA, then from the FAA to the NMCC, and then the NMCC to NORAD would have only taken a minute each. NORAD's order to scramble the Otis jets would have taken another minute. The jets should have been off the ground and pretty high up within 2 more minutes. Flying at top speed of 1,650 mph, they would have covered the 155 miles to Manhattan in no more than 6 minutes. Allowing 2 minutes for them to slow down before arriving makes it about 14 total minutes from knowledge of a hijack to arrival, which would have put them over the city by about 8:24 + 14, or 8:38 a.m. That would have been about 9 minutes *before* Flight 11 hit the North Tower, which occurred at about 8:47, and 25 minutes before Flight 175 hit the South Tower, which occurred at 9:03.

However, that did not happen; the Otis jets did not make it there in time. But why did they not make it there in time? The answer to that question appears to lie in certain other facts surrounding the handling of those Otis jets that strongly indicate that there was, in fact, intentional interference with standard protocol at several points along the way.

For instance, Lieutenant Colonel Tim Duffy, the pilot of one of the two jets scrambled at Otis, said that he was not alerted to the emergency until a full 11 minutes after the first hijack was known, or, he said, at about 8:35.[797] Due to that, even under ideal conditions, even if he left right away, he could not have intercepted the first hijack. He would have made it to the WTC at about 8:35 + 14, or 8:49, two minutes after that 8:47 crash.

But he still should have beat the second crash, which occurred at 9:03, by 14 minutes (9:03 – 8:49). Inexplicably, though, by all accounts, his plane was not airborne until 8:53, which was a bewildering additional delay of 18 minutes (8:53 – 8:35).[798] That made it impossible for him to intercept either of the planes, even if under ideal conditions and flying at top speed. Duffy further indicated that for most of that 18-minute delay, he was in his plane, sitting at "battle stations" on the runway, *waiting* for the order to take off.[799]

Worse than that, when the Otis jets were only about 40 miles out from Cape Cod, they were suddenly ordered by some unidentified interloper in the military chain of command to stand down and divert to a military holding pattern out over the ocean. This holding-pattern maneuver was the final blow. It virtually ensured that, even if the process of getting the Otis jets scrambled occurred perfectly concurrent with knowledge of first hijack, as potentially could have happened, there would have been no chance for an interception.

The spot they were sent to was located about 115 miles off the coast of Long Island.[800] And the jets remained in that holding pattern and did not head for New York City until 9:13.[801] That was about 26 minutes *after* Flight 11 had already hit the North Tower and 10 minutes *after* Flight 175 hit the South Tower. This strongly suggests a scheme to prevent interception was cooked up well in advance of the attacks and down to the minute by someone very familiar with military protocol for hijack-interception procedures, and who also had the means to carry it out.

The official explanation given for this odd holding-pattern order appeared in the report from the 9/11 Commission. But it was weak, to say the least.[802] It said that the reason these two jets were put in the holding pattern was because the FAA could not locate the hijacks on their radar due to the fact that the hijackers had turned off the planes' transponder tracking signals. But that is absurd. If it was so easy to defeat the US air defense system by turning off a plane's transponder signal, how good can that system be? That would mean that any aircraft from any country could invade the US at will just by turning off the transponder. In addition, it is known fact that military and civilian radar *can* track a plane without a transponder signal.[803] The identification number and altitude of the plane would not be there, but the blip will still appear on the screen.

Incredibly, this same kind of mismanagement in the chain of command also occurred with the Air Force jets that were sent to intercept Flight 77 as it was bearing down on the Pentagon.[804] Those two jets were ordered up from Langley Air Force Base in Virginia, and they should have reached their target in ten minutes. But instead, they were sent on a wild goose chase out over the Atlantic Ocean by some unidentified person. By the time they realized the "mistake" and made it back to the Pentagon, 130 people in that building were dead.

As a result of this appalling interference in the chain of command, the selection of Otis for the scramble order and the delays in notice and takeoff, Flight 11 was allowed to fly for 23 minutes from the time it was a confirmed hijack to when it hit the North Tower. And Flight 175 was able to fly unimpeded for some 21 minutes after it was confirmed a hijack until it hit the South Tower.

In that same vein, before it hit the Pentagon, Flight 77 flew for an astonishing 41 minutes after it was confirmed a hijack.[805] As for Flight 93, it crashed 27 minutes after its hijack was confirmed, without being intercepted.[806]

Hijackers Too Quickly ID'd

In the immediacy of the 9/11 attacks, there was an absolute and total lack of any hard evidence that Osama bin Laden and al Qaeda were responsible. None of the plane manifests that were issued to the media by American Airlines or United Airlines showed names of any of the alleged hijackers. And no international terrorist organization, including al Qaeda, claimed responsibility for the attacks. As will be shown below shortly, Osama bin Laden vehemently and consistently denied he had anything to do with it—which itself is strange; one would think that, if bin Laden was, indeed, the chief perpetrator, he would have like nothing better than to crow widely about what would have been the chief accomplishment of the fervent jihadi quest to which he had dedicated his life, as well as his considerable personal fortune; and his denial of involvement would have, to a great degree, be seen as a betrayal of the principles he had so strongly espoused to his followers.

All of this is why many find it highly suspicious that the FBI was able to identify the hijackers so quickly. Incredibly, within only three days of the attacks, on September 14, 2001, FBI Director Robert Mueller released to the media the following photographs and names of all nineteen alleged 9/11 hijackers.[807]

The 9/11 Hijackers

Source: The FBI

But how was this possible? Again, no terrorist group had even claimed responsibility for the attacks, including al Qaeda, and the plane manifests that were released by the airlines did not show any Arabic names. So who gave the names of the hijackers and their photos to the FBI?

Furthermore, at not one of the four sites where those planes eventually crashed was there any evidence found that those hijackers were actually on the planes. None of their bodies were ever recovered. Not even body parts. For instance, over 20,000 pieces of human flesh were found by medical examiners at the WTC after the attacks, but not one of those was ever found to have come from the ten hijackers who were said to have been on the two crashed planes.

The only physical evidence ever given that the hijackers were on the planes was the passport of Satan al Suqami, which was given to an FBI agent by a mysterious passerby a few blocks from the WTC. But it was in pristine condition, which defies logic.[808] For instance, the black boxes (flight data recorder, etc.) from Flights 11 and 175, which were virtually indestructible, were said to have been never found, as well as two of the four engines from the planes. So, is it believable that a paper passport could have survived the fireball crash of a plane, flew out of a hijacker's pocket, came out the other side of the flaming building and ended up on the ground, unscathed?

Even more bizarre is the fact that many of the alleged hijackers were found to be still alive after the attacks.[809] Typical of them is Waleed al Shehri, who, at the time of the hijackings, was working as a pilot for Saudi Airlines.[810]

Another was Mohammad Atta, who is accused of piloting Flight 11 into the North Tower. As will be described more fully shortly, it has been claimed that he made a phone call to his father in Egypt the day after the attacks.

Then there is the case of Abdulaziz al Omari, accused of being another Flight 11 hijacker. According to a September 23, 2001 BBC report, he turned up as an engineer working for Saudi Telecom.

According to that same report, both Saeed al Ghamdi and Khalid al Midhar also turned up alive.

Another British paper, The Telegraph, reported that Salem al Hamzi and Ahmed al Nami were found alive in Saudi Arabia after the attacks—al Hamzi in the city of Yanbou and al Nami in Riyadh.[811]

In fact, also according to that BBC report, by less than two weeks after the attacks, FBI Director Robert Mueller was forced to admit publicly that the identities of several of the suicide hijackers in his previously released list were "in doubt."

Was Bin Laden Framed?

Also pertinent to the question of whether the entirety of the 9/11 attacks was an inside job of domestic terror is evidence that backs up the charge that the Bush White House and the CIA were deeply involved in framing Osama bin Laden to take the blame.

As for Bush and Cheney's involvement, this charge stems from the fact that immediately after the attacks, without presenting any solid evidence, they launched into an extraordinarily intense media campaign meant to quickly establish in the public's mind that bin Laden was the perpetrator.

Obviously, that venture was successful, as is attested to by how widely accepted as fact that notion has become. In actual fact, however, when one digs into the issue of bin Laden's alleged 9/11 guilt, one finds that the only evidence the Bush administration used against him was nothing more than vague innuendo, based on his past history of militancy, and that he was likely telling the truth when, in the aftermath of the attacks, he contacted an international media source to proclaim his innocence. Indeed, when one gets deep into it, one finds that had bin Laden been captured and given a fair trial in a civilian court, it is very likely that he would have been found innocent for lack of evidence. Incredible as it may seem, the evidence shows that Osama bin Laden was entirely innocent of the 9/11 attacks.

There is no question that, at least in his later years, bin Laden was violently anti-American. That was made plain in an August 1996 fatwa he issued that called for a holy war of jihad against American interests in the Middle East. The justification he gave was that the US had continued to station its troops in Saudi Arabia after the 1990 Gulf War, specifically in two of Islam's most holy places, Mecca and Medina, which he considered an insult. He defined his fatwa as an act of "defensive warfare," which involved "defending what is most sacred through religion, at any cost," reasoning that "there is nothing more imperative, after faith, than to repel the aggressor who corrupts religion and life, unconditionally, as far as possible."[812]

That sentiment was brought to a higher level in February 1998 when he joined with a group of Muslim clerics and other militants in a second, more violent fatwa, saying:

> The ruling to kill the Americans and their allies—civilians and military—is an individual duty for every Muslim who can do it in any country in which it is possible to do it...[813]

These things are well documented, and no excuses will be given here that justify them. But as to the question of whether bin Laden was truly guilty of perpetrating the 9/11 attacks and deserved execution for that specific crime, one only has to take a look at his FBI "Most Wanted" page.[814]

Here it is:

FBI TEN MOST WANTED FUGITIVE

MURDER OF U.S. NATIONALS OUTSIDE THE UNITED STATES; CONSPIRACY TO MURDER U.S. NATIONALS OUTSIDE THE UNITED STATES; ATTACK ON A FEDERAL FACILITY RESULTING IN DEATH

USAMA BIN LADEN

Date of Photograph Unknown

Aliases: Usama Bin Muhammad Bin Ladin, Shaykh Usama Bin Ladin, the Prince, the Emir, Abu Abdallah, Mujahid Shaykh, Hajj, the Director

CAUTION

USAMA BIN LADEN IS WANTED IN CONNECTION WITH THE AUGUST 7, 1998, BOMBINGS OF THE UNITED STATES EMBASSIES IN DAR ES SALAAM, TANZANIA, AND NAIROBI, KENYA. THESE ATTACKS KILLED OVER 200 PEOPLE. IN ADDITION, BIN LADEN IS A SUSPECT IN OTHER TERRORIST ATTACKS THROUGHOUT THE WORLD.

CONSIDERED ARMED AND EXTREMELY DANGEROUS

Source: FBI

As you can see, there are no charges regarding 9/11 listed on it. And there never were, not ever; even up to the time of his death in May 2011.

In 2006, five years after the attacks, the FBI's Chief of Investigative Publicity, Rex Tomb, was asked about this odd discrepancy by an independent investigator named Ed Haas. His response should have been immensely unsettling to every human being on the planet. He said, "The reason why 9/11 is not mentioned on Osama bin Laden's Most Wanted page is because the FBI has *no* hard evidence connecting bin Laden to 9/11."[815]

The next day, INN (International News Network) *World Report* double-checked this astonishing news directly with Tomb, and he confirmed it.[816]

The fact of this inconsistency was, of course, known by President Bush and Vice President Cheney. Indeed, how could they not know? The Justice Department was operating under their watch. Besides that, this issue was written about in the *Washington Post* in August of 2006.[817] But neither Bush nor Cheney ever mentioned this conflicting information in public.

As for bin Laden, from the very beginning, he consistently denied he was involved in the attacks. His first claim of innocence came just five days after the fact. On Sunday, September 16, 2001, in a statement he issued to the Arabic satellite channel, Al Jazeera, he said this:

> The U.S. Government has consistently blamed me for being behind every occasion its enemies attack it. I would like to assure the world that I did not plan the recent attacks, which seems to have been planned by people for personal reasons. I have been living in the Islamic emirates of Afghanistan and following its leaders' rules. The current leader does not allow me to exercise such operations.[818]

By this time, as if innuendo could take the place of hard evidence, Bush had already called for bin Laden's extradition, telling the country there was no doubt that he was the perpetrator. But the Taliban, an Islamic religious group that was in control of Afghanistan at the time, balked, citing bin Laden's claim of innocence. As CNN reported on September 21,

The Taliban have defied the U.S. demand, refusing to hand over bin Laden without proof or evidence that he was involved in last week's attacks on the United States…The Taliban ambassador for Pakistan, Abdul Salam Zaeef, said Friday that deporting him without proof would amount to an "insult to Islam."[819]

CNN also noted that the Taliban claimed that bin Laden "could not have been involved" in the attacks, meaning he did not even have the logistical capability to carry out such a complicated plan.[820] And there appears to be a great deal of validity to that claim. For instance, it has been learned that by as early as mid-1998, after bin Laden joined in the second fatwa, the head of the Taliban, Mullah Omar, had become so uneasy that bin Laden's violent, anti-American diatribes were putting the regime in a bad light, that he took steps to muzzle him. He ordered bin Laden to stop his jihadist activities; he confined the man's movements to the area around Kandahar, which was near Omar's own location; he replaced bin Laden's own bodyguards with ten Taliban officers, who kept a close watch on him; and he confiscated his satellite phone.[821]

As for Bush and Cheney, the very first hint that something fishy was afoot with their accusations against bin Laden came within those first days after the attack, when they both demonstrated by word and action that they were determined to dodge anything that might mitigate the charges against him. First, they ignored his claim of innocence, even though the FBI had not formally charged him. Then, they tersely dismissed one Taliban request for evidence of his guilt after another.[822] Instead, they began a cynical effort to use the Taliban's refusal to hand him over as a lever to crank up the American public for a retaliatory attack on Afghanistan, saying it was in the national interests of the United States to capture the perpetrator of the 9/11 attacks, destroy his al Qaeda network, and eliminate the Taliban government that was sponsoring him.

Things began moving very quickly toward war, and by September 24, with the inevitable invasion of Afghanistan looming, bin Laden apparently felt compelled once again to publicly proclaim his innocence. In an interview with the Pakistani Urdu-language newspaper, *Ummat*, he said,

"I have already said that I am not involved in the 11 September attacks in the United States. As a Muslim, I try my best to avoid telling a lie. I had no knowledge of these attacks."[823]

This time, however, he went a bit further and gave the unmistakable impression that he thought the 9/11 attacks were an inside job, adding, "The United States should try to trace the perpetrators of these attacks within itself; the people who are a part of the US system but are dissenting against it."[824]

Although this statement was widely circulated in the Middle East, it got no traction at all in the US mainstream media. And it was completely ignored by Bush and Cheney, who continued their shell-game campaign for war by making appearances on various national TV news shows, keeping up the pretense that they had indisputable evidence against bin Laden, but without ever presenting any such thing.

Even after the invasion began, they continued the ruse, summarily rejecting in the most condescending terms any attempt made by the Taliban to negotiate a fair hearing of any evidence they might have had against bin Laden. For instance, on October 14, a week after the commencement of the bombing of Kandahar, the Taliban offered a compromise. They said they would hand bin Laden over to a third country for trial if the US would present evidence of his guilt for the 9/11 attacks and stop the bombing.[825] An agreement on that could have potentially safeguarded the more than two thousand lives of our military personnel who, as of this writing, have been killed in that conflict, as well as the lives of the untold thousands of innocent civilians who also would be lost. But when asked about that gesture of peace, Bush was not only unmoved, he was openly contemptuous. He callously brushed it aside, saying, "There is no need to discuss innocence and guilt. We know he's guilty."[826] But still, he again failed to produce any evidence of that.

The next day, October 15, at a secret meeting in Islamabad, Pakistan, Taliban Foreign Minister Wakil Ahmed Muttawakil made a last-ditch attempt at a compromise. The Taliban, he said, would drop the demand for evidence against bin Laden and would agree to turn him over to the Organization for the Islamic Conference (OIC) for trial.[827]

According to Gareth Porter of the *Asia Times*,

The OIC is a moderate, Saudi-based organization representing all Islamic countries. A trial of Bin Laden by judges from OIC member countries might have dealt a more serious blow to al-Qaeda's Islamic credentials than anything the United States would have done with him.[828]

But Bush also rejected this offer, out of hand. Again, he demanded that bin Laden be turned over to the US unconditionally, adding, "They must not have heard. There's no negotiations."[829]

The Strange Case of Khalid Sheik Mohammad

In actual fact, it was not until three years after the 9/11 attacks that the Bush administration offered any so-called "hard evidence" at all against bin Laden. And that proof was tenuous, at best. It came out in the July 2004 report from the 9/11 Commission investigation and was based solely on the coerced confession of a man named Khalid Sheikh Mohammed (KSM).[830]

KSM Prior to 9/11

Source: FBI

In its report, the commission claimed that KSM was the "principal architect" of the attacks, and that he went to bin Laden with the plan and got him to finance it.[831]

KSM was arrested without incident in Rawalpindi, Pakistan, on March 1, 2003. According to the commission's report, it was after his capture that he confessed to his and bin Laden's participation in the 9/11 attacks. However, it was not until the spring of 2007, about three years after the report was released, that it was revealed that the information the commission relied on to connect bin Laden to 9/11 was forcefully extracted from KSM by operatives of the CIA through the use of a medieval method of torture called waterboarding.[832]

Waterboarding is a particularly gruesome technique, so much so that its use was declared an international war crime by the Geneva Convention following World War II. In this procedure, the prisoner is laid on his back with his head slightly lower than his feet, and a cloth is held over his face. Water is then poured over the cloth, and with every breath he tries to take, the water enters his lungs, and he actually begins to drown. After one or two instances of this treatment, the realization of impending death and the sense of desperation that it creates in the victim will, according to experts familiar with the technique, invariably reduce him to squabbling gibberish as he tries to blurt out whatever he thinks the interrogator wants to hear. That is why this procedure has been used since the Middle Ages as a favored method for eliciting false confessions. And that is also precisely why any information gotten from it is not admissible as evidence in US courts.

Given that Cheney conspired with Giuliani to destroy the vitally important steel evidence from the WTC, and also given the fact that the torture of KSM provided the only official "evidence" against bin Laden, it is more than just a little interesting to note that the authorization to waterboard KSM came directly from President Bush. He admitted as much in his 2010 memoir, *Decision Points*, saying, "George Tenant [the head of the CIA] asked for permission to use enhanced interrogation techniques, including waterboarding, on Khalid Sheikh Mohammed. 'Damn right,' I said."[833]

This adds another level of intrigue to the situation, because it gives the distinct impression, not only that the White House was involved in a cover-up of the true cause of the WTC collapses, but that it also attempted to cover-up the truth about the entire range of the 9/11 attacks by fabricating false testimony against bin Laden.

The plot thickens even more when one learns of the extraordinarily intense effort that was put into the torture of KSM. So far as what has become known, the program overall did not involve other suspects' family members. In KSM's case, however, the CIA went to the extreme measure of also kidnapping his two young sons, Yousef, age 9, and Abed, 7.[834] And at one point, the torturers let KSM know that they were perfectly willing to kill the boys if he did not cooperate.[835]

KSM's reaction to this is not surprising. He sang like a bird. This vitally important fact was uncovered by investigative reporter Jane Mayer. In an August 2007 article in the *New Yorker* magazine entitled, "The Black Sites," she said that a former military officer who had insider knowledge of KSM's torture revealed to her that "Mohammad didn't resist. He cracked real quick. He was just a little dough boy. He couldn't stand toe to toe and fight it out."[836]

Ironically, as it turns out, the fact of KSM's fast capitulation presents even more evidence of White House involvement in a 9/11 cover-up and the framing of bin Laden. Both Bush and Cheney rationalized the use of waterboarding by saying it was necessary get actionable intelligence about future attacks that threatened the country. And they crowed about the successful results they got from it.[837] But, when one digs into the official record describing the nature of the waterboarding program that was specifically meted out to KSM, the fact of his quick capitulation presents a glaring contradiction to that. If, as the administration claimed, the true intention of KSM's torture was only to get actionable intelligence, one would think that if he "cracked real quick" and gave up the information on bin Laden right away, he might have been waterboarded maybe once or twice, if at all. But according to a report from the CIA Office of the Inspector General, he was actually waterboarded around six times a day for a solid month, for a mind-numbing total of 183 times.[838]

This reeks of an even deeper intrigue. It raises the question that if KSM capitulated quickly, what possibly could have been the need for that ungodly number of extra torture sessions?

In trying to judge what the White House's true motivation was for this unconscionable treatment of another human being, it is also significant to know that Cheney took a particularly keen personal interest in knowing how that torture program was progressing. In fact, the nature of his participation bordered on the bizarre. Not only is there evidence that he was updated about it on a daily basis, but he also may have even viewed videotapes of some of the sessions.[839]

The suspicion that Cheney was personally involved in the illegal torture program was raised considerably when a congressional committee was told that those CIA-produced tapes, ninety-two in all, were later destroyed with the involvement of his White House lawyer, David Addington.[840]

Of course, Bush and Cheney never mentioned their unusually cruel treatment of KSM. It stands to reason, however, that his torture could not have been to gain actionable intelligence, because such an extreme regimen of torture could not help but make any victim of it progressively less and less reliable as a witness, as his mental state deteriorates.

In fact, evidence has come forward from several sources which strongly indicates that, as far as KSM is concerned, that was exactly the case. In the first place, there is the record of a March 2007 military proceeding that was held at the Defense Department's detention center for terrorist suspects in Guantanamo, Cuba that appears to confirm that KSM had, in fact, become mentally unstable. At that hearing, his military lawyer read an incredible, over-the-top, laundry list of 28 terrorist attacks (in addition to 9/11) that KSM confessed to have either planned or helped carry out.[841] Included were plots to assassinate Presidents Carter and Clinton and Pope John Paul II, none of which ever came to pass. KSM also said that he was behind the Richard Reid shoe bombing incident, as well as the 1993 bombing of the North Tower.

He also claimed to have planned an attack on a "Plaza Bank" building in Washington state. The problem is, there was no bank in the state by that name until 2006.[842]

Most incredible of all, was KSM's claim that he was the one who beheaded *Wall Street Journal* reporter Daniel Pearl. Pearl was in Pakistan investigating a suspected connection between the secret police, the Inter-Services Intelligence agency (ISI), and terrorism when he was kidnapped in Karachi on January 23, 2002.[843] Nine days later, on February 1, 2002, he was murdered. However, by the time KSM made his confession in Guantanamo, the Pakistani Government had already captured, tried, convicted, and condemned to death a man named Omar Said Sheikh for that crime.[844]

In addition, Sheikh's widely publicized arrest occurred in July of 2002, some seven months before KSM himself was taken into custody, so KSM must have known about it when he was in a more lucid state. Yet, after the torture, he confessed to Pearl's murder anyway.[845]

KSM made another key mistake in his Guantanamo confession when he claimed that the video made of Pearl's killing actually shows him doing the beheading. His statement reads, "I decapitated with my blessed right hand the head of the American Jew, Daniel Pearl, in the city of Karachi, Pakistan…For those who would like to confirm, there are pictures of me on the Internet holding his head."[846] But this also does not fit the facts. The video, which is available online, only shows the hands of the person doing the beheading, not his face.[847] And there is nothing at all in it to indicate KSM was even there.

Furthermore, Randall Bennett, the head of security for the US Consulate in Karachi, who had a lead role in the investigation into Pearl's death, said he interviewed Sheikh and all of his convicted accomplices, and none of them ever mentioned KSM's name.[848]

In addition, a former CIA officer, Robert Baer, has come forward to testify that his contacts inside the agency told him "ninety percent" of the information gotten from KSM through waterboarding was considered "unreliable" by the agency.[849] Moreover, Baer has said that his former colleagues in the CIA "say with 100% certainty that it was not KSM who murdered Pearl."[850]

This apparent deterioration of KSM's mental condition makes some critics go so far as to speculate that his extended torture was a sinister attempt by Bush and Cheney, in particular, to render him certifiably insane so he would be unable at any future date to attempt to retract his "confession" that implicated bin Laden in the 9/11 attacks. In fact, the entire "Enhanced Interrogation Program" (as the administration was fond of calling the torture) may have been created to achieve the specific goal of framing bin Laden through false confessions.

As far-out as this notion may at first seem, there is some evidence to support it. In 2009, it was learned that there were actually professional psychologists present during many of the torture sessions.[851] At least one of them has been identified as James Mitchell, who worked as a CIA contractor after 2001.[852] In fact, reports are that it was Mitchell who personally waterboarded KSM.[853] It very well could have been that he reported back to the White House (most likely to Cheney) when KSM had finally lost touch with reality; meaning that the "evidence" against bin Laden had been secured.

The Secret Meeting in Dubai

The accusation that certain elements of the CIA might have taken an active part in framing bin Laden is also indicated by several incidents that occurred both before and after 9/11. Perhaps the most significant one of them surrounds an allegation that the agency had a secret meeting with him two months prior to the attacks.[854] According to the French newspaper *Le Figaro*, that meeting took place in July of 2001 when bin Laden surfaced at the American Hospital in Dubai to undergo treatment for a kidney condition. At some point during his ten days of treatment, he was visited by a CIA officer from the local station.

What is most mystifying about this incident is that at the time of this clandestine meeting, bin Laden was already on the FBI's Most Wanted list for killing more than 200 people in two 1998 bombings of US embassies in Africa, and a $5 million price tag had been put on his head by the Clinton administration. Yet, the CIA agent who met with him did not have him arrested. According to *Le Figaro*'s account, after their conversation, he simply allowed bin Laden to finish his treatment and then let him slip back into the ether. And bin Laden would not surface again until after he was accused of killing close to 3,000 more people on 9/11.

For its part, the hospital denies that bin Laden was ever treated there. But *Le Figaro* stands by its story, citing as its sources "a partner in the administration of the hospital" and "friends" of the agent, to whom he had bragged of his encounter.[855]

This story is also given some credence by the fact that the particular CIA officer involved in this incident was ordered back to Washington on the day after bin Laden allegedly left the hospital.[856]

The $100,000 Money Transfer

Adding to the charge that there was some CIA involvement in the framing of bin Laden is the stunning revelation of the circumstances surrounding a $100,000 money transfer that was sent to lead 9/11 hijacker Mohammad Atta on September 10, 2001, just one day before the attacks.[857] The fact of this peculiar payment was uncovered thirty days after 9/11, in October of 2001, by the intelligence agency of India. That agency discovered through cell phone records (and the FBI later confirmed it) that the money, which was wired from a bank in the United Arab Emirates to Atta's Florida bank account, was sent on the orders of General Mahmud Ahmad, the head of the Pakistani secret police—the InterServices Intelligence Agency (ISI).[858]

Aside from the obvious implication made here—that the ISI funded the 9/11 attacks and not bin Laden—this is an oblique indication that the CIA might also have been involved. For it is a matter of record that by the time of the 9/11 attacks, the ISI and the CIA had a close working relationship that went back several decades.[859] In fact, in its inception, the ISI was modeled after the CIA, which also financed its creation. That relationship got into high gear in the early 1980s with the CIA's funding, through the ISI, of local freedom fighters—known as the mujahedeen—who fought for ten long years against the former

Soviet Union's occupation of Afghanistan.[860] And it has been alleged that in the years leading up to 9/11, Ahmad was the CIA's handpicked proxy to head the ISI.[861]

In addition, it was also learned that General Ahmad had strong connections to the Bush White House and to some key members of Congress. He was sighted in Washington during the two weeks leading up to the 9/11 attacks, having high level meetings with people in the administration, one of whom was the head of the CIA, George Tenant.[862] And, strangely enough, at the exact time his apparent protégée (Atta) was allegedly crashing Flight 11 into the North Tower, Ahmad was having a breakfast meeting with certain members of Congress, some of whom were responsible for intelligence oversight.[863]

Interestingly enough, other information came forward a year after the attacks that strongly suggests that Ahmad's payment to Mohammad Atta could prove to be an important clue that might eventually help to unravel the mystery of the true nature of the 9/11 attacks, if it ever gets fully investigated. That information concerns Mohammad's father. The official story is that Mohammad died in a blazing fit of martyrdom, piloting Flight 11 into the North Tower. But in September of 2002, his father, who was a well-respected lawyer living in Cairo, held a widely attended news conference specifically to deny that charge.[864] He said that he had had a mid-day phone conversation with his son the day *after* the 9/11 attacks when Mohammad called him to say hello. If that is true, then Mohammad could not have been on Flight 11. And if that is so, then it is very possible that Ahmad's money transfer to him was a payoff made by a CIA/ISI faction in return for his participation in what very well could have been an insider-driven 9/11 conspiracy.

This notion that Mohammad Atta had connections to the CIA has never been fully investigated by any policing agency, including the FBI and remains an unproven accusation. On the other hand, however, some evidence did surface within a week of the 9/11 attacks which indicated that there may be something to it. Specifically, on September 16, 2001, the *Washington Post* reported that

Men with the same names as two other hijackers, Mohamed Atta and Abdulaziz Alomari, appear as graduates of the U.S. International Officers School at Maxwell Air Force Base, Ala., and the Aerospace Medical School at Brooks Air Force Base in San Antonio, respectively.[865]

If this news is accurate, it would be no small matter. With respect to Atta, a degree from the US International Officers School carries a lot of prestige. According the Maxwell Air Force Base official website:

> Many international fellows who attend Air University courses later become senior leaders and decision makers after returning to their home country. Air University's International Officer School maintains an honor roll of more than 400 foreign military students from 89 countries who have risen to senior positions—including equivalents to the U.S. Air Force chief of staff.[866]

If Atta did, indeed, attend this high-status school, with its international flavor, it does not seem a great leap in logic to presume that he would have also had the opportunity to rub shoulders with CIA officers and that his involvement in the 9/11 attacks and the $100,000 payment from Ahmad very possibly could have been a result of that.

The Phony bin Laden Confession Video

Another bit of evidence which indicates that the Bush White House and the CIA took an active part in framing bin Laden concerns a phony bin Laden "confession video" that was released by the agency two months after the attacks. It was alleged to be of bin Laden admitting his role in 9/11 during a meeting with associates in Afghanistan. President Bush was very quick to vouch for it, calling it a "devastating declaration of guilt."[867] But a later examination by experts roundly proved it was a fake; and not a very good one, at that. It was found that the physical and facial features of the man in the video did not match those of the real bin Laden.[868] He is much too heavy and his nose is of a different shape. In addition, the

APPENDIX F:

"bin Laden" in the video is seen writing with his right hand, while it is a known fact that the real bin Laden was left-handed.[869]

Furthermore, the Pentagon's transcription of the conversation that took place in the tape was found by experts in the Arabic language to be seriously inaccurate.[870] One of those experts, Dr. Abdel El M. Husseini, PhD, stated, "I have carefully examined the Pentagon's translation. This translation is very problematic. At the most important places where it is held to prove the guilt of bin Laden, it is not identical with the Arabic."[871]

Even in the face of this convincing evidence of fraud, Bush continued to defend the video. At a December 13, 2001 press conference, he complained that "it is preposterous for anyone to think that this tape is doctored. That is just a feeble excuse to provide weak support for an incredibly evil man."[872] His credibility, however, was seriously undermined by a later discovery that both the CIA and the Pentagon had, indeed, been involved in producing such fake films on bin Laden during this time period which were designed to discredit him in the eyes of the Muslim world. For example, at least one of them had "bin Laden" soliciting a sex act from a young boy.[873]

Years later, the confession video would also be debunked by an expert on bin Laden, Dr. Bruce Lawrence, PhD, at the time the head of Duke University's Religion Department. He had authored a 2005 book entitled *Messages to the World; The Statements of Osama bin Laden*, in which he presented over twenty of bin Laden's speeches and writings. In 2007, after examining the confession video, he concluded that the voice heard on it could not be bin Laden's.[874]

Moreover, he said that his conclusion was confirmed by his sources inside the CIA.[875]

The Question of Motive

Inevitably, the question that eventually comes up in all this is: Why would a group of conspirators tied to the White House perpetrate such a horrible false flag operation like 9/11 attacks? In reality, their motives could have been as varied as the number of conspirators involved, but there seem to be two main avenues of thought on that. In the first place, the most obvious objective would have been to gain a foothold in the Middle East through the use of the military in order to get control of a portion of that area's vast oil reserves for some of the Bush administration's most important corporate sponsors. And secondly, there was the potential for monetary gain for some of the major participants.

A War for Corporate Profits

Some evidence came forward a couple of years after 9/11 that suggested that just such a plot to gain control of Middle East oil for US and foreign corporations was being worked on within the very first weeks of Bush and Cheney taking office. This was brought to light in February 2004 by the further intrepid reporting of Jane Mayer. Again writing in the *New Yorker*, she cited an anonymously released Bush Administration document that ordered the National Security Agency (NSC) to cooperate with a secret task force on energy that was formed by Cheney—the so-called US National Energy Policy Development Group (NEPDG)—and to push for the "capture" of new and existing oil and gas fields in Iraq. The document cited by Mayer was dated February 3, 2001, only two weeks after Bush's inauguration as president.[876]

When pressed for information about Cheney's task force by some administration critics, the White House refused to release anything. But two years after the fact, in 2003, the group Judicial Watch (JW) won a Freedom of Information Act (FOIA) lawsuit and was granted seven documents from the meeting. The following map is one of them.[877] It suggests that at least one topic of discussion concerned the divvying up of Iraq into blocks for exploration by various international oil companies.

Iraqi Oil Fields and Exploration Blocks
Source: Judicial Watch

JW was also granted access to the following list. It details which companies had shown interest in Iraq for oil exploration. Notice how extensive is this list of Iraqi oil contract suitors. Obviously, this is not something that could have been whipped up in the two short weeks after Bush and Cheney took office. It must have been developed months or even years before that.

Foreign Suitors for Iraqi Oilfield Contracts
as of 5 March 2001

Country	Firm	Iraqi Oil & Gas Projects/Contacts Status	
Algeria	Sonatrach	Tuba	Discussions. PSC.
		Blocks 6 & 7	Collecting data.
Australia	BHP	Halfaya	Discussions. PSC.
		Block 6	Collected data.
Belgium	Petrofina	Ahdab	Technical/economic studies (China's CNPC awarded PSC).
		Block 2	Collected data.
Canada	Ranger	Block 6, other	Signed MOU with Baghdad.
	Bow Canada	Khurmala	Joint proposal w/Czech Republic's Strojexport
		Hamrin	Joint proposal w/Czech Republic's Strojexport
	Alberta Energy	Unidentified	None
	CanOxy	Ratawi	Discussions. PSC.
		Block 5	Collected data.
	Chauvco Res.	Ayn Zalah	Advanced talks by late 1996. Service contract for advanced oil recovery (gas injection project) in this aging field.
	Escondido	Ratawi	Discussions. PSC.
		Block 5	Collecting data.
	Talisman	Hamrin, E. Baghdad	Service contract negotiations October 1999.
	IPC	Hamrin	Discussions. Service contract
	PanCanadian	Unidentified	None
China	CNPC	Ahdab	Production Sharing Contract (PSC) signed June 1997.
		Halfaya	Bid for $4 bn, 23-year PSC.
		Luhais & Subba	Discussions. Service contract.
		Block 5	Collected data, discussions.
	Norinco	Ahdab	PSC signed June 1997 (CNPC consortium partner).
		Rafidain	Discussions. PSC.
	Sinochem	Rafidain	Discussions. PSC.
Czech Republic	Strojexport	Hamrin	Joint project with Bow Canada. Sent team to Iraq in Sept 1997.
		Khurmala	Joint project with Bow Canada
Finland	Neste Oy	Unidentified	None
France	Total Elf Aquitaine	Majnoon	PSC "agreed in principle" January 1997.
	Forasol SA	Saddam	Feasibility study presented to Baghdad in 1997, updated in 1998.
	IBEX	Hamrin	Technical discussions.
	Perenco	Rafidain	Discussions. PSC.
	Total Elf Aquitaine	Nahr Umr	PSC "agreed in principle" January 1997.
Germany	Deminex	Block 1	Collected data.
	Preussag	Ahdab	Technical/economic studies (China's CNPC later awarded PSC).
		Block 2	Collected data
	Slavneft	N. Rumaylah	Subcontractor to Lukoil consortium.
Greece	Kriti	Gharraf	Discussions. PSC.
Hungary	Hanpetro	Block 3	Collected data.
India	ONGC	Tuba	Advanced contract talks in October 1999 (ONGC drilled at least four wells in Tuba in the 1980s). PSC.
		Halfaya	Discussions. PSC.
		Block 8	Collected data.
	Reliance	Tuba	Discussions.
Indonesia	Pertamina	Tuba	Finalized discussions for a PSC in late 1997.
		Block 3	Collected data
Ireland	Bula	Block 4	Discussions.
Italy	Agip	Nasiriya	PSC initialed Apr 97. $2 bn, 23-year project (w/partner Repsol).
		Iraq-Turkey gas pipeline	Discussions.
		Block 1	Collected data, discussions.
	Snamprogetti	Luhais & Subba	Discussions. Service contract.

Suitors for Iraqi Oilfield Contracts

Source: Judicial Watch

434

The list continues:

Country	Firm	Iraqi Oil & Gas Projects	Comments/Status
Japan	Japex	Gharraf	Bid and technical/economic oilfield study submitted to Baghdad. March 1997. PSC
	Mitsubishi	Luhais & Subba	Discussions. Service contract.
Malaysia	Petronas	Ratawi	Discussions. PSC.
		Tuba	Discussions. PSC
		Block 2	Collected data, discussions
Mexico	Pemex	Unidentified	None.
Netherlands	Larmag	Subba & Luhais	Discussions. Service contract.
	Dutch Royal Shell	Ratawi	Discussions.
		Block 8	Collected data.
Norway	Statoil	Block 1	Collected data.
Pakistan	Crescent	Ratawi	Discussions. PSC.
		Block 5	Collected data.
Romania	Petrom	Khurmala Dome (Karkuk)	Apparently awarded service contract, project in advanced technical infrastructure design phase (setting equipment & materials specifications for project).
		Luhais & Subba	Discussions. Service contract.
		Block 4	Collected data, discussions.
		Qayyarah	Contract talks. Service contract for well drilling and engineering.
	Mol	Block 3	Discussions.
Russia	Kond Petroleum	Rafidain	Discussions. Russian firm Sidanko a possible partner. PSC.
	Lukoil	W. Qurnah	PSC signed March 1997. Topographic surveys in 1998.
		N. Rumaylah	Service contract negotiations to upgrade water injection facilities, develop additional geologic reservoirs.
	Zarubezneft	W. Qurnah	PSC signed March 1997 (Lukoil consortium partner).
		N. Rumaylah	Service contract negotiations (w/Lukoil consortium).
		Hamrin	Invited to bid in mid-1997. Service contract.
	Mashinoimport	W. Qurnah	PSC signed March 1997 (Lukoil consortium partner).
		Luhais, & Subba	Discussions. Service contract.
		N. Rumaylah	Service contract negotiations (w/Lukoil consortium).
	Tatameft	N. Rumaylah	Subcontractor to Lukoil consortium.
	Rostneft	N. Rumaylah	Subcontractor to Lukoil consortium.
	Sidanko	N. Rumaylah	Subcontractor to Lukoil consortium.
S. Korea	Sangyong	Halfaya	Bidding for $4 bn, 23-year PSC. Seoul in June 1997 invited Iraq Oil Minister to S. Korea for signing ceremony.
	Samsung	Halfaya	Bidding (part of Korean consortium). PSC.
	Pedco	Halfaya	" " "
	Hambo	Halfaya	" " "
	Yukong	Halfaya	" " "
	Daewoo	Rafidain	Discussions. PSC.
Spain	Repsol	Nasiriya	PSC initialed Apr 97. $2 bn, 23-year project (w/partner Agip).
		Block 4	Collected data.
Taiwan	CPC	Gharraf	Discussions. PSC.
		Rafidain	Discussions. PSC.
		Tuba	Discussions. PSC.
Tunisia	Setcar	Unidentified	None
Turkey	TPAO	Gharraf	Bid for PSC. Oilfield study completed January 1997.
		Mansuriya Gas Field	Service contract signed May 1997 to develop field, purchase gas
		Block 4	Reprocessed seismic data, conducting laboratory studies
UK	Branch Energy	Gharraf	Discussions. PSC.
	Pacific Resources	Rafidain	Discussions. PSC.
Vietnam	PetroVietnam	Amara	Service contract. Near signing Oct 1999

Suitors for Iraqi Oilfield Contracts
Source: Judicial Watch

In 2004, two other credible pieces of evidence came forward that corroborate the charge that the invasion of Iraq for its oil was being ramped up immediately after Bush took office. First there is the book, *The Price of Loyalty*, by Ron Suskind. In it, Paul O'Neil, the administration's first Secretary of the Treasury, is quoted as saying that he was actually a participant in that February 2001 NSC meeting noted above, and, at that time, he personally witnessed Bush make it clear that he wanted the US to invade Iraq and that he ordered the NSC to "find a way to do this."[878]

Subsequently, in late October 2001, after the attack on Afghanistan, Bush, Cheney, and their National Security Advisor, Condoleezza Rice, took that ambition into their own hands and started going around the country claiming that the president of Iraq, Saddam Hussein, was a national security risk. They said that he had weapons of mass destruction (WMD) that posed a threat to US interests in the area.

Moreover, they charged that Saddam was attempting to develop a crude type of nuclear device that presumably could be carried into an American city and ignited. They based this particular charge on an intelligence report which said that he had tried to buy raw uranium ore (known as yellow cake) from the African country of Niger. Furthermore, they said that Iraq had recently purchased a certain kind of aluminum tubes that could only have one purpose—that is to build the centrifuges that are necessary to refine the yellow cake into weapons grade plutonium. In the days leading up to the invasion of Iraq, Bush told a joint session of Congress that this threat was serious and that the US must do something about it before it came in the form of a "mushroom cloud" from a crude nuclear "dirty" bomb that could be smuggled into the country in a suitcase and detonated.[879]

Additionally, at the same time the Bush White House was making the case for WMDs, they began making insinuations that Saddam had a connection to bin Laden and al Qaeda, and that he had helped them perpetrate the 9/11 attacks.

As of this writing, all of the accusations that were leveled against Saddam have been proven to be false. After more than sixteen years of occupation of that country, evidence of WMDs had never been found.[880]

As for the "yellow cake" charge and the "mushroom cloud" threat, in late February 2002, diplomat Joseph Wilson traveled to Niger to investigate it. And he found the accusation to entirely untrue. In the end, it was discovered that that particular claim was based on fake documents that were obtained under suspicious circumstances from Italian intelligence sources.[881] And, regarding the aluminum tubes, it was found by government sponsored scientists to be too thick-walled and absolutely useless for building centrifuges.[882]

As for the allegation of Saddam's connection to 9/11, Bush himself put a closing nail in its coffin at press conference he held in mid-September 2003 when, in answer to a reporter's question on the subject, he rather blithely admitted that "We have no evidence that Saddam Hussein was involved with the 11 September attacks."[883]

The second credible piece of evidence that came out in 2004, which corroborated the accusations of Bush administration fraud regarding the need for the US to go to war in Iraq, was an insider leak that came from the British government. That leak was in the form of a document that referred to a meeting held in London before the invasion between Prime Minister Tony Blair and his top ministers. The document, which was written by a principle to that meeting, has since become known as the "Downing Street Memo." In part, it reads:

C reported on his recent talks in Washington. There was a perceptible shift in attitude. Military action was now seen as inevitable. Bush wanted to remove Saddam, through military action, justified by the conjunction of terrorism and WMD. *But the intelligence and facts were being fixed around the policy.*

It seemed clear that Bush had made up his mind to take military action, even if the timing was not yet decided. But the case was thin. Saddam was not threatening his neighbors, and his WMD capability was less than that of Libya, North Korea or Iran.[884] (Italics added)

Of course, all of these false allegations of Iraqi malfeasance were not debunked until after the invasion and the subsequent capture of Saddam, who was unceremoniously executed by hanging at the hands of his political enemies after he was turned over to them by the Bush White House.[885]

And finally, years later, in 2011, a CIA asset of some nine years' experience named Susan Lindauer came forward with insider information which clearly demonstrates the disturbing level of egregious duplicity with which the Bush White House lied the country into the war in Iraq.[886] During the course of her duties, she also learned that there was a clear warning of the 9/11 attacks that was known to the Bush administration for at least five months, but ignored, presumably out of a desire to go to war.[887]

A native of Alaska, Lindauer was from a politically prominent family; her father was once the Republican nominee for governor. She graduated from Smith College with a degree in public policy, and later attended the prestigious London School of Economics.[888] The relevant part of her story with the CIA began in the summer of 2000. That was when she was sent by her agency handler, Richard Fuisz, to New York City to secretly contact the Iraqi delegation to the United Nations (UN).[889] At the time, Saddam Hussein's government was still under economic sanctions that had been imposed after the first Gulf War, because he had refused to disclose his weapons of mass destruction (WMDs) and prove that he was destroying them. Saddam said he had none and offered to let the US into Iraq to inspect. After a series of back and forth messages relayed by Lindauer to each party, a November 2000 agreement on that was in place with the administration of President Bill Clinton.

By the time the Bush administration came into office in January 2001, Lindauer was the chief back-channel CIA asset dealing with the Iraqi UN delegation. But the new administration ignored Saddam's offer of inspections on WMD and began cranking up the pressure. In reaction, Saddam gave a little more. In February 2001, Lindauer reported to Fuisz that Saddam had further agreed to allow an FBI task force into Bagdad to investigate terrorism and arrest suspects. But again, Bush balked.

According to Lindauer, by April 2001, the CIA had learned that there was going to be an attack by Osama bin Laden on the WTC using hijacked planes. And she was instructed by Fuisz to warn the Iraqis delegation in the strongest terms possible that, if Iraq has any information about it, they had better tell her or, if there was an attack, the result would be war. She was also told to tell the Iraqis that this threat came from the highest level of the US government; the insinuation being that it came from the White House.

The Iraqis told Lindauer that they had no information on that, at all.

Subsequently, by July of 2001, Saddam had weakened further. Lindauer reported to Fuisz that he had suddenly offered to sweeten the deal; he was now offering many business concessions in return for lifting the sanctions, which were crushing Iraq's economy. He had offered to buy one million US automobiles a year for ten years and give American corporations lucrative contracts on many aspects of the Iraqi economy, like for example, telecommunications, pharmaceuticals, hospitals, etc. This could have averted war and been very beneficial to both countries, but again Bush refused the offer.

Lindauer also confirmed that in August 2001, the CIA delivered the Presidential Daily Brief (PDB) warning to Bush that bin Laden was "Determined to Strike in the US," a report that, she said, was partially written by her handler, Richard Fuisz. A month later, the 9/11 attacks occurred exactly as had been described to her by Fuisz, five months earlier.

As the invasion of Iraq loomed clearly on the horizon, Lindauer says that she felt a personal responsibility to tell what she knew about Saddam's peace offer in order to possibly avert that second war. To that end, she attempted to tell what she knew to several officials in Congress, including Senator John McCain and President Bush's chief of staff, Andy Card, who happened to be her second cousin. But this resulted in quite the opposite outcome as intended. Within thirty days, she was arrested at her home by the FBI under the Patriot Act and charged with acting as an "unregistered Iraqi agent," for initiating those contacts ordered by Fuisz. She was also accused of "misappropriation of government funds," because, as the FBI indictment accused, she had spent an unauthorized $92.90 on three lunches she had with the Iraqis UN Delegation.

After her arrest, Lindauer ended up spending eight months in a military prison at Carswell Airforce Base in Fort Worth, Texas. Later, she was transferred to the Metropolitan Correctional Facility in New York, where she spent another four months. Her lawyer was finally able to convince Judge Michael Mukasey to drop all of the charges against her, and she was released.

Lindauer has since intimated that her CIA contact, Fuisz, was paid $13 million out of Pentagon funds meant for Iraq to keep quiet about the July 2001 Iraqi peace offer and the April 2001 bin Laden threat against the WTC. She also says that, at one point after her detention, she was offered $10 million to keep quiet. But, standing on principal, she instead wrote a book about her experiences entitled *Extreme Prejudice*.

A War for Personal Gain

On the point that there would have been the potential for monetary gain for a lot of the major participants in a 9/11 insider plot, take Cheney, for one example. As noted in the Epilogue, he was prime example of that. As mentioned, before he became vice-president, he was the CEO of the firm Halliburton. Reportedly, when he left that company, it was facing the prospects of bankruptcy, and the value of his stock in it was estimated to be worth in the area of $250,000. But, after his former company received several huge no-bid contracts to provide services to the troops in the wars, the value of his stock skyrocketed to be worth about $8 million.[890]

Then, there is the question of the almost unfathomable amount of cash that was recklessly shipped into the war zone by the Bush administration and which subsequently disappeared without a trace. Reports are that, at one point, $9 billion in *unmarked* bills in denominations of $1, $5, $10, $20 and $100 were shipped into Iraq and lost.[891] It was flown in on military planes in shrink-wrapped bricks that were loaded onto pallets that weighed in the area of 1,500 pounds each.

But why fly that kind of money into a war zone without a system for accounting for it? And why unmarked bills? How many generals was it that pulled a brick or two off that pile? Did some of it make its way back to the White House on diplomatic flights that are not subject to search? Nobody knows.

There is also the question of the $2.3 trillion dollars that, in the months before the attacks, had been found to have gone missing from Pentagon funds.[892] That is a lot of money. So, who got it? The fact of this shocking loss of taxpayer money was announced by Secretary of Defense Donald Rumsfeld on September 10, 2001, just one day before the 9/11 attacks. The press release stated that the affair was under investigation. But when Flight 77 hit the Pentagon, it just happened to destroy the very offices that were handling the case. Due to that, all the records were lost; no records equals no investigation.

Then, there is the question of the mysterious and abnormally high volume of short selling of stock just before 9/11 in companies that were affected by the attack on the WTC. When stock in those companies dropped in price after the attacks, a lot of money was made by those "investors." For example, between September 6 and 7, six times the normal volume of put options—4,474—were placed on stock in United Airlines, the company which owned the plane that hit the South Tower. That raked in a profit of $5 million.[893] On September 10, 285 times the normal volume of puts were placed on stock in American Airlines, which owned the plane that hit the North Tower. Those orders made a profit of $4 million.[894]

It was also found that at least two companies who had offices in the North Tower also got shorted. Morgan Stanley, for one, experienced nine times the normal average number of put options, which paid out $1.2 million in profit.[895] And Merrill Lynch had ten times the normal average of puts ordered on its stock, which brought in $5.5 million.[896]

Another notable item of interest with regard to profit-taking coincident with the 9/11 attacks is the fact that President Bush's cousin Wirt Walker and his wife bought 56,000 shares of stock in Securacom (by then renamed Stratesec), in the days leading up to the attacks.[897] Soon after the attacks, that stock doubled in price. As was mentioned in the conclusions to Chapter 6, Securacom/Stratesec handled upgrades of security at the WTC in the year leading up to the attacks, and Wirt was a director of that company up to and including the day of the attacks.

Also as to the question of who benefited financially from the 9/11 attacks, there is the reported $4.5 billion that the lease holders of the WTC, Larry Silverstein and his partners, received in insurance payouts for their loss of the twin towers—structures that were unprofitable due to their age and had environmental problems that were expensive to fix.[898]

Additionally, coincident with the attacks, an enormous amount of gold and silver bars went missing from a highly secure, bomb-proof vault located four stories below WTC 4. Reportedly, those precious metals had a total value of close to $950 million.[900] But according to a later announcement by Mayor Giuliani, only $230 million was recovered by the NYPD and first responders.[901] So, who got the $720 million worth that went missing?

Incredibly, none of this alleged profiteering was ever investigated, not even by the FBI.

Notes

Introduction

[1] [Factor of safety was about 3.0] Thomas W. Eagar and Christopher Musso, "Why Did the World Trade Center Collapse? Science, Engineering and Speculation," *Journal of Materials* (JOM), 53 (12) (2001), 8-11, http://www.tms.org/pubs/journals/jom/0112/eagar/eagar-0112.html; "The World Trade Center New York City," *Contemporary Steel Design*, 1964, Volume 1, #4, http://www.engr.psu.edu/ae/WTC/AISI/WTCAISI 1.PDF (This document reveals that the perimeter columns, which were constructed of at least 45 ksi steel, had a minimum factor of safety of 5.4, and the core columns, which were constructed of 36 ksi steel, had a factor of safety of 1.8. Load distribution for the building was variously reported as being 40% to the perimeter columns and 60% to the core columns [by independent sources] or 50% to each [by NIST: NCSTAR 1-6, xlvii]. Thus, the minimum average overall factor of safety would be either 3.2 or 3.6, depending on the calculation. Based on this, 3.0 would be a conservative figure for factor of safety.)

[2] See Chapter 6, this volume, Section: "The Tower Was Designed to Survive the Plane Crash and Subsequent Fires," 196.

[3] Dr. Steven I. Dutch, PhD, *Vaporizing the World Trade Center*, Natural and Applied Sciences, University of Wisconsin-Green Bay, https://www.uwgb.edu/dutchs/pseudosc/911NutPhysics1.HTM

[4] Dr. Judy Wood, PhD, "Where did all the rubble go?," *Facebook*, 1/30/2006, https://www.google.com/webhp?sourceid=chrome-instant&ion=1&espv=2&ie=UTF-8#q=Wtc+dbris+pile+three+stories+high

[5] James Glanz and Eric Lipton, "City in the Sky: The Rise and Fall of the World Trade Center," Times Books (2003), 311.

[6] *Wikipedia*, "September 11 Attacks," http://en.wikipedia.org/wiki/September_11_attacks

[7] *National Commission on Terrorist Attacks Upon the United States* (aka "The 9/11 Commission Report"), "We Have Some Planes," Chapter 1, Section 1.1, http://govinfo.library.unt.edu/911/report/911Report_Ch1.htm

[8] *Wikipedia*, "September 11 Attacks."

[9] Ibid.

[10] Ibid.

[11] As to the number of deaths due to the collapses, it has been estimated that of the about 2,600 who died at the WTC, an estimated 300 to 400 died who were in the immediate area of the plane impacts. As many as 200 is said to have jumped from the burning buildings before the collapses and 174 died on the two planes, including 10 hijackers. *Wikipedia*, "Casualties of the September 11 Attacks," http://en.wikipedia.org/wiki/Casualties_of_the_September_11_attacks#By_the_numbers

[12] Shyam-Sunder, National Institute for Standards and Technology (*NIST*), NCSTAR 1, Executive Summary, xxxviii.

[13] See Chapter 6, this volume, Section: "Historical Examples," 245.

[14] *Architects and Engineers for 9/11 Truth*, http://www.ae911truth.org/; *Wikipedia*, "Architects and Engineers for 9/11 Truth," http://en.wikipedia.org/wiki/Architects_%26_Engineers_for_9/11_Truth

[15] See Chapter 6, this volume, Section: "Manipulated Computer Simulations," 261.

[16] *FEMA*, WTC Building Performance Study, Chapter 2, Section 2.2.1.2, "Fire Development, 2-22, https://www.fema.gov/media-library-data/20130726-1512-20490-7075/403_execsum.pdf

[17] Sadek, National Institute for Standards and Technology (*NIST*), "Final Report on the Collapse of the World Trade Center Towers," NCSTAR 1-2, "Executive Summary," lxxxiii, http://www.nist.gov/customcf/get_pdf.cfm?pub_id=909017

[18] *FEMA*, WTC Building Performance Study, Chapter 5, Section 5.1, 5-1, FEMA Final Report, http://www.fema.gov/media-library-data/20130726-1512-20490-2227/403_ch5.pdf

[19] Ibid, Chapter 5, Section 5.1, 5-1

[20] *C-SPAN*, Investigation of World Trade Center 7, 8/21/2008, http://www.c-span.org/video/?280569-1/investigation-world-trade-center-building-7

[21] *Architects and Engineers for 9/11 Truth*, "118 Witnesses to Explosions in the FDNY Oral Histories," http://www.ae911truth.org/images//PDFs/090116-118Witnesses.pdf

[22] The *New York Times*, "The Sept 11th Records (Oral Histories), http://graphics8.nytimes.com/packages/html/nyregion/20050812_WTC_GRAPHIC/met_WTC_histories_full_01.html

[23] Ibid.

[24] Ibid.

[25] Ibid.

[26] Ibid

[27] Ibid.

[28] Ibid.

[29] *YouTube.com*, "Final 5 Minutes: 911 Call in World Trade Center, While Tower ps://www.youtube.com/watch?v=RLW0jKKRXMo

[30] See Appendix D, this volume: "The High Factor of Safety," 359.

[31] *911 Research*, "The Fire's Impact," http://911research.wtc7.net/wtc/analysis/fires/steel.html

[32] NiFAST, "Do You Know What Will Not Burn in a House Fire?," http://www.nifast.org/blog/07/do-you-know-what-will-not-burn-in-a-house-fire/

[33] Eagar and Musso, "Why Did the World Trade Center Collapse? Science, Engineering and Speculation."

[34] NIST, NCSTAR 1, Chapter 3, Section 3.3, 38, http://ws680.nist.gov/publication/get_pdf.cfm?pub_id=909017

[35] See Chapter 6, this volume, Section: "High Factor of Safety Points to Use of Explosives," 235.

[36] Ibid.

[37] *Rethink911.org*, "New Poll Finds Most Americans Open to Alternative 9/11 Theories," August 2013, http://rethink911.org/news/new-poll-finds-most-americans-open-to-alternative-911-theories/

[38] Brendan James, "9/11 Conspiracy Theories: Inside the Lonely Lives of Truthers, Still Looking for Their Big Break," *International Business Times*, 9/11/2015, http://www.ibtimes.com/911-conspiracy-theories-inside-lonely-lives-truthers-still-looking-their-big-break-2091474
[39] *Wordpress.com*, "Scripps Howard Poll: What 33% Believe," https://prof77.wordpress.com/wtf/911-2/what-33-believe/
[40] 70 million is conservatively based on the 2000 Census; US Census Bureau, "Population by Age, Race, and Hispanic or Latino Origin for the United States: 2000," see Table 1, which has population over the age of 18 set at 74.3% of total population. http://www.census.gov/population/www/cen2000/briefs/phc-t9/index.htm
[41] See Appendix F, this volume: "9/11 Contradictions," 372.
[42] Sunder, *NIST*, NCSTAR 1, xxxviii.

Chapter 1
[43] Dr. R. L. Higginson, "Oxidation," http://homepages.lboro.ac.uk/~mprlh/
[44] "President Announces New Homeland Defense Initiative," *Web.Archive.org*, May 8, 2001, http://web.archive.org/web/20010630041038/http://www.usinfo.state.gov/regional/af/security/a1050878.htm; see also Michael C. Ruppert, *Crossing the Rubicon: The Decline of the American Empire at the End of the Age of Oil*, Gabriola Island: New Society Publishers (2004), 412-414.
[45] Ibid, 413.
[46] *Federal Emergency Management Agency* (FEMA), "Theodore A. (Ted) Monette, Jr.," June 11, 2012, http://www.fema.gov/leadership/theodore-ted-monette-jr
[47] Ruppert, *Crossing the Rubicon*, 417.
[48] Ibid.
[49] *FBI*, "Ten Years After; The FBI Since 9/11," The Federal Bureau of Investigation website, http://www.fbi.gov/about-us/ten-years-after-the-fbi-since-9-11/response-and-recovery
[50] *FEMA*, WTC Building Performance Study, Executive Summary, 2.
[51] Ibid, Cover/Publication Page, "Team Members."
[52] James Glanz and Eric Lipton, *City in the Sky* (New York: Times Books, 2003), 331; see also, testimony of Gene Corley, "Learning from 9/11—Understanding the Collapse of the World Trade Center," Committee on Science, U.S. House of Representatives, March 6, 2002, http://web.archive.org/web/20021128021952/http://commdocs.house.gov/committees/science/hsy77747.000/hsy77747_0.htm
[53] Eric Lipton, "Mismanagement Muddled Collapse Inquiry, House Panel Says," *The New York Times*, 3/7/2002, http://911research.wtc7.net/cache/wtc/groundzero/nyt_mismanagementmuddle.html
[54] Testimony of Gene Corley, "Learning from 9/11"; for the video of Corley's statement see also "9/11: WTC Evidence Destruction (C-Span)," *YouTube.com*, http://www.youtube.com/watch?feature=player_detailpage&v=ugCIIn6Nexs
[55] *FBI*, "Ten Years After; The FBI Since 9/11."
[56] *YouTube.com*, ABC News Special Report, As seen in: "9/11 - Time for Truth 2 (2011)," 41:03, https://www.youtube.com/watch?v=r0ngF9oVY7I
[57] *YouTube.com*, "9/11 Suspects: Rudy Giuliani," https://www.youtube.com/watch?v=6HZUc3AdBdc

58 Ibid, 2:07.
59 *National Institute for Standards and Technology* (NIST), Pitts, Butler, and Junker, NCSTAR 1, Appendix D, D-1.
60 David Khon, "Culling Through Mangled Steel," *CBS News*, February 11, 2009, http://www.cbsnews.com/2100-224_162-503218.html
61 Glanz and Lipton, *City in the Sky*, 329; see also testimony of Gene Corley, "Learning from 9/11."
62 "Boasteel Will Recycle World Trade Center Debris," *China.org.cn*, http://www.china.org.cn/english/2002/Jan/25776.htm
63 Ibid.
64 *Wikipedia*, "The Port Authority of New York and New Jersey," https://en.wikipedia.org/wiki/Port_Authority_of_New_York_and_New_Jersey
65 William Langewiesche, *American Ground: Unbuilding the World Trade Center* (New York, NY: North Point Press, 2002), 84.
66 Adam Nagourney, "Cuomo's Criticism of Pataki's Role After 9/11 Sets Off Furor," *The New York Times*, 4/18/2002, http://www.nytimes.com/2002/04/18/nyregion/cuomo-s-criticism-of-pataki-s-role-after-9-11-sets-off-furor.html
67 *FBI*, "Terror Hits Home: The Oklahoma City Bombing," https://www.fbi.gov/about-us/history/famous-cases/oklahoma-city-bombing
68 Langewiesche, *American Ground*, 94; see also *The Oklahoma Department of Civil Emergency Management* [report], "After Action Report Alfred P. Murrah Federal Building Bombing 19 April 1995 in Oklahoma City, Oklahoma," http://www.ok.gov/OEM/documents%20After%20Action%209Report.pdf
69 Anthony DePalma, "Ground Zero Illnesses Clouding Giuliani's Legacy," *The New York Times*, May 14, 2007, http://www.nytimes.com/2007/05/14/nyregion/14giuliani.html?pagewanted=all
70 Ibid.
71 Rudolph Giuliani, *Leadership*, Miramax (2002), 315
72 Ibid, 148.
73 Wayne Barrett and Dan Collins, *Grand Illusion*, Harper (2006), 103.
74 "9/11 Suspects: Rudy Giuliani," 4:58.
75 Giuliani, *Leadership*, 4.
76 Ibid, 44.
77 Langewiesche, 82.
78 Ibid.
79 Ibid., 66; Christine McKenna, "Mike Burton: A Lifetime Wrapped in a Marathon Inside a Year," *America Rebuilds*, PBS.org, http://www.pbs.org/americarebuilds/profiles/profiles_burton.html
80 *YouTube.com*, Interview with Mike Burton, Ground Zero-Shocking 9/11 History (Documentary), 5:11, https://www.youtube.com/watch?v=yBM0sJZx4C4
81 Langewiesche, 95.
82 Ibid.
83 Giuliani, *Leadership*, 4, 62.
84 *New York Times*, "The September 11th Records," Statements of Richard Zarillo, Abdo Nahmod and Steve Mosiello, http://graphics8.nytimes.com/packages/html/nyregion/20050812_WTC_GRAPHIC/met_WTC_histories_full_01.html
85 Giuliani, *Leadership*, 7.
86 Ibid, 6.

[87] *9/11 Commission*, Statement of Richard Sheirer, May 18, 2004, http://govinfo. library.unt.edu/911/hearings/hearing11/sheirer_statement.pdf
[88] Barrett and Collins, 31.
[89] Amanda Griscom, "Man Behind the Mayor," *New York Magazine*, http:// nymag.com/nymetro/news/sept11/features/5270/index1.html
[90] Barrett and Collins, 38.
[91] Ibid, 44.
[92] Ibid, 66.
[93] Ibid.
[94] The Port Authority Police Department (PAPD) lost 37 members and the NYPD lost 23, See: 9/11 Commission Report, Chapter 9, Section 9.2, http:// www.9-11commission.gov/report/911Report_Ch9.htm; For the number of fire-fighters killed, see Note 133.
[95] Barrett & Collins, 53.
[96] Ibid, 53, 54.
[97] Ibid, 54.
[98] Ibid, 56.
[99] Robert Kolker, "Stairwell A," *New York* magazine, 8/27/2011, http://nymag. com/news/9-11/10th-anniversary/stairwell-a/
[100] See Chapter 4, this volume, Section: "The Explosion in the Main Lobby," 128.
[101] Ibid.
[102] *NYFD*, World Trade Center Task Force (WTCTF), Interview with Joe Casaliggi, 1/9/2002, http://graphics8.nytimes.com/packages/pdf/nyre-gion/20050812_WTC_GRAPHIC/9110430.PDF
[103] Barrett and Collins, 31.
[104] Ibid, 32.
[105] Ibid, 31.
[106] Ibid, 33.
[107] The *New York Times*, "The Sept. 11 Records," Statement of Richard Zarillo, http://graphics8.nytimes.com/paages/html/nyrgion/20050812_WTC_GRAPHIC/met_WTC_histories_full_01.html
[108] *YouTube.com*, Barry Jennings Interviews (WABC-TV, 2001, LTW, 2007), https://www.youtube.com/watch?v=OmeY2vJ6ZoA
[109] 9/11 Commission, Staff Statement #14, May 19, 2004; see Barrett and Collins, 29.
[110] Barrett and Collins, 32,33.
[111] Giuliani, *Leadership*, 7.
[112] Ibid, 5.
[113] Ibid, 7.
[114] The *New York Times*, "The Sept. 11 Records," Statements of Richard Zarillo, Abo Nahmod and John Peruggia, http://graphics8.nytimes.com/packages/html/nyregion/20050812_WTC_GRAPHIC/met_WTC_histories_full_01.html
[115] Ibid.
[116] Ibid.
[117] Giuliani, *Leadership*, 5. (From other details the mayor gave, this 9:04 time for his meeting with Kerik seems reasonably accurate to within a minute. For instance, he also said that he was rushing south to the trade center in a car, and was at Canal Street when the 9:03 second crash hit. That put him about a

mile north of the WTC. If his car was going 60 mph, he would have arrived at 9:04. Even if there was traffic and they only averaged 30 mph, they still would have arrived by 9:05.)

[118] Bernard B Kerik, *The Lost Son; A Life in Pursuit of Justice*, Regan Books, 2001, 333.

[119] Ibid, 19.

[120] *YouTube.com*, "Barry Jennings Interviews (WABC-TV, 2001/ LTW, 2007)," https://www.youtube.com/watch?v=OmeY2vJ6ZoA

[121] Ibid.

[122] Ibid.

[123] Giuliani, *Leadership*, 20. David Ray Griffin, "The 9/11 Interview with Michael Hess: Evidence that NIST Lied about When He and Barry Jennings Were Rescued," 9/11Truth.org, 9/18/2008, http://www.911truth.org/the-91 1-interview-with-michael-hess-evidence-that-nist-lied-about-when-he-and-barry-jennings-were-rescued/

[124] *YouTube.com*, "9/11: Michael Hess live about Explosion at WTC 7," https://www.youtube.com/watch?v=F8u-pjN_rA8

[125] *Wikispooks.com*, "Barry Jennings, https://wikispooks.com/wiki/Barry_Jennings

[126] Ibid.

[127] Barrett and Collins, 297.

[128] Giuliani, *Leadership*, 4.

[129] Kerik, *The Lost Son*, 331.

[130] Giuliani, *Leadership*, 7.

[131] Ibid, 6.

[132] Bernard Kerik, *The Lost Son*, 331, 333; Barrett and Collins, 354; Mitchell Fink and Lois Mathias, *Never Forget*, Regan Books (2002) Santiago statement, 106; Giuliani, *Leadership*, 6; Bernard Kerik, "Bernard Kerik: 'I Was Looking Into the Gates of Hell,'" *Newsmax*, 9/9/2011, http://www.newsmax.com/Remember911/bernardkerik-9-11/2011/09/09/id/410390/; Annie Karni, "Lhota faced challenge of 9/11, the battled cancer," *New York Daily News*, 10/13/2013, http://www.nydailynews.com/news/election/lhota-faced-challenge-9-11-battled-cancer-article-1.1484470

[133] Kerik, *The Lost Son*, 333.

[134] Giuliani, *Leadership*, 6.

[135] Kerik, *The Lost Son*, 333.

[136] Fink and Mathias, *Never Forget*, 107.

[137] Ibid.

[138] Giuliani, *Leadership*, 10.

[139] *New York Times*, "The Sept. 11 Records," Testimony of Richard Zarillo.

[140] Ibid.

[141] Barrett and Collins, *Grand Illusion*, 32.

[142] *New York Times*, "The Sept. 11 Records," Testimony of James Yakimovich.

[143] Giuliani, *Leadership*, 8,9.

[144] Thomas Von Essen, *Strong of Heart*, 25.

[145] Kerik, The Lost Son, 333.

[146] *CNN.com*, "Former NYC Mayor Testifies Before 9/11 Commission," 5/19/2004, http://transcripts.cnn.com/TRANSCRIPTS/0405/19/se.01.html

[147] Kerik, *The Lost Son*, 331.

[148] Ibid, 334.

[149] Giuliani, *Leadership*, 7.

[150] Bernard Kerik, "Bernard Kerik: I Was Looking Into the Gates of Hell."

[151] David Silverberg, "Calm Amidst Chaos; Rudy Giuliani and 9/11," *Linkedin.com*, 9/11/2015, https://www.linkedin.com/pulse/calm-amidst -chaos-rudy-giuliani-911-david-silverberg

[152] Kerik, *The Lost Son*, 334.

[153] Karni, "Lhota faced challenge of 9/11, then battled cancer."

[154] Ibid.

[155] Kerik, *The Lost Son*, 332.

[156] *YouTube.com*, "9/11 Rudy Giuliani- FEMA at Pier 92 on Sept 10 for Planned Terror Drill," https://www.youtube.com/watch?v=vmPwwd1NdiU

[157] Giuliani, *Leadership*, 355.

[158] *9/11* Commission, Testimony of Rudolph Giuliani.

[159] Barrett and Collins, 108.

[160] Ibid, 108–109.

[161] Ibid, 109–110.

[162] Glen Stout, Charlie Vitchers, and Bobby Gray, *Nine Months at Ground Zero* (New York: Scribner, 2006), 102.

[163] Ibid.

[164] Ibid, 103–105.

[165] Ibid, 115.

[166] Ibid, 67

[167] Langewiesche, 11.

[168] Glanz and Lipton, 301.

[169] Langewiesche, 67.

[170] Stout, Vitchers and Gray, 104.

[171] Langewiesche, 67, 164.

[172] Ibid, 114.

[173] Ibid.

[174] For Burton's education, see Langewiesche, 65.

[175] Glanz and Lipton, 299.

[176] Barrett and Collins, 253.

[177] Ibid, 254.

[178] Ibid, 260.

[179] Ibid.

[180] Ibid.

[181] Ibid.

[182] *9-11, Time for Truth 2 (2011)*, See at 1:15:15, D:\WTC videos\9_11 - Time For Truth 2 (2011) - YouTube.html

[183] Barrett and Collins, 256.

[184] Ibid, 259.

[185] Ibid, 257.

[186] Ramon Gilsanz and Audrey Massa, *World Trade Center Building Performance Study*, FEMA Final Report, Appendix D, D-1.

[187] Ibid, Appendix D, D-13.

[188] Ibid

189 Lipton, "Mismanagement Muddled Collapse Inquiry, House Panel Says."
190 "911 Truth: Rudy Giuliani & the Feds Destroyed WTC Evidence" (video interview posted by clbackus, April 1, 2007), *YouTube.com*, http://www.youtube.com/watch?v=GxycV4fNPnQ
191 Testimony of Gene Corley, "Learning from 9/11."
192 Kohn, "Culling Through Mangled Steel."
193 Eric Lipton, "Mismanagement Muddled Collapse Inquiry, House Panel Says" (originally published at *The New York Times*, March 7, 2002), http://911research.wtc7.net/cache/wtc/groundzero/nyt_mismanagementmuddle.html; see also "Learning from 9/11," March 6, 2002.
194 James Glanz and Kenneth Chang, "A NATION CHALLENGED: THE SITE; Engineers Seek to Test Steel Before It Is Melted For Reuse," *The New York Times*, September 29, 2001, http://www.nytimes.com/2001/09/29/nyregion/nation-challenged-site-engineers-seek-test-steel-before-it-melted-for-reuse.html?n=Top%2FReference%2FTimes%20Topics%2FSubjects%2FT%2FTerrorism
195 Ibid.
196 Glanz and Lipton, *City in the Sky*, 331.
197 James Glanz and Eric Lipton, "A NATION CHALLENGED: THE TOWERS; Experts Urging Broader Inquiry in Towers' Fall," *The New York Times*, September 25, 2001, http://www.nytimes.com/2001/12/25/nyregion/a-nation-challenged-the-towers-experts-urging-broader-inquiry-in-towers-fall.html?pagewanted=all; see also *9/11 Commission Transcripts*, Public Hearing on April 1, 2003, Written statement of Kenneth Holden, http://www.sacred-texts.com/ame/911/911tr/040103.htm
198 Langewiesche, 135.
199 Robert D. McFadden, "A NATION CHALLENGED: THE FIREFIGHTERS; After Trade Center Scuffle, Charges Are Dropped or Reduced," *The New York Times*, November 4, 2001, http://www.nytimes.com/2001/11/04/nyregion/nation-challenged-firefighters-after-trade-center-scuffle-charges-are-dropped.html
200 Langewiesche, 146.
201 McFadden, "A NATION CHALLENGED: THE FIREFIGHTERS."
202 *9-11, Time for Truth 2*
203 Langewiesche, 150.
204 Ibid.
205 Ibid, 151.
206 Ibid.
207 Langewiesche, 151; see also "Putting Organizational Theories to the Test; An Explication of William Langewiesche's American Ground: Unbuilding the World Trade Center," *Boise State University*, 2003, 16, http://www.teachingpa.org/2004/Allen%20Heidemann%20Ingles%20Mills%20Paper%20%20American%20Ground.pdf
208 Langewiesche, 154.
209 Ibid, 164.
210 Ibid.
211 Ibid, 170.
212 Ibid, 70.
213 Ibid.

[214] Ibid, 174

[215] Ibid.

[216] FEMA, "World Trade Center Building Performance Study," Introduction, Section 1.1, 1-2, http://www,fema.gov/library/viewRecord.do?id=1728

[217] Manning, "Selling Out the Investigation"; see also Gilsanz and Massa, *WTC Building Performance Study*, Appendix D, "Steel Data Collection Spreadsheet."

[218] Gilsanz and Massa, *WTC Building Performance Study*, Appendix D, D-13 and D-1,

[219] Glanz and Lipton, *City in the Sky*, 330; see also "Learning from 9/11."; see also Glanz and Lipton, "Experts Urging Broader Inquiry."

[220] Glanz and Lipton, *City in the Sky*, 330.

[221] Lipton, "Mismanagement Muddled Collapse Inquiry, House Panel Says."

[222] Glanz and Lipton, *City in the Sky*, 330.

[223] Ibid.

[224] Ibid.

[225] Barrett and Collins, 252.

[226] Ibid.

[227] Bill Manning, *Firehouse Magazine*, "Selling Out the Investigation," 1/10/2002, http://www.fireengineering.com/articles/print/volume-155/issue-1/departments/editors-opinion/elling-out-the-investigation.html

[228] Stout, Vitchers, and Gray, *Nine Months at Ground Zero*, 253; see also "Ceremony Closes 'Ground Zero' Cleanup," *CNN.com*, May 30, 2001, http://articles.cnn.com/2002-05-30/us/rec.wtc.cleanup_1_ceremony-firefighters-tower?_s=PM:US

[229] Charles Doyle, "Obstruction of Justice: An Overview of Some of the Federal Statutes that Prohibit Interference with Judicial, Executive, or Legislative Activities," *Congressional Research Service*, 64, http://www.fas,org/sgp/crs/misc/RL34303,pdf

[230] *United States Department of Justice* (2003), Department of Justice Press Release on the Indictment of Jeffrey D. Arriola. United States Attorney's Office, Eastern District of Texas, March 5, 2003; see also, Joseph Richard Gutheinz, Jr, J.D, Stealing the Dream: The Consequences of Stealing Space Shuttle Columbia Debris, http://www.collectspace.com/resources/flown_stealingdream.html

[231] "New York Tightens Security, Will Restrict Bridge Traffic," *The Associated Press and The Washington Post*, via *The Seattle Times*, September 27, 2001, http://community.seattletimes.nwsource.com/archive/?date=20010927&slug=newyork27

[232] Giuliani, Leadership, 49.

[233] Leslie Miller, Associated Press, "Reconstructed TWA Flight Now Serves as a Teaching Tool," 5/4/2004, http://usatoday30.usatoday.com/tech/news/techinnovations/2004-05-04-twa800-teching_x.htm

[234] James Mash, "Plane Crashes Which Changed the Way Planes Are Now Made," *High Life*, 12/8/2013, http://www.therichest.com/expensive-lifestyle/plane-crashes-that-changed-the-way-planes-are-now-made/2/

[235] *911 Research*, "FEMA's Investigation," http://911research.wtc7.net/wtc/official/fema.html

[236] Ibid.

[237] Ibid.

[238] *FEMA* 403, World Trade Center Building Performance Study, Cover, http://www.fema.gov/media-library/assets/documents/3544

[239] "Learning From 9/11: Understanding the Collapse of the World Trade Center," *House Committee on Science*, 3/6/2002, Testimony of Gene Corley, http://commdocs.house.gov/committees/science/hsy77747.000/hsy77747_0f.htm

[240] *FEMA*, Building Performance Study, Executive Summary, 1.

[241] Glanz and Lipton, *City in the Sky*, 329.

[242] *House Committee on Science*, "Learning From 9/11."

[243] *Public Broadcasting Service*, "Why the Towers Fell," http://www.pbs.org/wgbh/nova/transcripts/2907_wtc.html

[244] *911blogger.com*, "Dusting Off Corley," http://911blogger.com/news/2010-05-31/dusting-corley-official-response-discovery-energetic-materials-wtc-dust#_edn16

[245] Ibid, Chapter 2, "WTC 1 and WTC 2," Section 2.2.1.4, 2-24.

[246] Ibid, Chapter 2, Section 2.2.2.5, "Initial Collapse," 2-35.

[247] Ibid, Chapter 2, Section 2.4, "Recommendations," 2-39.

[248] Wikipedia, "The Jersey Girls," https://www.google.com/webhp?sourceid=chrome-instant&rlz=1C1CHWA_enUS611US611&ion=1&espv=2&ie=UTF-8#q=The+jersey+girls&*

[249] *911Review.com*, "Executive Obstruction," http://911review.com/coverup/obstruction.htm

[250] Nadine M. Post and Sherie Winston, "$40 Million Needed to Study the Performance of the WTC Buildings," *Engineering News Record*, 3/18/2002, http://enr.construction.com/news/buildings/archives/020318b.asp

[251] House Science Committee Hearing, "The Investigation of the World Trade Center Collapse: Findings, Recommendations and Next Steps," 5/1/2002, http://commdocs.house.gov/committees/science/hsy78961.000/hsy78961_0f.htm

[252] S. Shyam Sunder, et al, *NIST*, "Final Report on the Collapse of the World Trade Centomcf/get_pdf.cfm?pub_id=909017

[253] Ibid, Chapter 6, Section 6.1, 82.

[254] C-Span, live broadcast with Shyam Sunder, "Investigation of World Trade Center Building 7," 8/21/2008, http://www.c-spanvideo.org/videoLibrary/mobilevideo.php?progid=193741; for an in-depth analysis of this controversy see Web Archive.org, http://web.archive.org/web/20110827060414/http://firefightersfor-911truth.org/?page_id=158

[255] NIST, "Questions and Answers about the NIST WTC 7 Investigation," 9/19/2011, http://www.nist.gov/el/disasterstudies/wtc/faqs_wtc7.cfm

[256] Ibid.

[257] Sunder, et al, *NIST*, NCSTAR 1, "Core Framing," 101 and Section 6.14, 144.

[258] Ibid.

[259] Sadek, NCSTAR 1-2, lxxxiv.

[260] John L. Gross and Therese P. McAllister, NIST, NCSTAR 1-6, Introduction, Section 1.2.11, 8, http://www.nist.gov/customcf/get_pdf.cfm?pub_id=101279

[261] *FEMA*, Building Performance Study, 2.2.1.2, 2-21, https://ia800500.us.archive.org/11/items/WorldTradeCenterBuildingPerformanceStudy/fema403wtc.pdf

[262] *NIST*, "Questions and Answers about the NIST WTC Towers Investigation, http://www.nist.gov/el/disasterstudies/wtc/faqs_wtctowers.cfm

[263] *9/11 Commission*, Statement of Richard Sheirer.

[264] Ibid, 3.

[265] Ibid, 5.

Chapter 2

[266] PAPD Transcripts, *Port Authority Police Department*, PAPD Main Desk, 9/11/2001, WTC Channel 08, 3541 LEFT, Transcript 36, 4–5, http://adam.pra.to/public/mir/www.thememoryhole.org/911/pa-transcripts/pa-transcript036.pdf; The 8:50 a.m. time of the call is confirmed by *The 9/11 Commission*, Folder of PAPD Phone Calls, 9-11 Commission Records Released Jan 14, 2009, http://www.911myths.com/images/6/61/NYC_Box15_PhoneCallTimeline_WTC-to-PA-Calls.pdf

[267] Hamburger et al., "WTC1 and WTC2," Section 2.2.1.2, "Fire Dynamics, 21.

[268] *9/11 Commission Report*, Barnes and Noble edition, 2006, Chapter 9, Section 9.2, 285.

[269] J Randal Lawson and Robert L Vettori, "The Emergency Response Operations," *National Institute of Standards and Technology (NIST) World Trade Center (WTC) Investigation, 2005*, NCSTAR 1-8, Section 5.3.1, 43. http://www.nist.gov/customcf/get_pdf.cfm?pub_id=101049

[270] *Wikipedia*, s.v. "Flash Point," http://en.wikipedia.org/wiki/Flash_point

[271] Ibid.

[272] Hamburger, et al., "Fire Development."

[273] See drawing, "1984 Site Plan" on page 89, this Volume.

[274] Please take note that all of the plans shown in this book, unless otherwise specified, are from the partial set of plans that were anonymously released by an insider to Dr. Steven Jones, then a professor of physics at Brigham Young University, who posted them on the Internet in March of 2007.

[275] Edward McCabe, written statement (spelling and punctuation corrected), Story #936, *The September 11 Digital Archives*, July 25, 2002, http://old.911digitalarchive.org/stories/details/936

[276] "The Basement Explosions," Loose Change 9/11: An American Coup - The Forums, http://s1.zetaboards.com/LooseChangeForums/topic/1701709/1/

[277] McCabe, Story #936.

[278] Hursley Lever, interview by David Alden, May 23, 2012.

[279] Ibid.

[280] "Inside the North Tower: Witness Accounts, Plaza level & Concourse Lobbies, Basements," https://sites.google.com/site/911stories/insidethenorthtower%3Awitnessaccounts,lobb

[281] Ibid.

[282] Lever, author's interview.

[283] "Inside the North Tower: Witness Accounts"; *see also "911: WTC basement explosion witness Phillip Morelli, YouTube.com, " http://www.youtube.com/watch?v=f3x8yG1qXww*

[284] Ibid.

[285] "911 Construction Worker Phillip Morelli – Elevator Shaft Explosion in the Basement" (video interview posted by 911InvestigationVids, July 15, 2011), *YouTube.com*, http://www.youtube.com/watch?v=KR3XCHRnae0

[286] Statements of Marlene Cruz and Arturo Griffith, "Inside the North Tower: Witness Accounts," https://sites.google.com/site/911stories/insidethenorthtower%3Awitnessaccounts,lobb

287 Lever, author's interview.
288 "911 Construction Worker Phillip Morelli."
289 "Inside the North Tower: Witness Accounts."
290 Lever, author's interview.
291 H. S. Lew, Richard W. Bukowski, and Nicholas J. Carino, "Design, Construction, and Maintenance of Structural and Life Safety Systems (Draft)," *National Institute of Standards and Technology (NIST) World Trade Center (WTC) Investigation*, NCSTAR 1-1 (Draft), Chapter 10, Section 10.4.4, 161, http://www.nist.gov/customcf/get_pdf.cfm?pub_id=908998
292 "Some Articles from Engineering News Record," *911 Research*, http://911research.wtc7.net/mirrors/guardian2/wtc/eng-news-record.htm

Chapter 3

293 "Learning from 9/11," 182.
294 Ibid.
295 *Scholars for 9/11 Truth and Justice* (STJ911), "Independent Investigators Release Suppressed Blueprints of Destroyed World Trade Center Tower," news release, March 27, 2007, http://911research.wtc7.net/press_releases/blueprints.html
296 Ibid.
297 911Blogger.com, "NYC Dept. of Buildings: Portions of WTC 7 Emergency Command Center "Plans" Withheld, Release Would "Endanger ... Life or Safety," http://911blogger.com/news/2011-06-24/nyc-dept-buildings-portions-wtc-7-emergency-command-center-plans-withheld-release-would-endanger-life-or-safety
298 Steve Watson, "WTC Blueprints Released by Whistleblower," *Infowars.net*, March 28, 2007, http://www.infowars.net/articles/march2007/280307blueprints.htm; one can do a Web search on "North Tower Blueprints" for many other websites.
299 *Architects and Engineers for 9/11 Truth*, "Table of World Trade Center Tower A Architectural Drawings," http://www2.ae911truth.org/WTC1_blueprints.php
300 "Collapse of the World Trade Center," Wikipedia, http://en.wikipedia.org/wiki/Collapse_of_the_World_Trade_Center
301 NIST maintained that the gravity load distribution between the core and perimeter columns was 50 percent to each. However, independent researchers have proven the ratio was actually 60 percent to the core and 40 percent to the perimeter columns. Chief among those researchers is the team of A. DeLuca, F.D. Fiore, E. Mele, and A. Romero, who published their findings in a paper entitled, "The collapse of the WTC Twin Towers: preliminary analysis of the original design approach," in *Stessa 2003: Proceedings of the Conference on the Behavior of Steel Structures in Seismic Areas*, ed. Federico M. Mazzolani (The Netherlands: Sweets & Zeitlinger Publishers, 2003). It can be found on the Web at: http://books.google.com/books?id=9Dc_cs5ucdEC&pg=PA84&lpg=PA84&dq=NOrth+tower+gravity+load+distribution&source=bl&ots=yIl8OzMHEY&sig=0_4N0Qyvdab5mrCsAtWuweT0&hl=en&ei=jZLmTLuyG4P4sAPT8c2xCw&sa=X&oi=book_result&ct=result&resnum=7&ved=0CEEQ6AEwBg#v=onepage&q=NOrth%20tower%20gravity%20load%20distribution&f=true, see also "Load Distribution

and Load Capacity in the Core of WTC1," Gregory Urich, BSEE, http://www.cool-places.0catch.com/911/loadDistribution_v1.pdf

302 "9/11: The WTC Elevator Key," *YouTube.com*, https://www.youtube.com/watch?v=sMvPHFbxnPM

303 See Appendix C, this volume: "The 50-, 6- and 7-Shafts," 341.

304 "Inside the North Tower: Witness Accounts, Plaza level & Concourse Lobbies, Basements."

305 "Witnesses Basement WTC, NBC 9/13, 12:27," *Today Show*, Interview with Matt Lauer, http://www.youtube.com/watch?v=xcGXlP6Zlgk

306 Ibid.

307 "9/11: The Elevator Key," (13:09 into film-Larry King interview with Arturo Griffith), You Tube.com, https://www.youtube.com/watch?v=sMvPHFbxnPM ; see also "Inside the North Tower: Witness Accounts."

308 Lawson and Vettori, "Emergency Response Operations. Federal Building and Fire Safety Investigation of the World Trade Center Disaster," *National Institute of Standards and Technology (NIST) World Trade Center (WTC) Investigation*, 2005, NCSTAR 1-8, 43, http://www.nist.gov/el/disasterstudies/wtc/wtc_finalreports.cfm

309 See *Appendix D*, this volume: "The High Factor of Safety," 359.

310 "William Rodriquez Speaks About 9/11," *C-Span*: American Perspectives, http://www.youtube.com/watch?v=MuqcERfdwrc

311 See Chapter 6, this volume, Section: "There Was an Explosion Before the Plane Hit," 201.

312 "William Rodriguez's Story" (Video posted by Wroudy, May 30, 2007), YouTube.com, *www.youtube.com/watch?v=wIZtqKiidlo*

313 NK-44, "The Basement Explosions," *Loose Change Forum*, http://z10.invisionfree.com/Loose_Change_Forum/index.php?showtopic=18745

314 Ibid.

315 Anthony Saltalamacchia, "WTC Survivor is Speaking out about 9/11." Video of speech at 2007 Justice, Peace, & Freedom Conference, the *Freedom Law School* in Dallas, TX, September 25, 2008; http://livefreenow.tv/past-conferences/september-11/anthony-saltalamacchia.html

316 NK-44 op.cit..

317 Ibid.

318 Ibid.

Chapter 4

319 Greg and Lauren Manning, Interview with Larry King. *CNN Larry King Live*, Aired October 1, 2002, transcript available at: http://transcripts.cnn.com/TRANSCRIPTS/0210/01/lkl.00.html

320 "Inside the North Tower: Witness Accounts."

321 Ibid.

322 Ibid.

323 Ibid.

324 "The Sept. 11 Records."

325 For film of the lobby damage, see "9/11: The WTC Elevator Key," *YouTube.com*, https://www.youtube.com/watch?v=sMvPHFbxnPM

[326] From the film "9/11," directed by James Hanlon, Rob Klug, Gédéon Naudet, and Jules Naudet (2002, Paramount).

[327] Ibid.

[328] See Appendix C, this volume: "The 50-, 6- and 7-Shafts," 341.

[329] "The Sept. 11 Records."

[330] Ibid.

[331] For the best view of those panels, see "9/11: The Elevator Key," YouTube.com, https://www.youtube.com/watch?v=sMvPHFbxnPM

[332] Averill, "Occupant Behavior," NCSTAR 1-7, Chapter 6, 86.

[333] NK-44, "The Basement Explosions: The 22nd Floor; see also Averill, "Occupant Behavior," NCSTAR 1-7, 86; see also Lawson and Vettori, NCSTAR 1-8, 48; Ibid., 35.

[334] Port Authority Transcripts, Transcript 48, 1, adam.pra.to/public/mir/www. thememoryhole.org/911/pa-transcripts/pa-transcript048.pdf; see also NK-44, "The Basement Explosions, The 22nd Floor.

[335] Curtis L. Taylor and Shawn Gardiner, "Heightened Security Alert Had Just Been Lifted," *Newsday*, September 12, 2001, http://www.newsday.com/news/ nationworld/nation/ny-nyaler122362178sep12,0,1255660.story

[336] "The Sept. 11 Records."

[337] NK-44, "The Basement Explosions, The 22nd Floor."

[338] Port Authority Transcripts, Transcript 48, 24," *Thememoryhole.org*, adam. pra.to/public/mir/www.thememoryhole.org/911/pa-transcripts/pa-transcript048. pdf; see also Port Authority Transcripts, PA Transcript 048, 24, z10.invisionfree. com/Loose_Change_Forum/ar/t4249.htm

[339] Ibid.

[340] Sarah Kugler, "WTC surveillance tapes feared missing," *Associated Press*, December 10, 2002, http://911research.wtc7.net/cache/wtc/evidence/fortwayne_ wtctapes.htm

[341] Statement of Alan Reiss, *911 Commission Report*, National Commission on Terrorist Attacks Upon the United States, May 18, 2004, http:// www.9-11commission.gov/hearings/hearing11/reiss_statement.pdf

[342] Ibid.

[343] Ibid.

[344] Lawson and Vettori, "Emergency Response Report," NCSTAR 1-8, 48, 200.

[345] PAPD transcripts, *Port Authority Police Department*, WTC Channel 09, Police Desk, 3541 Center, Transcript 37, 6, z10.invisionfree.com/Loose_Change_Forum/ ar/t4249.htm

[346] The transcript begins with Josie's call about the fire at the SCC, which was at 8:47. The report that no one was answering the phone at the OCC came in about 13 minutes into the transcript. So the OCC must have been abandoned by 9:00 (8:47 + 13 minutes).

[347] Port Authority Transcripts, Transcript 048, 8, adam.pra.to/public/mir/www. thememoryhole.org/911/pa-transcripts/pa-transcript048.pdf

[348] "The Heroism of William Rodriguez," *Arabesque: 911 Truth*, http://ara-besque911.blogspot.ca/2007/05/heroism-of-william-rodriguez-amazing.html

[349] Port Authority Transcripts, PA Transcript 048, 24, z10.invisionfree.com/ Loose_Change_Forum/ar/t4249.htm; see also Port Authority Transcripts,

Transcript 48, 24," *Thememoryhole.org*, adam.pra.to/public/mir/www.thememoryhole.org/911/pa-transcripts/pa-transcript048.pdf
350 "A Nation Challenged: Portraits of Grief: The Victims," *The New York Times*, September 28, 2001, http://www.nytimes.com/2001/09/28/nyregion/nation-challenged-portraits-grief-victims-dancing-their-way-through-life-with.html
351 See video report at "9/11 Security Courtesy of Marvin Bush," *Whatreallyhappened.com*, http://whatreallyhappened.com/WRHARTICLES/911security.html
352 Hursley Lever, interview by David Alden, May 23, 2012.
353 "The Sept. 11 Records."
354 "North Tower Blueprints," *9-11 Research*, http://911research.wtc7.net/wtc/evidence/plans/frames.html
355 Shyam-Sunder, NCSTAR 1, Executive Summary, xxxviii.
356 *YouTube.com*, "Interview with John Schroeder 9/11 Fireman," http://www.youtube.com/watch?v=DBb00PQR1zo
357 "The Sept. 11 Records."
358 Ibid.
359 Christopher Bollyn, "New Seismic Data Refutes Official WTC Explanation," *Rense.com.*, http://rense.com/general28/ioff.htm
360 All of the Engineering News Record drawings are taken from several articles that were written for that trade magazine in 1964. They were reprinted in the FEMA Final Report, Hamburger et al., *WTC Building Performance Study*, Chapter 2, Section 2.1.2, http://www.nist.gov/el/disasterstudies/wtc/wtc_finalreports.cfm
361 Szamboti, "The Sustainability of the Controlled Demolition Hypothesis."
362 "The World Trade Center New York City," *Contemporary Steel Design*, 1, no. 4, 1964, http://www.engr.psu.edu/ae/WTC/AISI/wtcaisi1.pdf
363 Glanz and Lipton, *City in the Sky*, 292–293.
364 William Rodriguez, speech, *C-Span*, August 17, 2007.
365 "WTC Victim Gartenburg Live On ABC," *Abovetopsecret.com*, http://www.abovetopsecret.com/forum/thread396336/pg1; see also "Accounts From the North Tower," Transcripts, Interview by Jim Dwyer, *The New York Times*, September /11, 2001, http://www.nytimes.com/2002/05/26/nyregion/26NTOWER.html?pagewanted=all
366 Ibid.
367 Ibid.
368 Sadek, NCSTAR 1-2 (Draft), Executive Summary, "Floor Truss and Slab Damage," Figure E-31, lxxxii.
369 For all references in this paragraph, see Chapter 6, "Further Evidence of Controlled Demolition," 311.

Chapter 5
370 Matt Lauer, *Today Show*, NBC-TV, Interviews September 13, 2001. "Witnesses basement WTC" (video posted by 11septembervideos, September 29, 2007), *YouTube.com*, http://www.youtube.com/watch?v=xcGXlP6Zlgk
371 *"911: WTC basement explosion witness Phillip Morelli," www.youtube.com/watch?v=9c3gyprsa9Y*

[372] Richard Korman and Debra Rubin, "Painful Losses Mount in the Construction 'Family'," *McGraw Hill Construction*, http://911research.wtc7.net/cache/wtc/analysis/construction_losses.html

[373] McCabe, Story #936.

[374] John Bussey, "Eye of the Storm: One Journey Through Desperation and Chaos," *Wall Street Journal*, 9/12/2001, http://online.wsj.com/public/resources/documents/040802pulitzer5.htm

[375] Quoted in Judith Sylvester and Suzanne Huffman, Women Journalists at Ground Zero (Lanham: Rowman & Littlefield, 2002), 19.

[376] Griffin, "Explosive Testimony"; original source, *the BBC*, September 11, 2001.

[377] *YouTube.com*, "9/11/-Pat Dawson NBC News 9/11/2001," http://www.youtube.com/watch?v=1sqi_BqKWPM

[378] Hamburger, et al., "Fire Development," 21.

[379] *9/11 Commission Report*, Chapter 9, Section 9.2, 289.

[380] Ibid, 290.

[381] Pitts, Butler, and Junker, *NIST WTC Investigation*, NCSTAR 1-5A, iii, http://www.nist.gov/el/disasterstudies/wtc/wtc_finalreports.cfm

[382] Lawson and Vettori, *NIST WTC Investigation*, NCSTAR 1-8, 36.

[383] Ibid.

[384] Ibid.

[385] Sadek, NCSTAR 1-2; also Gann et al., NCSTAR 1-5.

[386] Ibid.

[387] Johanna Zmud, "Technical Documentation for Survey Administration: Questionnaires, Interviews, and Focus Groups. Federal Building and Fire Safety Investigation of the World Trade Center Disaster," *National Institute of Standards and Technology (NIST) World Trade Center (WTC) Investigation*, 2005, NCSTAR 1-7B, 4.

[388] Ibid.

[389] Jason D. Averill, et al., "Occupant Behavior, Egress, and Emergency Communication. Federal Building and Fire Safety Investigation of the World Trade Center Disaster," *National Institute of Standards and Technology (NIST) World Trade Center (WTC) Investigation*, 2005, NCSTAR 1-7, Abstract, http://www.nist.gov/el/disasterstudies/wtc/wtc_finalreports.cfm

[390] *World Trade Center (WTC) Investigation*, 2005, NCSTAR 1-7, 81.

[391] Griffin, *9/11 Contradictions*, 245.

[392] Anthony Saltalamacchia, "WTC Survivor is Speaking out about 9/11." Video of speech at 2007 Justice, Peace, & Freedom Conference, the *Freedom Law School* in Dallas, TX, September 25, 2008; http://livefreenow.tv/past-conferences/september-11/anthony-saltalamacchia.html

[393] *World Trade Center (WTC) Investigation*, 2005, NCSTAR 1-7, 80.

[394] "United in Courage," People Magazine, September 12, 2001.

[395] Ibid.

[396] David Ray Griffin, *Debunking 9/11 Debunking: an Answer to Popular Mechanics and Other Defenders of the Official Conspiracy Theory* (Northampton, MA: Olive Branch Press, 2007), 179; Greg Szymanski, "WTC basement Blast and Injured Burn Victim Blows 'Official 9/11 Story' Sky High," http://prisonplanet.com/articles/june2005/240605officialstory.htm

[397] *YouTube.com,* "Interview with John Schroeder 9/11 Fireman," http://www.youtube.com/watch?v=DBb00PQR1zo

[398] Lawson and Vettori, NCSTAR 1-8, 10–12.

[399] Ibid, 11.

[400] *9/11 Commission Report,* Chapter 9, 302, and 549 note 137.

[401] *9/11 Commission Report,* Chapter 9, 281. (By simple ratio: PANYNJ/PAPD had 1,331 officers spread over 9 locations in New York City.)

[402] Ibid.

[403] Question 2, "Frequently Asked Questions." *NIST.*

[404] Jim Dwyer. "City to Release Thousands of Oral Histories of 9/11 Today," *The New York Times,* August 12, 2005, http://www.nytimes.com/2005/08/12/nyregion/12records.html

[405] *Wikipedia,* 9/11 (film), *World Trade Center (WTC) Investigation,* 2005, NCSTAR 1-7

[406] *The Fire Critic,* "9/11 Naudet film in its entirety online," http://www.firecritic.com/2009/09/19/911-naudet-film-in-its-entirety-online/Ibid.

[407] The *New York Times,* "The Sept 11ᵗʰ Records (Oral Histories).

[408] Ibid

[409] Ibid.

[410] Ibid.

[411] Ibid.

[412] Ibid.

[413] Ibid.

[414] Ibid.

[415] Ibid.

[416] Ibid.

[417] Ibid.

[418] Ibid.

[419] Griffin, *9/11 Contradictions* 240.

[420] "The Sept. 11 Records."

[421] Ibid.

[422] Griffin, *9/11 Contradictions* 244.

[423] Griffin, *Debunking 9/11 Debunking,* 313.

[424] Ibid.

[425] Greg Szymanski, "NY Fireman Lou Cacchioli Upset that 9/11 Commission 'Tried to Twist My Words," *Arctic Beacon.com,* July 19, 2005, http://www.arcticbeacon.com/articles/19-Jul-2005.html

[426] "The Sept. 11 Records."

[427] *YouTube.com,* "Interview with John Schroeder 9/11 Fireman," http://www.youtube.com/watch?v=DBb00PQR1zo

[428] "Frequently Asked Questions," *NIST.*

Chapter 6

[429] *The 9/11 Commission Report,* 305; see also Sunder, NIST NCSTAR 1, Section 6.14.4.

[430] Steven E. Jones, et al., "Fourteen Points of Agreement with Official Government Reports on the World Trade Center Destruction," *Open Civil*

Engineering Journal 2 (2008): 35–40, http://www.libertariansforjustice.org/stephenjones/14pointsCEJ.pdf

431 Graeme McQueen and Tony Szamboti, "The Missing Jolt, A Simple Refutation of the NIST-Byzant Collapse Hypothesis," *Journal of 9/11 Studies* 24 (January 2009), http://journalof911studies.com/volume/2008/TheMissingJolt4.pdf

432 David Chandler, "Destruction of the World Trade Center North Tower and Fundamental Physics," *Journal of 9/11 Studies* (February 2010), http://www.journalof911studies.com/volume/2010/ChandlerDownwardAccelerationOfWTC1.pdf

433 "World Trade Center Disaster," *Lamont Daugherty Earth Observatory*, (LDEO), (public domain material published in 2001), http://www.ldeo.columbia.edu/LCSN/Eq/20010911_wtc.html

434 Won-Young Kim, et al., "Seismic Waves Generated by Aircraft Impacts and Building Collapses of the World Trade Center, New York City," *Columbia University's Lamont-Doherty Earth Observatory (LDEO) report*, September 14, 2001, http://www.ldeo.columbia.edu/LCSN/Eq/20010911_WTC/WTC_LDEO_KIM.pdf; see also *911Research*, http://911research.wtc7.net/mirrors/guardian2/wtc/seismic/WTC_LDEO_KIM.htm

435 Glanz and Lipton, *City in the Sky*, 310–311.

436 Paul J. Lioy et al., "Characterization of the Dust/Smoke Aerosol that Settled East of the World Trade Center (WTC) in Lower Manhattan after the Collapse of the WTC 11 September 2001," *Environmental Health Perspectives* 110, no. 7 (July 2002): 703–714, http://www.ncbi.nlm.nih.gov/pmc/articles/PMC1240917/pdf/ehp0110-000703.pdf

437 Louisa Dalton, "Chemical Analysis of the Disaster," *Chemical & Engineering News*, October 20, 2003, http://pubs.acs.org/cen/NCW/8142aerosols.html

438 Stout, Vitchers, and Gray, *Nine Months at Ground Zero*, 65–66.

439 Interview for the film *9/11* by Jules and Gideon Naudet.

440 Christopher Bollyn, "Professor Says 'Cutter Charges' Brought Down WTC Buildings: Evidence of Thermite Uncovered at World Trade Center," *AmericanFreePress.Net*, http://www.americanfreepress.net/html/cutter_charges_brought_down_wt.html

441 "Aluminum Skin Sheaths World's Tallest Towers," originally published in *Engineering News Record*, October 29, 1970; from "Some Articles from Engineering News Record."

442 Glanz and Lipton, 321.

443 Bollyn, "Professor Says 'Cutter Charges' Brought Down WTC Buildings: Evidence of Thermite Uncovered at World Trade Center.

444 F R Greening, "The Pulverization of Concrete in WTC 1 During the Collapse Events of 9-11," http://www.911myths.com/WTCONC1.pdf

445 *YouTube.com*, "Trump and 9/11? New evidence found. HD," 9:52, https://www.youtube.com/watch?v=cPHpNijksVw

446 Langewiesche, 135.

447 *News.com. au*, "1000 9/11 victims 'Never Identified,'" *News.com. au*, http://911research.wtc7.net/cache/wtc/evidence/newsau_1000neverided.html

448 Langewiesche, 91.

449 Ibid, 165.

450 Barrett and Collins, *250*.

NOTES

Jim Hoffman, "The North Tower's Dust Cloud, Analysis of Energy Requirements for the Expansion of the Dust Cloud Following the Collapse of 1 World Trade Center," http://911research.wtc7.net/papers/dustvolume/volumev3_1.html
452 *NIST,* 2006, "Frequently Asked Questions,", https://www.nist.gov/property-fieldsection/national-institute-standards-and-technology-nist-federal-building-and-fire
453 "The Sept. 11 Records."
454 Therese McAllister, Jonathan Barnett, John Gross, Ronald Hamburger, Jon Magnusson, "Introduction," *World Trade Center Building Performance Study,* Chapter 1, 1–9.
455 Hamburger et al., *World Trade Center Building Performance Study,* Chapter 2, 2-1.
456 See *Appendix A,* this volume: "The Force Needed to Displace a Perimeter Panel." 331.
457 The panels covered three floors. Typically, they were about thirty-three feet long by ten feet wide. They consisted of three box columns connected by "spandrel" plates—steel bands that circled the building at each floor. The columns measured fourteen inches square throughout the building and at the upper floors—the likely location where the thrown perimeter panels in question came from—they were made of steel plate that was 1/4- inch thick. In the upper levels, the spandrels were 52 inches wide, and from the upper part of the plane impact zone to the top of the building, they were 3/8 inch thick. Using 1/4-inch plate for the columns—which weighs 10.20 pounds per square foot—and 3/8-inch plate for the spandrels—which weighs 15.30 pounds per square foot—the total weight for one panel calculates to be about 7,000 pounds.
458 *YouTube.com,* "The Last Secrets of 9/11," https://www.google.com/webhp?sourceid=chrome-instant&rlz=1C1CHWA_enUS611US611&ion=1&espv=2&ie=UTF-8#q=youtube+the+last+secrets+of+9/11
459 Ibid.
460 Ibid.
461 Glanz and Lipton, City in the Sky, 131.
462 Shyam-Sunder, NCSTAR 1, 20, 38. (Several times, both the FEMA report and the report from NIST use the figure of 10,000 gallons to approximate the amount of jet fuel on Flight 11. However, the NIST report shows a number that appears to be based on calculations. That is the figure used here.)
463 McAllister et al., *WTC Building Performance Study,* Chapter 1.
464 McAllister et al., *WTC Building Performance Study,* "Introduction," Section 1.5.2, 17.
465 Shyam-Sunder, NCSTAR 1, Section 5.3.2, "Aircraft Impact," footnote 8: Letter with an attachment dated November 13, 2003, from John R. Dragonette (Retired Project Administrator, Physical Facilities Division, World Trade Department) to Saroj Bhol (Engineering Department, PANYNJ), http://www.nist.gov/el/disasterstudies/wtc/wtc_finalreports.cfm
466 Ibid.
467 *Chicago Tribune,* September 12, 2001; Knight Ridder, September 12, 2001.
468 Glanz and Lipton, *City in the Sky,* 225.
469 Glanz and Lipton, *City in the Sky,* 2003, 135.

[470] Ibid, 138.

[471] Sadek, NCSTAR 1-2, xxxvii, which states that Robertson's "work included the development of the structural databases, the reference structural models, and the baseline performance analysis of the World Trade Center (WTC) towers."

[472] *9/11 Commission Report*, 460, Note 130.

[473] Ibid, 16.

[474] *NTSB* report, "Flight Path Study-American Airlines Flight 11," Feb 19, 2002, see at: http://www.gwu.edu/~nsarchiv/NSAEBB/NSAEBB196/doc01.pdf

[475] "9/11: The WTC Elevator Key" (at 19.49 into the film), *YouTube.com*, https://www.youtube.com/watch?v=smvPHFbxnPM; see also Dylan Avery, *Loose Change, 2nd Edition*, (42:49 into the film), http://www.youtube.com/watch?v=2IWJX879fOk

[476] Dylan Avery, *Loose Change, 2nd Edition*, (The Carr tape is discussed at 53:16 into the film), http://www.youtube.com/watch?v=2IWJX879fOk

[477] Dr. Crockett Grabbe, "Direct Evidence for Explosions: Flying Projectiles and Widespread Impact Damage," *Journal of 911 Studies.com*, http://www.journalof-911studies.com/volume/200704/GrabbeExplosionsEvidence.pdf

[478] Kevin Ryan, "High Velocity Bursts of Debris From Point-Like Sources in the WTC Towers," *Journal of 911 Studies*, June 13, 2007, http://www.journalof-911studies.com/volume/2007/Ryan_HVBD.pdf

[479] Sadek, NCSTAR 1-2, Executive Summary, "Floor Truss and Slab Damage," Figure E-31, lxxxii, http://www.nist.gov/el/disasterstudies/wtc/wtc_final-reports.cfm

[480] "9/11 Incontrovertible Truth the Government is Lying," NanoThermite911, March 3, 2009, *YouTube.com*, http://www.youtube.com/watch?v=8YaFGSPErKU

[481] "The Thermite Reaction," *The General Chemistry Demo Lab*, http://www.ilpi.com/genchem/demo/thermite/index.html

[482] "MEI Provides Assistance in Arson Investigations," *Mei Newsletter*, Spring 1996, http://www.materials-engr.com/ns96.html

[483] Ibid.

[484] See a complete explanation of the effects of the thermate reaction as it relates to evidence found at the WTC at: Steven E. Jones, PhD Physics, Brigham Young University, "Why Indeed Did the WTC Buildings Completely Collapse?" http://www.journalof911studies.com/volume/200609/WhyIndeedDidtheWorldTradeCenterBuildingsCompletelyCollapse.pdf

[485] Thomas Eagar, PhD and Christopher Musso, "Why Did the World Trade Center Collapse? Science, Engineering, and Speculation," JOM *(Journal of Materials)* 53, no. 12 (2001): 8–11, http://www.tms.org/pubs/journals/jom/0112/eagar/eagar-0112.html

[486] Jonathan Barnett, Ronald R. Biederman, and R. D. Sisson, Jr., "Limited Metallurgical Examination," *World Trade Center Building Performance Study*, FEMA Final Report, Appendix C, Figure C-1.

[487] JR Barnett, RR Biederman, and RD Sisson, Jr, *Journal of Materials* (JOM), JOM 53 (12) (2001), "An Initial Microstructural Analysis of A36 Steel from WTC Building 7, see at http://www.tms.org/pubs/journals/JOM/0112/Biederman/Biederman-0112.html

[488] Eagar and Musso, "Why Did the World Trade Center Collapse?"

[489] Barnett, Biederman, and Sisson, *WTC Building Performance Study*, Appendix C, Figure C-1.

[490] James Glanz and Eric Lipton, "A Search for Clues in Towers' Collapse," *The New York Times*, February 2, 2002, http://www.nytimes.com/2002/02/02/nyregion/ search-for-clues-towers-collapse-engineers-volunteer-examine-steel-debris-taken.html?pagewanted=all&src=pm

[491] Joan Killough-Miller, "The 'deep mystery' of melted steel," WPI Transformations, Spring 2002, www.wpi.edu/News/Transformations/2002Spring/steel.html

[492] Ronald R. Biederman, Erin M. Sullivan, Rick D. Sisson and George F. Vander Voort "Microstructural Analysis of the Steels from Buildings 7, & 1 or 2 from the World Trade Center," Microscopy and Microanalysis, 9 (Suppl. 02), p 550-551, (2003). http://journals.cambridge.org/abstract_S143192760344275X

[493] "911: NIST FOIA-Molten Metal at WTC 2" (video posted by cappucinokid100, May 25, 2011), http://www.youtube.com/watch?v=Tz8fvp7eDNE

[494] Sunder et. al., *World Trade Center Investigation*, NIST NCSTAR 1, Chapter 5, Section 5.5.1, Table 5-1, 67; see also *Contemporary Steel Design*, (American Iron and Steel Institute, 1964), Volume 1, Number 4, 7-8, http://www.engr.psu.edu/ae/WTC/AISI/wtcaisi5.pdf

[495] Ibid.

[496] Stephen W. Banovic and Timothy J. Foecke, "Damage and Failure Modes of Structural Steel Components. Federal Building and Fire Safety Investigation of the World Trade Center Disaster," *National Institute of Standards and Technology (NIST)* World Trade Center (WTC) Investigation, 2005, NCSTAR 1-3C, Chapter 6, 239, http://www.nist.gov/el/disasterstudies/wtc/wtc_finalreports.cfm

[497] Ibid.

[498] Ibid, 268.

[499] Ibid, 272.

[500] *Beautiful Iron.com*, "Using the Fire," http://www.beautifuliron.com/ usingthe.htm

[501] Jones, "Why Indeed?"

[502] "Images of the World Trade Center Site Show Thermal Hot Spots on September 16 and 23, 2001," 11/2/01, *USGS.gov*, http://pubs.usgs.gov/of/2001/ ofr-01-0429/thermal.r09.html

[503] Jones, "Why Indeed?"

[504] *US Department of Interior*, USGS, "Particle Atlas of World Trade Center Dust," http://pubs.usgs.gov/of/2005/1165/table_1.html

[505] Interview with Dr. Steven Jones, PhD, The film: "Zero: An Investigation into 9/11," at 24:23, https://www.youtube.com/watch?v=QU961SGps8g

[506] S Apperson et al., "Generation of Fast Propagating Combustion and Shock Waves with Copper Oxide/aluminum Nanothermite Composites," Applied Physics Letters, Volume 91, issue 94, http://apl.aip.org/applab/v91/i24/ p243109_s1?isAuthorized=no%20

[507] Jim Hoffman, "Explosives Found in the World Trade Center Dust," 911 Research.com, http://911research.wtc7.net/essays/thermite/explosive_residues. html#introduction; Niels H. Harrit, et al, *The Open Chemical Physics Journal*, "Active Thermitic Material Discovered in Dust from the 9/11 World Trade Center Catastrophe," (2009), 2, 7-31, http://www.911research.wtc7.net/mirrors/ bentham_open/ActiveThermitic_Harrit_Bentham2009.pdf

⁵⁰⁸ See the video of Robertson making this statement: "Proof that Leslie Robertson Saw Molten Steel at Ground Zero," http://911debunkers.blogspot. com/2011/03/proof-that-leslie-robertson-saw-molten.html; see also James M. Williams, "WTC a structural success," SEAU News VI, Issue II, October 2001, http://old.seau.org/SEAUNews-2001-10.pdf

⁵⁰⁹ Griffin, *9/11 Contradictions*, 266.

⁵¹⁰ Griffin, *Debunking 9/11 Debunking*, 181, 357.

⁵¹¹ Ibid.

⁵¹² Trudy Walsh, "Handheld app eased recovery tasks," *Government Computer News*, September 9, 2002, http://gcn.com/articles/2002/09/09/ handheld-app-eased-recovery-tasks.aspx?sc_lang=en

⁵¹³ Griffin, *Debunking 9/11 Debunking*, 181; see also Stout, Vitchers, and Gray, *Nine Months at Ground Zero*, 65, 66.

⁵¹⁴ Public hearing, *9/11 Commission Report*, National Commission on Terrorist Attacks Upon the United States, April 1, 2003, http://www.sacred-texts.com/ ame/911/911tr/040103.htm

⁵¹⁵ Jennifer Lin, "Recovery worker reflects on months spent at ground zero," *Knight Ridder*, May 29, 2002, http://911research.wtc7.net/cache/wtc/evidence/ messengerinquirer_recoveryworker.html

⁵¹⁶ Griffin, *9/11 Contradictions*, 266.

⁵¹⁷ "Mobilizing Public Health: Turning Terror's Tide with Science," *Johns Hopkins Public Health Magazine*, Fall 2001, http://www.jhsph.edu/Publications/ Special/Welch.htm

⁵¹⁸ Francesca Lyman, "Messages in the Dust," *The National Environmental Health Association* (September 2003): 40; http://www.neha.org/pdf/messages_ in_the_dust.pdf

⁵¹⁹ Marci McDonald, "Memories," *US News and World Report*, September 12, 2002, http://www.usnews.com/usnews/9_11/articles/911memories.html

⁵²⁰ Langewiesche, 32.

⁵²¹ "D-Day: NY Sanitation Worker's Challenge of a Lifetime," *Waste Age Magazine*, April 1, 2002, *WasteAge.com*, http://waste360.com/mag/ waste_dday_ny_sanitation

⁵²² "9/11 Incontrovertible Truth the Government is Lying."

⁵²³ Ibid.

⁵²⁴ *YouTube.com*, "The Physics of 9/11," 27:21, https://www.youtube.com/ watch?v=x-jWUzhtTIY

⁵²⁵ *WTC Building Performance Study*, Chapter 8, "Recommendations," Section 8.2.8.2, 11.

⁵²⁶ "Frequently Asked Questions," *NIST*, 2006.

⁵²⁷ *NIST*, "Questions and Answers About the NIST WTC Investigations," http:// www.nist.gov/el/disasterstudies/wtc/faqs_wtctowers.cfm

⁵²⁸ *NIST*, NCSTAR 1-5E, Abstract, iii, http://ws680.nist.gov/publication/get_pdf. cfm?pub_id=101033

⁵²⁹ *NIST*, NCSTAR 1-5F, Chapter 2, Section 2.1.8, 10, http://ws680.nist.gov/ publication/get_pdf.cfm?pub_id=101420

⁵³⁰ Ibid, "Executive Summary," xxxi.

[531] *NIST* NCSTAR 1-6, Figure 3-11, p49; See also: *Rethink911,* "Implausibility of the Official Theory," http://rethink911.org/evidence/twin-towers/implausibility-of-the-official-theory-twin-towers/
[532] *911Research.com,* "The Fires Severity," http://911research.wtc7.net/wtc/analysis/fires/severity.html
[533] Hamburger et al., *Building Performance Study,* Chapter 2, Section 2.2.1.4, "Structural Response to Fire Loading."
[534] *Contemporary Steel Design,* "The World Trade Center New York City."
[535] See *Appendix D,* this volume, 359.
[536] Sadek, NCSTAR 1-2, *NIST,* Figure E-1.
[537] Shyam-Sunder, NCSTAR 1, Section 6.4.3, 90.
[538] Ibid.
[539] Ibid.
[540] Susan Lamont, *The University of Edinburgh,* Edinburgh Research Archives, "The Behavior of Multi-story Composite Steel Framed Structures in Response to Compartment Fires," 12/2001, http://www.era.lib.ed.ac.uk/handle/1842/1485
[541] *The University of Edinburgh,* School of Civil and Environmental Engineering, 6/2001, http://www.civ.ed.ac.uk/research/fire/public_html/Cardington/main.pdf
[542] "The 1975 World Trade Center Fire," *What Really Happened.com,* http://whatreallyhappened.com/WRHARTICLES/wtc_1975_fire.html
[543] "Other Skyscraper Fires, *9-11 Research,* http://911research.wtc7.net/wtc/analysis/compare/fires.html
[544] Ibid; see also *Los Angeles Fire Department Historical Archive,* http://www.lafire.com/famous_fires/1988-0504_1stInterstateFire/050488_InterstateFire.htm
[545] "Other Skyscraper Fires."
[546] *YouTube.com,* "Trump and 9/11? New evidence found! HD," 0:00, https://www.youtube.com/watch?v=cPHpNijkeVw
[547] Sadek, NCSTAR 1-2, Executive Summary, Section E.7.1, lxxiv.
[548] Shyam-Sunder, NCSTAR 1, Chapter 2, 21.
[549] "Photographs of the North Tower Fires," *Google,* http://www.google.com/search?rlz=1C1CHNU_enUS364US368&sourceid=chrome&ie=UTF-8&q=photgraphs+of+the+North+tower+fires
[550] "September 11th FDNY Radio Transcripts" (Palmer report at 1:07:45 on tape), *Wikisource,* s.v., http://en.wikisource.org/wiki/September_11th_FDNY_Radio_Transcripts; For audiotape, see also "9/11: The WTC Elevator Key," *YouTube.com,* https://www.youtube.com/watch?v=sMvPHFbxnPM
[551] David Batty and Julian Borger, "NY Firefighters Reached the South Tower's Crash Zone," *The Guardian,* August 5, 2002, http://www.guardian.co.uk/world/2002/aug/05/september11.usa
[552] R. A. Grill and D. A. Johnson, "Fire Protection and Life Safety Provisions Applied to the Design and Construction of WTC 1, 2 and 7 and Post-Construction Provisions Applied After Occupancy. Federal Building and Fire Safety Investigation of the World Trade Center," *NIST Final Report,* 2005, NCSTAR 1-1D, p 19, http://www.nist.gov/el/disasterstudies/wtc/wtc_finalreports.cfm
[553] *Wikisource,* s.v. "September 11th FDNY Radio Transcripts."
[554] John L Gross, Theresa McAllister, *World Trade Center Investigation,* NIST NCSTAR 1-6, Chapter 6, Section 6.2.2, 167-176.

555 Sivaraj Shyam-Sunder, *World Trade Center Investigation*, NIST NCSTAR 1, Chapter 1, Section 1.2.2, Figure 1-10, 16.
556 Ibid, Figure 1-3, 7.
557 Robert Kolker, *New York* magazine, "Stairway A," 8/27/2011, http://nymag.com/news/9-11/10th-anniversary/stairwell-a/
558 Ibid, Chapter 6, Section 6.6.4, 97.
559 Ibid, 100.
560 Sunder, *World Trade Center investigation*, NIST NCSTAR 1, Chapter 2, Figure 2-12, 33.
561 Gross and McAllister, Figure E-5, lv.
562 Ibid, Section B.4.1, B-7.
563 "The World Trade Center New York City," *Contemporary Steel Design.*
564 Fisher, *WTC Building Performance Study*, Appendix B, Figure B-7, B-8.
565 "The World Trade Center New York City," *Contemporary Steel Design.*
566 Gross and McAllister, Chapter 3, Section 3.4, 41.
567 Sunder, *World Trade Center investigation*, NIST NCSTAR 1, Chapter 5, Section 5.5.2, 68.
568 Refer to the illustration at the end of Chapter 1 of this volume, which shows the panel arrangement of the North Tower's exterior wall design. The spandrels are clearly marked.
569 "The World Trade Center New York City," *Contemporary Steel Design.*
570 Sunder, *World Trade Center investigation*, NIST NCSTAR 1, Chapter 2, Figure 2-12, 33.
571 Sadek, NCSTAR 1-2, "Executive Summary," lxxxiii.
572 Ibid.
573 Ibid, Section E.7, lxxiii.
574 Ibid, Section E.6, lxx.
575 Ibid, lxxiii.
576 Ibid, Section E.7.2, lxxxiv.
577 Ibid.
578 Ibid, Section E.7.1, lxxiv.
579 Ibid, lxxii–lxxxii.
580 Sadek, NCSTAR 1-2, Chapter 7, Section 7.3.1, 178.
581 50 miles per hour is about 73 feet per second, and 73 ft/second x 0.215 seconds = 9 feet, 2/3 of 60 feet = 40, and 40 − 9 = 31
582 John Young, *Cryptome*, "Aircraft Wheel Punches Out a Steel Wall Section of WTC Tower," https://cryptome.org/info/wtc-punch/wtc-punch.htm
583 See *Appendix A*, this volume: "The Force Needed to Displace a Perimeter Panel." 331.
584 Refer to Note 421.
585 Shyam-Sunder et al., "Final Report of the National Construction Safety Team on the Collapses of the World Trade Center Towers. Federal Building and Fire Safety Investigations of the World Trade Center Disaster," *NIST Final Report*, 2005, NCSTAR 1 (Draft), Chapter 6, Section 6.14.1, http://www.nist.gov/el/disasterstudies/wtc/wtc_finalreports.cfm
586 Gross and McAllister, NIST NCSTAR 1-2, Section7.4, 196.
587 Sunder, NIST NCSTAR 1, Section 6.14.2, 144.
588 Ibid, 116.

[589] Steven W. Kirkpatrick et al., "Analysis of Aircraft Impacts into the World Trade Center Towers (Chapters 1-8) Federal Building and Fire Safety Investigations of the World Trade Center Disaster," *NIST Final Report*, NCSTAR 1-2B, "Executive Summary," lxx.

[590] Amanda Lin Costa, "Relics, Artifacts and Memories: A Year Spent With World Trade Center Steel," *Truthout.org*, September 11, 2011, http://www.truth-out.org/news/item/3254:relics-artifacts-and-memories-a-year-spent-with-world-trade-center-steel

[591] John Fisher, "Structural Steel and Steel Connections," *World Trade Center Building Performance Study*, FEMA Final Report, Appendix B, B-2.

[592] Ibid, B-11.

[593] Ibid, B-2.

[594] Ibid, B-9.

[595] Ibid.

[596] Ibid, B-11.

[597] Ibid, B-12.

[598] Ibid.

[599] Frank W. Gayle et al., "Mechanical and Metallurgical Analysis of Structural Steel. Federal Building and Fire Safety Investigation of the World Trade Center Disaster," *NIST Final Report*, NCSTAR 1-3, 85.

[600] Banovic, NCSTAR 1-3B, 40.

[601] Shyam-Sunder, NCSTAR 1, 88.

[602] Banovic, NCSTAR 1-3B, 42.

[603] See *Appendix B*, this volume: "The Force Needed to Shear NIST Samples C-46 and C-24," 339.

[604] Banovic, 72.

[605] See *Appendix B*, this volume: "The Force Needed to Shear NIST Samples C-46 and C-24," 339.

[606] Banovic and Foecke, NCSTAR 1-3C, 168.

[607] See *Appendix B*, this volume: "The Force Needed to Shear NIST Samples C-46 and C-24," 339.

[608] Gayle et al., NCSTAR 1-3, 6.

[609] See Chapter 6, this volume, Section: "High Strain Rates and WTC Steel," 280.

[610] Fisher, Appendix B, B-7.

[611] Banovic, NCSTAR 1-3B, 39.

[612] This documentary evidence used to be available from NIST at: Engineering Laboratory, *NIST Final Report*. But access to that file has been restricted. NIST's copy of the photo of Flight 175 in question, though, is available from a 2010 FOIA release at *911 Conspiracy.tv*, "9/11 Airplane Photo Gallery-"Flight 175"-2nd World Trade Center Attack," http://www.911conspiracy.tv/2nd_hit_photos.html

[613] "International Center for 9/11 Studies Secures Release of Thousands of Photos and Videos From NIST," *911Blogger.com*, August 31, 2010, http://911blogger.com/news/2010-08-31/international-center-911-studies-secures-release-thousands-photos-and-videos-nist

[614] See Christopher Bollyn, "The Huge 'Bullet Hole' in the South Tower and Analysis of Missile Evidence," *Christopher Bollyn: Journaliste Sans Frontiéres*, http://www.bollyn.com/the-huge-bullet-hole-in-the-south-tower-and-analysis-of-missile-evidence; see other websites as well.

[615] Avery, *Loose Change, 2nd Edition.*

[616] Bollyn, "The Huge 'Bullet Hole."

[617] Ibid.

[618] Avery, *Loose Change, 2nd Edition.*

[619] A paper touching on this subject was written by a Massachusetts Institute of Technology (MIT) student named Aden M. Allen. It was done as partial fulfillment of the requirement for his Bachelor of Science degree in Mechanical Engineering. Allen's conclusion was that there was no explosive device onboard the plane that hit the South Tower. He may be right; however, it is apparent from his logic that he did not read the official reports on the crash. If you take one of his critical calculations into account—that the amount energy needed to form the South Tower fireballs was equal to 12.5 percent less than the energy contained in 5,000 gallons of fuel (5000 x .125 or 4,375 gallons)—and combine it with certain conclusions arrived at by both FEMA and NIST—that only 3,000 gallons of jet fuel was consumed by the fireballs—the notion that a *missile* was fired into the South Tower a fraction of a second before impact does become a distinct possibility. And the power of that missile would had to have been equal to the energy contained in that missing 1,375 gallons (4,375-3,000); see: Aden M. Allen, "Yield Analysis of World Trade Center Crash," June 2002, paper submitted as a requirement for Bachelor of Science degree in mechanical engineering at *MIT,* http://dspace.mit.edu/bitstream/handle/1721.1/29588/52906608.pdf?sequence=1

[620] *WTC Building Performance Study*, Chapter 2, Fire Development, Section 2.2.1.2, 21. (Another section of this report gives the amount of fuel consumed by the fireballs as exactly 1,737. However, the figure 3,000 is used here because it is stated most often in the FEMA and NIST reports, and also because it gives a conservative estimate for the power of a possible missile.)

[621] Brian Dakss, "Speed Likely Factor in WTC Collapse," *CBS News*, February 23, 2002, http://www.cbsnews.com/stories/2002/02/25/attack/main501989.shtml; "Voice Recorders Could Provide Crucial 9/11 Clues," *Associated Press*, February 24, 2002, http://www.usatoday.com/news/sept11/2002/02/23/black-boxes.htm

[622] For an identifying photograph of Mr. Monette see "Theodore A. (Ted) Monette, Jr., *FEMA Press release* updated June 11, 2012, http://www.fema.gov/leadership/theodore-ted-monette-jr

[623] Ibid.

[624] Sadek, NCSTAR 1-2, Figure 7-82, 287.

[625] Margie Burns, "Bush-linked Company Handled Security for the WTC, Dulles and United," originally published in *Prince George's Journal* (Maryland), via *Commondreams.org*, February 4, 2003, http://www.commondreams.org/views03/0204-06.htm

[626] *Wikipedia*, s.v. "Larry Silverstein, http://en.wikipedia.org/wiki/Larry_Silverstein

[627] "America Rebuilds," Interview, *Public Broadcasting Service* (PBS), January 2004; see film clip at "Larry Silverstein admits WTC7 was pulled down on 9/.11." *YouTube.com*, http://www.youtube.com/watch?v=-jPzAakHPpk

[628] *Wikipedia*, "Larry Silverstein."

[629] Paul Joseph Watson, "Silverstein Answers WTC Building 7 Charges," *The New York Post*, January 5, 2006, http://www.prisonplanet.com/articles/january2006/050106silversteinanswers.htm

[630] "Silverstein's First Public 'Pull It' Response," *Killtown Blogspot*, September 23, 2005. http://killtown.blogspot.com/2005/09/silversteins-first-public-pull-it.html

[631] Ibid.

[632] "Decision to Stay Doomed Many," *The New York Times*, September 13, 2001, http://www.sptimes.com/News/091301/Worldandnation/Decision_to_stay_doom.shtml

[633] "Jackasses with Bullhorns: "WTC 2 is Secure!," *Whatreallyhappened.com*, http://whatreallyhappened.com/WRHARTICLES/jackasses.html

[634] *YouTube.com*, "Voices from Inside the Towers," 16:04, https://www.youtube.com/watch?v=BFOTneNSy3g

[635] See Chapter 1, this volume, Section: "The Skeleton in the Closet." 29.

[636] *YouTube.com*, "Where was Larry Silverstein on 9/11?", https://www.youtube.com/watch?v=9ScGZCqEyGM

[637] "'Power Down' Condition at the WTC on the Weekend Preceding 9/11," Serendipity.li, http://www.serendipity.li/wot/forbes01.htm; see also "Scott Forbes 911 power down in The Elephant in the Room" (video posted by TheFactsoverFiction, March 12, 2011), *You Tube.com*, http://www.youtube.com/watch?v=MUip4-Ibzk0

[638] "World Trade Center Employee Discusses Pre-911 Power Downs," *World911Truth.org*, September 15, 2010, http://911blogger.com/news/2010-09-17/world-trade-center-employee-discusses-pre-911-power-downs

[639] Avery, *Loose Change, 2nd Edition*.

[640] Taylor and Gardiner, "Heightened Security," http://web.archive.org/web/20050127000302/http://www.nynewsday.com/news/local/manhattan/wtc/ny-nyaler122362178sep12,0,6794009.story.

Epilogue

[641] "Learning from 9/11," the testimony of Gene Corley. (The fact that the plans were tightly held is indicated by Corley's statement that even his team of expert engineers could not get a copy of them for their own investigation until January of 2002.)

[642] *Controlled Demolition, Inc.*, "500 Wood Street," www.controlled-demolition.com/500-wood-street-building

[643] Ibid.

[644] (1590 Devices x 4) 2 Towers + (1590 Devices x 2) Bldg. 7 = 15,900 Explosive Devices; (595 Lbs x 4) 2 Towers + (595 Lbs x 2) Bldg. 7 = 5,950 Pounds

[645] 9/11 Commission Report, Barnes & Noble (2006), Chapter 9, Section 9.1, 280

[646] Shaila K. Dewan, "World Trade Center Makes a Vertical World of Its Own," *The New York Times*, 2/27/2001, http://www.nytimes.com/2001/02/27/nyregion/27TRAD.html?ex=1196485200&en=f7f1f4b52895f64e&ei=5070

[647] "The Heroism of William Rodriguez," Arabesque: 911 Truth, http://arabesque911.blogspot.ca/2007/05/heroism-of-william-rodriguez-amazing.html, Port Authority Transcripts, Transcript 48, 24," Thememoryhole.org, adam.pra.to/public/mir/www.thememoryhole.org/911/pa-transcripts/pa-transcript048.pdf; see also Port Authority

Transcripts, PA Transcript 048, 24, z10.invisionfree.com/Loose_Change_Forum/ar/
t4249.htm; "Power Down' Condition at the WTC on the Weekend Preceding 9/11,"
Serendipity, http://www.serendipity.li/wot/forbes01.htm; see also "Scott Forbes 911
power down in The Elephant in the Room" (video posted by TheFactsoverFiction,
March 12, 2011), You Tube.com, http://www.youtube.com/watch?v=MUip4-Ibzk0;
Susan Lindauer, "The Missing Security Tapes for the World Trade Center, Coto
Report, 8/1/2011, http://coto2.wordpress.com/2011/08/01/the-missing-security-tape
s-for-the-world-trade-center/
648 Curtis L. Taylor and Sean Gardiner, "Heightened Security Alert Had
Just Been Lifted," *New York Newsday*, 9/12/2001, http://web.archive.org/
web/20060107172607/http:/www.nynewsday.com/news/local/manhattan/
wtc/ny-nyaler122362178sep12,0,6794009.story
649 *Wikipedia*, "Stratesec," https://en.wikipedia.org/wiki/Stratesec; *9/11 Research.
com*, "WTC Security," http://911research.wtc7.net/wtc/background/security.html
650 Ibid.
651 Margie Burns, "Secrecy Surrounds a Bush Brother's Role in 9/11
Security," *The American Reporter*, January 19, 2003, http://web.archive.org/
web/20030202031922/http://www.american-reporter.com/2021/3.html
652 Ibid.
653 *The Raw Story*, 10/11/2005, http://rawstory.com/news/2005/Cheneys_stock_
options_rose_3281_last_1011.html
654 *Wikipedia*, Project for a New American Century, https://en.wikipedia.org/
wiki/Project_for_the_New_American_Century
655 Ibid.
656 *Wikipedia*, "Big Lie," https://en.wikipeda.org/wiki/Big_lie
657 Latasha Lennard, "Obama signs NDAA, indefinite detention remains," *Salon*, 12/27/1013, http://www.salon.com/2013/12/27/
obama_signs_ndaa_2014_indefinite_detention_remains/
658 2013 *YouGov* poll, "Majority of Americans Open to 9/11 Truth," https://yougov.
co.uk/news/2013/09/12/new-poll-finds-most-americans-open-alternative-911/;
Zogby International, "Zogby Poll: 51% of Americans Want Congress to Probe
Bush/Cheney Regarding 9/11 Attacks; Over 30% Seek Immediate Impeachment,"
9/6/2007, http://web.archive.org/web/20080918153848/http://www.zogby.com/
news/ReadNews.dbm?ID=1354
659 *Zogby International*, 9/6/2007, https://web.archive.org/web/20080918153848/
http://www.zogby.com/news/ReadNews.dbm?ID=1354
660 US Census Bureau, "Population by Age, Race, and Hispanic or Latino Origin
for the United States: 2000," see Table 1, which has population over the age of
18 set at 74.3% of total population. 106.6 equals 51% of the total population
over the age of 18; http://www.census.gov/population/www/cen2000/briefs/
phc-t9/index.htm
661 Glen Greenwald, "Justice Denied," the *Guardian*, https://www.theguard-
ian.com/commentisfree/2012/aug/31/obama-justice-department-immunit
y-bush-cia-torturer
662 Note from the Author: I can personally attest to the delivery of those books
because, as a member of that group, I sponsored 154 of them.
663 *Legistorm.com*, "Sen. Barack Obama (D-Illinois)-Staff Salary Data, https://
www.legistorm.com/member/76/Sen_Barack_Obama.html

[664] *Friends Committee on National Legislation*, "Do Emails to Congress Work?," http://fcnl.org/resources/toolkit/do_emails_to_congress_work/
[665] Obama: Bin Laden raid was a 55/45 situation," CNN, May 9, 2011, http://www.cnn.com/2011/WORLD/asiapcf/05/08/bin.laden.obama/index.html
[666] Ed Haas, "FBI Says, 'No Hard Evidence Connecting Bin Laden to 9/11,'" originally written for the Muckraker Report, via Global Research, June 6, 2006, http://www.globalresearch.ca/index.php?context=va&aid=2623 ; see also James Fetzer, The 9/11 Conspiracy: The Scamming of America (Illinois: Catfeet Press, (2007), xv.
[667] "Usama bin Laden Most Wanted," Federal Bureau of Investigation, http://www.fbi.gov/wanted/topten/usama-bin-laden
[668] Charles Krauthammer, "The Van Jones Matter," The Washington Post, September 11, 2009, http://articles.washingtonpost.com/2009-09-11/opinions/36802953_1_vanjones-white-house-wind-farms

Appendix A
[669] Fisher, *WTC Building Performance Study*, Appendix B, Section B.4.3, B-9.
[670] Ibid.
[671] Ibid.
[672] Ibid.
[673] Ibid.
[674] Ibid.
[675] Ibid, Section B.3.1, B4.

Appendix B
[676] Ibid, Section B.4.3, B-9.

Appendix C
[677] The drawings used in this section are from the North Tower plans that were released in 2007 and published on the Internet by Steven Jones.
[678] Lawson and Vettori, NCSTAR 1-8, (Draft), Executive Summary, Figure E-31, lxxxii.

Appendix D
[679] "The World Trade Center New York City," *Contemporary Steel Design*, 1964, http://www.engr.psu.edu/ae/WTC/AISI/wtcaisi5.pdf
[680] Ibid.
[681] Ibid.

Appendix E
[682] *NIST* NCSTAR 1-8, p 110, http://wtc.nist.gov/NISTNCSTAR 1-8.pdf; David Ray Griffin, *Debunking 9/11 Debunking*, (Olive Branch Press, 2007) p 312.
[683] *wtc7.net*, "BBC'S Premature Announcement of WTC 7's Collapse," http://www.wtc7.net/bbc.html

[684] Ibid.

[685] *FEMA*, World Trade Center Building Performance Study, Chapter 5, Section 5.1.

[686] *9/11 Commission Report*, Preface, p xiv.

[687] *C-Span*, live broadcast with Shyam Sunder, "Investigation of World Trade Center Building 7," 8/21/2008, http://www.c-spanvideo.org/videoLibrary/mobilevideo.php?progid=193741; for an in-depth analysis of this controversy see Web Archive.org, http://web.archive.org/web/20110827060414/http://firefightersfor-911truth.org/?page_id=158

[688] Ibid.

[689] *YouTube*, "Barry Jennings WTC 7 (Explosions) Interview-building 7," 2007 (uploaded 8/31/2011), https://www.youtube.com/watch?v=3Tr0TZa3WeI

[690] *Youtube.com*, videotaped statement of Kevin McPadden, http://www.youtube.com/watch?v=b4z-Wrp1pY8

[691] WKPFA Radio, Guns and Butter, Interview with Indira Singh, 4/27/2005, As seen in movie: "Under Occupation: 9/11 Reality," at 9:10, https://www.youtube.com/watch?v=yNuebABgJNs

[692] *Youtube.com.*, Interview with Craig Bartmer, www.youtube.com/watch?v=-IfgYhjQ9fE

[693] *Public Broadcasting Service* (PBS), Interview with Larry Silverstein, "America Rebuilds," January 2004.

Appendix F

[694] "Zogby Poll: 51% of Americans Want Congress to Probe Bush/Cheney Regarding 9/11 Attacks; Over 30% Seek Immediate Impeachment," *911truth.org*, September 6, 2007, http://www.911truth.org/article.php?story=20070906103632686; for actual poll numbers, see also: "Zogby America Likely Voters 8/23/07 thru 8/27/07 MOE +/- 3.1 percentage points," http://www.911truth.org/images/ZogbyPoll2007.pdf

[695] *US Census Bureau*, "Population by Age, Race, and Hispanic or Latino Origin for the United States: 2000," see Table 1 (which has population over the age of 18 set at 74.3% of total population), http://www.census.gov/population/www/cen2000/briefs/phc-t9/index.html

[696] *Global Research*, "Most Americans Open to 9/11 Truth," 9/1/2013, http://www.globalresearch.ca/new-poll-finds-most-americans-open-to-911truth/5348967

[697] For a video of the first time Bush said this, see http://www.youtube.com/watch?v=1xgk6bE58DQ; for a transcription of the second time he said it (in California), see *show-the-house.com*, "President Bush twice said he saw the first jet hit the North Tower World Trade Center 1," see, http://www.show-the-house.com/id53.html

[698] For the video, see: vodpod.com/watch/2792314-bush-saw-first-plane-hit-tower- - Cached; or http://911blogger.com/news/2007-05-04/bush-told-first-attack-911-he-left-florida-hotel.

[699] Bill Sammon, "Right Decision," *The Washington Times*, October 8, 2002, http://web.archive.org/web/20030210062733/http://www.washtimes.com/national/20021008-21577384.htm

Robert Plunkett, , "The president in Sarasota," *Sarasota Magazine*, http://
web.archive.org/web/20030210062902/http://www.sarasotamagazine.
com/Pages/hotstories/hotstories.asp?136; Bill Sammon, "Suddenly, a time
to lead," *The Washington Times*, October 7, 2002, http://web.archive.org/
web/20021124113636/http://www.washtimes.com/national/20021007-85016651.
htm; see also William Langley, "Revealed: What Really Went on During Bush's
'missing hours,' " *The Telegraph* (UK), December 16, 2001, http://www.telegraph.
co.uk/news/worldnews/northamerica/usa/1365455/Revealed-what-really-wen
t-on-during-Bushs-missing-hours.html

For this video, see: http://censored.strategicbrains.com/BushAnd911.cfm; or
http://www.whitehouse.gov/news/releases/2002/01/20020105-3.html.

See prospectus at: http://www.docstoc.com/docs/6409799/
Defense_Information_Systems_Agency.

For a comprehensive report on 911 Blimp.net's efforts in this matter, see:
http://911blimp.net/aud_BushImplicatesBush.shtml. (Note: Some may question
my use of this information because it can only be found in one rather obscure
website. But I have seen enough of these kinds of reports that, for me, it has the
ring of truth and deserves to be considered as credible until proven otherwise
by the FBI or other another governmental authority.)

Ibid.

Ibid.

Sammon, "Suddenly a Time to Lead.

Education Channel, "5-minute Video of George Bush on the Morning of 9/11,"
http://www.jesus-is-savior.com/Evils%20in%20Government/911%20Cover-up/
why_did_bush_just_sit_there.htm; see also Kevin Sack, "After the Attacks:
Missed Clues; Saudi May Have Been Suspected in Terror, Officials Say *The New
York Times,*," September 16, 2001, http://www.nytimes.com/2001/09/16/us/
after-attacks-missed-cues-saudi-may-have-been-suspected-error-officials-say.
html ; see also William Langley, "Revealed: What Really Went On During Bush's
'missing hours',," *The Daily Telegraph*, December 16, 2001, http://www.telegraph.
co.uk/news/worldnews/northamerica/usa/1365455/Revealed-what-really-wen
t-on-during-Bushs-missing-hours.html.

Bill Sammon, "Suddenly, a Time to Lead."

Eric Alterman, "9/11/01: Where Was George?" *Nation Magazine*, October
6, 2003, http://www.thenation.com/article/91101-where-was-george ; see also Bill
Sammon, "Suddenly, a Time to Lead."

Dennis Couchon and Martha Moore, "Desperation forced a horrific decision," *USA Today*, September 2, 2001, http://usatoday30.usatoday.com/news/
sept11/2002-09-02-jumper_x.htm

Ibid.

Bill Sammon, *Fighting Back: The War on Terrorism—From Inside the Bush
White House*, (Washington DC: Regnery Publishing, Inc.), 2002) 90.

"No one ever asked him about al-Qaida," *MSNB.com*, September 7, 2006,
http://msnbc.msn.com/id/14684993/page/2/.

"Bush 911 Speech on CNN," September 11, 2001, *YouTube.com*, http://www.
youtube.com/watch?v=cmH4vCuYcZ4

[715] "9/11 New Coverage: 8:30 PM: Bush Oval Office Address," (Video posted by Authentic History, January 30, 2011) *You Tube.com*, http://www.youtube.com/watch?v=ISGHcXeQFVI

[716] David Kohn: Interview with George W. Bush, "The President's Story," CBS News: 60 Minutes, September 10, 2009, http://www.cbsnews.com/2100-500164_162-521718.html

[717] "Bin Laden Determined to Strike in the US," President's Daily Brief, *The White House*, August 6, 2001, http://www.gwu.edu/~nsarchiv/NSAEBB/NSAEBB116/pdb8-6-2001.pdf; see also Thomas S. Blanton, "The President's Daily Brief," *The National Security Archives*, April 12, 2004, http://www.gwu.edu/~nsarchiv/NSAEBB/NSAEBB116/index.htm

[718] *Wikipedia*, "Limited Hangout," http://en.wikipedia.org/wiki/Limited_hangout

[719] "911 Commission: Trans Sec Norman Mineta Testimony," (video posted by derdy, February 20, 2006), *YouTube.com*, http://www.youtube.com/watch?v=bDfdOwt2v3Y

[720] "The September 11th Attack on the Pentagon," *Spacelist.org*, http *Pentagon.spacelist.org*,://pentagon.spacelist.org/

[721] *Wikipedia*, "Casualties of the September 11 Attack," see at: http://en.wikipedia.org/wiki/Casualties_of_the_September_11_attacks

[722] *In Memoriam Online Network*, "Victims of the Pentagon Attack," see at: http://www.inmemoriamonline.net/missing_Pentagon.html.

[723] Gregor Holland, 911truthmovement.org, "The Mineta Testimony: 9/11 Commission Exposed," 7/22/2005, see at: www.911truthmovement.org/archives/2005/11/post.php.

[724] *The 9/11 Commission Report*, (2004) p. 40.

[725] Ibid, p 464, note 213.

[726] *MSNBC.com*, "9/11 Commission finishes Bush Cheney Session," 4/29/2004, see at: http://www.msnbc.msn.com/id/4862296/ns/us_news-security/.

[727] Wikipedia, "Evan Thomas," see at: en.wikipedia.org/wiki/Evan Thomas.

[728] *Source Watch.org*, "Carl J Truscott, see at: http://www.sourcewatch.org/index.php?title=Carl_J._Truscott

[729] *The 9/11 Commission Report*, (2002), p 464, note 209.

[730] YouTube, "(Part ¼) Dick Cheney's Bush-Era National Security Speech At AEI (American Enterprise Institute)," 5/21/2009, https://www.youtube.com/watch?v=3VANII59j1c

[731] Alan Levin, *USA Today*, "Part One: Terror Attacks Brought Drastic Decision: Clear the Skies," 8/13/02, see at: http://www.usatoday.com/news/sept11/2002-08-12-clearskies_x.htm ; Glen Johnson, *The Boston Globe*, "Probe Reconstructs, Calculated Attacks on Planes," 11/23/2001, see at: http://www.boston.com/news/packages/underattack/news/planes_reconstruction.htm; *UPI*, 3/6/02 (according to Paul Thompson, *The Center for Cooperative Research*, "September 11: Minute by Minute," see at: www.benperi.eu/terror-database/911%20-%20Timetable%203.doc) *Wikipedia*, "Timeline for the Day of the September 11 Attacks," see at: http://en.wikipedia.org/wiki/Timeline_for_the_day_of_the_September_11_attacks

[732] *History Commons.org*, "8:19 a.m. September 11, 2001: Flight Attendant Betty Ong Describes emergency on Her Plane," http://www.historycommons.org/entity.jsp?entity=winston_sadler_1

[733] National Commission on Terrorist Attacks Upon The United States (aka the 9/11 Commission), "We Have Some Planes," Chapter 1, Section 1.1, http://govinfo.library.unt.edu/911/report/911Report_Ch1.htm

[734] *US Department of Homeland Security*, press release, "Assistant Director Carl J. Truscott announces Plans to Retire from the US Secret Service," 4/1/2004, see at: www.secretservice.gov/press/pub0704.pdf.

[735] Richard Clarke, *Against All Enemies*, (2004), p 1.

[736] *Wikipedia*, "The White House Situation Room," see at: http://en.wikipedia.org/wiki/White_House_Situation_Room.

[737] *Wikipedia*, "The Presidential Emergency Operations Center," see at: http://en.wikipedia.org/wiki/Presidential_Emergency_Operations_Center.

[738] *The White House Historical Association*, "White House Facts, http://www.whitehousehistory.org/history/white-house-facts-trivia/facts-white-house-dimensions.html

[739] Ibid.

[740] *Against All Enemies*, p 2.

[741] Ibid, p 6.

[742] Ibid, p7.

[743] Ibid.

[744] Ibid.

[745] Ibid.

[746] Paul Thompson, "Complete 9/11 Timeline," www.cooperativeresearch.org

[747] *YouTube.com*, "9/11-What happened to the Passengers?," 56:54, https://www.youtube.com/watch?v=mGB9A4ODmFo

[748] *Against All Enemies*, (2004), p 17

[749] Ibid.

[750] Ibid.

[751] Ibid, p 18.

[752] Lynne Cheney, "Notes by Lynn Cheney at Presidential Emergency Operating Center," 9/11/2002: see at: http://www.scribd.com/doc/12992809/Lynne-Cheneys-911-Notes-from-the-White-House-Bunker; Evan Thomas, *Newsweek*, "The day that changes American," 9/31/2001, see at: http://www.accessmylibrary.com/coms2/summary_0286-27266999_ITM.

[753] Aaron Dykes, "Norman Mineta Confirms that Dick Cheney Ordered Stand down on 9/11," see video at *The Jones Report*, 6/26/2007, http://www.jonesreport.com/articles/260607_mineta.html

[754] Robert J Darling, *24 Hours Inside the President's Bunker* (American Author, 2010), see photos at: //www.google.com/search?q=The+white+house+bunker+on+911&hl=en&rlz=1C1CHNU_enUS364US368&tbm=isch&tbo=u&source=univ&sa=X&ei=VtdJUaz8JqKg2gWDjIHICQ&ved=0CEUQsAQ&biw=1024&bih=677

[755] Larry King, "America's New War: Recovering From Tragedy," *CNN.com/TRANSCRIPTS*, September 14, 2001, http://edition.cnn.com/TRANSCRIPTS/0109/14/lkl.00.html

[756] David Ray Griffin, "Phone Calls from the 9/11 Airliners," *Global Research.com*, January 12, 2010, http://www.globalresearch.ca/phone-calls-from-the-9-11-airliners/16924

757 Massimo Mazzucco, *YouTube.com*, "The New Pearl Harbor ~ Full," at 1:38:36, https://www.youtube.com/watch?v=dWUzfJGmt5U

758 David Ray Griffin and Rob Balsamo, "Could Barbara Olsen Have Made Those Calls? An Analysis of New Evidence About Onboard Phones," Pilots for 9/11truth.org, http://pilotsfor911truth.org/amrarticle.html

759 *Youtube.com*, "9/11 Cell Phone Calls Impossible," https://www.youtube.com/watch?v=DHmrEGYoZAU

760 "The New Pearl Harbor ~ Full," 1:53:48

761 Ibid, at 1:54:28.

762 *Scribd.com*, http://www.scribd.com/doc/13499791/T7-B13-Flight-11-Calls-Fdr-Response-From-DOJ-to-Doc-Req-14-Calls-From-AA-11-and-77-and-UA-175-and-93-ATT-Wireless-UA-And-GTE-Airphone-Call-Record

763 *Federal Bureau of Investigation (FBI)*, Interview with Winston Courtney Sadler, 9/12/2001, http://www.scribd.com/doc/14094215/T7-B17-FBI-302s-of-Interest-Flight-11-Fdr-Entire-Contents

764 Ibid.

765 *Federal Bureau of Investigation (FBI)*, American Airlines: Interview by Larry Wansley with Nydia Gonzalez, 9/11/2001, http://www.scribd.com/doc/14094215/T7-B17-FBI-302s-of-Interest-Flight-11-Fdr-Entire-Contents

766 Ibid, Interview with Winston Courtney Sadler, 9/12/2001.

767 *YouTube.com*, Betty Ong's 9/11 call from Flight 11, https://www.youtube.com/watch?v=icfkIH3j-nk

768 *Federal Bureau of Investigation (FBI)*, American Airlines: Interview with Michael Woodward, 9/11/2001, http://www.scribd.com/doc/14094215/T7-B17-FBI-302s-of-Interest-Flight-11-Fdr-Entire-Contents

769 Betty Ong's 9/11 call from Flight 11.

770 *Federal Bureau of Investigation (FBI)*, American Airlines, Ibid, Interview with Evy Nunez, 9/12/2001, http://www.scribd.com/doc/14094215/T7-B17-FBI-302s-of-Interest-Flight-11-Fdr-Entire-Contents

771 Ibid, Interview with Jane Allen, 9/11/2001.

772 Ibid, Interview with Michael Woodward, 9/11/2001.

773 *9/11 Commission*, "Documents Requested By Commission Staffer Thomas Eldridge," http://911myths.com/images/e/ef/Team5_Box62_AliasesAndIDs-FBIIDshijackers-2.pdf

774 *Federal Bureau of Investigation (FBI)*, Interview with, Craig Marquis Marquis, 9/11/2001, http://www.scribd.com/doc/14094215/T7-B17-FBI-302s-of-Interest-Flight-11-Fdr-Entire-Contents

775 Ibid, Interview with unnamed AA employee, File #M-INT-00058946.

776 Betty Ong's 9/11 call from Flight 11.

777 *Federal Bureau of Investigation (FBI)*, American Airlines: Interview with Michael Woodward, 9/11/2001, http://www.scribd.com/doc/14094215/T7-B17-FBI-302s-of-Interest-Flight-11-Fdr-Entire-Contents

778 Ibid.

779 Ibid, Interview with, Craig Marquis Marquis.

780 Betty Ong's 9/11 call from Flight 11.

781 Ibid.

782 Ibid, Interview with Michael Woodward.

[783] Ibid.

[784] Ibid.

[785] "What do Autopilots do?", *Slate*, November 22, 1999, http://www.slate.com/ articles/news_and_politics/explainer/1999/11/what_do_autopilots_do.html

[786] "Hani Hanjour: 9/11 Pilot Extraordinaire, From the ridiculous to the sublime...," *What Really Happened*.com, http://whatreallyhappened.com/ WRHARTICLES/hanjour.html

[787] Jim Yardly, "A Trainee Noted for Incompetence," *The New York Times*, May 4, 2002, http://www.nytimes.com/2002/05/04/us/a-trainee-noted-for-incom- petence.html

[788] Ibid.

[789] *National Transportation Safety Board*, "Flight Path Study: American Airlines Flight 77," February 19, 2002, http://www.gwu.edu/~nsarchiv/NSAEBB/ NSAEBB196/doc02.pdf

[790] "Airtraffic Controllers Recall 9/11," *ABC News*, October 24, 2001, http:// abcnews.go.com/2020/Story?id=123822&page=1

[791] David Ray Griffin, *The 9/11 Commission Report, Omissions and Distortions*, (Olive Branch Press, 2005), 140.

[792] Ibid.

[793] Michael Ruppert, "Crossing the Rubicon, The Decline of the American Empire and the end of the Age of Oil," New Society Publishers (2004), 336.

[794] David Ray Griffin, Debunking 9/11 Debunking (Olive Branch Press, 2004), 35. (I am using Griffin's references in this section because his dissertation of these facts is extensive and he adds many interesting points which makes it required reading, but, for which, unfortunately, there is no space here to do it justice. His facts are based on the 9/11 Commission Report (2004); also see *NBC NEWS*, "9/11 Commission Staff Statement #17," http://www.nbcnews.com/ id/5233007#.UvHHe2JdW8A)

[795] *Wikipedia*, "McDonnell Douglas F-15 Eagle," https://en.wikipedia.org/wiki/ McDonnell_Douglas_F-15_Eagle.

[796] Griffin, *Debunking 9/11 Debunking*, 45.

[797] Ibid.

[798] Ibid, 58.

[799] Ibid, 46.

[800] Ibid, 59.

[801] Ibid.

[802] Ibid.

[803] *Midimagic*, "Radar FAQ, What Radar Can and Cannot Do," https:// midimagic.sgc-hosting.com/radarfaq.htm https://midimagic.sgc-hosting.com/ radarfaq.htm; *BBC*, "How Do You Track a Plane?," http://www.bbc.com/news/ world-asia-pacific-26544554

[804] Ibid.

[805] Ibid.

[806] Ibid.

[807] *Federal Bureau of Investigation* (FBI), "FBI Announces List of 18 Hijackers," 9/14/2001, https://www.fbi.gov/news/pressrel/press-releases/fbi-announce s-list-of-19-hijackers

808 *9/11 blogger.com*, "FBI Agent Dan Coleman Explains," http://911blogger.com/news/2011-11-14/fbi-agent-dan-coleman-explains-how-passport-911-hijacker-satam-al-suqami-was-found

809 *BBC News*, "Hijacks 'Suspects' Alive and Well,' 9/23/2001, http://news.bbc.co.uk/2/hi/middle_east/1559151.stm

810 Ibid.

811 David Harrison, "Revealed: the men with the stolen identities," *The Telegraph*, 9/23/2001, http://www.telegraph.co.uk/news/worldnews/middleeast/saudiarabia/1341391/Revealed-the-men-with-stolen-identities.html

812 Osama bin laden, "Declaration of War Against Americans Occupying the Land of the Two Holy Places," *PBS Newshour*, August 23, 1996, http://www.pbs.org/newshour/terrorism/international/fatwa_1996.html

813 "Osama Bin Laden's 1998 Fatway," excerpt from "Jihad Against the Jews and Crusaders," Statement of the *World Islamic Front, MidEast Web*, February 23, 1998, http://www.mideastweb.org/osamabinladen2.htm

814 "Usama bin Laden Most Wanted," *Federal Bureau of Investigation*, http://www.fbi.gov/wanted/topten/usama-bin-laden

815 Ed Haas, "FBI Says, 'No Hard Evidence Connecting Bin Laden to 9/11," originally written for the *Muckraker Report*, via Global Research, June 6, 2006, http://www.globalresearch.ca/index.php?context=va&aid=2623 ; see also James Fetzer, *The 9/11 Conspiracy: The Scamming of America* (Illinois: Catfeet Press, 2007), xv.

816 Griffin, *9/11 Contradictions*, 192, 318.

817 Dan Eggan, "Bin Laden, Most Wanted for Embassy Bombings?" *The Washington Post*, August 28, 2006, http://www.washingtonpost.com/wp-dyn/content/article/2006/08/27/AR2006082700687.html

818 "Bin Laden says he wasn't behind the attacks," *CNN.com*, September 17, 2001, http://archives.cnn.com/2001/US/09/16/inv.binladen.denial/

819 "White House Warns Taliban: 'We Will Defeat You,'" *CNN*, September 21, 2001, archives.cnn.com/2001/WORLD/asiapcf/central/09/21/ret.afghan.taliban

820 Ibid.

821 Gareth Porter, "How the Taliban Pressed bin Laden," *Asia Times*, February 13, 2010, http://www.atimes.com/atimes/South_Asia/LB13Df01.html

822 "Bush Rejects Taliban Offer to Hand Bin Laden Over," *The Guardian*, October 14, 2001, http://www.guardian.co.uk/world/2001/oct/14/afghanistan.terrorism5

823 Ummat, "Who Was Behind 9/11? An Interview with Osama bin Laden," *JUST Response Network, September* 28, 2001, http://www.justresponse.net/Bin_Laden1.html; see also http://www.911review.com/articles/usamah/khilafah.html

824 Ibid.

825 "Bush Rejects Taliban Offer to Hand Bin Laden Over," *The Guardian*.

826 Ibid.

827 "How Bush gave Osama a free pass," *Asia Times*, May 5, 52011, http://www.atimes.com/atimes/South_Asia/ME05Df01.html

828 Ibid.

829 Ibid.

830 For a discussion of the origins of and the controversies surrounding the commission, see Griffin, *9/11 Commission Report*.

831 *9/11 Commission Report*, National Commission on Terrorist Attacks Upon the United States, Chapter 5, *Al Qaeda Aims at the American Homeland*,

omelandHo145. For an in-depth report with reference notes, see *Wikipedia*, s.v. "Abdul Rasul Sayyaf," http://en.wikipedia.org/wiki/Abdul_Rasul_Sayyaf; also see *Wikipedia*, s.v. "Khalid Sheik Mohammed" at: http://en.wikipedia.org/wiki/Khalid_Sheikh_Mohammed

[832] "The Reason For This Cover-Up Goes Right To The White House," *Washington Blog*, March 18, 2010, http://www.washingtonsblog.com/2010/03/the-reaso n-for-this-cover-up-goes-right-to-the-white-house.html; see also Jane Mayer, "The Black Sites," *The New Yorker*, August 13, 2007, http://www.newyorker.com/reporting/2007/08/13/070813fa_fact_mayer

[833] George W. Bush, *Decision Points*, (Broadway, 2010), 170.

[834] Mayer, "The Black Sites."

[835] Ibid.

[836] "The Reason For This Cover-Up Goes Right To The White House," *Washington Blog*, March 18, 2010, http://www.washingtonsblog.com/2010/03/the-reaso n-for-this-cover-up-goes-right-to-the-white-house.html; see also Jane Mayer, "The Black Sites," *The New Yorker*, August 13, 2007, http://www.newyorker.com/reporting/2007/08/13/070813fa_fact_mayer

[837] Ibid.

[838] Professor Will Kuhn, "Stephen [sic] Bradbury's Torture Memos of May 10, 2005," *Akron Law Café*, April 21, 2009, http://www.ohioverticals.com/blogs/akron_law_cafe/2009/04/stephen-bradburys-torture-memos-of-may-10-2005/; see also memos, Steven G. Bradbury, Principle Deputy Assistant Attorney General, United States Department of Justice, "Memorandum for John A. Rizzo, Senior Deputy General Counsel, Central Intelligence Agency," May 10, 2005, http://msnbcmedia.msn.com/i/msnbc/sections/news/090416_Torture_Memo3.pdf and http://msnbcmedia.msn.com/i/msnbc/sections/news/090416_Torture Memo4. pdf; see also Emptywheel, "Khalid Sheikh Mohammed was Waterboarded 183 Times in One Month," *Firedoglake.com*, April 18, 2009, http://emptywheel.fire-doglake.com/2009/04/18/khalid-sheikh-mohammed-was-waterboarded-183-times-in-one-month/; see also John Helgerson, "Counterterrorism Detention and Interrogation Activities), *CIA Inspector General's Report*, http://graphics8. nytimes.com/packages/pdf/politics/20090825-DETAIN/2004CIAIG.pdf

[839] I personally watched a congressional hearing on C-Span about this and heard the testimony first hand of CIA contract agents who said they checked with the "White House" on a daily basis about their torture sessions. However, I have lost the reference to it.

[840] Jason Leopold, "CIA Destroyed More Torture Videos," *Consortium News. com*, March 2, 2009, http://www.consortiumnews.com/2009/030209a.html; see also *Associated Press*, "CIA Admits Destroying 92 Interrogation Tapes," March 2, 2009, http://www.msnbc.msn.com/id/29464930/ns/world_news-terrorism/; see also "The Reason For This Cover-Up Goes Right To The White House," *Washington Blog*.

[841] *Associated Press*, "Al Qaeda Chief Khalid Sheikh Mohammed Confesses to Planning Sept. 11, Gitmo Transcript," March 15, 2007, http://www.foxnews. com/story/0,2933,258817,00.html

[842] Lolita Baldor, "State bank on 9/11 terrorists' hit list," *Associated Press*, 3/14/2007, http://www.seattlepi.com/national/article/State-bank-on-9-11-terrorist s-hit-list-1231205.php

843 *Wikipedia*, "Daniel Pearl," http://en.wikipedia.org/wiki/Daniel_Pearl
844 Ibid.
845 Ibid.
846 Mark Mazzetti and Margot Williams, "In Tribunal Statement, Confessed 9/11 Plotter Burnishes His Image as a Soldier," *New York Times,* March 16, 2007, http://www.nytimes.com/2007/03/16/washington/16khalid.html
847 For the video, see http://www.liveleak.com/view?i=01e_1175818014 (WARNING: This video is very disturbing, so view it at your own discretion.)
848 Mayer, "The Black Sites."
849 Ibid.
850 Ibid.
851 Kuhn, "Stephen [sic] Bradbury's Torture Memos."
852 Marion Houk, "Abu Zubayda—Tortured—Implicated Khalid Sheik Mohammad," *Un-truth.com*, April 20, 2009, http://un-truth.com/human-rights/abu-zubayda-tortured-implicated-khalid-sheikh-mohammad
853 *MSNBC*, "All In With Chris Hayes," Interview with Jason Leopold (Vice News), 12/10/2014, http://www.msnbc.com/all-in/watch/will-dick-cheney-be-prosecuted-for-cia-torture--370220611654
854 Alexandra Richard, "CIA Agent Allegedly Met Bin Laden in July," *Le Figaro,* October 31, 2001, http://www.tenc.net/misc/lefigaro.htm
855 Ibid.
856 Ibid.
857 Manoj Joshi, "India helped FBI trace ISI-terrorists links,", *The Times of India*, October 9, 2001, http://articles.timesofindia.indiatimes.com/2001-10-09/india/27243646_1_isi-link-evidence-india
858 Ruppert, *Crossing the Rubicon*, 117.
859 Ibid, 103-104.
860 Ibid.
861 Ibid.
862 Amir Mateen, "ISI Chief's Parlays Continue in Washington," *The News* (a Pakistani newspaper), September 10, 2001, http://s3.amazonaws.com/911time-line/2001/news091001.html
863 Jake Tapper, "Spying Eyes and Ears," *Salon*, September 14, 2001, http://www.salon.com/2001/09/14/human_spies/
864 Kate Connelly, "Father insists alleged leader is still alive," *The Guardian*, September 1, 2002, http://www.guardian.co.uk/world/2002/sep/02/september11.usa
865 Guy Gugliotta, "Reconstructing the hijackers' last days," *The Washington Post*, September 16, 2001, http://web.archive.org/web/20011024161527/http://www.delawareonline.com/newsjournal/local/2001/09/16reconstructingt.html
866 Lt. Colonel Tricia York, "Air War College's international festival fosters cultural understanding," March 29, 2013, http://www.maxwell.af.mil/news/story.asp?id=123342237
867 "Bush: Tape a 'devastating declaration of guilt," *CNN.com*, December 14, 2001, http://edition.cnn.com/2001/US/12/14/ret.bin.laden.video/index.html
868 "'Fatty' bin Laden," *9/11 Research.com*, http://911research.wtc7.net/disinfo/deceptions/binladinvideo.html

[869] "Bin Laden 'Confession' Tapes," 9/11 *Hard Facts.com*, http://www.911hard-facts.com/report_19.htm; For the actual part of the video showing bin Laden writing with his right hand, see also, 9/11 Blimp.net, "Faked Video Confession," http://911blimp.net/vid_fakeOsamaVideo.shtml

[870] Craig Morris, "9/11: bin Laden 'confession' video mistranslated and manipulated by the CIA," *The Empire Strikes Black*, December 23, 2001, http://empirestrikesblack.com/2011/05/911-bin-laden-confession-video-mistransla ted-and-manipulated-by-the-cia/

[871] Ibid.

[872] *CNN.com*, December 14, 2001.

[873] Jeff Stein, "CIA Unit's Wacky Idea: Depict Saddam as gay," *The Washington Post*, May 25, 2010, http://voices.washingtonpost.com/spy-talk/2010/05/cia_group_had_wacky_ideas_to_d.html

[874] Steve Watson, "Expert Goes on Record; bin Laden 9/11 Confession is Bogus," Infowars.net, February 19, 2007, http://infowars.net/articles/febrary2007/190207Osama_tape.htm

[875] Ibid.

[876] *National Security Council*, document dated 2/3/2001; Jane Meyer, *The New Yorker*, 2/16/2004; Asia Times, "U.S. Eyes Still on Iraqi Prize," 5/9/2007.

[877] *Judicial Watch*, "*CHENEY ENERGY TASK FORCE* DOCUMENTS FEATURE MAP OF IRAQI OILFIELDS," Jul 17, 2003, see at: *www.judicialwatch.org/ printer_iraqi-oilfield-pr.shtml.*

[878] *Wikipedia*, "The Price of Loyalty," http://en.wikipedia.org/wiki/ The_Price_of_Loyalty

[879] *C-SPAN*, "Bush Mushroom Cloud," Bush Speech Video, 10/7/2002, http:// www.c-span.org/video/?c4484367/bush-mushroom-cloud

[880] *CNN World*, "Report: No WMD stockpiles in Iraq," 10/7/2004, see at: http://arti-cles.cnn.com/2004-10-06/world/iraq.wmd.report_1_nuclear-weapons-charles-duelfe r-iraq-s-wmd?_s=PM:WORLD.

[881] *Wikipedia*, "Niger Uranium Forgeries," http://en.wikipedia.org/wiki/Niger_ uranium_forgeries; Joseph C. Wilson 4th, *New York Times*, "What I Didn't Find in Africa," 7/6/2003, see at: http://www.nytimes.com/2003/07/06/opinion/ what-i-didn-t-find-in-africa.html; *BBC News*, "White House 'warned over Iraq claim'," 7/9/2003, see at: http://users.eastlink.ca/~fedwards/blog/2003/07/sheesh-bb c-news-americas-white-house.html; *The Sunday Times of London*, "'Forgers' of Key Iraq War Contract Named," 4/9/2006, see at: http://www.timesonline.co.uk/ tol/news/uk/article703553.ece

[882] Union of Concerned Scientists, "Evidence On Iraq's Aluminum Tubes Misrepresented," http://www.ucsusa.org/scientific_integrity/abuses_of_science/ aluminum-tubes-in-iraq.html

[883] *BBC*, "Bush rejects Saddam 9/11 link," 9/18/2003, see at: http://news.bbc. co.uk/2/hi/3118262.stm.

[884] *The Sunday Times* (of London), "The Secret Downing Street Memo," May 1, 2005, see at: http://www.timesonline.co.uk/tol/news/uk/article387374.ece

[885] *Wikipedia*, "Execution of Saddam Hussein," http://en.wikipedia.org/wiki/ Execution_of_Saddam_Hussein

[886] *YouTube.com*, "Extreme Prejudice-CIA Whistleblower Susan Lindauer," 8/6/2011, https://www.youtube.com/watch?v=G43zl4fzDQg

[887] Ibid.

[888] *Wikipedia*, "Susan Lindauer," https://en.wikipedia.org/wiki/Susan_Lindauer

[889] Note from Author: Fuisz has refused to "confirm or deny" that he ever worked for the CIA, but he did admit that Lindauer did come to his office on several occasions to discuss the Iraq situation, among other things. See: David Samuels, "Susan Lindauer's Mission To Bagdad," *The New York Times*, 8/29/2004, http://www.nytimes.com/2004/08/29/magazine/susan-lindaue r-s-mission-to-baghdad.html?_r=0

[890] *The Raw Story*, 10/11/2005, http://rawstory.com/news/2005/Cheneys_stock_ options_rose_3281_last_1011.html

[891] Donald L. Barlett and James B. Steele, "Billions over Bagdad," *Vanity Fair*, October 2007, http://www.vanityfair.com/politics/features/2007/10/ iraq_billions200710

[892] Aleen Sirgany, "The War on Waste," *CBS News*, 1/29/2002, http://www. cbsnews.com/news/the-war-on-waste/

[893] Dr. Hugh McDermott, "9/11 Terrorists Made Millions on the Stock Market," Independent Australia, 11/10/2011, http://www.truth-out.org/news/item/475 4:911-terrorists-made-millions-on-the-stock-market

[894] Ibid.

[895] Ibid.

[896] Ibid.

[897] *FBI*, "FBI Briefing on Trading," 8/15/03, See the film: "9/11 Trillions: Follow the Money," at 24:39, https://www.youtube.com/watch?v=n3xgjxJwedA

[898] "Silverstein Makes a Huge Profit Off the 9/11 Attacks," *WhatReallyHapened. com*, https://whatreallyhappened.com/WRHARTICLES/silverstein.html

Select Bibliography

Barrett, Wayne, and Dan Collins, *Grand Illusion: The Untold Story of Rudy Giuliani and 9/11*, HarperCollins, 2006.

Bergen, Peter L, *Holy War, Inc.: Inside the Secret World Of Osama Bin Laden*, Touchtone, 2002.

Burke, Jason, *Al-Qaeda: The True Story of Radical Islam*, I. B. Tauris & Co, Ltd, 2003.

Clarke, Richard A, *Against All Enemies: Inside America's War on Terror*, Free Press, 2004.

Dunbar, David, and Brad Reagan, eds. *Debunking 9/11 Myths: Why Conspiracy Theories Can't Stand Up To The Facts*, Hearst Books, 2006.

Dwyer, Jim and Keven Flynn, *102 Minutes; The Untold Story of the Fight to Survive Inside the Twin Towers*, Time Books, 2005.

Federal Emergency Management Agency (FEMA), *World Trade Center Building Performance Study*, Federal Emergency Management Agency, US Government Printing Office, 2002.

Fetzer, James H., ed, *The 9/11 Conspiracy: The Scamming of America*, Catfeet Press, 2007.

Fink, Mitchell and Lois Mathias, *Never Forget; An Oral History of September 11, 2001*, Regan Books/Harper Collins, 2002.

Giuliani, Rudolph, Leadership, Miramax Books, 2002.

Glanz, James, and Eric Lipton, *City in the Sky: The Rise and Fall of the World Trade Center*, Times Books, 2003.

Griffin, David Ray, *9/11 Contradictions: An Open Letter to Congress and the Press*, Olive Branch Press, 2008.

———— *Debunking 9/11 Debunking: An Answer to Popular Mechanics and Other Defenders of the Official Conspiracy Theory*, Olive Branch Press, 2007.

———— *The New Pearl Harbor: Disturbing Questions About the Bush Administration and 9/11*, Olive Branch Press, 2004.

———— *The 9/11 Commission Report: Omissions and Distortions*, Olive Branch Press, 2005.

Griffin, David Ray, and Peter Dale Scott, eds, *9/11 and American Empire: Intellectuals Speak Out*, Olive Branch Press, 2006.

Gunaratna, Rohan, *Inside Al Qaeda*, Columbia University Press, 2002.

Kerik, Bernard B, *The Lost Son; A Life in Pursuit of Justice*, Regan Books/Harper Collins, 2001.

Langewiesche, William, *American Ground: Unbuilding the World Trade Center*, North Point Press, 2002.

Marrs, Jim, *The Terror Conspiracy: Deception, 9/11, and the Loss of Liberty*, The Disinformation Company Ltd, 2006.

Mitchell, Elizabeth, *Revenge of the Bush Dynasty*, Hyperion, 2000.

Morgan, Rowland, and Ian Henshall, *9/11 Revealed: The Unanswered Questions*, Constable & Robinson Ltd, 2005.

Murphy, Dean E, *September 11: An Oral History*, Doubleday, 2002.

National Commission on Terrorist Attacks Upon the U.S, *9/11 Commission Report*, U.S. Government Printing Office, 2006.

National Institute of Standards and Technology (NIST), *Final Reports from the Investigation of the World Trade Center Disaster*. National Institute of Standards and Technology, Department of Commerce, US Government Printing Office, 2005.

Olbermann, Keith, *Truth and Consequences: Special Comments on the Bush Administration's War On American Values*, Random House, 2007.

Ruppert, Michael C, *Crossing the Rubicon: The Decline of the American Empire at the End of the Age of Oil*, New Society Publishers, 2004.

Stout, Glenn, Charles Vitchers, and Robert Gray, *Nine Months at Ground Zero*, Scribner, 2006.

Sylvester, Judith and Suzanne Huffman, *Women Journalists at Ground Zero*, Rowan & Littlefield Publishers, 2002.

Unger, Craig, *House of Bush, House of Saud*, Scribner, 2004.

———— *The Fall of the House of Bush*, Scribner, 2007.

Von Essen, Thomas, *Strong of Heart; Life and Death in the Fire Department of New York*, Regan Books/Harper Collins, 2002.

Index

Abel, Jennifer, 234
Addington, David, 402, 425
Afghanistan,
  attack on, 326
  Taliban in control, 419
Ahmad, Mahmud, General, 428
Alfred E Murrah Building, 25
Allbaugh, Joseph, 19
Allen, Jane, 407
Al Jazeera, 419
Al-Shehri, Waleed, 416
Al-Suqami, Satan, 416
American Society of Civil Engineers
  (ASCE), 22
Army Corps of Engineers, 25
Arteburn, Tom, 229
Ashley, Victoria, 107
Astaneh, Abolhassan-Asl, 60
Atta, Mohammad, 428
Avery, Dylan, 39
Baer, Robert, 426
Banaciski, Richard, 178
Barnett, Jonathon, 216
Becker, Brian, 181
Beijing Mandarin Oriental Hotel, 246
Bennett, Randall, 426
Bermas, Jason, 39
Biederman, R.R., 213
Biegeleisen, Shimmy, 315
Bin Laden, Osama
  accused, 3, 382
  framed, 417, 422
  claims of 9/11 innocence, 415
  fake confession video, 430
  death of, 328
  FBI Most Wanted page, 418
  meeting in Dubai, 427
Blaich, Peter, 148
Blair, Tony, 437
Borhrer, David, 400
Booker Elementary School, 373
Bovis Road, 65

Building Performance Study team (BPS)
  began investigation, 22
  denied access to evidence, 66
Brady, Gregg, 179
British Steel (BS), 244
Building 7,
  Location, 1, 362
  official cause of collapse, 365
  BBC report, 363
  Fox News report, 364
  witnesses to explosions, 366
Burger, Ron, 229
Burton, Mike, 28, 56, 58
Bush, George W
  authorized waterboarding, 423
  August, 6, 2001 PDB, 382
  At Booker Elementary School, 373
  defends fake bin Laden video, 430
  gave Cheney authority over WTC, 19
  ignored bin Laden's claims of
    innocence, 420
  lied to American people, 381
  saw Flight 11 hit the North Tower, 373
  Office of National Preparedness, 19
Bush, Marvin, 322
Bussey, John, 165
Butler, Bill, 181
Byrne, Robert, 153
Cacchioli, Lou, 181
Cachia, Edward, 178
Calderon, Edward, 145
Carbonetti, Tony, 50
Carr, Ginny, 203
Card, Andrew, 373, 379, 439
Cardington Tests, 244
Carlson, Craig, 180
Carswell Airforce Base, 439
Casaliggi, Joe, 191
Cazzaniga, Luigi, 217
Central Intelligence Agency (CIA)
  phony bin Laden confession video, 430
  InterServices Intellgence Agency (ISI), 428

KSM, Office of the Inspector General
   report, 424
   waterboarded, 423
Chandler, David, 186
Chang, Kenneth, 62
Cheney, Lynn, 387, 400
Cheney, Richard "Dick"
   destruction of evidence, 25
   monitored Flights 11 and 175, 389
   Office of National Preparedness
     (ONP), 19
   stalled WTC investigation, 58
   torture tapes, 425
   TriPod II, 51
Clarke, Richard, 392
Clifford, Ronnie, 130
Clinton, Bill, 69, 427
Coard, Daria, 317
Corbett, Gary, 316
Corbett, Glenn, 60
Corcoran, Marty, 53
Corley, Gene, 23
Cosgrove, Kevin, 8
Coyle, John, 180
Cruthers, Frank, 180
Cruz, Marlene, 114
Culley, Kevin, 33
D'Agostino, Sal, 181
Daniels, Sandra, Kay, 378
Darnowski, Kevin, 179
David, Felipe, 120
Dawson, Pat, 165
Defense Information Systems Agency
   (DISA), 376
DePalma, Anthony, 52
Department of Design and Construction
   (DDC), 26
DeRubbio, Dominick, 7
Deshore, Karin, 7
Dixon, Brian, 179
Doyle, Danny, 2
Dragonette, John, 199
Duffy, Tim, 413
Dwyer, Jim, 161
Eaton, Keith, PhD, 228
Electron-backscattered Diffraction, 18 224
Emery Roth & Sons, 200

Evans, Stephen, 165
Farias, Jeff, i
Fairbanks, Evan, 308
Farmer, John, 31
Federal Emergency Management Agency
   (FEMA)
   airplane parts recovered, 309
   fireballs in the North Tower, 81
   first investigation of WTC collapses, 5
   held back plans, 106
   ignored B4 witnesses, 164
   ignored evidence of thermate, 216
   ignored high strain rates in WTC
     steel, 280
   ignored molten steel at WTC, 222
Fenyo, Christopher, 195
Fenzel, Mike, 396
Fertig, Beth, 165
First Interstate Bank Building, 246
Fitzpatrick, Thomas, 6
Fleischer, Ari, 378
Forbes, Scott, 316
Fountain, Ben, 316
Fuchek, Greg, 228
Fuisz, Richard, 438
Gage, Richard, 107
Gallagher, Kevin, 64
Ganci, Peter, 45
Gartenburg, James, 160
Geyh, Alison, MD, 229
Giambanco, Salvatore, 125
Giuliani, Rudolph
   Benevolent Dictator, 26
   broke federal law, 68
   controlled WTC, 22
   destruction of evidence, 22
   Fresh Kills landfill, 24
   DDC coup, 25
   TriPod II, 51
   75 Barclay Street, 41
Glanz, James, 56
Godfrey, Richard, 42
Goldschmidt, Hans, PhD, 211
Gorman, Kevin, 179
Grabbe, Crockett, PhD, 206
Gray, Bobby, 54
Greene, William, 132

INDEX

Gregory, Stephen, 7
Griffin, David, Ray, 327
Griffith, Arturo, 115
Gross, John, L, PhD, 229
Haliburton, 324
Hall, Bobby, 99
Hamburger, Ronald, 71
Hanjour, Hanni, 410
Hanson, Greg, 153
Hanson, Peter, 404
Haas, Ed, 419
HCC Insurance, 323
Hess, Michael, 38
Hirsch, Charles, 193
Hitler, Adolph, 325
Hoffman, Jim, 194
Holden, Kenneth, 26, 228
House Select Committee on Science, 23, 106
Hughes, Karin, 380
Hussein, Saddam, 436
Husseini, Abdel, El, M, 431
Jennings, Barry, 38, 366
Jet fuel (facts), 83
Jones, Hermina, 141
Jones, Steven, PhD,
    released the North Tower plans, 108
    Thermate at the WTC, 184
Jones, Van, 328
Josie (SCC witness), 140
Kaminski, John, 316
Keane, Sue, 180
Kerik, Bernard, 30
Kirby, John, 188
King, Larry, 129
Kravette, David, 130
Krauthammer, Charles, 328
Lamont, Susan, 245
Langewiesche, William, 28, 229
Lauer, Matt, 114
Lawrence, Bruce, 431
Lamont Doherty Earth Observatory
    (LDEO), 186
Lever, Hursley "Chino", i, 93
Levy, Malcom, 195
Lhota, Joe, 7
Liedig, Charles, 395
Lim, David, 159

Lindauer, Susan, 438
Lipton, Eric, 56, 159
Loizeaux, Mark, 228
Long, Kirk, 142
Lopez, Pablo, 159
Lyles, Cee Cee, 404
MacKinlay, Janette, 225
Maffeo, Jennieanne, 131
Maggio, Mike, 45
Manning, Bill, 67
Manning, Lauren, 129
Marquis, Craig, 408
Massachusetts Institute of Technology
    (MIT), 11, 308
Matalin, Mary, 402
Materials Engineering, Inc (MEI), 212
Mayer, Jane, 412, 432
Maxwell Air Force Base, 430
McCabe, Edward, 87, 16
McCain, John, 439
McPadden, Kevin, 368
McQuillan, Dara, 314
Meeker, Greg, 226
Melisi, Sam, 54
Mendes, Lou, 56
Mineta, Norman, 383
Minter, Vanessa, 406
Mitchell, James, 427
Mohammed, Khalid, Sheikh, 422
Monette, Ted, 20
Morelli, Philip, 95
Moussaoui, Zacarias, 403
Mueller, Robert, 21
Muttawakil, Wakil, Ahmed, 421
Mutuanot, Vasana, 130
Nahmod, Abdo, 36
National Aeronautics and Space
    Administration (NASA), 224
National Military Command Center
    (NMCC), 385
National Institute of Standards and
    Technology (NIST)
    Second Bush investigation, 6
    Answers to Frequently Asked Ques-
        tions (2006), 231, 320
    manipulated computer simulations, 261
    fireballs in the North Tower, 80

paint-cracking study, 241
piston theory, 207
public hearings, 173
thermate ignored, 217
Naudet, Jules, 131
New York Police Department (NYPD), 22
North American Air Defense Command
   (NORAD), 411
Northeast Air Defense Sector
   (NEADS), 411
North Tower
   1975 fire, 246
   1993 bombing, 26
   50-Shaft blocked, 113
   50-, 6-, and 7-Shafts, 113
   6 and 7-Shafts blocked, 117
   AA Flight 11, 4
   architectural drawings released, 108
   collapse, 4, 184
   factor of safety, 359
   official explanation for collapse, 17
   plans withheld, 106
   seismographic evidence, 201
   sky lobby system, 109
   speed of collapse, 2, 183
   Security Command Center (SCC), 139
   explosion before plane crash, 201
Nunez, Evy, 407
Obama, Barack, 327
Ober, Michael, 179
Occupational Safety and Health Admin-
   istration (OSHA), 56
Office of Emergency Management
   (OEM), 26
Office of National Preparedness (ONP), 19
Olsen, Barbara, 403
Olsen, Ted, 403
Omar, Mullah, 420
One Meridian Plaza, 246
O'Neil, Paul, 436
Ong, Betty, 406
Operations Control Center (OCC), 139
Organization for the Islamic Conference
   (OIC), 421
Otis Air Force Base, 412
O'Toole, Joe, 228
PAN AM Interntional, 410

Palmer, Orio J, 12, 251
PAPD (Port Authority Police Depart-
   ment), 80
Pataki, George, 25, 192
Pearl, Daniel, 426
Pecoraro, Mike, 171
Pentagon,
   AA Flight 77, 4
Plaugher, Edward, 31
Polls
   2013 YouGov Poll, 14
   2006 Scripps Howard Poll, 14
   2007 Zogby Poll, 327
Pontecorvo, Andrew, 159
Port Authority of New York and New
   Jersey (PANYNJ), 25
Porter, Gareth, 422
Puma, Patricia, 160
Quinlan, Willey, 188
Rice, Condoleezza, 386, 402, 436
Reiss, Alan, L, 315
Rivera, Daniel, 178
Robertson, Leslie, 199, 228
Rodriguez, William, 118, 173, 201
Rogers, Kenneth, 178
Rossberg, James, A, 61
Rotanz, Richard, 34, 45
Rumsfeld, Donald, 324, 441
Ruppert, Michael, 411
Ruvolo, Philip, 228
Ryan, Kevin, 206
Sadler, Winston, 406
Saltalamacchia, Anthony, 172, 122
Sammon, Bill, 379
Sanchez, Jose, 93
Santiago, Hector, 42
Satan al Suqami, 416
Schapelhournan, Harold, 193
Schroeder, John, 181
Securacom, 313, 322, 441
Sheikh, Omar Said, 426
Sheirer, Richard, 30
Silverstein, Larry, 313, 323, 371
Singh, Indira, 369
Sisson, R.D., 213
Skeen, Thomas, PhD, i
Skilling, John, 200

INDEX

Smith, Carl, Wayne, 376
Smith, Sam, 314
Stafford, Brian, 397
Stanley, Jane, 363
Structural Engineers Association of New York (SEAoNY), 59, 232
Suskind, Ron, 436
Sweeny, Amy, 406
Sweeny, Brian, 404
Sunder, Shyam, PhD, 72, 366
Szamboti, Tony, 185
Taliban, 419
Tardio, Dennis, 177
Tenant, George, 423, 429
Thermate, 211, 225
Tomb, Rex, 328
Truscott, Carl, 387, 391
Tully, Peter, 191
Turilli, Thomas, 179
Turner, Lee, 229
Ummat (Pakistani newspaper), 420
University of Edinburgh's School of Civil and Environmental Engineering, 245
U.S. Geological Survey (USGS), 226
USS Cole, 4
Valiquette, Joseph, 310
Varonne, Patty, 42
Veliz, Teresa, 173
Viola, Stephen, 180
Vitchers, Charlie, 54, 228
Wakil Ahmed Muttawakil, 421
Walker, Wirt, 322
Wall, William, 179
White, Kim, 173
Wilson, Joseph, 437
Woodward, Michael, 407
Worcester Polytechnic Institute (WPI), i, 213
World Trade Center Task Force (WTCTF), 6, 177
Worthington, Skilling, Helle, & Jackson, 197
Yakimovich, John, 45
Yamasaki, Minoru, 109
Yarembinsky, Michael, 141
Young, Dennison, 42
Zarillo, Richard, 36

Zelikow, Philip, 386
Zoda, Patrick, 177
9/11 Commission,
    August 6, 2001 PDB, 382
    confession of Khalid Sheikh Mohammad, 422

About the Author

DAVID ALDEN has a Bachelor of Science degree in civil engineering from Worcester Polytechnic Institute. He has worked a variety of jobs related to the subject of this book, ranging from structural design to construction engineering. *The North Tower* represents six years of research and writing on the World Trade Center collapses.